KILL BROTHER SISTER

LELAND E. HALE

Epicenter Press Inc.
Alaska Book Adventures™

KENMORE, WA

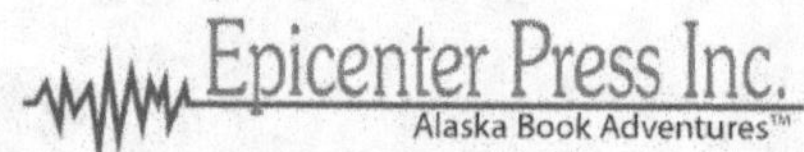

6524 NE 181st St., Suite 2, Kenmore, WA 98028

Epicenter Press is a regional press publishing nonfiction books about the arts, history, environment, and diverse cultures and lifestyles of Alaska and the Pacific Northwest.
For more information, visit www.EpicenterPress.com

Kill Brother, Kill Sister

Cover design: Scott Book
Interior design: Melissa Vail Coffman
Cover image: Michael McDermott / Anchorage Daily News

Library of Congress Control Number: 2024940272

ISBN: 978-1-684922-38-3 (Trade Paperback)
ISBN: 978-1-684922-39-0 (Ebook)

Kill Brother, Kill Sister *is dedicated to all the families touched by this unspeakable tragedy. The Anchorage cops also deserve a shout out: working in the shadow of Robert Hansen's heinous murders, they ensured that no stone was left unturned. I would be remiss if I didn't include the journalists whose diligent reporting contributed considerable nuance to this sprawling story. And, most importantly, I dedicate this work to the archivists at the Alaska Court System, whose deep dive into the official records delighted me at every turn.*

Acknowledgments

Stan Jones and Kim Rich, who "made me do it"; Doug Pope, eloquent eyewitness to the precipitating crime; my wife, Lorraine Miller, for her keen Canadian eye; the intrepid journalists at the Anchorage Times and the Anchorage Daily News, including Kim Rich, Sheila Toomey, Larry Campbell, Paul Fanning, Earl Swift, Kris Capps and Rosanne Pagano; Seattle Times writer Stanton H. Patty; private detective Steve Goodenow; linguist Roger Shuy; APD Cpl. Don Langdok; Pamela Cravez, author, The Biggest Damned Hat: Tales from Territorial Alaska Lawyers and Judges; The National Archives for the Trust Territory of the Pacific Islands; and the librarians at Eastern New Mexico University, who generously found and digitized a copy of the New Mexico Crime Commission Report (1985), "The Colacurcio Organization: An Organized Crime Group Tests New Mexico."

1

Anchorage, Alaska, October 12, 1985

Capt. Robert Pfeil nudged his Boeing 727 into the Alaska Airlines gate, the final leg of his daily schedule. He'd flown to Nome and Kotzebue, gliding past the Arctic Circle and skirting the Chukchi Sea. Spied an empire of rivers. Witnessed the tundra, red with fall colors. Glanced ice tickling shorelines. Once the ground crew blocked in the aircraft, he finished his log and strode into the waning light of the Anchorage evening.

At the employee lot, he chatted briefly with a fellow pilot, then struggled his six-foot-four frame into his daughter's Mazda. He swung the car onto International Airport Road and headed east. The snowy magnificence of the Chugach Mountains dipped in shadows as he drove. The captain soon turned south, past a string of glacial lakes. Sand Lake. Sundi Lake. Jewel Lake. Campbell Lake, his final destination, was the diamond in the crown.

Thirty years a pilot, Capt. Pfeil's life had taken him to the top of his profession. He was, in fact, Alaska Airlines' most senior pilot. But his perfect life was fraying around the edges. Odd visits and bizarre encounters were beginning to haunt him. One came two years previous, when a man pulled a gun after a traffic incident.

Another came in August, when a stranger troubled his home at 6:30 a.m. The doorbell rang; his wife Marianne answered from the garage. She saw an unfamiliar face. A face that asked, "Robert Pfeil?" Marianne called after her husband. The captain didn't know the man, who said "I want to talk to you," then walked away and said, "I will see you at work."

Bob called the cops and started to take precautions. One of them was to place a pistol under his pillow.

Today they were waiting for him. They'd parked at a supermarket, their battleship of faded Detroit luxury facing the roadway. They briefly worried about a woman who stared from a red Corvette. Soon forgot her. The chase began the second they spotted him, their rusty iron beast roaring to life. The gradual slope down Jewel Lake Road slipped inexorably toward its lakeside terminus. The clunker rumbled past view homes and a shock of trees as it pulled closer. Its occupants knew they had to catch the Mazda at the stop sign, one thousand feet away. Had to catch him or they'd miss their chance.

When Capt. Pfeil reached the "T," where Jewel Lake Road meets North Point Drive, he was almost home. Take the left and drive 600 feet. He'd be there. The time was 7:52 p.m.

The large boat of a car pulled up on his left. Stopped beside him. Blocked his exit. Then came the muzzle flash of a .45 caliber semi-automatic. The squeeze of the trigger sent two shots, then three more in quick succession. At least five shots. Five shots because the shooter was nervous and failed to make the first one count. The sawed-off shotgun he'd brought as backup sat on the floorboard. Unused.

One of the .45 caliber rounds shattered the driver-side window of the Mazda. Another four penetrated the door and dove toward Robert Pfeil's lower extremities. He was hit six times. Four times in his left thigh. Once in his right thigh. Once in his shoulder. His wounds were torn by three of the bullets and shrapnel from the other two gunshots.

Charles Booth, eating dinner at his nearby home, heard several quick rounds and ran to the door. Saw two vehicles in the lingering dusk. Moving to his deck, he noticed that one was considerably larger. Soon, the land yacht was gone, speeding east on North Point Drive in a cloud of oil and rubber. It was an older model, with two clusters of taillights, its left turn signal still blinking.

Only the silver Mazda remained at the intersection.

Booth and his wife Phyllis—herself an EMT—rushed to the scene. As Charles Booth arrived, he spied glass scattered on Pfeil's parka, and bullet holes in his clothing. He and a neighbor held up the pilot's head, while Phyllis went into lifesaving mode. She directed her husband to remove

Pfeil's clothes, so she could stanch the bleeding. Charles used a knife to cut through his uniform. He sensed the man was dying.

Capt. Pfeil told his rescuers he was paralyzed. Said he wanted an ambulance. Charles Booth directed a bystander to make the call. The captain kept talking, polite and very much in control. Being in command was an instinct, honed by his many years on the flight deck. Phyllis Booth kept him in conversation as she administered his wounds.

"Who did this?" she asked.

"He hired it done," Bob Pfeil responded, his voice weak but resolute.

"Who hired it done?" Phyllis wanted to know.

"Neil Mackay . . . he finally got me. Get my wife and kids."

Just before 8:00 p.m., one of the neighbors ran to the Pfeil home. Told Caroline Pfeil about her father, just feet away at the intersection. Marianne Pfeil heard her daughter shout. "Mom, daddy has been shot." They sprinted to the intersection of North Point Dr. and Jewel Lake Road. They recognized the shattered car. It belonged to Kristina, their oldest daughter.

The police were already there.

Anchorage Police Department (APD) Investigator Joe Hoffbeck was first on the scene. He recognized the man in the car. Capt. Pfeil was a fixture in the community. Their paths had crossed before, going back to Hoffbeck's stint in the Alaska State Troopers.

At forty-four years old, Hoffbeck was also a grizzled veteran of police work. He immediately noticed multiple gunshot wounds, one in Bob's shoulder, one in his groin area and a vast amount of blood. Hoffbeck further noticed that Bob Pfeil was very calm as he said that his left arm hurt. Repeated the words that he was paralyzed. The paramedics arrived within five minutes.

APD Investigator Joe Austin was next to arrive. A nine-year veteran of the force, he was on his way home when he heard the dispatch call about a shooting. Austin quickly cordoned off the entire area. He, too, knew Robert Pfeil. Had even taken his call after the strange man visited his door.

When Sgt. Mike Grimes arrived shortly thereafter, he took over scene command. As APD's chief homicide investigator, he'd spent more than a decade working the dismal side of Anchorage. Not just murders, but cases involving after-hours gambling joints, sex workers and drug-dealing motorcycle gangs. He also knew the travails of Capt. Robert Pfeil.

The cops knew him because, nine years earlier, Robert Pfeil's youngest sister was killed in a still-unsolved car-bombing. A car-bombing in which Muriel Pfeil's ex-husband, Neil Mackay, was a prominent suspect. Now Neil Mackay's name was once more on the tips of their tongues.

A squad of investigators soon packed the scene. Part of the recently formed Homicide Response Team—created in the aftermath of APD's failure to identify serial killer Robert Hansen—they were primed for results. A core team of five homicide investigators was now joined to a group of technical specialists. A lawyer, a forensic pathologist, a fingerprint expert, a computer expert, a videotape team, and a photographer. They favored expertise over rank and seniority. Threw everything they had at a crime; worked two or three days around the clock. Then kept going.

Leo Braden was there to take videos. His camera swept across the car to take in the larger view, focusing on the left-hand turn onto North Point Drive. Evidence specialist Larry Arend, meanwhile, retrieved two .45 caliber shell casings from the scene. He noted four bullet holes in the door and a graze mark from a fifth round. Inside the Mazda, he found glass under the door and recovered one spent bullet from the front seat. A foot search of the area failed to turn up more shell casings, but Arend knew from experience that the other shell casings could have ejected back into the gunman's vehicle.

After the scene walkthrough, Sgt. Grimes and Arend made their way to the Pfeil residence. They noticed a fist-sized hole in the garage window. Using a flashlight, the cops followed a footpath to an area where the landscaping had been disturbed. They also noted that, from the outside, the garage looked like a living area. These were early indications that the person who'd knocked on their door was unfamiliar with the house.

As is often the case with such incidents, a confusion hovered over everything. At least one of the witnesses, who was in his living room when the shots rang out, thought he heard shotgun blasts. Some witnesses described the Pfeil car as white; others said it was green and yet others said it was gray. Several witnesses described the getaway car as a late model sedan, possibly a Chevrolet; others said it was an older vehicle. Nearly all agreed about the profusion of taillights at the rear of the shooter's car, but there was little consensus about how many people were inside. Most had only seen the shooter. The hive mind was leaning toward two, with a shooter and a driver.

Crime scene processors were still working past midnight.

The aid car rushed Robert Pfeil eight miles northwest, to Providence Hospital, where he immediately underwent emergency surgery. The Anchorage Police Department had already stationed a 24-hour armed detail to protect him. Marianne and the kids arrived with a police escort shortly afterwards.

Police soon got a visit from Russellyn Carruth—one of Robert Pfeil's attorneys. She rushed to the hospital with the news that Capt. Pfeil had come to her office within the last few days. Told them he'd talked about a "new development" in the murder of his sister. Bob Pfeil let on that an unknown subject had approached him, claiming he'd been contacted by someone boasting about a job he'd done in Alaska. A job that Bob thought was a match for the Anchorage bombing that killed his sister Muriel.

Carruth also informed the police that Pfeil had just won a large sum of money in civil litigation with Neil Mackay. The settlement amounted to $175,000, which Mackay was to repay to Muriel Pfeil's estate. The details mounted. Neil Mackay had appealed the Alaska Superior Court ruling in Federal Court and lost. U.S. District Court Judge Russel Holland had, in fact, handed down his decision only six weeks previous. He had been unstinting in his contempt for Neil Mackay.

"Suffice it to say that the Court concludes on the entire circumstance of this case that (Mackay's) complaint was brought as a last-ditch attempt to evade the lawful final judgments of the Superior Court of the State of Alaska and for the purpose of harassing the defendants."

Even with the surgery, Bob Pfeil was in critical condition. The bullet that hit his spine, paralyzing him, was too difficult to remove. APD Investigator Joe Hoffbeck was nevertheless given the delicate task of interviewing him in the intensive-care unit. It was an awkward setting—a doctor and a nurse continued to work on the captain while Hoffbeck conducted his interview. The ICU itself afforded little in the way of privacy—it was an open bay, closed off only by curtains, filled with the life-saving medical equipment of the day.

Hoffbeck's presence, in this claustrophobic space, was a sign that police—and medical professionals—considered Robert Pfeil a man at risk. The cops needed to talk to him at once. Hoffbeck placed himself as close to the hospital bed as he could, dangling a portable tape-recorder near Bob Pfeil as he hovered over him. "Bob, I just turned on a tape recorder," Hoffbeck announced, "I want you to tell me as much as you can about the shooting again for me, will you please?"

There was a pause before Bob Pfeil answered, a look of pain tattooed across his face. "I stopped . . . at, at the stop sign," Bob said, struggling to gather his thoughts. "A car pulled up probably behind me . . . and it was right along the left-hand side . . . and he shot and drove off at a high speed. I don't know."

"Describe the car as best you can for me, will you, please . . ." Hoffbeck asked, thrusting the recorder closer to Bob's face. Pfeil was quicker this time, as if the interlude had focused his energies.

"It was a white sedan. I don't know if it was two door or four door," he responded. In the adjacent space—what there was of it—a doctor and nurse were prepping additional procedures. They needed to address Bob's collapsed lung. Hoffbeck would vie for space, yielding only when he had to. There were so many questions.

"Okay. Did you see the people inside of it?" Hoffbeck asked.

"Well, ummm, yeah," Bob replied. The fog of the event left certain details wanting. "I—I couldn't make out anybody, though."

"[O]kay could you please . . ." the nurse said, edging up to the left side of the hospital bed. "Just give us room here," she commanded. They needed to make an incision in his left side, between the ribs, so they could insert a chest tube.

With Bob in position, things started to careen toward medical intervention, the ticks and tocks that could save his life. The two of them moved in a Mayo table and methodically arranged an array of medical supplies. There was a 15-blade knife with a small, curved cutting edge, perfect for making short, precise incisions. Several Kelly clamps, which they'd need to open the incision and insert the chest tube. Sutures for securing the tube. Gauze for sponging and protecting the incision once the clear plastic tube was inserted. Local anesthesia for numbing the area where the doctor would make his incision.

Hoffbeck kept going, eking out every answer he could. "Have you ever seen that car before, Bob?"

"No. No," Bob replied.

The doctor and nurse moved closer to their supine patient, lifting his gown to get a closer look at the spot where they'd make the incision. They were looking for the "safe triangle," a space between the nipple, ribs, and armpit, where they could make a cut, insert the chest tube, and not damage any internal organs. The doctor probed the externals of the region with his fingers. Hoffbeck turned off his tape-recorder.

Though paralyzed from the waist down, Bob Pfeil was acutely aware of the pain in his torso. When Hoffbeck resumed his recording, Bob was in the process of telling the ICU team to go "easy."

"I'm sorry," the nurse apologized.

"Oh . . . God, my hands hurt," Bob complained.

"Let's put this one leg down," the nurse interrupted, commanding the man now in her care. "We're gonna take your pulse again."

For Hoffbeck, it was a small window of respite. An opening for more questions. "You mentioned some time ago that, ah, you feel that you know who—who, ah, had this done," he noted. He knew what Pfeil had reported at the crime scene, but that was then, when the shock of being shot had overwhelmed him.

"Oh, Neil Mackay did," Bob answered emphatically.

"Is that just an assumption or do you know that as a fact?"

"I don't know," Bob said. "I think he had my sister killed, too, about ten years ago."

"I'm aware of that," Hoffbeck replied. There was a buzz behind him, as the medical staff conferred on the vital procedure ahead of them.

"Has anybody been bothering you or harassing you or following you lately?" Hoffbeck asked. It was the string that could tie the shooting to a person or a motive. A possible clue for the cops to follow.

"No," Bob answered, his mind gone blank. The doctor was busy at his side, trying to bathe the incision site with antiseptic. "We need to get that arm up out of the way there," the doctor said, moving Bob's arm back and away from his left side. Bob's pain eclipsed his response.

"Oh, Jesus . . . uh . . . oh, Jesus," he exclaimed. Joe Hoffbeck paused. He could see that the doctor was starting to work on Bob, making the incision that was a precursor to inserting the chest tube. They had to release the air pressure that was building up in Bob's chest, shoving his vital organs to one side and causing him great discomfort. Hoffbeck could also see that Bob Pfeil was looking at him and then he broke. He suddenly broke. "Oh, Jesus . . . Is Sergeant here?" he asked. "Is the doctor here yet?"

"Doctor's here," the nurse cooed comfortingly.

"The doctor's working on you now," Hoffbeck repeated. The doctor and nurse worked an intricate ballet as the incision was made and the chest tube readied. "My mouth is very dry. Oh, Jesus," Bob moaned.

"You ready?" the nurse asked, holding the chest tube in her gloved hand. The parallel worlds of medicine and police work were now at full overlap.

"Any of your beliefs or assumptions or anything at all that might help us?" Hoffbeck asked, the medical procedure now a routine he had to interrupt whenever he could. Bob said, "no." Hoffbeck asked if anyone had been following him. "Somebody came to the house early one morning. You know, ah . . ." But Bob Pfeil couldn't think about that now. There was something else going on. Something he couldn't ignore.

"What's going on with my chest now?"

"Okay . . . he's putting a tube in your chest," the nurse told him. "'cause it nicked one lung and made it collapse. He's putting a tube in to make it re-expand."

"Okay," Pfeil said weakly.

"Making it . . . You'll find yourself . . . Breathing easier in a few minutes. Okay, Bob?"

"Ouch . . . oh . . . ohhh . . . oh. Where am I?" Bob replied. Joe Hoffbeck shut off his tape recorder. That's all he was going to get. His family was now ready to see him. Robert Pfeil waited until his mother arrived to make his announcement, "I am going to die," he proclaimed. It was daughter Caroline who cried the unrehearsed response. "No, Daddy. No."

The next morning, Marianne Pfeil found a rock inside her garage. It matched an impression in the mud outside the house. And corresponded with the broken window that gaped nearby. Police subsequently found footprints from what they described as a "very distinctive type of boot." Officer Arend made a plaster of paris impression. The prints, they would learn, belonged to a special boot.

In a nearby wooded area, they found more evidence. A piece of plywood. An empty Pepsi can. Likely a surveillance spot for the Pfeil residence. Someone—or multiple someone's—had been watching the comings and goings at the Pfeil home.

Police also canvassed residents of this affluent neighborhood, looking for more clues. One witness identified the shooter's possible escape route. A route that led the shooter's car to Dimond Boulevard, a main east-west corridor. Police were soon asking for the public's help in finding that vehicle.

2

Anchorage, Alaska, October, 1985

DESPITE THE TALK ABOUT NEIL MACKAY, Sgt. Grimes soon came up with another suspect. They'd interviewed Alaska Airlines pilot Ted Parsons, who'd chatted with Pfeil in the employee parking lot after he came in from Nome. It was Parsons who gave Grimes the name of the man from the traffic incident, the man who'd pointed a handgun at his fellow pilot.

Marianne Pfeil confirmed that the man's name was Charles Hutchins. Capt. Pfeil, it seemed, had the man arrested on a citizen complaint for the traffic incident. Pfeil lost the criminal case, but it wasn't long before Hutchins sent the Pfeil's a demand letter. Court records indicated that Hutchins wanted $25,000 in damages. Grimes knew right away they needed to talk to this guy. He assigned an Investigator to follow up on him. That case had recency and real threats of violence.

Grimes put investigator Ken Spadafora on the Hutchins follow-up. After studying the case report, Spadafora learned that Charles Hutchins had pointed an unloaded .38 caliber pistol at Bob Pfeil. That, instead of a traffic accident, it was a near miss collision on a main thoroughfare. One in which the captain and his passenger chased Hutchins' car, forced it off the road and then called the police. It was Hutchins who was arrested and charged with third-degree assault. His bail was set at $3,000. Significantly, Hutchins' last demand letter was sent in May of '85.

Even so, Spadafora interviewed the man on October 13th. Hutchins had an alibi for the date and time in question. He declined Spadafora's offer to take a polygraph. The police immediately put him under surveillance and kept it on him for eleven days straight.

Back at the hospital, meanwhile, Bob Pfeil's condition was improving. Doctors upgraded him from critical to serious within two days of his admission. "He's coming along," Marianne Pfeil told reporters. "His brain's good. He's talking. We're taking it day by day right now. I haven't lost my faith."

Asked about the relationship between his ambush and Muriel's murder, Marianne was diplomatic. "I don't really have any idea who would do something like this," Marianne Pfeil said. "I'm just in shock right now. It's a bad world out there."

"Certainly, he was interested in solving Muriel's death." she added, speaking of her husband. "That's only natural, I think. Anybody would be that way."

The Anchorage police were no less coy. While insisting they didn't yet have any clues to the shooting, they admitted to the possibility the two crimes were related. "That is one avenue we're looking at," an APD spokesman said. "It's not the only one, but it is there."

Neil Mackay, however, had not lived in Alaska since 1978. He was, in fact, residing in Hawaii. That fact alone presented multiple challenges. First, it was no simple matter to interview him. The Anchorage cops couldn't simply go waltzing over to Mackay's Waikiki apartment and start in with the third degree. That would require the cooperation of Hawaiian authorities. That would require more facts on the ground and that was exactly what they didn't have.

What police were hoping for, though, was a link back to the getaway car. If someone had spotted it, they wanted to know when and where. With the help of a scene witness, they produced a composite sketch. The drawing suggested an early 60s Chevrolet without being overly explicit. They put the message out to Crimestoppers, which produced wanted posters. They put the drawing on local TV. And in the newspapers. It was a cream, light tan or "off-yellow" vehicle, their plea for help announced. It might have rust spots on the right-hand side.

They immediately got some bites.

Several observant citizens called police and told them they'd spotted a similar car at the Carrs-Payless shopping center on the day of the shooting. It was seen in the parking lot at the corner of Jewel Lake Road and Dimond Boulevard. It was parked there from at least 5 p.m. onwards.

"There were two men in the car, and they were parked backwards so they could watch the traffic on Jewel Lake," Sgt. Grimes announced. "The way folks have described it, it was like they were looking or waiting for something."

Waiting for something indeed.

That the suspect's car was there for almost three hours before the shooting told the cops something else. His attackers had likely learned that Pfeil's Alaska Airlines schedule was unpredictable. The shooter's stake-out of his house bore that out. Police also learned that, while all Alaska Airlines employees had to park in the employee parking lot, it was difficult to get the same spot day after day. Bob Pfeil had no predictable parking place either.

Given this reality, his attackers had to catch Capt. Pfeil where they could. The two assailants—and the police were now certain there were two of them—had been reduced to the crudest tactics imaginable. Sit. Watch. Wait.

It took two weeks for Bob Pfeil's condition to improve enough to warrant his release from Providence Hospital. By then the Crime Stoppers reward for information leading to the arrest and indictment of the perpetrators had gone from $20,000 to $50,000. The cash bump came from Pfeil's friends and fellow pilots, all of whom wished to remain anonymous.

"We have a lot of good friends out there," Marianne Pfeil said in announcing the reward on October 25th. "It makes me feel wonderful. I hope it helps."

Bob's paralysis appeared permanent. "We can always hope for miracles, but I don't know," Marianne said. "He is in good spirits, though. He's a fighter."

When Robert Pfeil checked out of Providence Hospital on Friday, October 25, police refused to discuss his discharge. The hospital said they did not know where he was. "I would say, given the nature of the incident, he doesn't want anybody to know either," said a hospital spokeswoman.

They were, in fact, moving him halfway across the country, to the Mayo Clinic in Minnesota. Mayo was known to work miracles. Maybe they could work one more.[1]

---

1 That same day, Caroline Pfeil started at center for her high-school basketball team, the Dimond Lynx. An away opener against the Palmer Moose, the contest was decided by a pair of free throws in the final 43 seconds. Caroline scored 12 in a 45-43 loss.

3

Anchorage, Alaska, December 31, 1968 – August 31, 1976

Neil Mackay was smitten with Muriel Pfeil almost the minute they met. She was hard to miss. Attractive and athletic, she was a force in Alaska's fast-moving business environment. She came from money, but hers was the same money Neil Mackay came from. From the bottom-up and working hard money. She had one thing he did not: she came from a pioneer family which, in the hermetic world of Alaska's elite, meant they had physically domiciled in the state for at least "twenty accumulative years." It was a slippery requirement: the Pioneers of Alaska organization had only formed in 1907.

That detail notwithstanding, their social circles overlapped. Both counted prominent Alaskans within their coterie of friends and acquaintances. Real estate and property development served as connecting fabrics. Muriel's father built one of Anchorage's first department stores in 1923 and a string of apartment complexes after that. Neil Mackay was an upcoming real estate and property magnate in his own right.

When Muriel opened a travel service, she rented a space in a building that Neil Mackay owned. It was the same building where he kept his law practice. They couldn't avoid each other. She was there a lot. "Ten hours a day is a minimum," she told an *Anchorage Daily Times* reporter in 1968. "Six days a week." It was the same work ethic that Neil Mackay practiced.

She was not, however, just a workhorse. A charming, outgoing woman, she was periodically voted among the best dressed in Anchorage. "I buy what I like," she asserted of her best dressed award, "regardless of the current rage." A pretty brunette who stood 5-foot-5, she'd been known to wear her hair in a beehive. On a slim 125-pound-frame, wearing high, slim heels, she looked even taller. She was quite the catch.

Muriel Pfeil was worldly in a way many of her contemporaries were not. An international affairs graduate from the University of Colorado, Boulder, she went on to study at the University of Erlangen, in Bavaria, Germany. She was there on scholarship and took it seriously, becoming a fluent German speaker. While there, she also roamed the continent with her sister Caroline, a nurse at the Stuttgart Army Hospital. For the better part of three years, they traveled country to country in a Volkswagen. Avid skiers—Muriel was an Alaska ski racing champion in high school—they'd schussed all over Europe. After her European venture, Muriel took a stint at the National Planning Association in Washington, D.C.

Muriel Pfeil had, in other words, traveled in worlds few experienced. She had stared at the emerging post-war world up close. Pairing her with Neil Mackay would, at the very minimum, join two powerhouses. There was at least one problem, though. Neil Mackay was still married.

If there was a sparkle of hope, it was that Mackay's long-suffering wife, the former Barbara Hayes, had gently nagged him for a divorce. It took him three years to get there. Neil Mackay was so besotted with Muriel that he finally granted it, almost without explanation. Once that was out of the way, he asked one of his influential acquaintances—the chief justice of the Alaska Supreme Court, no less—to speak to Muriel, knowing the judge was a close family friend. Something worked. With a license but no wedding plans, Muriel and Neil were married in a near dare on New Year's Eve in 1968. She was 33; he was 45.

After the marriage, they led the good life. "Neil was a charming man and he was wealthy," Edgar Paul Boyko, a former Alaska state Attorney General, told journalist Sheila Toomey. "It was a logical thing for a successful businesswoman to do . . . They were able to live in top style. They seemed a happy couple."

When they were married, it was a union to envy. Until it wasn't. "They were both strong-willed people," another attorney, later a judge, observed. "Neither one of them seemed to back down."

And when, in 1973, Muriel found herself pregnant, the rocks in their marriage became boulders; the crags became crevasses. They were ultimately polar opposites. Muriel social, gregarious, worldly; Neil cloistered and content to retire into the folds of their fourteenth-floor penthouse in the Mackay Building. In the shock of her expectancy, Muriel moved out of the penthouse. Lived with her brother Bob and sister-in-law Marianne, sometimes for three weeks at a time. Capt. Pfeil urged her to leave Neil Mackay. Found him antisocial, a recluse barely willing to attend their treasured Sunday family dinners. Muriel ultimately moved back, at least until the birth of their son, on March 11, 1973. She was thirty-seven when Scotty was born. Neil Mackay was forty-nine.

She left Neil Mackay almost the moment Scotty was out of her womb.

Their divorce was the longest—and costliest—in Alaska history. They kept fighting even after their divorce was granted, stretching it through three years of tempests and storms. They fought over custody of their son. Fought over visitation rights. Fought over slights, real and imagined. There were allegations of drug abuse. Rumors of confrontations that rapidly spun out of control. Intimations of medical and mental infirmities. The judge eventually sent them both for psychiatric evaluations.

One of their last legal contretemps was a hearing on August 31, 1976. Neil won the right to take Scotty away for a month—but not until the child was five. That was almost two years away.

4

Anchorage, Alaska, September 30, 1976

ON SEPTEMBER 30, 1976, ANCHORAGE WAS its usual fall self. The sky a gauzy grey. Clouds maybe. Wind maybe. Temperatures hovering near a daily high of 42 degrees. Weather still not sure what it wanted to be. Snow at least a month away.

Only one thing was certain.

It was Thursday. Every Thursday morning Muriel Pfeil dropped three-and-a-half-year-old Scotty at nursery school, then drove another five-minutes to her downtown travel agency. By 11:30 a.m. she was back on the road, picking up Scotty, taking him to day care, just yards from her newly rented apartment. It was a joyful part of her day, being with her son, so beautiful and bright. So like herself.

On a lark, she stopped at the Nordstrom department store on her way back to the office. A new life was beckoning. With the pipeline and oil money surging through Alaska, the town was booming. Her business was booming, too. By the numbers, it was one of the most successful travel agencies in the state and the travel awards kept coming.

Still, in the back of her mind, there was something else. Neil Mackay. Never much of a father, Scotty's daddy wanted his son like a toy, like a possession, like a lost part of himself. It was as if his wild seed had finally settled into a surprise. It was true, he hadn't wanted kids. Didn't like kids. Didn't know kids. Now, Scotty was everything.

Muriel had other ideas. She tried to ignore her ex when she could and fight him in court when she couldn't. She gave as good as she got. Only weeks before, she'd appealed the court decision that steadily expanded her ex-husband's visitation rights. Muriel wanted to keep Scotty away from Neil Mackay as long as possible.

She had her reasons. "Scotty can have all the money in the world," she once said, referring to her ex-husband's wealth, "and be destroyed by a man that doesn't know love or how to exist within the society we function in."

Neil Mackay would try to convince her otherwise. She would share Scotty with him. It wasn't like he'd been stingy. She'd extracted a cash settlement of more than $750,000 from him and monthly child support payments of $500. He would persuade her. Or the courts would. There were always the courts.

Yes, there were always the courts, but today Muriel had other things on her mind. This very day, twenty-two years previous, her father had died as his hunting companion tried to take off on a foggy Lake Spenard in his Piper Super-Cruiser float plane. It was a family tragedy, long remembered. There were happier things, too. Like a new boyfriend. He was married, yes, but he'd given her a ring. A nice ring. A show-off ring. Of course, there was the new coat from Nordstrom. Oh, you have to see it, she told her staff. It's from their latest fall line.

Except she couldn't show them. She didn't have it. She'd absent-mindedly left it in her car.

"I'll go get it," she declared.

Muriel made the quick jog to her car, which was not in its usual place behind the travel agency. Construction work had forced her to take a more conspicuous spot, in a small lot across the street, within walking distance of the Anchorage courthouse complex. She was, as it turned out, temporarily borrowing a parking place reserved for one of her employees.

Luckily, her car stood out in that sea of bland American vehicles. It was a statement car. The bright orange one. Her new Volvo station wagon.

Surprisingly, she returned to the office only seconds later. Without the coat. Her car was locked. She'd forgotten her keys. Not that she was going anywhere. Her employees noticed she'd also left her purse and glasses behind. She'd never go anywhere without them.

This Thursday was different. It wasn't just Muriel's seeming forgetfulness. Today someone was watching her.

Muriel entered her car close to 2:10 p.m. Rather than simply grabbing her coat and returning to the travel agency, she clambered into the driver's seat. She was apparently going to move it to another spot. The key slid into the ignition, her right hand poised to turn it, her left hand on the steering wheel.

One hundred feet away, in his second-floor law office, Doug Pope sat in a swivel chair, his feet propped on the windowsill. On the phone with a fellow attorney, he was talking about court cases. Suddenly, their conversation collapsed.

"I heard this WHOOMPH—more than just a *whoomph*," Pope recalled. "I just kind of turned my gaze because my window overlooked the parking lot. I saw the hood of the car going up like—when I was a kid, we used to put firecrackers in a lead pipe and drop a can into them. The firecracker would go off and shoot the can out. It reminded me of that. Here was this hood going up in the air, it must have gone five or six stories in the air, because I just kept watching it, and it was kind of slowly rotating and then it reached its peak and then it came down."

Pope told the man on the other end of the line that he had to go.

"And then I looked out. People were there already. At least one. There was some—there was a woman down at the car. She had her hands to her face. So, I ran out to see what I could do. Or if there's anything."

One man ran toward the blast after the bomb exploded and quickly reached the smoldering wreckage. He found Muriel Pfeil sitting in the driver's seat, "still holding the steering wheel." The driver's door was closed and, he thought, possibly locked. The fingers on her right hand were nearly severed. The rest of her body was intact, although her legs were almost detached at the knees by the force of the blast. Doug Pope arrived seconds later.

"Another guy got there first," Pope said, "and looked like he was trying to help somebody in the car. I ran over there and saw there was nothing anybody could do for her. She was dead."

Long-time Pfeil family friend Gene Shackleton, on his way to visit Muriel, also heard the blast and, to his horror, watched her car explode. "My imagination is far too meager to know why anybody would do this to Muriel," he told a reporter. "They were an old-time family, good settlers like. I knew them all."

The bomb had blown off part of the engine block and blown out the car's doors. The front end of the vehicle was, for the most part, gone. Its right-front quarter panel was missing. Debris from the hood spread 250 feet around the car. The safety glass of the windshield shattered like pond ice; the frame buckled as the force rocketed through the car's interior. The explosion itself was followed by a concussive force that blew out several windows of an adjacent house and shook multiple buildings at the western edge of downtown Anchorage.

At the bomb site, Doug Pope immediately surmised that the person who set the charge was an expert. His college experience as a road builder told him the blast was aimed inward and toward the victim. It was, in his words, a directed blast. A blast targeted at one person and one person only.

AMBULANCE AND EMERGENCY PERSONNEL reached the scene within two minutes. APD Corporal Don Langdok was close behind. Arriving at 4th Avenue and L Streets, Langdon spied the hood of a car in the middle of the road. Parking his squad car, he activated his emergency lights, and then sprinted toward the still-smoking Volvo.

Pieces of flesh were everywhere. A shard of steel had pierced Muriel's chest, pinning her body to the seat. An autopsy later revealed that shrapnel had severed her aorta, the main artery carrying blood from the heart.

By now, a crowd of witnesses hovered nearby. One of them was Helene Woods, from Muriel's travel office. She was visibly shaken by the gruesome scene before her. Still in shock, she admitted that they couldn't see the parking lot from the office, but that Muriel's car, "had been parked in the lot for about an hour. We didn't know she was going to move the car."

Personnel from nearby law offices were there, too, having seen the explosion from inside their workplaces. They'd all rushed out, trying to help; were now speechless in anguish. At one point, Doug Pope volunteered to Langdok that there was no one around the car just prior to the explosion and that no one ran away after the bomb went off. When he heard Langdok speculate that, "Maybe the carburetor blew up, or something," he had to interrupt.

"Can't you smell the cordite," Pope asked. "Can't you smell it?" That comment would briefly make Doug Pope a suspect. He seemed to know too much.

Police investigators soon arrived in force. They immediately closed off the area and, within 30 minutes, were sifting through the vehicle's remains, looking for clues on the explosive fashioned for Muriel Pfeil's demise. That's not all they did. They walked through the entire lot, toting plastic bags, kneeling to pick up every scrap of evidence. As part of their protocol, they also searched an entire line of cars, looking for more bombs, their hoods lonesome soldiers pointing toward the sky. No other bombs were found.

It was now a full-court press, with an investigative team that soon grew to 13 members. There were Anchorage police detectives. Alaska State Troopers. Federal Bureau of Investigation agents and, of course, U.S. Alcohol, Tobacco, and Firearm Agency personnel. The bomb experts.

Their investigation was interrupted only once. That was when Fathers Frank Wilkes and Augustine Hartman of the Archdiocese of Anchorage arrived to administer last rites to Muriel Adele Pfeil. She was 41 years old.

God of mercy,
hear our prayers and be merciful.
to your daughter Muriel, whom you have called from this life.
Welcome her into the company of your saints,
in the kingdom of light and peace.
We ask this through Christ our Lord.
Amen.

5

Anchorage, Alaska, September 30 – October 1, 1976

TELEPHONES RANG ACROSS NEIGHBORHOODS, EACH A buzz of trouble. Bob Pfeil was in his garage. On the line was a guy whose business was next to Muriel's, saying there'd been an explosion. It's your sister's car, he added. Bob Pfeil took off immediately. Marianne rushed to her mother-in-law's house. She did not want Grandma Pfeil to be alone.

It took Bob thirteen long minutes to reach *Muriel Pfeil's Professional Travel Service.* There was much to think about. Who would want to do this? Who would want to harm his sister? He already had his suspicions.

The scene at the corner of 4th Avenue and L streets was a study in organized chaos. Red lights were flashing. One police vehicle blocked L street. A half-dozen police cars surrounded the parking lot, hemming it in on three sides. Several firetrucks lingered nearby. While men in suits swept the lot, investigators in trench coats gathered at the Volvo. Several firemen stared stone faced at the wreck from behind a fragile chain link barrier.

Bob Pfeil made a beeline to the nearest officer. Told him who he was.

Twelve blocks to the east, a parallel scenario was unfolding in the penthouse offices of Neil S. Mackay. On the phone to Mackay's legal secretary was an attorney and friend of Mackay's. A man close enough to have been Mackay's best man when he married Muriel. He, too, had an office in Muriel's building.

"Did you hear about the bombing in the parking lot?" Frank Nosek asked. Neil Pfeil's legal secretary and confidant, Virginia "Virg" Zawacki, got up and looked out their fourteenth-floor window, thinking Nosek was talking about the parking garage across the alley. It was then that Nosek asked to speak to Neil. The time was, in Virginia's recollection, sometime after two o'clock.

When Neil Mackay emerged from his office moments later, he was, Zawacki said, "flustered because he didn't—Frank didn't know for sure that it was Muriel's car, that Muriel was in the car herself, and Neil was worried about Scotty, was Scotty in the car." Ten minutes later, Nosek called back. It was Muriel's car, he said. Muriel was inside but not Scotty. For the next few hours, Virginia said she was, "in a kind of a state of shock, you know, a lot of things run through your mind, you just sort of move around and you don't know what you're doing."

Grandma and Marianne Pfeil meanwhile, were hovering at grandma's house, a mere three blocks from the crime scene, awaiting an update. Even before Marianne arrived, an Alaska Airlines pilot had called, asking for Marianne. When Marianne got there, grandma relayed the message. Call the Alaska State Troopers.

It was 3 o'clock by the time Bob Pfeil clambered up the stairs of his childhood home. He felt the gravity of his news. It was not just the anniversary of his father's tragic death; they were only days from his mother's birthday. He was crying; tears flowed down his face.

"Muriel is dead," he said. Then, later, he added, "I can't believe that Mackay would be that evil."

Grief was soon overtaken by action. The Pfeil's knew that Scotty was Muriel's life. They'd seen the change come over her as soon as she became pregnant. Scotty was only six weeks old when she'd left Neil Mackay for good. They'd stood by during her fractious divorce. Knew that she would not countenance having Scotty cast overboard to her ex-husband.

Bob and Marianne immediately drove the six minutes south to Scotty's daycare. The woman who ran the daycare, Rena Jane Bertram, knew them. They'd been there before. They were ingrained in Scotty's life. They loved him. The Pfeil's wanted Scotty in their home, where he would have two older cousins, aged eight and ten. They also knew the details of Muriel's last will and testament, believed it would grant them custody. Yes, they were acting preemptively. There was no hesitation when they whisked him away.

The Pfeil's did not, however, take Scotty to their home on Campbell Lake. In that moment, it seemed one trauma too far. They instead took him 150 feet down the street, to Muriel's apartment. Scotty knew the place. His things were there. The smells of his mother were there and the Pfeil's had a key.

Even before Scotty was in transit with the Pfeil's, Virginia Zawacki had started a search of her own. She was on the phone from her lofty perch in the Mackay Building, calling around, looking for Scotty, trying to find out where he was. She started with babysitters, but they were immediately at a disadvantage. In her own words, "we never knew the actual name of Scotty's babysitter." She spent a lot of time in the phone book, trying to find a name that sounded like, "Bertrand or on that order and trying to check addresses." She also called his nursery school. Scotty was not there.

Virginia Zawacki could not find him. Never did find him.

It wasn't until after five o'clock that Neil Mackay finally learned of Scotty's whereabouts. An Anchorage police officer called and advised him that Bob Pfeil had Scotty. But Mackay did not call the Pfeil's to check up on his son. He called Ted Pease instead. Muriel's divorce lawyer. Pease was not available, though he was able to talk to another attorney at the same law firm. That attorney urged Mackay to call back later.

Neil Mackay finally reached Ted Pease the following day. They discussed Scotty, albeit briefly. If Pease was diffident, he had reason to be. There were changes afoot. That same day, October 1st, the Pfeil's gathered up Scotty's toys and his clothes. They took him to their lakeside home. They made a bedroom for him.

By their own account, the Pfeil's were a normal family. They had family dinners together, took vacations together. Went skiing with their girls. Went hiking, fishing, and clam digging out of their cabin on the Kenai Peninsula, across from the Homer Spit. Scotty would be part of this. Had already been part of this "normal, happy, low-profile life," as Marianne Pfeil once told a reporter.

It fell to Marianne to bear the bad news.

She told Scotty his mother had died in a car accident. After that, she said, Scotty always looked for his mother, but asked no questions. He knew his mother was gone. He'd heard of the explosion and knew something of the car. Marianne presented it as gently as she could. Still, he asked, "when is mother coming back?" Then he said, "mother is in heaven."

THE TOW TRUCK HAULING MURIEL PFEIL'S ORANGE VOLVO rumbled through Anchorage, gliding past Grandma Pfeil's house as it made its way to the police garage. Even before it got there, her car presented a litany of questions. None of them trivial. At the top of the list was trying to piece the shattered vehicle back together. That, in turn, might provide insight into how the bomb was placed and detonated. It was something they needed to know.

Working backwards from the explosion, investigators already had a rough timeline. Travel agency employees said Muriel returned to the office "shortly after noon." She left to retrieve her new coat at approximately 2:00 p.m., came back briefly to get her car keys, and reached her car at about 2:10 p.m. From most accounts, the explosive device detonated once Muriel Pfeil entered the car. During those two hours no one saw anyone approaching or leaving her Volvo. At least, no one they'd interviewed so far had seen anyone.

That suggested the bomb was placed beforehand. That raised a new set of issues.

For one, the bomb's timing seemed designed to miss Scotty Mackay. It was designed, in fact, to kill Muriel Pfeil and only Muriel Pfeil. That seemed to leave the bomber a narrow window of opportunity: those fleeting moments when the two of them were separated. To complicate matters, on this day Muriel had deviated from her usual routine. Had stopped to shop, however briefly, for that new coat. This raised the possibility that the bomb was already in place.

A large bomb, set on a fixed timer like a clock of some type, raised the risk of collateral damage. Imagine that the timer was off by even a few minutes. Imagine it going off in the middle of downtown Anchorage, killing not only Muriel but Scotty. More than that, killing or injuring bystanders, too.

That's not what happened.

Investigators now considered a third option: a remote-controlled device. With such a device, someone could wait nearby, within radio range, ready for Muriel to appear. Wait for the right moment and the designated target. Wait for her to be alone and vulnerable. Wait for the streets to be empty or nearly so. Then, in that instant of opportunity, hit the switch that would trigger instant death.

Lending credibility to this thesis was the realization that, on the Volvo, an inside knob had to be turned to open the hood. That implied that the bomber would first have to get into the car's interior and open the hood. Then, and only then, could that person—or persons—plant the bomb. Doing that on the day of the bombing carried a high risk of discovery. The bomb site was a well-traveled, high-density street.

So, there it was. The perfect theory. The bomb was planted in advance of the act, possibly at night while Muriel slept. Attached to a radio-controlled detonator. Now the bomber could kill at leisure. Could kill with precision.

Within two days of the bombing, investigators came across another tantalizing bit of information. On September 5, 1976, Alaska State Troopers in Fairbanks responded to the bombing of an abandoned car. That vehicle, a 1964 Rambler sedan, was found on a remote road. Was it a practice run? They had a name for the Rambler's registered owner. They were investigating. Troopers checked travel manifests between Fairbanks and Anchorage, on the lookout for potential suspects.

Nor could investigators ignore another possibility. That the explosive was set to go off as a scare tactic. It was just a tragic coincidence that Muriel Pfeil was in the vehicle as it exploded. The motive? Someone wanted Muriel to sell her travel agency. She'd refused.

For some, these theories were distractions. The fact that Scotty was not involved seemed portentous. Just as portentous was the fact that Muriel was the only victim. Even the earliest press accounts could not help but hint at the possibility her ex-husband was somehow involved. One of the first articles to hit the stands, the October 1, 1976, edition of the *Anchorage Times*, contained this tempting tidbit.

"In an affidavit filed April 16," the newspaper reported, "Anchorage resident Nobby Segelhorst said he saw Mackay and Mrs. Pfeil in a heated discussion April 3 in which there was apparent physical contact. Mackay was clearly excited, he stated in the affidavit."

Other news accounts pointed out that, "Mrs. Pfeil and Mackay have had recent court battles concerning the attorney's visitation rights to their

3 ½ year old son Scotty." As time went on, reporters started describing "a bitter divorce trial and child custody battle." The fuel was there.

Investigators did, of course, bring Neil Mackay in for questioning. At one point, they asked if he'd take a polygraph. He said he'd consider it but he wasn't talking. Investigators made it abundantly clear he was a focal point in Muriel's murder investigation. In fact, they hinted, he might be their prime suspect.

That made Virginia Zawacki's alibi statement even more important. On the Thursday of the bombing, she told an APD investigator, Neil Mackay went to Lyon Optical in downtown Anchorage to pick up a pair of glasses. She said he left the office at about 1:40 p.m. and was gone for about an hour. He was, she added, back in the office around 2:40 or so. That was about the same time, she thought, that Frank Nosek called to tell them about the explosion. Asked if she was certain of those times, Zawacki said yes, saying she'd written them down after they'd learned of the homicide.

"I jotted down the times when Mr. Mackay left the office," she insisted. "And when he returned,"

Asked why she wrote them down, she replied sharply. "Well, for the reason that the victim was Muriel Pfeil, Neil's former wife. There had been a hotly contested divorce, they had just gone over a hotly contested motion to enlarge his visitation rights, and of course one would look to an ex-husband, especially with heated court battles going on."

Investigators faced other challenges. Whatever else he was, Neil Mackay had friends in high places. Friends who would vouch for him. Defend him and testify on his behalf. There was always this: why would a man seemingly as intelligent and well-placed as Neil Mackay risk everything by murdering his ex-wife? That was a question that would get asked over and over.

Then came a setback. On the afternoon of Muriel's murder, Virginia Zawacki called the APD. She asked for the investigator who'd done her original interview. Told him she wanted to update her statement. Insisted she'd do it person, if necessary. The officer accepted a telephonic revision.

After the investigator left their office, Virg now told him, she realized she'd made a mistake. She'd been a "whole hour off" on the timing of Neil Mackay's visit to Lyon Optical. Neil Mackay hadn't left at 1:40 and returned at 2:40, like she'd said. Neil had left for Lyon Optical at 12:40 p.m. and returned closer to 1:40.

What she didn't say was that was just enough time to drive his Lincoln from Lyon Optical to the corner of 4th Avenue and L Streets, detonator in hand. Neil Mackay was back on the map. Except for one detail. The call from Frank Nosek.

Mackay's penthouse apartment was, as the crow flies, a mile away from the murder scene. With downtown Anchorage's warren of one-way streets, there was no crow and no direct path between the two sites. At least five minutes separated them. The explosion and the Nosek call, however, barely overlapped. Both came just after 2:00 p.m.

Neil Mackay couldn't be in two places at once.

6

Anchorage, Alaska, October 4 – November 14, 1976

Life did not stand still in Anchorage. Employees at Professional Travel Service posted a notice in the local newspapers, announcing they were open as usual to serve their many friends and customers. Bob Pfeil posted a reward in both Anchorage papers. He offered $20,000, "For information leading to the arrest and conviction of the person or persons responsible for the bombing death of my sister, Muriel Pfeil (formerly Mrs. Neil Mackay) on September 30, 1976, in Anchorage, Alaska."

Bob Pfeil left his personal phone number as a 24-hour contact point and directed respondents to "put a digit number on letter and on lower corner. Cut off corner with number as your receipt." The ad ran for 15 days straight.

That wasn't all. Within four days of Muriel's death, Bob Pfeil asked the court to appoint him personal representative of her estate. That would give him authority over Muriel's wealth and make him executor of her will. It was a logical first step. Soon enough, Bob Pfeil went further. He and wife Marianne filed petitions for guardianship and adoption of Scotty. That was a recipe for trouble and, for one person in particular, a step too far.

Neil S. Mackay hadn't counted on the reactions of Bob Pfeil and his wife. Not only did the Pfeil's keep their nephew in the same nursery school and use the same daycare Muriel used—on the premise that continuity was important—they started calling him Scotty Pfeil. After all, Scotty was merely a nickname, given in honor of his father's Scots heritage. He already had Pfeil as part of his given name, Neil Pfeil Mackay. That not-so-subtle change was a potent of a deeper intent.

Neil Mackay learned of that intent on October 5th. After finally reaching Muriel's former divorce lawyer, he was told that the Pfeil family was going to keep Scotty and that he should contact Muriel's new attorney, Doug Baily, if he wanted details. He immediately did just that.

"Mr. Baily advised me that Robert Pfeil was going to keep the custody of Scotty," Mackay complained, outraged. "I inquired about my visitation rights and Mr. Baily advised me that there would be none."

Upon learning of Bob Pfeil's petitions for guardianship and adoption, Mackay went full lawyer, the typewriter his chosen instrument. His goal was simple: he wanted the existing custody agreement—which gave full custody of Scotty to Muriel—to be tossed. It was Neil Mackay's view that he had assumed full legal custody of Scotty on September 30, 1976. The day Muriel was murdered.

Neil Mackay also knew—and, in fact, the reality of the situation demanded—that he had to go through the courts.

"There is a very serious situation existing which makes it absolutely mandatory that this matter be brought to the court's attention as rapidly and practically possible," he tapped onto the page. "I am being denied all access to my minor son, Neil P. Mackay, hereinafter referred to as 'Scotty.' It serves no purpose to dwell on tragedy, but it must be recited herein that the mother of Scotty met with death on Thursday, September 30, 1976."

Unbidden, he also wrote that he'd made an October 5th appointment with two psychiatrists. Not for himself, of course, but for Scotty. He wanted to do everything humanly possible to "ease the mental suffering which Scotty is suffering." He ended up going to the psychiatric appointment alone because, he noted, "I could not get Scotty in my physical custody."

How did he know Scotty's mental suffering without having seen or talked to him? Mackay had a ready answer. It was a searingly personal revelation that had an eerily familiar ring.

"From my own personal experience," Mackay wrote, "I know how it feels to lose a parent. My father was unexpectedly killed in an automobile mishap when I was approximately five years old. I still have clear and unpleasant memories surrounding my father's death, but I do have the fondest remembrances of him."

Hector William Mackay died on August 28, 1928, in a one car accident in Whittier, California. He was on his way home from his lineman's job. The cause of death was a "crushing-in of front of skull . . . driving own car." Now Scotty was one with his father's history. The automobile, the tender age—it was an almost a too-on-the-nose tragedy. Neil Mackay pivoted to his personal anguish. "I am being deprived of seeing my boy," he pleaded, "and the last time I saw Scotty was on my last visitation, September 29, 1976."

The day before Muriel Pfeil was killed.

By October 5th, Muriel's autopsy was complete, and a Certificate of Death issued. It said she died of "explosion injuries," that the hour of death was 2:10 p.m., that the approximate interval between injury and death was "seconds." At least now they knew she hadn't suffered.

They buried her the same day. It was a private ceremony, beyond the reach of gossiping eyes.

The murder investigation, meanwhile, settled into what the lead detective called "a long, drawn-out affair." Police Lt. Ralph Christianson said his detectives continued to obtain samples of Muriel Pfeil's wrecked Volvo to send to the Federal Bureau of Investigation laboratory in Washington, D.C. He added that they had already compared the characteristics of the Pfeil bombing with that September 5 bombing in Fairbanks.

"The only real similarities are that both vehicles were station wagons, and they were both bombed," Christianson said. No one was injured in the Fairbanks incident. The Fairbanks explosion involved an abandoned auto, with the payload placed under the seat, not the engine compartment.

Things were, in fact, changing before their very eyes. Police were now openly speculating that a dynamite explosion had killed her. Anchorage police chief Charles Anderson told reporters that the dynamite could have been detonated by a fuse or an electric cap. That it could have been set off simply by turning the key in the ignition, turning on the car lights or opening the car door. "All it needs is a battery source," the chief noted. Anderson also said that dynamite was easy to obtain and that "virtually anybody could use it."

"We're still interviewing possible witnesses," Anderson added. He said that besides the businesspeople located in the area surrounding the parking lot, many windows of the Captain Cook Hotel, located a short distance away, overlooked the bomb site. "We're still tracking many of those people down," he said.

"We're also considering using a polygraph to test certain people who may be involved," Chief Anderson said. He declined to name any possible suspects.

One of those suspects named himself.

IN A NOVEMBER 9TH DEPOSITION OCCASIONED by his renewed custody claim, Neil Mackay ventured to the Anvil Building in Anchorage. Perched on a gentle slope between the court complex and the city's industrial core, the building hid its workings behind reflective glass. Mackay headed to a conference room at R & R Court Reporters, where a long table, utilitarian chairs, a microphone, and two opposing lawyers awaited him. He said "yes" to an offer of coffee. Decaf. Took a seat. Lit a cigarette. He was dressed casually. No suit. No tie.

His attitude was evident from the first exchange. Doug Baily asked him to give his full name and spell his last name for the record. "That's pretty hard to do," Mackay smirked, "but my name is Neil Mackay. It's spelled N-E-I-L, the last name, M-A-C-K-A-Y."

After providing his address, though, he asked to go off the record. They didn't get much farther. After the Court Reporter waved them back on record, Doug Baily asked the most pro-forma of deposition questions.

"You are the Petitioner, are you not," Baily asked, "of the action pending in the Superior Court for the Third Judicial District entitled Neil S. Mackay, Petitioner, versus Robert Pfeil et al, Defendants?"

"Yes, counsel," Mackay replied, his manner diffident. "And I'd like to read something into the record before we proceed any further. I'm going to refuse to answer any questions submitted to me for the reason that I am the focal point, if not the prime suspect, in the homicide of my former wife Muriel, also known as Muriel Mackay. For this reason, I decline to answer any and all questions on the grounds that same might tend to incriminate me . . ."

Doug Baily was nothing if not resolute. "Mr. Mackay," he asked again, interrupting, "are you the Petitioner in the legal action pending in the

Superior Court for the Third Judicial District, Anchorage, Alaska, entitled Petitioner versus Robert Pfeil?"

". . . Also, I want to be as courteous as possible," Mackay forged on, ignoring Baily. "And I stated my position in the record, and as far as any answers are concerned and as far as I'm concerned that's where it's going to stay. I'm not going to change that position, and I'm going to drink my cup of coffee and I'm going to leave."

"Mr. Mackay," Baily persisted, "are you the Petitioner in that certain legal action entitled Neil Mackay, Petitioner, versus Robert Pfeil, et al, Defendants, which is presently pending in the Superior Court for the Third Judicial District at Anchorage, Alaska?"

"Counsel, you have my previous answer, and my answer's going to remain the same, and it's not going to change. I've now drank my cup of coffee, and I appreciate the cup of coffee from the lady, and I just about finished my cigarette. And . . ."

"Mr. Mackay, what's your present . . ."

"I'm leaving," Mackay declared. "I've finished my cup of coffee, I've finished my cigarette, and in all due respect to opposing counsel and the very gracious lady that gave me the cup of coffee, I will now be leaving."

That's exactly what he did.

DAYS LATER, FEDERAL BOMB EXPERTS INFORMED Anchorage police that the blast that killed Muriel Pfeil was equivalent to about three or four sticks of dynamite. They also suggested it would only take a moment to hook up such a device. The hood of the locked Volvo opened from the inside, Investigator Robert Clemens told a coroner's inquest. However, he testified that officers using a coat hanger on a similar Volvo were able to reach through the car's grill and quickly open the hood.

The idea of a remote detonation was quickly fading into the dust.

The *Seattle Times* newspaper had picked up another story that was too good to pass up. Their claim was that organized crime was involved. Their reporters wrote that police were considering the idea Muriel Pfeil had died because she would not sell Professional Travel Service to the mob. It was not far-fetched.

Muriel's agency was one of Alaska's most successful. Crime figures happened to like travel agencies. Liked them because they could use their assets to book gambling junkets to casinos, with airfare, ground transportation, lodging and meals available at rates far below market. It was a lucrative pipeline, too good to pass up. Investigator Clemens rejected the idea, saying that the possibility was considered but, "there doesn't seem to be any truth to the allegation."

Then came another vehicle explosion. Once more it was an abandoned car. In Fairbanks. That wasn't the only news coming out of Fairbanks. On September 13—just two weeks before Muriel's murder –troopers recovered two hundred fifty pounds of dynamite stolen from the Alyeska pipeline and 4,000 feet of fuses. With the oil pipeline going in, it was easy to obtain dynamite.

The news kept rolling in. During the two hours preceding Muriel's death, police learned that someone had loudly and repeatedly proclaimed that a bomb was going to go off within two blocks of the Captain Cook Hotel. Muriel's office was, in fact, just down the street from the Captain Cook.

At the time, people close to Donny Wayne Pitts didn't believe him. An hour after the bombing, he made additional proclamations, including one insisting that the bomb should have gone off by now. When the bombing was reported, police brought him in. He was interrogated. Pitts told the cops that he had passed plans for the bomb to another man. That, the previous Sunday, he had collected a hundred dollars from that man for planning the bombing.

Under questioning, however, Donny Pitts recanted. A scheduled polygraph was subsequently cancelled. Pitts was schizophrenic. Indeed, he was soon returned to the adolescent ward of the Alaska Psychiatric Institute.

Another incident also taunted investigators. APD Investigator Robert Gray observed approximately $15,000 in cash being exchanged in an Anchorage restaurant within six days of Muriel Pfeil's death. The transaction involved two men, who got away before Investigator Gray could identify them or determine the circumstances of their transaction.

Then there was the story of a downtown Anchorage businessman who was spooked by Muriel's murder. The owner of the Baronof Lounge, he was convinced that the bomb was meant for him. His life had already been threatened. He drove a vehicle very similar to Muriel Pfeil's car. He left Alaska out of fear that another attempt would be made on his life.

These reports were only the prelude. By mid-November, someone suddenly confessed to a bombing. The car bombing that killed Muriel Pfeil. And he knew more than he should.

Things started unremarkably, when a Marine Corps fugitive was arrested in Seattle on burglary charges. Identified as David Brian Lee, the 18-year-old used several aliases, including Robert Penny, Jim Finley, and Peter Conley. That was strange enough, but there was something else about him that rattled investigators. He had recently lived in Anchorage. Had, in fact, allegedly stolen $1,500 from Turf News on Fourth Avenue. The Turf News address was less than a half-mile from the murder scene and only four minutes by car.

Details were initially sketchy, but Lee let on that he was paid $5,000 by an unnamed man at an Anchorage bar to commit the murder. Lee admitted picking up the bomb at a storage locker, planting it in Muriel Pfeil's car and watching it detonate. He was paid, he said, at another Anchorage bar.

There were discrepancies in his story. He got the color of Muriel's Volvo wrong. But, it turned out, he was color blind. Police sources in King County, Washington, confirmed that Lee's account "seems to be checking out real good."

Cops in Alaska couldn't find the storage locker where Lee said he picked up the bomb. The description of the individual who allegedly paid Lee for the killing was vague. He eventually gave them a name. That name proved to be fictitious. Anchorage police immediately sent an officer to Seattle. So did the Alaska State Troopers, who already had an officer stationed in Washington State. After an Anchorage polygraph expert interviewed Lee, they learned the man's story was fictitious.

David Lee ultimately recanted his confession. Indeed, he admitted to fabricating the story to get attention. Said he wanted to die or be sent to prison for life. Lee also told cops he got the idea from newspaper accounts of Gary Gilmore, the Utah prison inmate who, at the time, was awaiting death by firing squad.

When APD Investigator Joe Acton conducted a follow-up, David Brian Lee revealed something else. He alleged that he was really two persons,

David Lee and Crazy Bob. Investigator Acton concluded that David Lee did not commit the bombing. But that Crazy Bob might have.

"It didn't take a mental giant to see that the man was lying," Acton added. "He wanted to die. He thought murderers in Alaska were hanged or shot by a firing squad."[2]

2 The State of Alaska did not have a death penalty and hasn't had one since its 1959 admission as a state.

7

Anchorage, Alaska, October 23 – 24, 1985

THE APD HOMICIDE RESPONSE TEAM GOT THEIR FIRST break in the Robert Pfeil shooting on October 23, 1985. A concerned citizen called. Said her sister knew something about the shooting. Mentioned something about a handgun. A possible murder weapon. The caller's credentials seemed impeccable; she was a system control technician for the Alaska Railroad. Not one of the usual flakes.

Anchorage police immediately made arrangements to speak to the informant's sister.

That very same day eighteen-year-old Joanne Harris made her way to APD Headquarters. It was there that she faced Sgt. Mike Grimes and Investigator Ken Spadafora. She knew something, alright. While housesitting at a local lawyer's home, Harris told them, she went into the master bedroom, looking for marijuana. It was a breach of trust, and she knew it. She was also this family's babysitter, trusted to watch their kids while they were gone. She cringed as she made the confession. Investigator Ken Spadafora let it ride. There were bigger fish to hook.

What Joanne found at the lawyer's house, she said, was not marijuana. What she found in that bedroom drawer was a shiny, nickel-plated Colt .45. A semi-automatic pistol, one of the best guns Colt made. Her mistake, she now knew, was telling her boyfriend about the discovery.

Her boyfriend's name, she told the cops, was Tyoga Closson—she called him "Ty." He often came by the residence while she was housesitting. Used to stay overnight with her, sharing the attorney's bedroom. The critical nugget, however, was that shortly after her discovery, the weapon turned up missing. Stolen by Tyoga Closson. Then, sometime in mid-October, Ty started to intimate that the stolen pistol was used in a murder. The murder of the "airline pilot."

New questions were raised in quick succession. Who wanted Pfeil killed? Do you know? No, Joanne insisted, she did not. But she was not oblivious to the import of what she *did* know. "My mother," she said, "filled me in on why Pfeil got shot and the previous one a couple years ago."

Ken Spadafora didn't miss a beat. He bluntly informed Harris what her boyfriend was up against. Neil Mackay "has got millions," he told her. "The type of person we're dealing with, we're talking about a powerful person with a lot of money, and Ty is no match for these people, not at all, and these people use little people all the time, they chew 'em up and they spit 'em out."

Shocked into a new reality, Joanne Harris spilled a torrent of details. Ty, she said, had been making numerous statements claiming that he and a "guy named John" had committed the Pfeil shooting. "I was paid to hurt this guy," she said, quoting Closson. "Me and my friend went and blew this guy away."

Joanne admitted that she didn't believe him. Her doubts were fueled by the fact that his admissions came after the two of them smoked "a lot" of marijuana. While Harris thought Closson was relatively in control of his faculties at the time, she had only a vague recollection of the conversation. She added that she was "shocked and amazed" by his assertions. She also noted she was mostly skeptical that "he would try to make somebody believe that he did something like that."

There were other statements, filled with curiosities she couldn't let pass. One time, he implied he had driven the shooter's car. At another point, he implicated himself more deeply, suggesting that she could call Crime Stoppers. Should turn him in and collect the $1,000 reward. He'd wrecked her car, he said; it would be a kind of payback. She still didn't believe him. He frequently told stories and bragged about his "tough guy" exploits.

Then she dropped the bombshell.

At the time of the shooting, Tyoga was roommates with another young man. A young man she identified as Robert Betts. Both of them, she thought, were somehow involved in this mess. Joanne also revealed that the two friends often hung out a local pool hall. If not there, at an apartment just off E. Tudor Road. A sort of crash pad.

The Anchorage Police put out surveillance that very day. Put an officer in an unmarked car and parked it at a glass and steel office building near the junction of E. Tudor Rd. and B Streets. The hope was to find Tyoga Closson meandering the thoroughfares of Midtown Anchorage. They wanted to talk to him.

Tyoga Closson thrust himself into APD headquarters the following day. Acknowledged that he knew the police wanted to talk to him. He was not placed under arrest, but Sgt. Grimes and Investigator Joe Austin put him in a chair. Confronted him. "You've been bragging down at the pool hall," Grimes sneered. "Claiming you had something to do with the shooting of that airline pilot." Grimes sat close, using his body to block any notion of escape.

Then Investigator Joe Austin butted in. "Your friends say you've claimed responsibility for this."

Closson denied any knowledge of the shooting. Insisted that all he knew was what he'd read in the newspaper. "Oh, Pfeil's fucking with Mackay," he replied. "And that's about all there was to it, you know. Word of mouth says that a few years ago, a girl blew up downtown, dropped . . . Um, all I heard was that he was on his way home when he got shot."

Grimes played hardball. Told him that if he got up to leave, he would be arrested. Investigator Austin handcuffed him to the chair. Tyoga Closson said he might need a lawyer. Was told that he could not have one. Grimes went further. Told him that failing to cooperate would leave him "a dead beaver."

Grimes also made sure to impress upon him the danger of being involved in a conspiracy with the likes of Neil Mackay. It was a variation of what they had told Joanne Harris. "Do you know what people you're dealing with here?" he exclaimed, thrusting himself forward.

"Yeah," Closson replied, filled with the false confidence of an eighteen-year-old.

"Do you know this Neil Mackay?" Grimes snorted.

Tyoga Closson was stuck at Grimes' previous question, blurting out, ". . . stealing and . . . and murdering thieves and . . ."

"Know Neil Mackay?" Grimes interrupted, his body now hovering close to Closson's.

"No, I don't know Neil Mackay," Closson replied, then haltingly countered, "I went to school with a Lee Mackay. Daddy owned a hardware store."

"Dude's got money," Grimes hammered. "He's got power . . . Okay."

When Assistant District Attorney Stephen Branchflower arrived at the interrogation room, he took one look at Tyoga Closson and stopped in his tracks. He was immediately concerned about his youth. "How old are you, Ty?" he asked. When Closson replied that he was eighteen, Branchflower caught his breath and made him an offer. He would give him immunity from prosecution for the gun theft and he'd give him something else. He knew that Closson had a pending assault charge. He would, he said, arrange to have the Municipality of Anchorage drop the assault charge in exchange for his cooperation in the investigation.

Closson agreed to the deal. The police granted him immunity, in return for which he agreed to be wired. While he said he'd cooperate, he still had reservations. Reservations driven by a fear of his co-conspirators.

"I got the gun and I'm gonna get stiffed," Closson told the cops.

"Not if you, we can work together here guy," Sgt. Grimes promised. "If you weren't involved in it, we can do a lot."

"Sure, I'll help you back here behind," Closson replied. "But there's no way in hell I'll let anybody know what I'm doin.'"

"No one's gonna know," Grimes assured him. "But you gotta be straight up with us. Just totally cooperate with us. You cooperate with us, we'll get these people off the street, they won't touch you, I'll guarantee you that."

"I don't want any publicity," Closson insisted. "I don't want anybody knowing I was involved in any of this garbage."

Tyoga Glenn Closson then started to talk more freely. After stealing the .45, he now admitted, he bragged to friends about his score. One of those friends was his nineteen-year-old roommate, Robert Betts. It wasn't long before the two of them had a visitor. Shortly before the October 12 attack on Pfeil, Closson said, Robert Betts introduced him to a man he knew only slightly. That man asked him if he wanted to make some money doing something illegal.

"I said, 'How illegal . . . What are you talking about?'"

"He says, 'Well, I need a driver 'cause I need to shoot somebody,'" Closson said, adding, "I told him to get fucked."

At this point, Closson continued, he thought he was done with the guy he now knew as John Bright. Robert Betts soon countered with an offer he could not refuse. "I was still sittin' in my car, all right, and then my friend came up to me and wanted to borrow the gun. Said he'd have it back to me by Saturday and it'd be worth seventy-five bucks. I figured, OK, worst thing he could probably do is go rob a Qwik Stop or something."

That was a Friday, the day before Capt. Pfeil was gunned down near his Campbell Lake home. On Saturday afternoon, Betts came back and said he had to keep the gun for one more night.

"He says, 'Well nothin' happened. I'm gonna need it again tonight.' . . . and I said, 'What do you mean nothin' happened?' He says, 'Well, we threw a rock through this guy's window, and he didn't come out.'"

"I told him right then, I want it back, don't be shootin' nobody with that fuckin' gun and he says, 'Well, I'll give it back to you tomorrow.'"

Two days later, Betts returned the gun to Closson. Told him to get rid of it. Tyoga said he tossed it into the bay and confirmed something else. He had learned from Betts that the shooting was done for money. It was time to go before a judge. Tyoga Closson's cooperation had only just begun.

The cops hauled Tyoga Closson before Judge David Stewart in support of a search warrant that authorized the use of wires against co-conspirators Robert Betts and John Bright. First, they had to establish Tyoga Closson's credibility. Grimes told the magistrate that certain information was public about the shooting of Robert Pfeil. Other information had been withheld.

"All right," Judge Stewart replied. "So, the items that were not made public would be the information concerning the boots, the broken window episode, the type and character of the bullet, the surveillance scene that you've just described, all those things, correct?"

"That's correct," Sgt. Grimes replied. Then he piled on the details. "Regarding the type and character of the bullet," he said, "it is significant that Mr. Closson knew that the bullets were .45 caliber copper-jacketed hollow points. Knew it because he's the one that loaded the gun, and it was loaded when he loaned it to Betts."

Judge Stewart ultimately approved a search warrant to record conversations between Closson and Robert Betts and between Closson and John Bright. John Bright, however, could not be found. Everything was now riding on Robert Betts.

8

Anchorage, Alaska, October 24 – 30, 1985

THE TAPED CONVERSATIONS BETWEEN TYOGA CLOSSON and Robert Betts took place at a Safeway grocery store on 9th and Gambell, just blocks from downtown Anchorage. Ty Closson was fitted with a transmitter. Police set up their surveillance van in the parking lot. As the two roommates spoke from the relative privacy of the Safeway coffee bar, the anodyne sounds of the grocery store clattered around them. Carts rattled. Cash registers clicked. There was a muffled chatter of footsteps as people rushed to their daily bread.

Closson started by bitching out his former roommate. He was angry—righteously angry—that the .45 was used in a shooting. Not some ordinary, gangster-style shooting. This was a big deal, on all the TV stations. Robert Betts was having none of it.

"I told you exactly what I was going to do," Betts shot back.

Ty upped the ante. Let on that the police had recovered the gun and linked it back to him. Then he reeled out another piece of bait. They were in trouble, both of them. Maybe Joanne, too. There was something that could save them. The reward. Not any old reward. The $20,000 reward for information on the Pfeil shooting. With their insider knowledge, Closson hinted, the two of them were in line for that reward money. There was more.

"The other thing you get, is the plea bargain," Closson added. "Whoever the partner is, that did not pull the trigger, will walk away from the other one, rich enough that he'll never have to work again . . ."

Ty then moved up the hierarchy of guilt. Glided, in fact, to the very top of the guilt stack. It was one of his police-directed scenarios: get Betts to name the source of the contract. Significantly, when he mentioned Mackay as the source of the shooting, Betts did not answer. Not the first time. Not the second time, either. Closson tried another tack.

"I want to know who shot, who shot the motherfucker," he demanded. This time, Betts did not hesitate.

"John did," Betts replied, referring to John Bright. The same John Bright who'd tried to recruit Tyoga Closson as his driver.

"Why?" Closson asked.

"Why? You wanna know really why?" Robert Betts seemed to be daring him.

"Yeah," Closson replied, sidling up to the challenge.

"Okay, I'll tell you why," Betts responded, this time with a hint of insider knowledge. Referring to Capt. Pfeil, Betts said it was "the dude's union. He's trying to raise some hell in his union. His bosses don't like it. His bosses in the union just so happen to be part of the family. It was taken care of. The dude started—started a lot of shit. Okay?"

Robert Betts revealed something else. John Bright, he confessed, was none too happy with him. He'd been talking too much. It was poolhall talk, but any talk was too much. And if there's one thing Robert Betts understood, it was that John Bright was a dangerous man. Indeed, Robert Betts was aware that he might be in physical danger.

The police sensed an opening. After his first contact with Betts ended, they directed Closson to admit that he was cooperating with the police. Moreover, to tell Betts that they might be "willing to make a deal with the driver."

Two days later, on October 26, Betts made a confession. "I was the driver, man." In the police surveillance van, they also heard Closson's reply: "The driver will walk away. Unless they're feeding me another bullshit story, that's what they tell me," Closson said. "I can't lie to you, and say I know this for sure. I don't. That's what they tell me."

Later that day, Betts told Closson he wanted him to call the police and ask about "making a deal" for the getaway driver. "So you can't make any deals," Betts wondered out loud, "the district attorney has to?" Closson repeated the ground rules for Betts' benefit, "The district attorney is willing to work with the driver and make him a deal but you're going to have to tell what you know first."

Closson telephoned the Anchorage police and got on the line with Investigator Austin. Closson, purporting to speak for Austin, again told Betts that the police could not make any deals, but that the district attorney could do that. Closson, through Austin, added that the district attorney was "willing to work with the driver and make him a deal."

Betts went for the offer. There was a smidge of resignation in his demeanor.

The "wires," however, revealed something unexpected. Revealed that Closson had lied about the disposal of the weapon. No one had thrown it in the bay. The truth, it soon became clear, was Closson sold the .45 to a drug dealer named Jack. For a gram of cocaine. He eventually explained that the reason he committed perjury was "to protect Jack."

It was not a good sign. Closson was immediately taken back before Judge Stewart. He corrected his false testimony. Stewart ratified the previously issued warrants and, in the process, Tyoga Closson lost some of his bravado.

When Robert Betts showed up at the police station, the first words out of Sgt. Grimes mouth were, "You're not going to get any deals." There was, Grimes added, ample evidence to prosecute him for his role in the attempted murder. He'd bragged about the job and even told someone he pulled the trigger. Investigator Austin added the clincher. "Either you can be on our team, or you can be out in the cold."

If there was any softening to be had, it was when Grimes told Betts that he wasn't going to arrest him, that he was free to go at any time. Of course, there was a catch. "The more you cooperate with us now and do just what we say," Grimes added, "the sooner this is gonna be all over and you'll be able to go right about your life."

From that time on, Betts considered himself "a member of the police team" and agreed to secretly tape other suspects. Before any of that could happen, though, Betts had to take care of some pressing police business.

On that October 26, 1985, Robert Allen Betts gave a full statement to the Anchorage police. It ultimately stretched to forty pages. Betts told them that a man he knew as John Bright had been hired to rough-up or scare Robert Pfeil. Betts said he had agreed to be, and was, the driver of the car when Bright opened fire on the Alaska Airlines pilot. He claimed he didn't know that in advance. Betts also confirmed police theories regarding surveillance of the Pfeil residence, and the rock through the garage window. Betts reported that during the surveillance, Bright wore military boots similar to the footprints found at the Pfeil property.

The instigator of the scare attack on Robert Pfeil, according to Betts, was a man named "McKenzie," who was associated with a union to which Pfeil also belonged. Having already heard a different name from Tyoga Closson, the cops asked Betts for the source of that information. "John Bright," he said confidently. Betts added that Mr. "McKenzie" worked with Wien Airlines—in itself a puzzling detail, since Robert Pfeil had only flown for Alaska Airlines—and then confidently added that Pfeil had started some trouble in the union. That's why he was shot.

Robert Allen Betts kept going, adding detail upon detail. The biggest one was that he was paid $1,000 to be the driver and that John Bright was the one who paid him. Betts used that money, he said, to buy a motorcycle, cocaine, and marijuana.

Betts added that the car they drove to the shooting was a light-colored Lincoln Continental—not the Chevrolet portrayed in the newspapers. He also told police that the Lincoln Continental belonged to a friend of Bright's known to him only as "Larry." The police asked whether "Larry was the guy that kind of brought this McKenzie and John together." Betts replied that he was. It was also Larry, Betts told them, who provided Bright with a Mossberg-brand 12-gauge pump action shotgun, outfitted with a pistol grip. It was to be Bright's "backup weapon."

Bright, Betts added, considered this Larry person his "partner." The cops wanted to know what role Larry played in the shooting. "None," Betts answered. "It was just his car." He added knowingly, "John drove it more than Larry did."

Crucially, Betts explained that it was a "contract" shooting, arranged through a friend of John Bright, a person known to Betts as "Junior."

By the end of the day, Betts agreed to conduct recorded conversations and otherwise work with the police. After Betts told them about John Bright's participation in a liquor store shooting, and that he might have killed someone else, the cops wanted Bright even more.[3] But the man could not be found. Police soon learned that John Bright had left the state.

They turned their focus to Larry, the owner of the Lincoln and applied for more search warrants. On October 27, Betts showed up at Larry Gentry's trailer—parked behind his father-in-law's house—and demanded he be paid the money he was still owed for the Pfeil job. He never got farther than the front porch. Gentry denied knowing what Betts was talking about.

"Well, I know," Betts explained in his slightly fractured English. "See John was supposed to pay me some money that I help him do."

"I don't know nothing about nothing what you're even talking about," Gentry insisted. "I don't know you and I don't even know what you're talking about."

"Well, we're talking about Robert Pfeil," Betts told him.

"Who's Robert Pfeil?"

"All I know is that John had me help him do a job," Betts told him, "and I was supposed to get paid a thousand dollars."

"Okay, if it's something illegal, don't be talking to me about it." It was the first hint that Larry Gentry knew more than he was letting on.

"I want to get my money," Betts demanded.

"What money? I don't even know what the fuck you're talking about. I have not the slightest idea what you're talking about. Now you want to tell me what it is? If it's something illegal, you don't want to tell me. I'm telling you, you don't want to tell me if it's something illegal. My sister is a cop."

Betts wouldn't—couldn't—let it rest. He added details, pertinent details. Robert Pfeil was the airline pilot who'd been shot, he explained. Shot by John. The doughy-faced 33-year-old bartender and construction worker continued with his denials.

"Like I said, dude, I ain't involved in it," Gentry said in his gentle

---

3 The alleged incident was a liquor store shooting that occurred on September 13, 1985, just a month before the attack on Robert Pfeil. At 6:30 p.m. that evening, 30-year-old Pyong An was found shot in the neck at the Bootleggers Cove Liquor Store, located within the Anchorage Hilton hotel. An was rushed to a local hospital by Anchorage Paramedics, where he died as a result of the gunshot wound. According to the police, no one in the hotel had heard a gunshot.

Kentucky drawl. Robert Betts once more pushed for his payoff. Gentry lashed out, exclaiming, "I was told you got everything, every fucking dime."

Gentry warned Betts not to bother him again. "You better handle this different," he said at one point. "You came to my home . . . You know what I feel like doing right now . . . Next time, you remember your fucking manners."

Betts left Larry Gentry with a thinly veiled threat. If he didn't get his money, he was going to start talking.

The next day, October 28, 1985, Betts and Gentry spoke again. This conversation was somewhat friendlier. During the course of their recorded chat, Betts stated that he had already spoken to "McKenzie," the alleged source of the contract. Gentry responded curtly that he had never heard of "McKenzie." Gentry again warned Betts not to bother him—or he'd be sorry. Then, on a grace note, Larry said, "I'll see what I can do for you."

It was hard to know who was playing whom. The Homicide Response Team had an idea.

On October 29, 1985, they helped Robert Betts write a letter—in Betts' handwriting—that implicated Larry Gentry and provided details of the Pfeil shooting. These words—and the photo of the Colt .45 that police helpfully included in the envelope—finally scared Larry Gentry into doing something he never intended.

9

Anchorage, Alaska, October 29 - November 2, 1985

LIKE TYOGA CLOSSON AND ROBERT BETTS before him, Larry Gentry was not the sharpest tool in the shed.[4] He had an IQ of about 86 and limited comprehension abilities. An early diagnosis said he had a slight mental disability. His family rejected that characterization, but acknowledged he was slow, easily led and, they thought, easily tricked. A linguist who spoke with him later said that "with an incomplete high school education, a low IQ, a strong tendency to comply, and a penchant for cooperativeness, Gentry was an easy target."[5]

After the confrontation with Betts at his house, for example, Gentry made a harassment complaint to police on the advice of his sister, Anchorage Police patrol officer Janet Perkins. Perkins did not know her brother was a suspect. She took him to the station, where her brother told police he didn't know what Betts was talking about.

When, at Sgt. Grimes' request, Betts taped his threatening letter to the back of a newspaper stand at a Tudor Road Qwik Stop, Gentry again called his sister. It was Janet Perkins who drove him—in her patrol

4 It didn't help that Gentry had fallen into the street life on Anchorage's notorious Fourth Avenue. A street that actor-comedian Bob Hope once described as "the world's longest bar," Fourth Avenue was a haven for drugs, sex workers and pimps.

5 Sociolinguist Roger W. Shuy specialized in legal cases that included language evidence. In a forty-year career he focused on the language implications of police interrogations and confessions. His work acknowledged that wily investigators and prosecutors can play, and win, vocabulary games with less sophisticated suspects.

car—to pick it up. Among the letter's explosive accusations was the following:

> "Larry said he crushed the car. John told me that Larry fucked up and owed money for cocaine and because John and Larry were partners, they took the job to pay back the money and give cash. A guy named McKenzie hired them to take care of Pfeil because he was causing trouble in the union."

When Perkins saw the reference to Pfeil in the letter, she took it and her brother to Sgt. Grimes, delivering what she believed was a new lead in the most important case then under investigation.

At the police station, Gentry denied any knowledge of the shooting, but made several contradictory and incriminating statements. He admitted talking to John Bright by phone about an hour after Robert Pfeil was shot. He admitted meeting Bright at a grocery store on Arctic Boulevard, near the airport, and taking back a shotgun, pillow and blanket he'd loaned Bright. Gentry claimed he had specifically warned Bright not to use the shotgun to kill anyone. Larry Gentry further acknowledged that Bright had been living at his trailer home and using his Lincoln.

There was also, Grimes thought, something wrong about Larry Gentry's bland assertions. He was evasive. Omitted information that would incriminate him. What worried Grimes more was the possibility that Gentry was planning to kill Robert Betts and was setting up a self-defense case. Gentry nevertheless told police they could "come over there and go through my house, do anything you want."

The cops let Larry Gentry go but took him up on the offer to search his trailer.

Once there, the police asked Larry and his recent bride, Susan, about John Bright. The Gentry's said he'd moved out a few months previous, just after they got married. Asked if Bright had taken everything with him, Susan Gentry pointed them to a storage shed and said that Bright had left some things behind. It was there that police spotted a pair of boots they expected would match the footprints at the Pfeil property. They also grabbed some dark clothing that Bright was reportedly seen wearing just before the shooting. The Gentry's gave the police permission to take Bright's belongings. From all appearances, Bright had abandoned them.

That wasn't the end of the Larry Gentry's strange adventures.

At another point, police directed Betts to set up a meeting with Gentry at a Sizzler Restaurant on Northern Lights Boulevard. Gentry told his sister, who told her patrol supervisor, who ordered patrol officers to stake out the restaurant. When homicide investigators learned of the stakeout, the meeting had to be called off.

Four days later, on November 2nd, Gentry again came to the police station. This time, the police had pointedly asked him to come in and clarify his earlier statements. When Larry Gentry faced Officer Joe Austin, he didn't know that they already had him marked as part of the Pfeil shooting.[6]

In the cramped interview room, Gentry was shown shots of his car and title. Was told what two co-conspirators had already told the police. Was played excerpts of the tapes made with Robert Betts. Was told about the boots they'd found at his trailer and how they matched prints found outside Robert Pfeil's house. Austin informed him that they suspected those boot prints belonged to his former roommate, and partner in crime. That they belonged to John Bright.

Then they told him someone was trying to kill Robert Betts. That Larry might be next. Larry Gentry suddenly started talking.

WHAT LARRY GENTRY BEGAN TO REVEAL, his body now consumed by nervous energy, were the outlines of a half-assed, yet ultimately successful, attempt to shoot Robert Pfeil. There was at least one small irony. The site of Larry's revelations, in the police headquarters building, was familiar to him. This was his sister's place. A cop's place.

But not that day.

That day, Larry Gentry was on the hook to expose the next rung in the ladder. The rung occupied by "Junior," full name Gilbert Kapualoha Pauole, Jr. An affable Hawaiian, Pauole was, more than anyone, the man everyone

---

6 Joe Austin was named Police Officer of the Month in 1979 for his "consistent high standard of performance as a patrol officer." His specialty was talking to witnesses and organizing investigative materials for courtroom presentation. In contrast to his boss, Sgt. Mike Grimes—who tended to be hard-edged and badgering—Austin was more like a priest at the confessional.

seemed to be pointing toward. A man well-known to the police, because of his affiliation with multiple topless-bottomless clubs in Anchorage.

"I can't even remember how it all started now," Gentry admitted, his face often cupped in his hands, his body rocking. He had already revealed that he'd worked for Junior, both as a doorman and bartender. The rest dribbled out in a steady, if sometimes anemic, stream. The cops were only slightly surprised to hear Larry admit to using a gram of cocaine a week. It wasn't exactly addict territory, but it marked him as more than a casual user.

"It just started over some drugs and shit," Gentry admitted. "I think maybe Junior had something to do with it. It's the reason we wind up gettin' ripped off. Junior gave me an ounce of coke to sell . . . he came up to John one day and asked him if he wanted to do somethin' for him and John said, 'sure.' Junior looked at me and said, 'Do you want to hear about it?' I said, 'No I don't,' so I left."

"So, Junior fronted you this ounce of coke?" Investigator Austin asked.

"Right, and it got stolen. John made a deal with him," Gentry insisted. "John said he was gonna pay Junior off for this job he was gonna get paid for. I said, 'Well great, then we ain't got nothin' to worry about.' So that there was taken care of there and that was the last we heard about that."

"Did you know what job he was referring to?"

"No, I did not," Gentry insisted.

"Did he tell you it was gonna be for Junior?" Austin wondered.

"No, he did not. I found out later. I figured it was for Junior. I figured it out myself. I done been told if I opened my mouth or anything I'd get killed . . . John told me that night he shot the guy and shit and then he started hollerin'. He figured Junior wasn't gonna pay."

As the questioning continued, Sgt. Grimes interjected to tell Gentry that, "The more you cooperate with us now and do just what we say, the sooner this is gonna be all over and you'll be able to go right about your life." Larry Gentry did just that. He talked and talked and talked. He talked as if to save his life.

"Ok," Austin continued, "did John indicate to you how much he was getting paid or did Junior . . ."

"Yeah, John told me it was going to be $10,000," Gentry confirmed.

"That Junior was going to pay him?"

"Yeah," Gentry said, then paused for effect. "Ten grand."

"What did John tell you as far as who the ultimate person that hired them," Austin asked, trying to reach the top rung of their ladder. "Did he tell you who?"

"Nah, Junior did. About, I think it was a week or so later," Gentry noted, before continuing in a halting series of half sentences. "He said that it was a, I asked him, I said did you get this guy, you . . . I said so and so, he's the one that hired you to have this guy knocked off and he went . . . yeah you know, and I went are you nuts . . . I said what the hell's wrong with you. I said man you should never have done this shit. He goes, well I told John it was gonna be a hot one. He goes, he said, I told you guys it was gonna be a hot one. I said I didn't know nothin' about no hot one, you know."

Austin kept probing, stacking question upon question. This time he explicitly asked Larry to name the person who hired Junior Pauole to shoot Robert Pfeil. Slowly, very slowly, Larry stretched out his revelations. There was, his sisters would later say, an urge about their brother to be accommodating. They would later accuse the police of manipulating him.

"Well, I read the paper," Gentry admitted. "It seemed, you know, who this guy was connected to, Pfeil, was connected to his wife being killed in a car."

There was one person who fit that "killed in a car" description. Muriel Pfeil. Austin dug deeper. Asked the follow up. "And that article referred to Mackay, is that correct?" In court, that would be called a "leading question." They were not in court.

"Right," Gentry answered. "And he said yeah, but Mackay is, I'm not sure he said Mackay's name or not, you know, I can't swear to that, it'd be like lying to you or somethin', so I don't really, I can't really tell you."

"Well, the best as you can recall though, what . . ."

"Was something about . . . the way I remember," Gentry said, hesitating, averting his eyes, waiting a beat before going all the way. "He did mention Mackay was the one that hired him from what I can remember of it."

There were other tidbits, one seemingly more tantalizing than the rest. Gentry asserted that, after the shooting, Junior Pauole claimed there were people in Hawaii who wanted other jobs done. Jobs just like the Pfeil shooting. Pressed for specifics, Gentry said Pauole planned to have John Bright do a killing in Portland, Oregon. According to Gentry, the beneficiary of the prospective killing in Oregon "does not know nothing about it. This here's just somethin' Junior's gonna do on his own."

Gentry quickly let out another little morsel. He tied Bright to the killing of an Asian man in downtown Anchorage. Counting Betts, they now had two people telling the same story. It confirmed their sense that John Bright was a clear and present danger. They'd heard enough.

At the end of Larry Gentry's long day in hell, Anchorage police asked him to wear a wire during any future conversations with John Bright or Gilbert Pauole. Gentry agreed. Then they took him to Judge David Stewart's courtroom, just as they had the others. They got their search warrant.

There was one unusual request. The cops asked the judge to permit Gentry and his wife to execute phone taps without police supervision. "The situation we have," Grimes told Judge Stewart, "is that due to a large number of applications and limited police resources, it would be almost impossible for a peace officer to sit at Larry Gentry's home 24 hours a day to monitor the phone."

They got their request, but that still didn't solve the problem of Robert Betts. Betts had mentioned the union prominently. Had mentioned it insistently. To date, the police investigation had barely touched that angle.

Sgt. Grimes did, however, contact Alaska Airlines on the last day of October, asking them to check for any active union members named "McKenzie." Airline officials confirmed that they were involved in a lengthy strike during the summer of 1985. There had been a few incidents, they said, but airline officials characterized them as non-violent.

When the airline's security head finally reported back on November 4, he left a message saying there was no one named "McKenzie" affiliated with Alaska Airlines in Anchorage. Their ladder now led them inexorably toward Gilbert K. "Junior" Pauole. If it led farther, so be it.

10

Anchorage, Alaska, November, 1985

THE HOMICIDE RESPONSE TEAM KNEW ALL ABOUT Junior Pauole. He was a fixture on the Fourth Avenue "Strip." He'd managed multiple strip clubs, including one called the Wild Cherry, since 1979. The Cherry and its ilk overflowed with men, money, naked women, and booze. Their patrons included a freewheeling swarm of workers down from the North Slope. Guys intent on spendthrifting their way from bar to bar and club to club.

They also knew that Junior's boss was a Seattle crime figure named Frank Colacurcio. That Colacurcio had a hidden interest in various strip clubs because, as a felon, he couldn't hold a liquor license. That Colacurcio also supplied the clubs with dancers and skimmed a hefty percentage of the take. Skimmed, that is, until the Alaska Beverage Control board decided to shut the whole thing down.

In Junior's world, trouble was never hard to find.

From the time the Wild Cherry opened in 1978, to the time it closed in 1983—to become a no-booze strip club called the Fancy Moose—the APD investigated 88 disturbances at the club. They ranged from larcenies, to bomb threats, shootings, assaults, and arson. In June of 1982 cops responded to an incident in which a patron, angry for being booted from the club, emptied a 9 mm pistol into the front door, barely missing Junior Pauole. The shooter did manage to hit one of his dancers in the leg. She survived.

It wasn't just the Wild Cherry. At the Alaska Express across the street, police were called 207 times between 1977 and 1982. One of them involved a prostitution-related shooting in which one man was killed. Then there were the rapes and more sex beefs and more murders. One of Junior's other clubs, the Good Times, had 52 police calls in three years. A shootout at the Red Garter left the manager and bouncer hospitalized. The shooters were members of a motorcycle gang. A club called Moby Dicks was torched, but not before legions of violence, some of it spilling out onto the street.

It got so bad that the clubs stopped reporting and that was another problem.

In the early eighties, a serial killer named Robert Hansen prowled these very same clubs. On November 16, 1981, a dancer named Sherry Morrow showed up at the Wild Cherry for her 11:00 p.m. shift. She told her boyfriend she had a doctor's appointment the next day, so she'd be spending the night at a girlfriend's house. Unbeknownst to anyone, she'd also agreed to a date with Robert Hansen.

At her friend Lisa's house, Sherry confided that a man she'd met offered her $300.00 for a photo shoot. She was to meet him in a downtown restaurant at noon the next day. A week later, Sherry's boyfriend reported her missing. She hadn't shown up for her doctor's appointment. She was nowhere to be found. Soon enough, the cops were on it, including Joe Austin. He ended up talking to Junior Pauole multiple times. By that time, a string of dancers, including Sherry Morrow, had gone missing from multiple clubs.

Sherry was found the following fall, in a shallow grave on the Knik River. There were many more, just like her. Robert Hansen had been lurking under the noses of Anchorage police for a decade. It was, in fact, that very debacle which birthed the Homicide Response team. The APD was now taking a no-holds-barred approach to killers in their midst. They were depending on Larry Gentry to lead them to the next rung on their ladder.

Larry Gentry didn't have much trouble finding Junior Pauole. He was his former boss. Their first conversation was recorded on November 5, 1985, when Junior called Larry and Larry clicked "record." Junior started off in classic fashion.

"Are you in bed?" he asked. "You have your dick in your hand?"

Junior was calling about a piece of crime-related business. Something about a plane ticket that John Bright was supposed to return. Something about Pauole cashing that ticket and sending the proceeds back to Bright. Gentry didn't know what Junior was talking about but now that he had him on the line, he jumped to Robert Betts.

"I need to talk to you, guy," Gentry insisted. "It seems like John might have forgot to pay his driver and he's been over here bugging me."

"Well," Pauole replied, "that's something you don't know about, right?" After a back and forth in which Gentry insisted he'd told Betts he was clueless about his claim, Pauole added, "You just tell the guy, hey, don't come around my house any more man. I don't know, that's something you and John have to work out. I don't know nothin' about nothin' man."

Gentry was insistent that the two of them meet and suggested a nearby Sears store. Pauole wanted to meet at his club, the Fancy Moose, instead. It was a no go. Until Larry mentioned the letter that Robert Betts had dropped off.

"Am I in the letter?" Junior asked.

"Yeah, the way . . . yeah. Got you in there and Mackay in there. John's done some talkin' to this damn kid."

"You kiddin'?" Pauole asked, his voice a near quaver.

"No, I'm not kiddin'," Gentry replied. "It says that, uh, you hired John and him to do the fuckin' job and that Mackay hired you to hire them and that I let John use my car to fuckin' do it."

"Did you tell John that?" Pauole wondered.

"Yeah . . . He said he was gonna be up here in a couple of days to take care of all that." Gilbert Pauole immediately distanced himself, saying, "Well I don't know nothin' about nothin' like that."

"Yeah, so I don't know if you want to see the letter or not?"

"Nope," Junior replied. "Just get rid of it."

The attempted murder of Capt. Pfeil led some to describe them as the "gang who couldn't shoot straight." But that moniker belonged to only one of them. To John Ian Arthur Bright. And John Bright was in exile. There was a reason. At least one good reason.

Robert Pfeil was still alive and Junior Pauole was reluctant to pay him. "No way," Bright replied, indignant, "I shot him five times, he shouldn't be alive." That changed quickly; Bright made plans to finish the job. He ended up alone, at the airport, headed to Houston, Texas. No wonder the cops couldn't find him.

He wasn't alone for long. Within days, Larry Gentry sent Bright's girlfriend, dancer Theresa "Sassy" Marshall, down to meet him. Her job was to deliver an envelope. They met in a rental car at the Houston International Airport. Sassy was there when he opened the envelope, saw that it held dozens of hundred-dollar bills.

"Important papers, huh?" Sassy asked. John Bright just smiled. The kind of smile, Sassy said, that meant "don't ask." She didn't. She had a feeling she already knew what that money was for.

Once, while driving around Anchorage with Bright, he'd pointed out a jogger and told her he'd been hired to kill that man. "Before I left, he told me that he was going to do the shooting and I didn't believe him," Marshall later told authorities. "Then when I took him the money, I felt that could have been why I give him the money. Because it was part of the payoff. So, I didn't ask any questions."

Sassy Marshall didn't like Houston, though. Said the people were snobs. John's mother lived there, though, so it was a logical place to start an exile. Soon enough they were off to Florida. John Bright had spent time there as a youth. Had *done* time there. At age 16, he stole a Corvette Stingray and led police on a high-speed chase. Tried as an adult, he was sentenced to five years in prison. That wasn't the only evidence of a life headed off the rails. Bright admitted to pulling off a series of Florida burglaries with his older brother.

His initial arrival in Alaska didn't go well either. He didn't like it. He was soon back in Florida and getting in more trouble. Yet something about Alaska called him and, when he was released from the Florida correctional system, he flew to Anchorage. Went straight into the woods to clear his head.

In the rumble-tumble life of John Ian Arthur Bright, one thing always led to another. His first job in Alaska was a food warehouse near the Anchorage International Airport. It was a forty-minute bike ride from his Government Hill apartment. He found the Wild Cherry a good place to stop on the way back. It was beers and video games and, of course, topless dancers. That's where he met Larry Gentry. Fate held all the cards.

Because John Bright cultivated the image of a tough guy, he was hired as a bouncer at the Cherry. It was no ordinary topless/bottomless establishment. The Colacurcio's brought in a new crop of dancers every week. They needed someone who would chase off the pimps who sought to steal those dancers and recruit them as sex workers. John Bright, with his long hair and tattoos, not only looked the part. He acted it.

According to those who knew him, "John Bright projected the image of a sidewalk commando, who could handle any problem that would come his way." He was macho. A street person. He told stories of taking a mop ringer to someone who'd bothered him. He always had knives and guns on his person.

If there was one thing that distinguished John Bright from his cohorts, though, it was his intelligence. His mother said they'd done IQ testing when they lived in Connecticut. Judy Douglas said, "John tested out at 140 or 150." He was nine years old at the time. That score put him in the highly gifted range.

Be that as it may, Bright had clearly gone astray. Maybe it was his jail time, which put him in with hardened criminals. Maybe it was his abiding resistance to authority. He readily admitted to being a white supremacist. Admitted he belonged to the Odinist Society, an extremist group devoted to "keeping racial lines pure."[7] Whatever his views, police knew they had to keep him in their crosshairs.

They put a tap on Sassy Marshall's telephone and hit paydirt. John Bright called her soon after she returned to Alaska. This time, curiosity finally got the best of her. She asked about the money. He told her it was the rest of his payoff. Told her that he'd driven down the road and pulled up alongside Robert Pfeil and shot him. Shot him five times with a .45. That the shots came from inside Larry Gentry's Lincoln Continental. He also told her his total payment was $7,500, but that he only received $2,500. The rest went to pay off a cocaine debt.

That wasn't the only phone tap the police had. They also had one on a telephone belonging to a Pauole associate named Matthew Vickers, who'd allegedly passed on the Robert Pfeil assassination attempt. This was the same Matthew Vickers who'd been paid by Junior Pauole to beat up pimps,

7 Portions of John Bright's biography courtesy of journalist Earl Swift of the *Anchorage Times*.

at the rate of $200 per broken bone. Things like that put Bright and Vickers in the same league.

In one of those conversations, Bright told Vickers about the shooting of Robert Pfeil. Bright said that he'd used a handgun, but that he'd "fucked up" because he wasted several shots, turning the shooting into a "big mess." Bright additionally told Vickers that Gentry was in charge of picking up his car after the shooting, then disposing of all the evidence. The vehicle, the guns, the clothing.

It was Vickers who told the cops that, in early October, Bright left him a package to safeguard. Vickers' wife eventually opened it and found that it contained C-4 explosives. Bright later explained that the material was to make a bomb as "backup" for a job he had taken. Had Junior Pauole not intervened, John Bright would have used that very explosive at the hospital where Bob Pfeil lay severely injured.

Strangely enough, not everyone saw the danger lurking in John Bright. His friends and family professed that he was more bark than bite. "If you worried about every time John said he was going to kick somebody's ass or kill somebody, the police wouldn't have time to deal with anybody but John Bright," claimed Janet Perkins, Larry Gentry's sister. "It's all such a joke if you know John, because he's all hot steam."

Larry Gentry's wife, Susan, agreed. "I never saw any violence," she asserted. "He always talked a lot of bull, but I never saw him do anything."

Bright's father, Robert, made similar claims, saying that his "son has these fantasies of being a big-time hoodlum and sometimes he takes credit for crimes he really didn't commit."

Somehow, the protestations of John Bright's friends and family no longer made sense. They were reminders of benign encounters, experienced years before. That John Bright no longer seemed to exist if, in fact, he ever did.

11

Anchorage, Alaska, October 28, 1976 – November 30, 1976

NEIL MACKAY'S CUSTODY FIGHT WITH ROBERT PFEIL was a battle for the soul. There was an abiding, even overwhelming undercurrent of anger and scorn. Things were bad enough that the judge who got the case, Judge Roy Madsen of Kodiak, was offered a police escort to the Anchorage hearings and was told that nobody was to know where he stayed when he was in town. The 1976 bombing incident loomed in the background, a warning to anyone who came near.

From the outset, Neil Mackay was insistent on one thing. Scotty was his. "Judge Compton's ruling found I was a fit and proper person," Mackay noted of the judge who presided over his divorce. "I received a copy of the document from Judge Compton stating I have full care and custody of Scotty. I have a certified copy of that document."

There was one inconvenient truth, however. Mackay had preempted Judge Compton. Compton had no authority to issue further orders. That's why Judge Madsen was there.

And Madsen knew he had a complex, emotional case before him. His gut told him the parties needed a cooling off period, so they could approach this matter more dispassionately. He also needed to move quickly. He had to get the parties to agree to a third way. One that involved a temporary custodian for Scotty as well as someone to independently represent Scotty's interests during the custody matter.

The judge quickly reached two solutions. He got Alaska Supreme Court

Justice Robert Erwin and his wife to take temporary custody of Scotty. The Erwin's had known the Pfeil family since the mid-forties. They also knew Neil Mackay, having met him in 1964. The justice was also very aware of the divorce proceedings, calling them the longest, bitterest divorce case in Alaska's history.

When it came to the subject of Scotty's representation, only one name came up. Robert Wagstaff.[8] Madsen called the man to his chambers. Madsen requested that he act as Scotty's legal representative. Stated he was familiar with his work. Said he wanted him to represent Scotty because he wanted a fighter.[9] Wagstaff thought about it—and was advised by other attorneys to stay out of this fractious matter. After discussing it with his law partner, however, Wagstaff called Madsen back. He was in.

Judge Madsen now had his quick fix in place.

The Erwins, however, suddenly found themselves in the middle. They had known and liked Muriel. Muriel had told them a great deal about Neil. She did not use the word, "hate," the judge insisted. Judge Erwin had also taken the time to tell Neil Mackay how Muriel felt. He'd talked to Neil for hours at a time.

But Scotty's stay at the Erwin's was traumatic. Visitation alternated between the Pfeil family and his father. Each party had visitation for three days a week. It was a whirlwind of conflicting loyalties. Within two weeks, Scotty came up sick. The Erwins called the Pfeils for assistance; they also called Neil Mackay. They were on their own.

Increasingly, the Erwin's got the impression that Neil Mackay could not trust himself. They told him that if the boy wanted to visit him at the Mackay Building, they would take him. Mackay initially said, "no." Eventually they got him to pick up Scotty at 8 or 9 a.m. and then return him at 1:00 p.m.

Even then, it seemed strained. Neil always came with his brother-in-law, Alfred Willis, or the Willis' son. Mackay had difficulty getting up the driveway and onto the porch. Would support himself by holding onto the

8 In 1975, Wagstaff successfully argued a landmark case before the Alaska Supreme Court concerning the right of children to retain counsel, independent of parental input.

9 During one juvenile custody hearing, the master excused Wagstaff from the proceeding. Wagstaff refused to leave. He was escorted out by a security bailiff.

fence. Mackay had particular difficulty on the ice. Knowing this, in the wintertime the Erwin's tried to have Scotty ready to go when his father arrived. Even then Mackay insisted that they dress Scotty in a coat that he'd bought him.

The Pfeil's, on the other hand, came to the Erwin house many times. Had dinner with them at the Erwin's request. The Judge and his wife got to know them fairly well. Noted that they agreed to any limitations on visits. That Scotty got along with them.

All was not right with Scotty. At one point the Erwin's found him wandering down the street. They went out and got him. They brought him home.

Then there was the phone call, the one where Mackay berated Judge Erwin. Called him names, said his conduct was questionable. In fact, accused the Justice of a conspiracy to take Scotty from him. The judge later said, "I listened." Mackay went on to declare that Caroline Pfeil—Scotty's aunt—should not be allowed to visit the boy and declared that the Erwin's were only in it for the money.

Judge Erwin adamantly rejected Mackay's accusation. They accepted no money for foster children in their home. Indeed, the Erwin's felt they'd done Neil Mackay a favor.

"He was not the most popular man in the area," the judge noted. "He was knocking on doors, looking in windows. He was looking for Scotty's babysitter. Then there was the telephone call and strange things at my house. I heard things breaking. Mackay was conducting surveillance. I have a great deal of trouble understanding him."

Madsen made no secret of his impatience with the fractious Mackay custody matter. Cases like this tried the resolve of even the most patient judge. Even a brief review of the Mackay divorce file gave him a glimpse of what he faced. Bob Pfeil's answer to the habeas corpus petition quoted revelations that Mackay had "psychological characteristics indicative of a child abuser." In that same document, Pfeil noted that Neil Mackay had denied, in times past, "that he was in fact the natural father of the child."

For those who opposed Neil Mackay, reality was a ticking timebomb. They had to find a way to hold Neil Mackay accountable. To hold his feet to the bonfire. Robert Wagstaff wanted the experts to weigh in not only on Mackay's fitness for parenthood but also hear from anyone who could speak to Muriel Pfeil's homicide.

The latter was a reach, and Wagstaff knew it. He also knew it would make him few friends among the Neil Mackay partisans. He said it anyway. Even put it in writing. "Whether or not Neil S. Mackay was involved in the death of Muriel Pfeil, or who else might be involved," Wagstaff told the court, "is relevant to the best interests of Scotty Mackay, here being litigated." At a minimum, he was convinced Neil Mackay was not fit to have custody of his son. That his condition was not temporary. That Mackay would stop at nothing to get what he wanted.

It wasn't going to be simple. It would never be simple. There was—and always will be—an understandable urge to award child custody to a biological parent. Overturning that could not—should not—be on the basis of whim or an inherent dislike for the surviving parent. Wagstaff and Baily knew they had to present the full range of Mackay's medical and psychiatric diagnoses. Had to get that information before the court prior to any final decision was reached. Had to convince, moreover, a judge who was reluctant to dig deeper.

The maneuvering was full speed ahead.

Mackay took aggressive steps to suppress the medical and psychiatric testimony taken during his divorce. He wrote letters to two doctors at the Elmendorf Air Force hospital, men who'd treated him in the past. Warned them of an upcoming deposition that "will be for the purpose of obtaining evidence which may or may not be used against me." Then added that, "Irrespective of the merits of the taking of said deposition, I must, as a matter of fact, claim the doctor-patient privilege."

His was a preemptive move and it worked. When Dr. Pollock—his attending physician at Elmendorf Air Force Base—was called in to Judge Madsen's November custody hearing, he refused to testify. In court, he read from Mackay's demand letter instead. A letter which said, in part, "I hereby invoke the doctor-patient privilege and object to your giving any and all information which you acquired, either directly or indirectly, as the result of your being one of my physicians."

That gag on physician testimony—combined with Mackay's refusal to testify, combined with Judge Madsen's disallowance of any medical or psychiatric evidence from Neil and Muriel's divorce action—meant that the record before the court was incredibly thin. Mackay's strategy paid off. He now had Judge Madsen where he wanted him.

Judge Madsen reverted to the decree of Judge Allen Compton, who had noted in October that "It would be an anomalous situation if the surviving parent, who by law is entitled to custody at this point in time, could not obtain evidence of that right from the court that had previously limited his right . . . Defendant's Motion for Modification is hereby granted, and Defendant is restored the care, custody and control of Scotty."

On November 16, 1976, Madsen took the next step. He approved Mackay's Writ of Habeas Corpus and, in the process, awarded full custody of Scotty Mackay to his father.

12

Anchorage, Alaska, November 16 – 30, 1976

ROBERT WAGSTAFF TOOK JUDGE MADSEN'S PRECIPITOUS decision straight to the Alaska Supreme Court which, in Anchorage terms, was only steps away. He appealed the Kodiak judge's ruling. Over the objections of Neil Mackay—who claimed that Wagstaff was no longer a party to the matter—he won a reprieve. It was, by any measure, a resounding defeat for Scotty's biological father.

The Supreme Court ordered a full inquiry into Neil Mackay's fitness, not the constrained one Judge Madsen had meekly approved. That inquiry was to include all "relevant information, past and present." The divorce, his military treatment history. His family dynamics, everything. The Court also ruled that Mackay had waived his physician-patient privilege. The medical professionals were now cleared to testify. He couldn't even rely on testimonial privilege against self-incrimination. As the Court noted, "that privilege was improvidently invoked by Neil S. Mackay at the Superior Court proceeding."

The *coup de grace* was the Supreme Court go ahead for the appointment of "two independent medical examiners." There would be fresh eyes. With impending updates on Neil Mackay's fitness for parenthood.

With the Supreme Court ruling in hand, Wagstaff and Baily were at the ready. They had the ongoing hostility between the man and wife on background. They were also armed with subpoenas for the physicians, psychiatrists, psychologists, and other professionals who'd testified during Neil's divorce from Muriel. There were ten in all. They would bring them back. They were poised to reach out for additional medical examinations.

Even without that, their quiver was full. The divorce file had the deposition of the doctor who'd catalogued Neil Mackay's drug abuse. There was another doctor who'd documented Mackay's overdoses. One who said there was evidence of diffuse brain tissue loss. Based upon that information, the doctor concluded that Mackay lacked the insight to function effectively as a parent. It got worse.

Another doctor had said, during the divorce proceedings, that Mackay should not be allowed to see Scotty. There was yet another doctor who said that Mackay's drug problems affected his propensity for violence. There was more. One psychologist diagnosed Mackay as "very, very close" to being a paranoid. More important was her evaluation of the Neil Mackay's emotional stability and anger:

"I have, however, gotten the distinct impression," she wrote, "and this is in my area, that Mr. Mackay is fixated at the level of emotional development of an under five person, that he is quite capable of having temper tantrums, and that his psychological organization is perhaps most similar to maybe a 3 ½, 4-year-old, in terms of frustration tolerance and ability to cope with feelings of anger."

A psychologist at the Langdon Clinic in Anchorage opined that: "There is strong evidence of the presence of an acute and relatively severe psychosis of thought disorder type", which includes elements of paranoia and sadomasochism. The doctor also said that "The presence of brain damage, which while scorable only in the borderline range . . . points toward a pervasive, somewhat disabling condition." He found Mr. Mackay to have a "very fragmented personality" which caused him to function "almost on a psychotic level."

The doctor concluded that Neil Mackay was "capable of impulsive acting out with poor judgment," which he defined as "doing things impulsively without intellectual control."

Before his separation from Muriel, there were, in fact, allegations of physical abuse. When she finally filed for divorce, Muriel Pfeil asked for, and received, a temporary restraining order against Neil Mackay. Psychiatric reports ordered by the court found that Mackay had "propensities to violence and irrational conduct," and "a tendency to violence in stressful situations."

One incident stood out. A mere three months after Scotty's birth, Neil was already making demands. He called the travel service and insisted on a visit with Scotty. Muriel rebuffed him. Gave him what Mackay characterized as "the run around." Neil stormed out of the penthouse and rushed over to Muriel's travel office.

"I'm busy," she told him when he got there. He ignored her. Demanded that she call her mother and arrange a visitation. He wanted to see his son. He was adamant.

"I'm busy," she repeated impatiently.

Neil Mackay angrily grabbed a nearby pile of paperwork. Tore it up and tossed it in the air. Then stamped out of the office in a fit of fury. Muriel chased after him. Threatened to call the cops, saying, "You can't do that in my office."

Neil Mackay became even more enraged, yelling "it's my building," and "you can't tell me what to do in my building." With that, he went full-on raging bull. Pushed his way back into the office. Started throwing furniture. Slammed her adding machine against the wall. Tossed her typewriter too.

"I pushed everything off on the floor," he later admitted, even shoving her telephone off the desk.

It wasn't the first time he'd erupted. In the summer of 1974, during the height of divorce proceedings, Neil Mackay physically barricaded himself in the penthouse apartment of the Mackay Building. According to court records, he "willfully failed and refused to appear in court, in violation of a court order."

There was also the time he "caught" Scotty playing with a doll at his maternal grandmother's house. It made sense for his grandmother to have dolls. She had two granddaughters. Witnesses said that Mackay picked up the doll, which was laying among other toys, and threw it across the room. He declared he didn't want his son playing with dolls.

Grandma Pfeil recounted—under oath—the time Muriel came home at 8 or 9 o'clock, her face red because Neil had struck her. "I'm going to call the police," her mother said. Muriel said, "No." Grandma Pfeil called one of Neil's closest friends instead, Judge Occhipinti. She told the judge about the red marks on her daughter's face, about Neil striking her.

"Tell Muriel not to go back to Neil," Occhipinti advised.

In 1974, just one year into the divorce proceedings, Muriel told the court she feared for her son's safety.

Neil Mackay responded by suing Bob and Marianne Pfeil for destroying the "father-son relationship." He also filed an affidavit in response to Muriel's no-visitation request. His counter argument, which alluded to real estate magnate and future governor Walter Hickel, was no doubt intended to highlight the absurdity of his wife's allegations. It struck some observers as both frightening and bizarre.

"The entire Pfeil family will be absolutely positive that if Mrs. Pfeil were to be found dead," Mackay wrote, "they would know exactly who did it, of course, it would be none either than Walter J. Hickel. Mrs. Pfeil [Sr.] lives in deadly fear of Walter J. Hickel. This syndrome appears to be contagious and now Muriel speculates 'that the defendant will sooner or later cause bodily harm to her or her mother or the baby.'"

Mackay went on to add that, "I have tried to be tolerant and have made excuses to my family as to why they could not visit Scotty, but the time has now come where tolerance has reached an end."

THE BREAK CAME IN THE RUNUP TO CHRISTMAS 1976. The Erwins, it seemed, had plans to visit Hawaii over the holidays. There would be eight of them voyaging to a rented condominium in Maui. Their plans, they added, had been in place since June of that year. In a letter to Judge Madsen, titled "Vacation in Hawaii," they made their position clear.

"We want to take Scotty with us, but we wish to state strongly that we do not intend to go on the vacation if it means in any way that Scott will be removed from our home prior to a permanent solution of the custody problem. We think it would be extremely detrimental to the boy to shift temporary custody at this time, and we would rather forego our vacation than to risk any harm to Scott."

Neil Mackay went ballistic. His first complaint was that his visitation rights with Scotty had been cut off. That was true. There was still too much dissention between the parties and Judge Madsen had called for a time-out. The central issue of his complaint went to deeper issues, to what looked for all the world like primeval fears. Speaking of himself in the third person, Neil Mackay wrote a bitter letter to Judge Madsen.

"Mackay wants to point out to the court that he has never been able to spend any Christmas Eve or Christmas Day with Scotty," he wrote. He had someone to blame. "Mr. Wagstaff's unauthorized letter of November 23, 1976, terminating his Friday visitations prevents Mackay from spending Christmas Eve with his son."

"Christmas Day," he added, with microscopic attention to detail, "falls on a Saturday, which is Mackay's scheduled visitation day with Scotty. If a positive clarification of this court's order of October 29, 1976, is entered and allows Justice Erwin and his wife, Monica Erwin, to take Scotty to Hawaii, it would, of course, prevent Mackay and Scotty from spending any portion of the holidays together, let alone Christmas Eve and Christmas Day.

"Further, a positive clarification would do great damage to the father-son relationship between Mackay and Scotty. What would be Scotty's emotional and mental state of mind should he be surreptitiously taken away from Mackay by the Erwins!"

Judge Madsen knew there was trouble dead ahead. His first instinct was to contact another of Neil Mackay's friends, Judge C.J. Occhipinti. Occhipinti had performed the marriage between Neil and Muriel. He also knew that the judge had helped take Neil to the hospital on "a couple of occasions due to adverse reactions to drugs." That Occhipinti had been involved in the divorce and property settlements between the two parties.

To get to that settlement, Occhipinti had to bar Muriel and Neil from the meetings. "They had tied up the court system for months," he recalled. "Being sympathetic to both parties, I banged heads together and we settled it."

So it was that Madsen called Occhipinti and asked if he could recommend another custodian for Scotty, "If I should decide to relieve the Erwins of this responsibility so they could make their planned trip to Hawaii." He called again three days later and Occhipinti told him he hadn't found anyone but added "that he and his wife would be willing to assume the responsibility."

Judge Madsen's hands were tied, however, by his very own haste to rid himself of this case. With his hands firmly clapped back by the Alaska Supreme Court decision, and hesitant to further aggravate the already corrosive visitation arrangements, Madsen reached in another direction. He was leaning toward a solution that awarded the next round of temporary custody to reestablish "a permanent association with a blood relative or relatives."

He didn't have Robert and Marianne Pfeil in mind. Instead, he awarded temporary custody to Carolina and Alfred Willis, Scotty's paternal aunt and uncle. Madsen had seen them in court. Had taken their measure. It was Scotty's third custody change in as many months. The fourth if one counted his mother. By all accounts that was three too many.

Carolina and Albert Willis were about to visit hell. They'd already seen glimpses.

13

Anchorage, Alaska, December 6, 1976 – April 1977

NEIL MACKAY'S LAIR WAS AN ELABORATE PENTHOUSE at the top of the Mackay building. Among its features was a large water fountain—a leftover from his time with Muriel—and a law office that was inextricably attached to the living quarters. That's how he liked it: the two modes of his existence carelessly intertwined.

A keen observer would notice he kept odd hours. He was in and around the office all the time but might take a one- or two-hour nap in the middle of the day. While his legal secretary knew there was no pattern to his sleeping, his preference was to work late, from 9:00 p.m. to 3:00 a.m.

"He won many of his cases by just outworking the other attorney," Judge Occhipinti noted. "You'd see him at 4 o'clock in the morning in his office, working."

It was perhaps no surprise, then, that his office was a clog of law books, depositions, and Westlaw quarterlies. That mess was interwoven with paperwork—subpoenas, motions, and memoranda in various states of readiness. The quiet hum of his legal research was interrupted only by the sound of his Smith-Corona typewriter.

These days, his biggest client was himself. All of his recent tangles were waged against one or more members of the Pfeil family. The first was the divorce action, *Muriel Adele Mackay v. Neil S. Mackay*, filed in August 1973. The next one began shortly after Muriel's death. He'd thought his chief target was Robert Pfeil, but the field was spreading.

He was now determined to take advantage of that shift. With temporary custody moving to his sister, he sensed an opening which, while short of his ultimate goal, was trending in his direction. If he could get rid of Bob Wagstaff, he still had a chance to prevail in Judge Madsen's court. In a December 6 letter, he wrote:

NEIL S. MACKAY hereby moves the court to terminate the servies [sic] of Robert H. Wagstaff of the law firm of Wagstaff & Middleton as attorney for Neil P. "Scotty" Mackay, the natural son of petitioner.

He followed that with a December 21 memorandum that took things even further. It was an *ad hominem* attack and it was vicious. "Mr. Wagstaff has not been representing Scotty in order to protect Scotty's rights," Mackay claimed. "Rather, he has spent all of his time with Mr. Baily and/or representing the interests of Justice Erwin in this matter."

He continued in the same vein:

"There is no doubt where Mr. Wagstaff of the law firm of Wagstaff & Middleton finds himself, i.e., right in the hip pockets of Justice Erwin and a politically influential attorney whom Mackay understands was a good geologist. Mr. Wagstaff is doing nothing constructive relative to this particular proceeding. As a result of his intellectual dishonesty, there is strong animosity between Mr. Wagstaff and Mackay. It should be clear to the court that Mr. Wagstaff is representing himself first, the interest of Mr. Baily second, the interest of Justice Erwin third."

It was, Mackay pointed out, all about the money:

"Mr. Wagstaff knows just as well as everyone else that the bottom line of this proceeding is the estate of Muriel A. Pfeil, deceased. There are assets available . . . Mr. Wagstaff has a money-making machine so long as he is the attorney for Scotty."

Mackay's obsession with money was, in fact, legendary. One critic told journalist Sheila Toomey that Mackay was "a sharp, perhaps unethical lawyer and real estate speculator who would do anything for a buck."

Asked during his custody trial about contributions to his ex-wife's reward fund, Mackay answered, "Why should I contribute to reward money? Why should I? Publicity and want-ads are unwise. They have nothing to do with the dead."

Neil Mackay's sister did not share her brother's apparent obsession with money. She was by all accounts a humble and religious woman. A woman who had raised two children. Who'd come north to help Neil manage the Mackay Building—an unwieldy holding that soon consumed them—and care for their mother, residing in a nearby care facility. Now, with temporary custody of her nephew, she and her husband were cast into the center of a storm.

They didn't exactly understand why they were put there. How was it that Judge Madsen had picked them? He had, to their reckoning, picked them out of the blue without even discussing it with them. It was their daughter who called to say Judge Madsen had awarded them custody of Scotty. Mackay attorney Arthur "Dave" Talbot who brought over the Court Order and explained it to them. Talbot told them they had to follow the Court Order or Scotty would be placed in another home. Carolina and Alfred thought the whole thing bizarre.

But the Willis' vowed to do their best to follow the judge's orders. As part of that, they decided to move Scotty out of his father's apartment and into their own unit, one story below in the Mackay building. Going to another apartment was very disturbing to Scotty. His bedroom was upstairs. His toys were upstairs. His father was upstairs. Still, Scotty seemed to be handling it better than his father.

Neil Mackay took it badly, very badly. If they were going to carry out the Order of Court, Carolina quoted her brother, "I could get my ass out and kiss his." On December 13, while in Scotty's bedroom, Neil came in and gave Carolina an envelope. Told her it was their termination checks. They thought of Scotty. For his sake, they hated to move again but the Willis' moved to an apartment complex in Eagle River a month later, taking a position as apartment managers. They were now 14 miles from downtown Anchorage. It proved a difficult adjustment for everyone concerned.

Neil insisted that Carolina and Alfred were terminated for "economic reasons." Accused his sister of saying things he didn't like. Particularly galling was her assertion that he and Muriel had brought all of this on themselves. "That really got to me," he said. "It irritated me." His venom, once reserved for Robert Wagstaff and Robert Pfeil, now included anyone else who stood between him and Scotty. Including, it turned out, his own sister.

No matter what Neil Mackay claimed, Scotty was struggling to come to terms with his mother's death. It was inevitable. A three-year-old doesn't have a wealth of experience to fall back on. At one point Scotty was seen by a psychiatrist, who observed him in an undirected play exercise, during which he played games, drew pictures, and amused himself in a sand tray. Based on that play exercise, psychiatrist Dr. Barry Mendelsohn reached some disturbing conclusions.

"A major area of anxiety is in relation to the loss of Scotty's mother," Mendelsohn noted. "He has a strong sense of loss and a magical expectation that his mother will return. He has a desire to join his mother. I observed him playing in the playroom with a castle. He knocked everything down. He said, 'things are bombed and on fire.' A child of this age ascribes causation to himself. That comes from the notoriety of this case. Scotty listens for his name on TV and feels a great deal of responsibility."

The real danger was that Scotty would get lost in all the maneuvering.

14

Anchorage, Alaska, February 23, 1977

THERE WAS NO SECRET SAUCE IN BOB WAGSTAFF'S encounters with Neil Mackay. Every time he had a chance at the man, he pressed him about Muriel Pfeil's murder. Neil Mackay was, usually, evasive, even smug. He was not a man to suffer fools. Things were different on February 23, 1977. They were once more at the offices of R & R Court Reporters. The time was 9:30 a.m.

The parties were gathered for another deposition of Neil Mackay. Robert Pfeil's attorney, Doug Baily, was there. Robert Wagstaff was there, as well as Mackay's attorney, Dave Talbot. The room was crowded with the attendees, a court reporter and one guest. Robert Peter Pfeil.

At six-foot-four and 200 plus pounds, Robert Pfeil towered over the five-foot-nine Neil Mackay. Both had been athletes in their day—Pfeil a star high school basketball player who played lacrosse at the U.S. Military Academy, Mackay a high school varsity baseball player. Since that heyday, however, Neil Mackay had suffered a cavalcade of physical maladies. A court-ordered review of his medical records revealed an ankle fracture in 1948; a cerebral concussion in 1955; a shoulder dislocation in 1958; and a compression fracture of his L1 vertebrae in 1961. He had a metal plate in his skull from a World War II related accident at a Navy base in California.

About an hour into the proceedings, Bob Wagstaff once more directed his questions to the topic of Muriel Pfeil's death. He asked Neil Mackay if he had the "name of anybody that might have been involved in Muriel's death? Have you gotten any names from sources?"

Mackay wanted to know if they were back on the record. They were. Mackay was coy. "I hate to place a stigma on anybody in relationship to the bare-naked allegations," he replied, "but . . . is that your question?" Mackay asked.

"That's certainly a portion of it," Doug Baily responded. If Neil Mackay had any doubts about what he was up against, they were certainly fading by now. It was going to be three against two.

"Well, I think the question was," Wagstaff continued, "since Muriel's death, since the death of Muriel Pfeil, your former wife, have you received any information from any source concerning the identity of the person or persons who were responsible for her death?"

Neil Mackay's face belied a smirk, his impatience beginning to show. "Well, counsel, if I relied on the information that I have received," he said with a sneer, "we would be here for fifteen days."

There was a pause for effect and an implicit "but" in his next utterance. "It's my understanding that it's a possibility there was a mistake in the identity of the car, that the car was parked in the wrong place at the wrong time. I have received—I've been queried as to whether Bob Pfeil might have been responsible for it."

Bob Pfeil immediately launched from his chair. He leaped in Neil Mackay's direction. Mackay grabbed Bob Pfeil's shirt in a defensive reflex. "Stay here Bob," Doug Baily commanded. Mackay's attorney hopped in, trying to stop the melee. "Bob," he clamored. Then the court reporter chimed in. "Bob." Followed by Baily, demanding. "Bob."

"Take it easy you guys," Dave Talbot admonished, his voice rising. Bob Pfeil was now in Neil Mackay's face.

"You've got your hand on me," Pfeil shouted.

"I never touched you," Mackay replied, but he had crossed a barrier he should never have touched. The two of them were now fighting against the deposition room table. The microphone wobbled and the tape recorder temporarily went silent. The two men continued to tangle. Neil Mackay doubled his fist to hit Bob Pfeil. Pfeil punched him in the face. Dave Talbot tried to calm his client, tried to get between them, shouting, "Neil."

Doug Baily, hovering around the edges of the conflict, used a calming voice. "Let's cool it," he said. "Let's cool it."

Robert Pfeil now loomed over Neil Mackay. Glared at him with every ounce of disgust he could muster. "You rotten bastard," he seethed. "This is a rotten bastard," he repeated. Neil Mackay finally left the room, more in retreat than victory. The deposition was over. Done. Finished.

When Neil Mackay counted his wounds, he realized he'd been struck in the head, face, and body. Five days after the encounter, he started experiencing headaches. Ten days after the deposition, he took a fall in his apartment. He ended up at Elmendorf Hospital complaining of a loss of equilibrium, slurred speech, and headaches. He would, through his attorney, blame the attack on Robert Pfeil and seek a protective order against him.

"On every single occasion on which I have appeared for Mr. Mackay in this litigation," Dave Talbot declared, "Mr. Pfeil has appeared to be extremely tense and hostile, and I have been fearful from the very start that Mr. Pfeil would lose control and attack either Mr. Mackay or myself. I believe Mr. Mackay and I have an unquestioned right to attend and participate in all depositions, free from assaultive behavior by Mr. Pfeil."

Robert Pfeil had different memories. Memories of Neil Mackay's deep well of menace. He summed it up in court documents when he said he considered the man "a very violent person." Bob Pfeil remembered one incident in detail. He had visited Mackay's apartment during his separation from Muriel. Mackay promised Bob "monetary measures" if she stayed with him.

"Then his temper snapped," Bob Pfeil recalled. "He cursed me, told me if I ever crossed him, he'd have me and when he was through with me, I'd look like I'd been run over. And if didn't get out of his way, he'd have me taken care of."

To Bob Pfeil, those weren't idle threats. They were the very threats Neil Mackay had visited on his sister.

With Judge Madsen's appointment of two "medical examiners," both psychiatrists, there was at least an opportunity to reassess Scotty's father. There was always the chance that Neil Mackay had rid himself of his earlier demons. He had, for instance, given up the alcohol that plagued his relationship with Muriel. There was always the chance that the recent outburst between the two antagonists—Mackay and Pfeil—was an aberration.

Dr. Norman N. Janzer, a Seattle physician who specialized in psychiatry, had even seen Mackay in the past. Had, in fact, concluded in an earlier assessment that Mackay was "fit and competent in supervision for 5-year-old child." Janzer now testified that, after recent psychological and psychiatric visits, "I changed my impressions considerably. Mr. Mackay is ignorant as a father. He has not tried as a father with his child."

Janzer testified that Mackay also tried to bribe him, telling him that "experts are entitled to compensation." Janzer took it as a direct threat. Mackay, having said, "I know this is not a doctor-patient relationship," reached for his wallet.

"I was shown a carrot," Janzer said, "and I was shown the stick."

In an insight into how Mackay's background figured into his current dilemma, Janzer noted that Mackay had a hard going in life—with poverty, a struggle for money, and mistreatment in his home environment. His mother whipped him with a belt, Janzer said, and that affected his feelings toward women. According to the good doctor, it gave him a sense and need for power.

After talking to Mackay's sister Carolina, Janzer gleaned even deeper insights. "Mrs. Willis talked of their early life. Mr. Mackay hated his grandmother," Janzer learned. One time she turned the water off to their house.

"Mr. Mackay does not seem to need women," Janzer added, "and that's not good for Scotty." He didn't want children when he was growing up, the doctor noted, and he saw no visible change in that now. Indeed, Janzer said Mackay didn't have much time for women or children. More ominously, Mackay indicated that there was "nothing stopping him from taking a big trip" with his son.

Scotty, meanwhile, was beginning to show signs of trouble. Dr. Marian Witt, his pediatrician, had grounded him for three days of rest. He was having night terrors, with men coming to get him and kill him. The two families were also fighting over his last name. Was it Pfeil or Mackay? Both families tried to make name changes in Dr. Witt's office. On top of that, Scotty did not like it that his governess was a woman. Demonstrated persistent issues with behavioral limits. When two adults were talking, Scotty thought they were talking about him.

"Scotty has more than seven parent figures in his life right now," Janzer told the court. "That's too much for a child."

If there was a positive in all of this, Janzer felt it was Carolina Willis. He considered her Scotty's psychological mother. "Her coaching is excellent," he said. The doctor added, all the adults were catering to Scotty. Except Carolina Willis. His only regret was Carolina's age, he said, adding that "she's very competent."[10]

Dr. Allen Lieder, a Seattle-based physician and psychiatrist, had his own take on Scotty's father. Neil Mackay, he said, was "highly motivated as a parent—but unprepared for the task. He wants to do what is best for his child," Lieder said, "but he does not know what it is . . . He's concerned that the child will not like him. He wants the child to love him very much—but is fearful of talking about his mother's death."

In Leider's telling, the father also wanted to remake the son in his own image. "He wants to teach his son how to work," Lieder explained. "He's a workaholic. He has psychological needs for his son. But there is a time and place for everything. And children do better when their parent is not so concerned."

More damning was Lieder's take on witnessing Mackay's in-court testimony. He called it, "Inarticulate." Said he witnessed, "emotional turmoil within the plaintiff. He was barely functional at the beginning—that's what I heard."

When asked how Mackay would react to not having custody of Scotty, Lieder said, "That's not acceptable to Mr. Mackay. He would continue till he had his son. I think he might take the child and leave the state or country."

The biggest reveal came when the elephant wandered into the courtroom. Not an elephant, actually, a mastodon. Things kicked off when Wagstaff raised the issue of Nazis with Dr. Lieder. Dave Talbot interrupted to sputter that he'd stipulate to Neil Mackay's assertion that the Pfeil's were Neo-Nazis.

Robert Wagstaff read out loud from Lieder's deposition. Lieder agreed with everything Wagstaff read. "'The Pfeil's are Neo-Nazis.' Yes, he said that."

It wasn't the Nazi's who thwarted Neil Mackay. It was Neil S. Mackay himself. On March 7, 1977, he was hospitalized at Elmendorf Air Force

10 Carolina Mackay Willis was 51 in 1977. Her husband Alfred was 53.

Base after suffering from migraine headaches, slowness in answering questions, slight confusion, a slight staggering gait when he walked, and slow, hesitant, and slightly slurred speech. A blood screen was ordered. Barbiturates were found in his system.

When confronted with this finding, Mackay denied that he had knowingly or willfully ingested barbiturates. He claimed the test was a false reading due to "belladonna" present in his prescribed medication. There were also allusions to the fistfight with Robert Pfeil. In the following days, Virginia Zawacki pointedly noted that Mackay's physical maladies arose shortly after that confrontation.

Whatever the underlying cause, Mackay was ordered to present himself to Alaska Medical Laboratories for another blood and urine sample. The second sample showed the presence of 5.4 milligrams of barbiturates. On April 23, 1977, Mackay took a third blood screen. That one showed 4.1 milligrams of barbiturates.

According to the attending physician, a 5.4 milligram blood level of phenobarbital was consistent with a person who takes the drug regularly for a prolonged period of time. In layman's terms, Mackay was either a barbiturate abuser or an addict.

Like all good druggies, Neil Sutherland Mackay was in denial.

15

Anchorage, Alaska, May 6, 1977

OVER EIGHT DAYS OF TESTIMONY, JUDGE MADSEN heard from the medical professionals, from members of both families and from Scotty's attorney. He'd also heard from Neil Mackay himself. Madsen's decision got easier with each passing hour.

Dave Talbot admitted in court that Neil Mackay "has not told the truth regarding his use of drugs." Talbot added, one of Mackay's physicians—with whom he'd discussed Mackay's drug abuse—was not willing to testify. Talbot continued, "If I disclose this, he'll withdraw as Mr. Mackay's physician." Asked about another doctor, who seemed most willing to provide Mackay with prescription drugs, Talbot's answer was also revealing. 'Yes," Talbot admitted. "'Dr. Nembutal' has seen Mr. Mackay."

Carolina Willis, meanwhile, told the judge in all sincerity that she did not want to adopt Scotty or alienate him from his family. "Scotty needs his family," she insisted. "I do not want to take his mother's place in Scotty's life. He still speaks of her. All parties would have to do this in love for Scotty."

Then she revealed the issues that haunted her. She had fibrosis of the breast and might have to get surgery. Her husband had been ill and under a doctor's care. "Now he's healed," she said. "Healed by Jesus Christ."

Her biggest concerns, though, were her brother and Scotty.

Carolina and her husband Alfred had already seen glimpses of the emotional maelstrom surrounding Neil Mackay. Had seen it firsthand during the divorce and visitation battle between Neil and Muriel. On one of those occasions, Alfred found himself in the midst of a physical confrontation between the two spouses. It was what Judge Madsen would later call the "watch cap" incident. It wasn't something they wanted to go through again.

On the last day of September 1974, after an early snow hit Anchorage, Neil and Alfred had shown up at Grandma Pfeil's house. No sooner had they arrived than Mackay surged in Scotty's direction. He started arguing with Muriel, saying he wanted to see Scotty, and struggling with Alfred Willis, who had placed himself between them.

At that point, the two of them were interrupted by Alaska State Trooper Buddy Harrel, there to serve a subpoena on Carolina Willis. Trooper Harrel put down the pad carrying his subpoenas and tossed it into a chair. Neil Mackay turned his attention to Harrel. Asked who he was. Asked what his business was. Harrel told him. All the while, Mackay continued to struggle with Alfred. Finally, about five minutes later, Neil and Alfred left the house and moved toward their car, Scotty in tow.

Scotty was now wearing the infamous watch cap, a cap which Neil Mackay claimed Scotty did not want to wear. Of more immediate concern, though, was that the child was carrying a stack of vinyl records and not holding onto the handrail as he clambered down the stairs. Neil worried he would fall. He would claim he was unprepared for what happened next.

Muriel followed them outside. She was not finished with their argument. The fight spilled into the yard, with Muriel closing the door behind her. It was then that Neil Mackay snatched the watch cap from Scotty's head and threw it in the snow. In a fit of pique, he proclaimed it was a silly thing for Scotty to wear. Muriel yelled. Told him the hat should be on. She moved in on him. Neil yelled an incomprehensible insult about Muriel's aunt. Muriel came out swinging.

Alfred ended up in the middle, grabbing Muriel, trying to separate her from Neil. He ended up taking punches, all the while calling out to Grandma Pfeil. "Get Scotty," he told her. "Take him into the house."

Somehow, Alfred managed to get Neil into the car. They drove around the block. "No visiting today," Alfred told him. Alfred's memory of that day was, he said, "instant hate." There was a lot of anger, all around, all the time.

On the eve of Judge Madsen's ruling, Carolina now told the judge the biggest problem was her brother's recurring illness. Which had, in turn, affected his scheduled visitations. Neil was to have twelve visits in the month of March alone, she said. He only kept three of them. At least, she said, things were better now with Scotty, though they were rough the first few days after leaving Anchorage. He no longer screams at night, she said. He no longer wears out Alfred.

"I've never told him he was going to stay with us," Carolina revealed, "but he has asked if he can call me and Alfred 'Mom and Dad.'"

There were still things that unnerved her.

Like when Scotty made a scene in a café, after their initial move to Eagle River. He'd looked at his plate and said, "my food is wrinkled." No, she told him, it's not. Before Carolina knew it, he was kicking and screaming on the floor. "He got on the floor like a little animal and screamed, don't touch me. Don't come near me. And he just laid there and screamed on the floor and that is—there are witnesses to that fact. My husband picked him up in his coat and carried him out. And I was sitting there crying, telling them we've never laid a hand on this child."

Carolina had additional worries, like kidnapping. Scotty's picture had been in the newspaper. The night it came out, the Willis' received four phone calls. The world now knew the boy was independently wealthy. She was concerned about him. This wasn't a child she could leave just anywhere. He was not just any child. People recognized him.

On May 6, 1976, Judge Roy Madsen finally handed down his decision. There were two opposing issues before his bench. Neil Mackay's *Writ of Habeas Corpus* and Robert Pfeil's *Guardianship and Adoption Petitions.* Someone was guaranteed to be unhappy. Maybe more than one someone.

The kindest thing the judge could say about Neil Mackay was that he enjoyed financial success due to his hard work. Among the downsides, the judge recounted, "He is impulsive, has taken actions without first considering the effect of those actions on his child, such as the abrupt firing of his sister and brother-in-law shortly after they were awarded custody of Scotty."

Madsen was just getting warmed up.

"Neil S. Mackay," he continued, "has an inflexibility of will or character, evidenced by his persistence and work drive, which makes it difficult for him to disperse his time and energy in a balanced way with respect to work and manifests itself in his inability to have exchanges with other persons or have close or intimate relationships with other persons."

The temperature got hotter.

Judge Madsen recognized the medical witnesses, saying Neil Mackay was a "borderline psychotic," had an "explosive personality," was "manipulative," "impulsive," and was unable to deal with stress, "as evidenced by his firing of his sister and brother-in-law, the use of barbiturates, and his "lack of judgment" in hiring Scotty's governess, who was a 52 year old nurse who'd spent 32 years in a supervisory capacity, had never been married and who had minimal experience with small children. The judge also took note of his "pushing and shoving match" with Muriel over Scotty's watch cap. The incident where he threw the typewriter in Muriel's office. The angry conversation with Justice Erwin in which he accused the Justice of a conspiracy to take Scotty from him.

In a balancing comment, he acknowledged that, while Mackay was once an alcoholic, he'd conquered it some fourteen or fifteen years previous but the alcohol had been replaced by barbiturates. Madsen noted pointedly that Mackay was once hospitalized for an unintentional overdose. He also referenced the time blood screening found barbiturates in his blood.

"When confronted with this finding, he categorically denied that he had knowingly or willfully ingested any barbiturates whatsoever and that the test must have received a false reading from the 'belladonna' present in his prescribed medication."

On the other side, the judge noted that Alfred and Carolina Willis, with four months of custody under their belts, had effectively served as Scotty's surrogate parents. That they had "established a bond of love and affection toward him, have evidenced their concern in all dealings with the adults involved, and have accommodated the wishes of the adult relatives of Scotty to the best of their ability, thereby providing stability and continuity for him during the interim."

If this sounded like things were trending in the Willis' direction, though, there was one problem. The issue, the judge noted, was this: "The right of parents to the care, custody and control of their children is an important and substantial right protected by the U.S. and Alaska Constitutions."[11]

11 It should be noted, however, that these rights are not enumerated in either document. Rather they are implied rights, upheld by multiple judicial rulings.

Madsen straight-out denied the Pfeil's petition for adoption. That wasn't his only denial. He concluded that the evidence established that it would be "detrimental at this time to place Scotty with his natural father." Put simply, Neil S. Mackay was unfit to function as Scotty's sole parent.

For the time being, Scotty Mackay was to be left in the temporary care and custody of Alfred and Carolina Willis. That wasn't all. Neil Mackay was ordered not to remove Scotty from the State of Alaska without posting a performance bond of $250,000. Judge Roy Madsen's ruling explicitly acknowledged the threat that Neil Mackay posed. The medical folks had declared it loud and clear. Neil Mackay, they warned, would leave the State, with Scotty in tow, if he didn't get his way.

Anchorage, Alaska, May 25 – August 19, 1977

Carolina and Alfred lasted little more than a month. By May 25th they were back in court.

Something was not right with her brother, Carolina insisted. She blamed the drugs. "I went to Neil and said what are we going to do about your problem?" she testified. "He said, 'what problem?' I said, 'let's go to specifics.' He said it was the belladonna. I said, 'no.'"

There were other issues. Observed issues. She mentioned the night before the judge's May 6th order, when she picked up Scotty and learned he had a bloody stool. Scotty's pediatrician said it could be caused by anxiety. She talked about how she'd once visited Neil's apartment—and learned that Scotty wanted to fly down to the street to meet them in his Batman cape. How she had to explain that he must stay away from the windows. There was another incident when Neil let Scotty light his cigarette and one where Neil encouraged Scotty to hit him.

"How can we know what is happening with Scotty," she asked, referring to Scotty's visits with his father, "if someone is not present for the weekend?"

After all that, Judge Madsen changed little in the terms of the custody agreement. No one needed to supervise Neil Mackay's visits, he ruled. Neil Mackay had preference in the choice of babysitters when the Willis' had conflicts. Then, in a bit of remedial action, he spelled out the exact days those visits were to be had.

It would not work. By June 26, 1977, the Willis' had withdrawn as temporary custodians of Scotty Mackay. There was an abiding sense that Neil had convinced his sister to withdraw as co-guardian by using Scotty as a weapon. There was no court order, just a handover.

Neil Mackay's tendentious personality had now fully subsumed his relationship with Carolina. In a deposition taken on August 3, 1977, Neil sought to establish the righteousness of the new custody arrangements. It was a tense exchange.

"Didn't you think it was a good idea that you relinquish your temporary custody," he asked Carolina, "and that the father have the custody of the boy?"

"How could I say that the father have the boy," Carolina answered, "when the boy was placed in our home because the father couldn't have the boy in the first place . . . Why did you ever not have the boy? Why did I have the boy? Ask me. Why did I have the boy in the first place? Why was he in our home?

"Do you remember my question?" Neil Mackay demanded.

"Do you remember mine?"

Robert Pfeil was even more blunt. In an August 19 deposition, he said he'd had numerous discussions with Alfred and Carolina about their temporary custody experience. He gave Dave Talbot a long, detailed response.

"Their opinion as to why they quit," Pfeil told Talbot, "as to why they could not continue to function as the guardians and custodians of Scotty Mackay was due to the fact that you, Mr. Talbot, harassed and intimidated them, lied to them, and that Mr. Mackay caused psychological problems with the little boy by destroying the relationship between the boy and the Willises as the guardians of the child. The boy was confused as to where he should be because his father told him that Mr. and Mrs. Willis were stealing him.

"I think she did the wrong thing in letting the child go to the father because," Bob Pfeil added, "of all the people in Anchorage, there's only one person in this matter that's been determined to be unfit to have the boy and that's the father."

When asked about Neil Mackay's fitness, Robert Pfeil was equally terse.

"I have no way of knowing . . . He seems to be the same recluse he's been for years. I never see him on the street, I don't see the boy on the street uptown, and I don't hear anything as to how the boy is making out."

Scotty was now a virtual recluse, like his father, in the Mackay Building. Judge Madsen was in no mood to change that. Though the Pfeil's appealed the dismissal of their adoption request, there was little sense anything would change. That is, unless Neil Mackay totally failed to meet the conditions he'd set. A no drugs mandate, parenting classes, an acceptable governess, an acceptable home.

Failure was not an option.

16

Anchorage, Alaska, September 1977

FIFTEEN SUSPECTS, 81 BAGS OF EVIDENCE, an 18-inch case file, 950 investigation hours, one séance, four investigative agencies and a $20,000 reward. The Muriel Pfeil case looked good by the numbers. Until one realized it was still unsolved. These were the numbers of a failed investigation.

Robert Pfeil responded in March of 1977 by bumping the reward offer to $50,000. "I feel whoever is responsible was paid in the same vicinity," Pfeil said, "and that's what it's going to take for someone to come forward."

By the September anniversary of Muriel's death, that reward still stood unclaimed. Anchorage police Capt. Ralph Christianson told reporters the chances of solving the murder were slim, "but there's always the chance that if the right person comes along with the right information, it can be solved."

Christianson added that, while investigators were still following leads in the case, "most are anonymous-type tips with someone claiming to have information on the bombing." None of those tips had led investigators any closer to finding Muriel's killer. The police investigation had indeed been thorough. At least seventeen different suspects had been identified. Almost as many motives had been unearthed.

Lawyer Karl Johnstone, soon to become a judge, speculated to police that he may have been the intended victim. Johnstone routinely parked his car in the lot where Muriel was killed. Adding to his suspicion was the fact that he had been involved in litigation adverse to the interests of the Teamsters in Alaska. He'd received threats shortly before the blast.

Investigative reports also turned up a relationship between Muriel Pfeil and man named Joachim Peiper, the latter a former lieutenant colonel in an armored division of Hitler's Waffen SS during the Second World War. Peiper was involved in the massacre of American soldiers at Malmedy, Belgium, during the Battle of the Bulge, and was subsequently convicted as a war criminal. After his death penalty sentence was commuted to life imprisonment, he was released from incarceration. Peiper met Muriel and Caroline Pfeil on one of their excursions through Europe. Met him because, as a higher up at Volkswagen, he helped them acquire a vehicle for their travels.

Muriel Pfeil had, moreover, discussed Peiper with a friend—a friend who revealed the unsavory details of Peiper's past. That story naturally found its way into police files. Adding intrigue to that lead, Peiper's past caught up with him on Bastille Day, July 14, 1976. He was killed when his lodge in eastern France was firebombed by French partisans. Was it a coincidence that less than two months later, on September 30, 1976, Muriel Pfeil was also killed? Some thought not but investigators could not make a connection—partly because Peiper was burned beyond recognition in the ensuing fire.

And then there was Louis Edward Dickinson. Court documents identified him as the married boyfriend of Muriel Pfeil at the time of her death. The man who had given her the ring. Police learned that their relationship was in trouble because of its impact on Dickinson's marriage. Dickinson's wife knew that her husband was having an affair. Knew it at the time of Muriel's death. The wife declined to take a polygraph exam to clear her name. Said she was experiencing "psychiatric problems," as a result of the strains placed on her marriage by her husband's affair.

Beyond that, the list of other possible sources was a flurry of ifs, ands and maybes. The still mysterious $15,000 restaurant transaction. The two mentally ill "suspects." The spooked Baronof Lounge owner.

A new one had it that the bomb that killed Muriel Pfeil was actually meant for a female reporter investigating corruption in the Fairbanks Teamsters organization. The reporter had in fact gone to Fairbanks to meet with a covert source but was thwarted when the source failed to show. He was subsequently "located" during a spring thaw, having been murdered. All that was academic, except that the reporter was based in Anchorage, drove a car very similar in appearance to Muriel Pfeil's, and always parked in the lot where the blast occurred. A lot in which Muriel Pfeil seldom parked.

Christianson, a cop with a knack for extracting confessions, had his own reservations. In 1973, he got 22-year-old Charles Meach to confess to the beating death of a grocery clerk. Nine years later, Meach would return to Christianson and admit to the murder of four teenagers in Anchorage's Russian Jack Springs Park.

This wasn't that kind of case. No hard evidence had been uncovered.

"We're no closer in knowing who did it, or why," admitted Joe Acton, the police investigator assigned full-time to Muriel Pfeil's homicide. Most of the suspects turned out to be cranks who got a thrill out of boasting to their friends that they committed a big-time crime.

Acton had spent more than his share of time chasing dead ends. Conversations overheard in Alaska bars sent eavesdroppers sprinting to his office. He got tips from narcotics officers about "heavy dudes in crime circles" who might be involved. The clues proved unfounded.

Joe Acton knew he had reached the desperation phase when he attended a séance. "I've only been to one, and I won't go to another," he said of his trip into the spiritual world. "The guy claimed to have made contact with Muriel Pfeil, but it all went in circles. Obviously, it was no lead."

Still, Acton filled a casefile with the heading "psychics and other phenomenon." It showed the depths he'd probed to solve the murder. "I've spent so much time on this case," Acton confessed, "I probably know Muriel Pfeil just about as well as anyone."

"This is not Kojak," Acton added, referring to a late 70s TV crime drama, "where a case is solved between commercial breaks. People think cops are inherently smart, but Abbie Hoffman once said cops couldn't catch a cold if someone didn't help and he's absolutely right. I think sooner or later we'll find the killer of Muriel Pfeil, but we're open for any and all assistance."

His relative optimism notwithstanding. the lack of progress clearly bothered him. "It gets to you," Acton admitted. "I get up in the morning and I think about it. I think about it all day. Then, I get in bed and stare at the ceiling and count the squares. We're at the stage now where physical evidence isn't going to turn the case. Someone is going to turn up who wants to talk to us."

THEN THERE WAS THE CLINCHER. "A bombing is the hardest case to investigate," Acton admitted, "usually because of lack of evidence and the fact that the perpetrator is not often in the area."

Even with their frustrations, the police had learned a lot. They were now confident that the cars detonated on lonely roads around Fairbanks were not linked to the Muriel Pfeil case. Capt. Christianson further noted that the Muriel Pfeil explosion wasn't set off by remote control, as was speculated originally.

On closer inspection, investigators found two wires to the coil of Muriel's Volvo that didn't belong there. Federal authorities suggested it would take only a moment to hook up the explosive device once the hood was open. They now knew it was fairly easy to open the hood from the outside.

Complicating matters, Alaska was a gold mine for explosives. Although the Alyeska Pipeline Service denied allegations about massive thievery on the pipeline project, that didn't explain how 250 pounds of explosive was stolen from a pipeline haul road near Fairbanks. There were other suppliers, closer to home. On July 14, 1976, Hess & Son held a public auction of the X-Demex Corporation's inventory in Anchorage. It featured "demolition explosives compounds, supplies and components." Among the sales items were "shaped charge cans," favored in petroleum exploration because of the explosive jets they produce. Those explosives could have created the directed charges found on Muriel's Volvo.

Yes, the cops had checked out the bidders.

As the investigation progressed, however, a new finding redirected their course. The Bureau of Alcohol, Tobacco & Firearms (ATF) concluded that a high velocity explosive, probably a military explosive such as C-3 or C-4, had been planted under the hood of Muriel Pfeil's car. A blasting cap connected to the explosive was wired to the engine in such a way that hitting the ignition switch detonated the device.

While plastic explosives like C-4 can be used in civilian applications, they are more expensive than dynamite. For most commercial uses, dynamite performs just as well. The Alyeska dynamite theft in the months before Muriel's assassination was now relegated to footnote status.

Suddenly the military angle seemed worthy of pursuit. Plastic explosives like C-3 and C-4 had found their earliest use in the military, during World War II. Their primary advantage was they could be easily molded into any desired shape, which allowed a skilled user to control the direction of the explosion. That wasn't the only advantage. Plastic explosives are fairly impervious to impact, so the risk of accidental detonation was diminished. Field troops in Vietnam even used C-4 as fuel for heating rations since it merely burns unless detonated with a primary explosive.

There were two military bases in Alaska, one in Fairbanks and one just north of Anchorage. That barely accounted for the total number of veterans in the state. World War II veterans. Vietnam War veterans. The fact that plastic explosives were more expensive than dynamite added yet another wrinkle. The idea that Muriel's murder was a professional hit had only grown in likelihood. Bob Pfeil's steps to increase the reward were a stark reminder of that truth.

Still, the best suspect they'd had so far was the Marine fugitive who confessed to the crime in Seattle. And his confession was a hoax.

17

Anchorage, Alaska, November 7, 1985

All the chatter about Robert Betts had Junior Pauole spooked. He called Larry Gentry on November 6th and told him that he "oughta come and talk to me." In Pauole speak, that meant ditch the phone and meet in person. There was an immediacy in his request. He said, "today, now," then added, "or later." Larry Gentry stalled. Seeing Gilbert Pauole in person meant he had to wear a wire. That was going to take some setup. Gentry put their meeting off until the following day.

What the police also knew, even as they prepped Larry Gentry for his visit, was that John Bright had called Junior the previous evening. Had called and, their wiretap revealed, made threats to Junior and his girlfriend Amy. Angry about Pauole's lack of response to the Robert Betts threat, Bright said he was going to come back from Florida and "take care" of anyone who'd crossed them. He demanded a plane ticket, so he could do what everyone else had failed to do.

Robert Betts' ersatz demands, the cops now knew, were a psychological grenade, slowly ticking among the conspirators.

Larry Gentry arrived at Junior Pauole's modest triplex at noon on November 7th. Plopped in a humble neighborhood south of downtown Anchorage, it was fifteen minutes from Junior's Fourth Avenue club and only six minutes from where Robert Pfeil was shot.

According to court documents, Gentry engaged Pauole almost at once. The immediate topic was, once again, Robert Betts. Of Betts, Gentry opened by saying, "that guy is talkin' crazy." Unfortunately, the transmission was spotty. The recording device had bad batteries. The TV was on. The cops reinterviewed Gentry shortly after the conversation ended, trying to reconstruct the conversation. They would later reconstruct the tape itself.

In the reconstructed tape, the conversation meandered, crackled, broke up and broke off but snippets drifted into earshot. The police picked up what they could. At one point, when Gentry said, "fucking Mackay's gonna come over here and fuckin' wipe us out," Junior deliberately shifted gears.

"The paperwork never come from Mackay, though," Junior insisted.

"Well, who did it come from?" The tape went wobbly. Gentry turned out to be a facile talker. "I thought you told me it came from Mackay. It didn't come from Mackay?"

"No," Junior replied.

Gentry kept digging and revealed his own deep fears. Fears about John Bright. He quoted a conversation where Bright told him, "he was going to take care of everything if he has to go to jail." Gentry continued in that vein, telling Junior that he'd told Bright, "hey, I don't want nobody being shot at, or anything up here. Okay? I said I don't want no more to do with this damn shootin' shit, 'cause I've had enough."

And then Larry's fears reverted to their default. "Mackay is gonna send somebody," he burbled. "He ain't like John. This motherfucker is gonna come and blow us away."

"But Mackay's not where the thing's coming from," Pauole repeated. "It's coming from right here." The tape went silent for a few seconds, but when it returned, Larry Gentry was incredulous, "Right here . . . are you serious? A union. Are you sure?"

"They want him out of the way," Pauole whispered.

"They want him out of the way?" Gentry asked.

"Yeah," Junior replied.

"What for?" Gentry wanted to know. "I can't figure that out. Just vote him out."

"Because they can't. The airlines will vote him in."

That revelation brought another shift. Where Gentry was once concerned about blowback from Neil Mackay, he was now concerned about unknown forces. "Do we have anything to worry about these union guys," he asked.

"Nothing to worry about the union guys," Junior assured him. Then, suddenly, Pauole took a left turn, a turn so quick Gentry was momentarily confused. Junior suddenly asserted, "I haven't been able to get ahold of Neil Mackay in ah, four years."

"But you did know him four years ago."

"Yeah," Junior said, admitting the connection. "He's the same one that used to own the Wild Cherry."

Larry Gentry kept pressing. Pauole stuck to this story. Insisted the paperwork never came from Mackay. That, instead, the union wanted to set up Neil Mackay as the fall guy. That they wanted Mackay to be, in Pauole's words, "the patsy."

Gentry, seemingly confused, shot back with a question. "Well, why didn't you tell me that in the first place, it was the union?"

"I don't want nobody to know, but now you say you getting so nervous, now I'm telling you that, now I'm telling you."

For the police who were listening in, it was frequently difficult to tell whether the information Pauole was relaying to Gentry was intended for Gentry's ears—or for Robert Betts.' Betts was always there as a specter, as an underlier. What if Betts goes to Mackay, Larry wondered.

"Neil Mackay," Junior cautioned, "if he, if he talks to Neil Mackay, Neil Mackay gonna laugh at him. He won't believe him. He's gonna laugh at you. You know? You know what he's gonna tell you? 'Hey, you better call up the newspaper company. To give him fifty thousand dollars for information leading and the arrest of.'"

Larry Gentry mumbled, "yeah," but Pauole wasn't finished. Whenever he was excited or animated, he broke into the pidgin English of his Hawaiian youth.

"You know, that's what he's gonna tell him. You know, but you're the only one that's getting scared. Nobody else is getting scared and I never bring you in this. Your buddy bring you in this. (Your buddy) John. You was out of it, you was out of it, you was always out of it. And if you remember correctly I'm the one that went get rid of the car. You know? I told him not to use that car. And he told me he wasn't going to use that car. He told me he was going to steal one car. You remember when he said that?"

"Yeah," Gentry muttered. He seemed exhausted or, if not that, his imagination had run dry. He just let Gilbert K. Pauole keep talking, offering only one- or two-word responses for much of their remaining conversation. It was just enough to keep things going until the next day.

AT 9:05 P.M. ON NOVEMBER 8, 1985, GENTRY SPOKE with Pauole again, this time by phone, with the cops at his side. Going according to script, Larry swung back to the Robert Betts story. Said that Betts had just called him, saying he wanted not only the money that very night, but a plane ticket to L.A. Junior responded by saying, "that's not in the cards."

Then, abruptly changing his tune, Junior said, "Tell him what kind of guarantee we got he's gonna go?"

From the side, the police were handing Larry notes. Telling him to say he couldn't get a hold of Betts. Gentry took the cue, said he couldn't reach Betts, "'cause he wouldn't let me have his number."

"He's shakin' you down, you know," the streetwise Pauole admonished. But he was starting to buy it. He asked what name Betts wanted on his airplane ticket. And then, after a stretch where he complained about being out the extra $700 for the plane ticket, he decided to give him the ticket he'd purchased for John Bright. A ticket, Pauole insisted, that used "a Mexican guy's name."

Suddenly, that was the plan. Gilbert and Larry would go to the Anchorage International Airport. They would change John Bright's ticket over to Robert Betts. Then they could tell Betts it'd be waiting for him at the counter. All Betts had to do was present his ID. And meet them within the hour.

That was the beginning of a wild ride.

For this to work, the cops needed to get Larry Gentry hooked up again. Junior called Larry back twenty minutes before the police had him ready. His wife Susan took the call instead. And stalled. It was an uncomfortable place for her to be. The two of them were newly married. One month to be exact. They had known each other exactly four months prior to getting hitched. She had to sit by and watch as Larry was put in increasingly uncomfortable situations. She noted with despair that the police had to write notes telling Larry what to say. He couldn't remember his lines.

And now, suddenly, they were in a race to find Junior, with both Larry and the cops going through their list of contacts. They called Junior's house. "Not even at home," Gentry exclaimed. They called one of their mutual friends. No dice. They called the Wild Cherry. Still no dice.

"Okay guys," Larry said in exasperation. "I've tried the numbers. I don't know where that man's at."

Then, suddenly, the cops were following Larry's car in their surveillance van. Junior was back at his triplex. It was dark, though, and Larry had trouble finding the place. The tape was rolling as they drove. "I believe this is the one I want," Larry declared. "If it ain't, I'll try it again. Yeah, the one I want is one more over. Don't . . . believe so . . . One more street over . . . and we'll have it. Okay . . . Yep, this is the one. Here we go . . . gentlemen, here we go . . ."

Larry walked toward the door. Heard noises. It was the same problem they'd had during the last recording. "Damn," Larry proclaimed. "TV's on again." At Gilbert Pauole's house, the TV was the soundtrack of life. This time it turned out to be less problematic. The TV, that is.

They began by chattering, predictably enough, about Robert Betts. Junior wanted to get it over with. Quick. Wanted the kid to meet them within the hour. Larry insisted the kid wouldn't go "for the one-hour deal," because he feared a trap. Junior decided that, rather than wait for Betts, they'd go to the airport and get a ticket under Larry Gentry's name. Then they'd hand it over to the kid. Larry started referring to him as the "little fucker." A dog barked in the background, momentarily interrupting the flow.

Pauole's brain was racing toward the perfect pressure campaign. "I'd tell him . . . hey pal, I wasn't there . . . and you was. You understand . . . I never do the crime . . . you did."

Amid these very adult seeming conversations, Pauole's girlfriend, Amy Shotwell, thrust herself into the picture. She needed to do a drug delivery. The two of them bantered, with Junior saying her errand would take too long, that she would end up dragging things out with "talk, talk, talk." What he and Larry needed to do, Junior added, was more important. He had to go to the airport and exchange a plane ticket. Because, he said, he didn't want John Bright coming back. Didn't want John Bright and his threats of violence to visit them again. Still, they haggled. There was a deeper reason than the usual bumps and grinds of a relationship.

"Well, you just go on to the airport," Amy declared. There was a pause, and then she turned to Larry Gentry. "How's your mom?" Larry didn't realize she was addressing him. Seemed lost in the room. It was a beat before he answered.

"Oh . . . they're haven't scheduled her for her operation yet . . . way it looks they're gonna operate on her again, or somethin' . . . something wrong with the colon, it's not right or somethin' . . . so . . . they haven't found out . . . they haven't told her the schedule yet . . . when they're gonna operate on her."

Amy and Junior slid back into hassling, going back and forth about the drug delivery. "No, it's not gonna take me three hours," Amy insisted. "Take me about an hour. I'm stopping nowhere now. Don't do that to me. When I say something, I mean it. I ain't givin' you no fuckin' ass either."

Larry Gentry moaned. He and Junior left right after that, with the Hawaiian checking to make sure he had the airline ticket and Larry complaining when Amy's dog peed on his car tire. It wasn't long before Larry realized he was driving the wrong way. The cops in the surveillance van scrambled to keep up.

Over their eight-minute drive to the airport—made longer by their missed turn—Junior kept up a nonstop diatribe. He told Larry the cops would never identify Gentry's car as the shooter's car, even though Gentry's own sister had called it a "cop killer's car."

The more they drove, the more worried Larry acted. He returned like a bird dog to "The Union," the one topic he was primed to stress. It was all about the union. He asked Junior if it was Robert Pfeil's union that arranged the shooting. "That's none of your business," came the reply.

At the airport, the two revealed themselves as hapless bumblers, going from one airline counter to the next. At 10 o'clock p.m., the Anchorage International airport was deserted. There were no agents in sight. When they finally found one, at Northwest, there was a problem. The ticket had John Bright's name on it. Tickets were non-transferable. Besides, the ticket was paid for, in cash, on another airline. On Western Airlines. You might be able to get a refund from Western Airlines, the agent offered.[12]

"You bring the cash I can sell you a ticket for anybody you want, any place you want," she explained.

They sauntered off to the Western Airlines counter. Quibbled about who was going to pay for the new ticket. Coach, one way. The price? $530

12 Both carriers are long gone, each subsumed by Delta Airlines.

plus $29.80 tax. Junior won the dispute, saying Larry could argue with John when he saw him. "If I ever see him, I'll take a baseball bat to him," Gentry chuckled.

By the time they left the ticket counter, Gilbert Pauole was singing a new tune. The ticket, he said, was now for Larry Gentry to use as he pleased. A one-way ticket to Los Angeles. It came with one caveat. "But don't call me no more," Junior demanded. Larry Gentry was confused on multiple levels. Was Junior really suggesting he get out of town? Was he really suggesting they cut off all contact? Were they, more importantly, just deciding to blow off Robert Betts?

Yes, Junior said. "You got a plane ticket. All you need is one more . . . All you need is one more for your wife and disappear. Because that guy [Betts] don't know where I live, he don't know my phone number."

There was nothing left to say. They ended their night on a trenchant note. Junior told Larry he was leaving town. He didn't know when, but he was leaving. The Wild Cherry, he explained, was being sold to Koreans. There was nothing to keep him in Anchorage.

Left unsaid was his deeper motivation. The threat of John Bright. In fact, John Bright was headed back to Anchorage that very night.

18

Anchorage, Alaska, November 8, 1985

THE JOHN BRIGHT WHO RETURNED TO ANCHORAGE was John Bright the crazy man. He immediately lodged himself in another unit at Pauole's triplex and borrowed Junior's van. When that van ran out of gas, he called Larry Gentry. There was at least a facsimile of trust between them. Larry made sure he was wired up before he arrived. Let his police handlers in on his itinerary. At 4:45 that afternoon, the police recorded their chat. It was a fateful conversation, one in which Gentry told Bright he was going to surrender to police but not before a telling exchange about the threatening letter "sent" by Robert Betts.

"Okay," he confided in Bright, "he told me there was another name in this letter I didn't even mention to Junior." He paused for effect, baiting the hook. "Who's McKenzie?"

"That's the dude, Mackay is who he's thinking of, Mackay."

"Mackay," Gentry repeated, his voice betraying no emotion.

"Yeah. The guy that you don't like that had his sister-in-law blown up or his wife blown up."

"But do you know who the fuck hired, hired this shit done or not?"

"Yeah," Bright answered.

"Who?"

"Mackay," Bright said matter-of-factly.

"Mackay? Junior told me it was the fucking union."

"Yeah, this guy's the head of the Flyer's Union, man." Then Bright moved on to his chief concern. Robert Betts. Bright started to say, "This dude . . ."

But Gentry interrupted him. "Junior said the union."

". . . is trying to bust somebody for the fucking reward is all he's doing," Bright continued, overrunning the topic. "He's trying to bust me and then get and blackmail you. He's going against the law to get, to mess with you, and then trying to bust me."

When Larry called Pauole, later that evening, Junior seemed to be running on anxiety and paranoia. That sense was betrayed by Pauole's expression of a new fear not for himself, for Larry Gentry. That fear was named John Bright. "You know, I mean, you know," Junior said, referring to John Bright, "he's got that, you know, come over here, talk to me."

Junior begged Gentry to come to his house. To talk to him at his house. Larry wanted no part of that. He knew all about John Bright the crazy man.

"Hey Junior, I ain't going to take no chances, man," Larry replied.

"Okay, well if that's the way you feel then that's good you do that, okay? That I understand, okay? And I told him distinctly, I told him clear, I got right off in his face, and I told him. I said, 'Larry has nothing to do with nothing. Don't go around his house. Don't call him. Leave him alone.'"

Gentry was relieved, but still on the police leash and in this building sense of desperation, the cops had Larry push one more button. After assuring Junior that he was "fine," Larry said he was going to keep a low profile and try to find John Bright. He then revealed why. The ruse was that he wanted John Bright to deliver the airplane ticket to Robert Betts. The bet was that Bright's imperiousness would get the better of him.

"I'll drop this ticket off to [John]," Larry declared, "and I'm gone . . . You know, I'm gonna go bury myself somewhere for a while."

"Well good, because that's what I'm going to do, you know," Junior replied. "You know, the way that I look at it is, you know, if everybody's drop outta sight and boo, boo, boo, then there is nobody, right? [And] that guy over there, you, I can't help it if you gotta crazy friend, you know?"

"So, tell John I'm trying to find him," Larry replied, dashing past Junior's warning. "And tell him I'll get a hold of him where he was at today . . . Just tell him I'll drop it off where he was at today, Junior. Just tell him to be out, you know, I'll call there and see if he's there. I'll drive by and hand it to him and I'll be gone."

"Larry, he doesn't have any wheels," Junior responded. "He's using my van and I can't even find him."

"All right. Okay. I'll, let me think about it. I'll call you back and if he's there, then we'll work something out then."

"No, well he's not here."

"Yeah, he's not there?" Gentry asked.

"No. He's not here."

ANCHORAGE POLICE HOMICIDE DETECTIVES HAD ALREADY decided it was time—past time—to play their closing scenario. At 6:30 p.m. they moved an unmarked car to a cross street, catty-corner from Junior's triplex. They would surveil every car that came, every car that left. Then, in a coordinated operation, they pulled in homicide investigators and the Anchorage Metropolitan Drug Enforcement Unit. Twenty-some officers were now slipping into place.

With military precision, they established a highly armed perimeter around 711 W. 75th Street. Junior's residence. The outer perimeter covered six square blocks, stretching north to south. The inner perimeter was two square blocks with the triplex at its center.

Once everything was in place, Larry Gentry confronted Junior Pauole on the telephone. He had worked himself into an exasperated state. His goal was to push Junior into a big reveal. It would take thirty-eight minutes—and a series of phone calls—for the scenario to play itself out.

The first call was from Larry Gentry to Junior Pauole at 8:52 p.m., on Friday, November 8, 1985. There was no small talk. No beating around the bush. Larry Gentry went straight at it, as if to be done with this forever. Gentry was, in fact, operating under the notion that helping the police would get him off the hook. Why waver?

"Junior?" he asked when Pauole came to the phone. "Larry again. I've been thinking things over guy and, you know . . .

"Come on and talk to me," Junior insisted. "I no can hear you."

"I said I've been thinking things over," Gentry repeated, raising his voice several decibels. "And I've come to the conclusion you're right. I don't know nothing about this stuff and I want to go to the police and turn myself in."

"No! No, Larry don't do that," Junior exclaimed. Gentry just kept going, taking a bulldozer to their edifice of deception.

"'Cause you and John did this shit," Gentry told him. "I'm gonna turn myself in and get out of it."

"Larry, don't do that Larry. You don't need to do that."

"Why Junior?" Gentry implored. "I gotta save my family honor here and stuff."

"Damn it Larry, you have your family honor, okay. Larry, you're gonna get me in trouble . . . It's already straightened out. The guy left. John went and took the guy to the airport, and he left. Don't do that Larry. Please!" Gilbert Pauole was lying straight up to Larry Gentry. John Bright had not taken Robert Betts to the airport. Robert Betts had not left. The police knew that. Larry Gentry knew that. Gentry plowed ahead.

"Junior, I'm running around town here like a scared chicken. I've had enough, God damn it."

"Okay, it's over with, Larry. Please don't do that. Don't do that, please. You know, what about my family? What about my wife and kids? Huh? What about my wife and kids, Larry? It's over with. Don't do that. It's over. What about my wife and kids? You gonna take me away from my wife and kids? I have five kids Larry."

Junior did, indeed, have five kids. Several by his first wife. Two more with his current wife but neither of these women were named Amy Shotwell. Junior's current wife was Melanie. She lived in Seattle, with his second batch of kids. Junior Pauole led a complicated life.

"What about my wife?" Larry Gentry countered. He too was in a sticky place. As newlyweds, he and his wife were in way over their heads.

"I know. That's, but Larry, there is nothing Larry. You, you have nothing to do, nothing to worry about. It's over with Larry, just, just leave it alone. You the only one that's making something out of it."

As Junior tried to convince Larry that the only thing on Robert Betts' mind was blackmail, Larry threw a strange piece of truth back at him. A truth he knew about Robert Betts and that John Bright seemed to have figured out.

"Yeah," Gentry said bleakly. "John's fucking talked to Betts' girlfriend and tells me the fucking guy's wired."

Junior Pauole immediately offered to put John Bright on the phone. After insisting that Bright wasn't around, Junior was now claiming he could get ahold of him. Miracle of miracles. You can get ahold of him?

Gentry asked. Yes, Junior said. "He's next door."

"Did you, what you lying to me? He was there all the time?" Gentry sounded aghast.

"No, he wasn't here all the time Larry, he's next door . . . Hang on, let me go get him. Hang on, okay? Wait. Please wait. Please Larry, don't do something that stupid . . . You're really making me scared, you know?"

Scared is where they wanted Gilbert "Junior" Pauole. Scared is where they needed him. The quaver in his voice. The scamper from emotion to emotion. The callout to his family. Then there was the way he could jump from topic to topic with little hesitation. The way he could riff on his emotions. The way he could squirm to a different solution as each new problem arose. It was like having a salesman on the line. Or an actor. One had to wonder: if the cops hadn't been watching over Larry Gentry's shoulder, would he have fallen for Junior's ever-expanding promises? Gilbert Pauole, it seemed, was fully capable of offering the known universe on a string.

Whatever else Junior Pauole was, he was quite convincing. So convincing that he got caught up in his own monologue and forgot everything but his own immediate needs. Larry had to remind him of the topic at hand. It wasn't Junior Pauole or the known universe.

"Where's John at?" Gentry demanded. "I want to talk to him."

John Bright came on the line friendly as could be. Casual even. The two of them were more than roommates. They had a shared sense of familiarity. Considered themselves running buddies. To most observers, it was Larry Gentry who led that procession. Larry Gentry who was top dog. John Bright was, by all accounts, the follower.

"Hey buddy," Bright said as he took the phone, ever the smooth criminal.

"Yeah," Larry replied. "I'm about fed up here John, and I'm up to my fucking neck fed up."

John Bright ran through a ramble of reassurances. Told Larry he had everything under control. Told him that's why he flew back. That he was here to get things under control. It soon became clear that John Bright was in no position to do the things he promised. When Larry let slip that he'd talked to Robert Betts again, Bright's response was "where is he?" He asked again. "Where is he?"

"He won't tell me," Larry said. John Bright laughed. The cops breathed a sigh of relief.

"I'm fixing to take care of it," Bright insisted. "I asked you to do it, the way I asked you to do it and you didn't even do that man. Just please let me handle it, okay? I told you, you're not taking no heat, okay? You don't have nothing to do with nothing . . . I dropped my house, I dropped my job, I dropped my car to come all the way back here to alleviate the strain off you in this, okay? I told you that on the phone. I come all the way this way just to straighten this out so that you can live happily ever after. Okay? So can you just be patient a couple of days, just be mellow and everybody will be gone and you can live happily ever after. Okay? Please?"

"Okay John. I'm going, this, I want to think things out for about five minutes, all right? Get my head together here and I'll call you guys back and give you my decision on this." He was stalling. Purposely stalling. The cops wanted Junior and John to sweat a while. John Bright thanked him. Then handed the phone back to Junior Pauole, who resumed his begging, his pleading, his whining. Larry Gentry promised to call him back and hung up the phone.

The minute the phone call ended, Junior Pauole and John Bright knew something was up. What it was, Pauole later told police, was less than certain. But both men were nervous. Junior was walking back and forth in the living room of his apartment. John Bright was there with him. He too was pacing.

"It wouldn't surprise me that he's not at the police department already," Junior said.

"Well," John seethed, "if I have to shoot him, like, Gentry *and* Susan, I will."

At that point, Junior Pauole didn't know what he felt. He later admitted he didn't care. He didn't want to hear the truth about Larry Gentry. He had a feeling Gentry was at the police department because of the way he was acting. Because everything was out of control.

"I just have this feeling," he thought. "I just know. I just know." And yet Junior seemed paralyzed.

19

Anchorage, Alaska, November 8, 1985

DURING THE BREAK, THE COPS SCRAMBLED a new script for Larry Gentry. They needed him to close the deal. Worries were a swirling storm above them. Worries about Robert Betts. Worries about John Bright. Worries about Gilbert Pauole. They knew they were on the right track when, on the 9:14 p.m. call back, Junior immediately asked Larry why he was mad at him.

"Just let me talk to John right now," Gentry demanded. There was method to his madness. The cops wanted Bright to stay where he was. Wanted him contained in Junior's triplex.

With Bright on the line, Larry said there was something he wanted to know. Then he confronted him about the murder of the Korean liquor store clerk. Bright demurred. There was a chance, in that moment, that he was on to them. That he had a heightened sense that Larry was with the cops. Larry trudged on, demanding. "Did you kill that damn Korean?"

"Well, I'm not going to say now," Bright responded. "I'm not going to say anything. I'm not going to . . . On that. Or anything like that."

The notes from the cops kept coming. Soon, Larry shifted back to Robert Betts. The man whose name was never enunciated. The opportunity came when John Bright once more insisted he was going to "straighten it out," because he wanted to make sure, "he never bothers you again."

"Yeah," Larry asked. "Did you ever find him or not?"

"Yeah, I gotta go see him right now," Bright announced, again dropping a subtle hint that he was on to something. "'Cause I wanted to stop by and pick up the ticket on the way, just so he goes away and nothing else."

"Mmm, let me talk to Junior then." It was John Bright's turn to beg Larry Gentry. "But you can't . . . You can give me a couple of days at least to get this cleaned up before you start really wigging out on me, man."

If Gilbert Pauole was an expert at free association, Larry was showing his command of an anger that welled up and spilled over. With Junior back on the phone, Larry was figuratively in his face. Smoldering.

"Junior," he seethed. "I asked you to do something for me last night and you wouldn't do it."

"What's that?"

"I wanta know the fucking guys, the union guys. I wanta now 'cause I'm fucking scared, I told you."

"Okay," Junior muttered. "There is no union guys Larry. I just told you that not to, not to scare, try to get you away from . . ."

"What, you fucking lying to me again, huh?"

"Larry, Larry! You know what Larry? You making me scared. That's the reason . . . You know I'm fucking scared in my fucking pants."

"Well, who in the fuck did this then? I wanta know who I gotta watch out for, all right?"

"Okay. Hey, if I tell you who you gotta watch out for, you drop it, you forget it and you leave it alone completely?"

"Okay, you tell me. I'll leave it alone completely."

"You promise me Larry, you swear on your first child's head? You swear on your first child's head and you swear on your father?"

"Yeah," Gentry said blandly. It wasn't good enough. Junior made him swear three more times.

"I swear to God," Gentry finally said with force. Gilbert K. "Junior" Pauole took a deep breath. Then almost whispered his revelation. "You was right the first time," he declared.

"That it was Mackay?"

"Right."

"Yeah," Larry replied. He was looking at the note from the cops. He asked their question. "When was this? When you were over there last time?"

"Two years ago, when I was over there to talk to him."

"Well, how much did you get?" Larry asked, reading from the new note hovering at eye level.

"Exactly right there, the ten, that's all I get," Junior insisted. "That's why this ain't even fucking worth it. You know I ain't got fucking nothing, I gave you guys everything . . . You know, that's all I got. I ain't got a fucking dime outta this . . ."

"Okay, so you got the cash two years ago, right?" Larry continued.

"No, I didn't get the . . ."

"I thought you said you got it two years ago?"

"No, you asked me how long I know him," Junior corrected. "I told you I know him two years ago. You see? You know, the cash was mailed. Man, I never even see the fucking guy, you know what I mean?"

"Oh, he mailed the cash?"

"Yeah, he mailed it. He talked to me two years, three years ago about it and he says, 'Well, whenever you want the money, just mail it, I'll mail it to you.' And he said, 'When I mail it to you then you just, you know, do whatever you want with it.' And that's what I did, man."

It was time to bring the hammer down. APD Investigators, assisted by the Anchorage Drug Enforcement Unit, had Junior Pauole's triplex in their sights. Were in contact with officers monitoring the Gentry conversation. They knew things were reaching a climax. Within fifteen minutes of that call, Gilbert K. Pauole and John Ian Arthur Bright were on the lam.

The two men left the triplex almost in unison. Junior headed south on Arctic Avenue in a borrowed Chevy El Camino. Bright took Junior's van north on the same street. There were cops at both ends of the thorofare. Waiting. The cops surrounded them in two exquisitely choreographed squeeze moves. Had more guns than either suspect had ever seen in their lives. John Bright would later refer to his arrest as an "abduction at gunpoint."

Pauole's description was equally graphic. "There was more than a dozen guns pointed at me at the time of my arrest," Pauole would later say. "Everyone was yelling. I was told to slowly turn my car engine off and crawl out my car door." At the scene, police found multiple guns in the van Bright was driving. Which was actually Junior Pauole's van. They also seized the $23,500 that Junior was carrying. Some in cash, some in traveler's checks, some in the form of a $14,000 cashier's check.

Larry Gentry and his wife Susan, meanwhile, were given $400, driven to the airport by the cops and told to get out of town. They rented a Mercury Topaz and drove north, to Wasilla. Their vacation was to be short-lived. Things were happening fast.

20

Anchorage, Alaska, November 8, 1985

Gilbert Kapualoha Pauole, Jr. and John Ian Arthur Bright were handcuffed and brought to the Anchorage Police headquarters, on the first floor of the Public Safety Building in downtown Anchorage. Built in the early sixties to bring police, fire, and municipal courts to a single location, it was already showing its age. It had survived the 1964 earthquake, during which it served as a command post, but officers were now stacked like firewood. Their evidence room was overflowing. The fire department had already escaped to a new facility. Soon, the police would do the same but for now, this was it. A dingy collection of interview rooms and offices, bathed in a dim blue fluorescence.

By 10:07 p.m., Gilbert Pauole was in the custody of lead homicide investigator Sgt. Mike Grimes. He was just at the beginning of what would become a two-and-a-half-hour ordeal. "The time will be 2207 hours on 11/8/85," Grimes declared into the microphone. "This recording is made in reference to case no. 85-92725. Persons on this recording will be Sgt. Grimes on the Homicide Unit, Assistant District Attorney Steve Branchflower, and the defendant Gilbert Pauole, P-A-U-O-L-E, a/k/a Junior Pauole. Why don't you come on in here, Junior?"

"Here" was a cramped interview room, with several chairs and the requisite recording equipment. Grimes beckoned Pauole to enter. The stout Hawaiian complied, but he remained standing, as if in defiance of what was sure to come.

"All right, Junior, you know me, right? Okay. I'm Sgt. Grimes, I'm in charge of the Homicide Unit."

"Okay," Junior replied, a dull monotony in his voice. Then Grimes introduced the other man in the room. "This is Steve Branchflower," the sergeant announced. "From the District Attorney's office, okay? As I understand it, when you were brought in here, you asked for an attorney already?"

For the first time, Junior Pauole gave more than a one-word reply. "Yes, because—well, first, before I ever bring on an attorney, tell me what am I being arrested for?"

"Okay," Grimes told him. "You're being arrested for the crime of attempted murder and solicitation of murder . . ."

"I never do," Junior interrupted.

". . . of Robert Pfeil," Grimes continued.

"No way," Junior insisted.

"Okay. Junior," Grimes told him, "Go ahead and have a seat." Junior resisted the request. Grimes repeated it. "Go ahead and have a seat."

"Now I want my attorney," Junior declared.

"Okay fine," Grimes said.

Junior Pauole now made the first of many insistent protestations about his innocence. "I never do nothing like that," he proclaimed. Grimes offered him a phone book, so he could call his attorney. Junior didn't want it. He had his own phone book, with his attorney's number written for quick retrieval. He was in the bar business. The topless bar business. Having a personal attorney was second nature.

It was then that Steve Branchflower addressed the room. After volunteering to find Junior's personal address book, he smacked Junior with another slice of reality. "And while I'm doing that," he announced, turning to Grimes as he stepped out to get Junior's address book, "you might tell him the crime that he's under arrest for."

"Like I said," Grimes repeated, "you're being charged with solicitation of murder and also attempted murder of Robert Pfeil."

"Oh, no," Junior exclaimed.

"And when you call your attorney," Grimes continued, "I want you to tell him that we have—some of the evidence that we have against you is every conversation that you've had with Larry Gentry."

That got Junior Pauole's undivided attention. He wanted to talk. He desperately wanted to talk. "Okay, well, I am going tell you," he started. Sgt. Grimes interrupted Junior with a warning: Call your attorney before you make any statements. It was standard cop talk. Miranda warning talk. Between them, Grimes and Branchflower would repeat that warning eighteen times over the next half hour. Eighteen times—or once every two minutes—they had to tell him to stop babbling.

"No, I'm going to tell you—I'm going tell you everything, okay," Junior insisted, "because I am not gonna go to jail for something that I never do, okay? You know, and . . ."

"Play the tape," Branchflower declared. "Just listen to yourself. Shut up."

The next sound was a telephone ringing on the recording and then the sound of voices, coming from Junior's conversation with Larry Gentry.

Gilbert Pauole: Come on, talk to me, no one can hear you.

Larry Gentry: I said I've been thinking things over.

Gilbert Pauole: Yeah.

Larry Gentry: And I've come to . . .

"I already know all that, okay?" Junior interjected, talking to the room. The tape rolled on.

Larry Gentry: . . . a conclusion you're right.

"Do you remember the other part of that tape?" Grimes asked.

"Yeah," Junior admitted. The recorded conversation rambled on. It was hard to take that in—if your name was Gilbert "Junior" Pauole.

Larry Gentry: I'm going to go to the police and turn myself in.

Gilbert Pauole: No! No, Larry, don't do that, 'cause . . .

Larry Gentry: You and John did this shit, I'm gonna turn myself in and get out of it.

Gilbert Pauole: Larry, don't do that, Larry. You don't need to do that.

Grimes punched the stop button. The tape snapped to a halt. But it was not the end of Junior's protestations. "I'll tell you guys everything, okay? I'll tell you guys everything because I never do that, I didn't even want to do that," he insisted. Once more the warning came. Don't talk, Junior. Wait until your attorney arrives. Then a sudden shift in Junior's consciousness. A realization that a new reality awaited him.

"Can I call my wife?" Junior asked. She's in Seattle, Junior said, again denying his involvement. Again, he was admonished. "Okay, well, I want you to talk to your attorney," Grimes declared.

"Well, I'm going to tell him, I'm not a murderer," Pauole said, as he finally acknowledged the admonition. "No way am I a murderer."

"I just wanted you to understand you ain't here on a bum rap," Grimes countered, his voice suddenly confrontational. "I've got you bought and paid for, and that's why I want you to call your attorney."

"Yeah," Junior admitted. "Well, I'm not saying that you, you know, but it's not like what—what it says, what it says there, that I did anything. I never do nothin.' Yes, I did have knowledge of it, you know, and I'll testify . . . I just don't want to go to jail for something that I did not do, you know. I have common knowledge of it and I'll tell you guys everything, how it all came about, just so I won't go to jail, because I just don't want to go to jail for something I did not do. I will testify."

Branchflower returned with Junior's address book. The time was finally at hand. Pauole dissembled. He wanted to call Amy Shotwell, his girlfriend. It was a local call, he reasoned. Grimes and Branchflower turned him down. Flat. Fearing possible destruction of evidence, they didn't want anybody at his house. Junior could no longer stall but he was too nervous to dial the phone. Steve Branchflower offered to do it for him.

"Yes, Anchorage," Branchflower told the telephone operator, "I need Richard Kibby please, residence. Yes. Kib—yeah. 345-4909. Okay. Yeah. Thank you. Three," Branchflower called out.

Junior dialed the numbers, repeating after Branchflower. As the phone rang, Junior's mind wandered to another of his immediate concerns. "Is somebody in my house? Are you guys in my house right now?"

"Nope," Grimes declared. Suddenly, they lost Junior Pauole to more pressing matters.

"Yes, is Mr. Kibby there, please?" he said, his voice breaking. "It's an emergency. Yes, it is definitely an emergency." There was a pause, then Junior was chattering. "Hello, Dick? This is Junior. I'm in the police station. I have been put under arrest for attempted murder for Mr. Pfeils [sic]. Please. Yes, will you please come down here?"

"Let me talk to him," Branchflower interrupted. After a beat, Junior handed over the phone.

"Dick? This is Steve Branchflower. We've got your client down here and he's going to be arrested and we're about to talk to him and he's asked for a lawyer, so will you be able to come down?" There was a slight pause at the other end of the line. "Okay, where do you live? [It's] 10:31—okay, so it will be a while, huh? He's down at 625 C Street, and we won't question him, we'll wait for you to get here. Okay, great. Goodbye."

At the end of the call, Junior immediately pushed another request. This time, he asked to call Amy Shotwell. He apparently thought that, once he'd talked to his lawyer, he'd somehow get the go-ahead. Grimes told him otherwise.

"That's one thing you have no right to," Grimes said, slamming him with a rejoinder, "and you have no right to have your girlfriend present down here, okay?" They instead played another snippet of his taped conversation with Larry Gentry.

Larry Gentry: I—I gotta save my family honor here and stuff.

Gilbert Pauole: Larry, Larry, you have your family honor, okay? Larry, you gonna get me in trouble.

Larry Gentry: Gonna get you in trouble? What kind of trouble am I in?

Gilbert Pauole: You're not gonna—you're not in any trouble. It's already straightened out. The guy left.

Larry Gentry: The guy left?

Gilbert Pauole: Yes, he—John went and took the guy to the airport, and he left. Don't do that, Larry, please. I . . .

Grimes hit stop. And Junior went back to his desperate diatribe. It was almost non-stop. I have nothing to hide, he said. I'm gonna tell you guys everything, he insisted. I never shoot nobody, he declared. I'm going to tell you how all this came about and the whole thing. It became a constant call-and-response. Pauole declaring full transparency, the cops reminding him they didn't want to hear anything from him until his attorney arrived.

Junior was having none of these niceties. "I will fuckin' tell you everything, I mean, you know, I'll tell you from the beginning how, who, what and everything, you know, because I'm not in—I didn't want this thing, you know, that—that—you know, I didn't want this thing, I didn't want to even do this trip, you know? . . . I am volunteering the information, and I'm gonna volunteer more information, you understand? Because I never did it and I will testify to it, too, because I never—I never do that, you know, I just never do that, you know, and I have proof where I was and what I was doing and everything at that time, you know. I had no common knowledge of what that guy was—he was gonna do something that's fuckin' stupid, you know."

Finally exhausted from his solitary protestations, Junior settled into a somewhat more sensible pattern. In a moment of calm, Grimes asked Junior if he wanted a cup of coffee. It was a clichéd offer, but there it was. Junior wondered aloud whether they had his Certs. Then, turning to Grimes, Junior declared, "I thought you was working the streets for prostitutes."

"Well, I—I've been in the Homicide Unit for about a year and a half now."

"Oh," Junior answered, confounded.

Minutes went by. Grimes stayed. Junior glanced over at the tape recorder. Said he didn't care if it was on. Made another statement for posterity. This time, he was referencing the man in the other room. Mr. John Bright. "Okay, because I'm telling you, man, I never, I never wanted to do this, I didn't want to have anything to do with it, I told him not to fool around, that it was dangerous and it's not good, bad karma, you know, and that's he's—that crazy, fuckin' guy in there, he's nuts."

He paused. "I wish I'd never come back to this place."

Gilbert K. Pauole was on a ramble. On a discontinuity. His mind shifting perilously. He suddenly asked about the El Camino he was driving when he was arrested. It wasn't his car, he said. He had borrowed it.

"Well, I'll let you call them after your attorney gets here," Grimes told him. "And I'll guarantee you that we're gonna have it overnight anyway."

"Okay," Junior acknowledged, then shifted his focus. Again. "Why do you guys come down on people? I mean—I mean—why do you guys gotta rush people with so many guns? You know what that—you know what that feels like when you . . ."

"Well," Grimes declared matter-of-factly, "we just take shootin' people pretty serious when we're arresting somebody for shootin' somebody."

They were almost to the end of the tape. There was a pause while Grimes turned it over to the other side. The time was 10:39 p.m. Thirty-two minutes had transpired.

21

Anchorage, Alaska, November 8-9, 1985

THE POLICE TAPE OF JUNIOR PAUOLE'S MEANDERING assertions continued until just past midnight. Slowly, inevitably, things slipped into the small talk of people who wanted to be somewhere else. Junior talked about his worry for his dog, a pit bull named Caesar. Grimes wanted to know if he'd bite. Junior was more concerned something would happen to the dog if it did. In the ensuing tedium, Grimes asked Branchflower to bring him another cup of coffee. Then asked, "Is that other guy still running his mouth?"

"Yeah," Branchflower responded.

"Who's that," Junior asked, suddenly curious. "John? Larry?"

"You got it right the first time," Grimes answered.

In the boredom of their forced companionship, Junior started pacing, then walking in slow circles. Grimes asked him about it, but then was suddenly called aside. Junior's attorney had arrived. In his place came Investigator Austin, who was briefed by Grimes just before he left. "I've got that recorder on," he told him. "There should be another 20 minutes left on that side."

"I'll be glad to get this over with," Junior muttered on learning his attorney had finally arrived. "This is crazy. I never seen so many guns in my whole life."

Conversation now gravitated toward the truly mundane. Austin announced, apropos of nothing, that he was "starting to stink, I can't stand myself. I've been here since 8:00 o'clock this morning." Junior asked for some Rolaids. Investigator Austin admitted he had some in his office. It was one of the things that bound them. Next up, Junior wanted to use the bathroom. Someone had to accompany him. Austin turned off the recorder in the meantime. The time was 11:02. When Junior returned, Austin resumed. "The tape recorder is back on," he spoke into the ether. "The time is 11:09."

Behind them, the tape recorder picked up random police voices in the room. "One of those non-smokers had a girl," they caught on tape. "So instead of giving out cigars, they give out suckers." There was laughter. There was a break while Austin fussed with the tape. It was defective. Junior needed to make another trip to the restroom. He complained, "Jesus, can't a guy go to the bathroom alone?" Austin did some complaining of his own, repeating "I can't stand myself anymore." Someone offered him some aftershave. Then, gradually, the two of them started talking about the one thing they truly had in common. Crime.

"So, you're selling the Fancy Moose, huh?" Austin asked.

"Well, I was tryin' to get out of here and I just, you know, stay away from Alaska. Alaska has been a very unlucky place for me and I just want to get away, just get, you know, just get away from all of this."

"Who are you selling it to?" Austin wanted to know.

"Oh, the Koreans bought it."

"Which? Which Koreans?"

"The Ambassador Club, they bought it," Junior told Austin. "Not for very—not for very much, they just pay—they're just paying $25,000 for it. Because there's—there's no value there, the only value that's there is the lease. You know, there's no value of—of the building, it belongs to Lake Bluff, Inc.,[13] and you know, we're only making three, four hundred dollars a day. I don't want to be in the bar business anymore, I don't want to be in any of that business anymore, I just want to get away, you know. The last nine years I've been used as a patsy for everything that I was a sucker for."

Junior was getting nostalgic now, thinking about his wife and kids. Realizing he would never make a life of it in Alaska. Not with his criminal history. He started fantasizing about becoming a lone laborer, taking

13 Lake Bluff, Inc. was a Neil Mackay holding company.

mindless orders from a boss. Austin, meanwhile, kept smelling himself. He questioned one of the female officers: "You didn't bring deodorant with you, did you? I can't hardly stand myself anymore."

Then, Austin was suddenly obsessed with his hunger. It had been a long day. He'd only had a half bag of pistachios. At one point, Austin admitted "smoking so much my hands are turning yellow." Junior, meanwhile, contemplated the hermit life. Then it was back to the one thing they had in common.

"People are funny," Junior rhapsodized. "You know, they come, people, all kinds of people, you know, you—all kinds of people, they always come—they always come to Junior and ask Junior for this or ask Junior for that. I don't know why people think that I'm the steppingstone to something, but they all come. I'm serious, you know, even if—you know, even the officers, the police department, if they have something related to go-go's, right, a missing girl or a vice ring or some such, the first place they come to is Junior's."

"That's 'cause you've been around here longer than anybody else."

"Yeah, and I know all the girls, you know."

"Oh, I remember I've come to you several times to talk to you about girls," Austin admitted. "We came and talked to you—I've talked to you several times about the girls, particularly at the time we had all those girls missing, Hansen's victims." [14]

"Yeah," Junior said blandly. He knew it was more than that. His was a world of cold realities and so, by extension, was Joe Austin's. They stood on opposite sides of the street and sometimes met in the middle. They started reminiscing about a guy who'd come to the Wild Cherry, tweaked out and ended up shooting at the cops. Shooting, in fact, at Joe Austin.

"Yeah, and he was lucky he didn't kill anybody," Austin concluded.

"This bozo here is lucky he didn't kill anybody, too," Junior responded, referring to John Bright. "Stupid, stupid!"

Steve Branchflower suddenly stuck his head into the interview room. He had a look of urgency on his face. Austin sensed its meaning. "They're here?" he asked.

"We're here," Branchflower announced.

---

14 Serial murderer Robert Hansen had been arrested, and then convicted, only two years previous. Some of the victims worked at Pauole's clubs.

"We're going to shut the recorder off," Austin declared. "The time is now 12:37."

At this point there was, in fact, a newfound urgency to these proceedings. The news reporters were already on the scent. They'd learned about the early evening arrests on the street outside Junior's triplex. They were whispering about major developments in the shooting of Robert Pfeil. It was the nature of this beast that they would out-compete each other for the biggest and best headline. Their clamoring for details had quickly reached a fever pitch.

The cops had to make their next move before the news stories broke. Joe Austin would soon take on his next assignment. He would build airline miles hunting down witnesses.

22

Anchorage, Alaska, November 9, 1985

STEVE BRANCHFLOWER WANTED JUNIOR TO CALL Neil Mackay at his Ilikai condo in Honolulu. Wanted him to pressure the man. The call would, of course, be recorded. To make sure they got Mackay to compromise himself, Branchflower drafted the questions in advance, intending to prompt Junior while he talked. Branchflower had to whisper his cues instead. Junior was effectively illiterate.

Things kicked off at 4:23 a.m. Alaska time, 3:23 a.m. Hawaiian time. Branchflower had already seen the early headlines trumpeting the news. MCKAY NABBED IN MURDER PLOT. CHARGES SAY HE PAID $10,000 FOR PFEIL'S LIFE. They couldn't wait.

Knowing that Neil Mackay was a night owl helped. The likelihood was high that he would not only be awake, but alert. The initial call lasted thirty-two minutes. The first sound on the tape was a message crafted to reinforce bureaucratic tedium.

To complete your call as dialed, please check the number, and dial again. (dial tone) (ring).

Neil Mackay answered on the third ring, his voice giving no sign of drowsiness or confusion. Scotty, they would later learn, was not there. His father had a habit of prevailing upon others as built-in care givers. Scotty was, as it turned out, spending the night at a next-door neighbor's condo. Neil Mackay and Junior Pauole could talk without fear of interruption.

After a few words, during which Junior quickly identified himself, they dove right in. "I'm in real serious trouble," Junior said, emphasizing his panic. It was a tone he would maintain for thirty minutes straight.

"What's the matter?" Mackay replied, his voice alert, focused. This was precisely the response Junior wanted. The hook was set.

"Um, this guy, um, I just got back here last night, and I'm hiding from uh, I'm hiding from the Anchorage Police Department," Pauole said, his voice quavering. "Two of those guys rolled over, and I thought they left town but they didn't and I'm scared to death. I need some help real bad. This guy's read everything that is in the newspaper and they're implicating you. They said that I hired them, and that I got the money, and I paid 'em. I need some help, real serious help."

"God almighty," Mackay replied. "What the hell's happened? I don't know what the hell, what are they talking about?"

"Well, ah," Junior started, then paused for emphasis. "It's, I don't know, you know, they just, uh, uh . . . Neil I'm scared. I'm real scared you know because they're pointing the finger at me, they're saying that I did it, that I'm your hit . . . I'm your contractor, I'm your hit man. Uh, and uh, and all that kind of stuff, you know."

There were any number of possible responses to Junior Pauole's assertions. Most get couched in terms of what an "innocent man" would do. Or what an innocent man would say. Would he leap into adamant denials? Repeat, in no uncertain terms, his earlier incomprehension? Change the response to "I don't know what the hell *you* are talking about?" Hang up? But that's not what Neil Mackay said or did.

"Well, where are you calling from?" he asked. This was a presence of mind response. The thrust of his question soon became evident.

"Where am I calling from?" Junior asked. "I'm hiding in Anchorage right now; I'm calling you from a pay phone. I used my calling card to call you, but I . . ."

Neil Mackay interrupted. "They'll be able to check that out," he replied. There was no sign of befuddlement in his affect.

"Well, I been . . . I waited this late in the morning because that's the only time that I thought would be safe, but I'm . . . If I sound like I'm panicking, I am, because I'm scared to death these people gonna charge me with murder and that's what, that's what they're charging those other two guys with murder."

"Oh, there's two other guys involved?" Mackay asked.

"Yeah, I, what I did was, I, you know . . ."

"Don't say too much, you know," Mackay advised. "You're gonna implicate yourself."

There were at least two ways to read Neil Mackay's last two utterances, starting with the "two guys involved" question. Any time multiple people are involved—especially in a murder—it's a field day for the cops. Somebody is going to break. Somebody is going to tell. A good attorney knows that. Any attorney *should* know that.

With that as background, one can posit that Neil Mackay was comfortably taking on the role of Junior's counselor. He had, in fact, acted as Junior's informal legal counselor in the past. In that interpretation, he was worried on *behalf* of Junior, He was cautioning Junior against statements that would incriminate him in this murder he was talking about.

There was another reading. more ominous. These things Junior was saying were *personally* worrying to Neil Mackay. Hence, his follow-up admonition was a plea for silence. If you implicate *yourself*, he seemed to be saying, you also implicate *me*. Except, of course, none of that mattered to Junior Pauole.

For Junior, it was time to start piling on. Branchflower was impressed. Junior was convincing. The man was readily coming up with the details, without prompting.

"I'm afraid that if I go down that you're gonna go down, you know," Junior insisted. "That's why I'm so scared because I know, I mean, you know these people, uh, I thought they were, I thought they were, you know, I thought they were professional people. Um, Neil, I'm scared to death. I need help, you know, I need your help, that money that I . . . you know."

"Well, Jesus," Mackay exclaimed, "don't be saying too much like that on the phone. Before you know it somebody gonna pick this crap up and believe it. See they probably got me wired too."

"No, I'm at a payphone," Junior reassured him. "I'm at a payphone clear across town. I'm in Muldoon."

"Yeah 'cause," Mackay said, then changed course. "But they could bug me here, they probably may have me bugged here at the . . . where I am."

At this point, Junior was little concerned about Mackay's reservations but the cops were looking at him. Steve Branchflower was looking at him. There was nothing for him to do but keep pressing the case.

"Yeah, I don't want to go down, Neil. If I go down, you gonna go down with me because that $10,000, you know I never got nothin' out of this whole thing. Now, Neil, you know I love my family, too. You know so if I go, you know, I don't . . . you know if I go down, I know you gonna go down, you know. But I can't . . . you know, you know, uh, that $10,000 and you know . . ."

"That $10,000 you keep talking about," Mackay replied, taking on a cautionary tone. "God, Junior, you know, let's use our head and let's calm down."

"Neil, you know I can't, you know I can't. I don't want to lose my family. If I go down, I'm telling you, you gonna go down, too. That is a fact, OK? I'm scared to fuckin' death they gonna charge me with murder."

"Well, how can they charge you with murder if you didn't have nothing to do with the goddamn thing?"

Pauole needed an answer for this one. Branchflower needed an answer too. Mackay's response was a potential conversation ender. Only it wasn't. "Well, these guys are tellin' em everything, I guess," Junior responded, throwing a life ring to himself. "They put two and two together. And, uh, and, and," Junior was stalling. It was time to repeat one his themes. "And that, you know, I know your phones ain't bugged because . . . Uh, you know, you know. And I'm at a payphone, you know, and it's using a . . ."

"My phone over here may be bugged."

"No," Junior insisted.

"They got private detectives working over here."

Junior quickly switched gears. Told Mackay he needed a plane ticket. Wanted him to wire the money. Mackay implied it was too risky, saying "anything I do right now, just . . ." Junior stayed on script. He was scared. The suspects were trying to make it sound like he—Junior—had tried to murder "this guy."

Neil Mackay now said what he should have said all along. "Well see, here's the situation. I don't know nothin' about nothin.' I . . . you're just get[ting] me in a real bad position." Even after a passionate monologue from Junior about how the cops had been to his house and "jacked up my girlfriend, they threatened my bartender," Neil Mackay held steadfast in his denials.

"But here's the situation," Mackay repeated. "You're talking about somethin' I don't know anything about."

Junior turned on a dime. I need your help, he pleaded. Are you gonna help me? Mackay wanted to know how he could do so. Because, he said, anything he did would leave the impression "that I am involved." Junior had him.

"That means that I'm gonna go to jail and it's the end of it," Junior said.

"Now wait a minute," Mackay counseled. "Now you're all panicked, and you're all worked up right now."

Junior mentioned his wife in Seattle, his kids. Told Mackay he was "freezin' my ass out here in the telephone booth," said he didn't even want to be talking to him, except that he didn't know where else to turn. Soon, he was into a stream-of-consciousness ramble, weaving from his confiscated van to confiscated Wild Cherry files, to an indirect reference to Muriel Pfeil's murder. Neil Mackay tried in vain to slow him down, but Junior's panic had an implacable reality to it. The best lies, after all, are close to the truth.

The trick now was to put Neil Mackay at ease. The problem was clear enough. He didn't trust that his phone wasn't bugged. He'd said it more insistently as the call continued: "This phone is bugged," he repeated, an incessant refrain that kept him plugged, gagged, circumspect. Now Junior was offering him an alternative. Just give me a number to call, he said, so we can talk. "You know, you, you, you said that you had a number."

Mackay was still afraid. Junior promised Mackay that, if he gave him another phone number, it would be "the last time I'm gonna call you." Then he put strings on it: "You give me $2,000 and I can go. You know, that's all I want, you know."

Those words did not comfort Neil Mackay. It was, to him, just another tie in to the "other people." Another trap he'd rather avoid. Junior's next words were calm, soothing, seductive.

"Nobody's going to get tied in," Junior assured him. The only person the other people knew was him, Junior Pauole, and besides, those guys were in jail. All their information was coming from the newspaper. "They got upset because they read that the estate is one million dollars or something and they feel they are getting tricked. You know? See and I never, I never told nobody no details or anything, you know. So, when they read the newspaper, they say one million dollars, and then they turn around and these people are giving up $50,000 . . . Neil, give me another phone number so I can talk to you!"

"All right," came the reply. "Just a second."

NEIL MACKAY EXITED HIS ILIKAI CONDO, trundled down the elevator, crossed the lobby and ensconced himself in "his" phone booth. There, he could be sure the phone was not bugged. There was something else: the payphone was within easy reach. He wasted no cycles getting there. Junior waited the agreed upon five minutes. The time was 4:55 a.m.

Mackay answered on the first ring.

This time, Junior tried even harder to convince Mackay to send him the $2,000. What he needed, Junior said, was a plane ticket. He insisted his problems were bigger than that. "What am I gonna do," he asked. "I can't even go to my club, I can't go home, my girlfriend doesn't even want me around, I can't even leave, I can't go to the airport, I can't even rent a car. I can't do nothin.'"

"Well," Mackay responded, maintaining his calm demeanor, "what would the $2,000 do?"

Junior suggested he could get someone to drive him across the Canadian border. The real problem was getting the money. It was the weekend, Mackay pointed out. The banks and everything else were closed. Junior kept pushing. He suggested Mackay send him a "speed pack" in an envelope and move it via Western Airlines. He could pick it up in baggage claim and disappear. "I'll be in the Canadian Border tomorrow night, and you'll never hear from me again. I'll never ask for another penny."

"But here, here's the situation," Mackay explained. "How the hell do you get cash on the weekend, there's no cash here. See the banks are closed."

"Are you saying you don't have no cash, is that what you're saying?"

"Right. That's right."

"Well, I'll wait till Monday," Junior insisted. The cops were choking on that one, but Junior kept riffing. "You know, I can hide till Monday."

Neil Mackay stayed cautious. He told Junior he was trying to think of way to help him without getting himself tied in. When Junior mentioned that he did this as a favor to Mackay, Neil told him not to say too much on the phone. Junior launched into a passionate diatribe that referenced a conversation the two of them had while Junior was in Seattle.

"I mean, when I was in Seattle, you know, I thought everything was fine when I talked to you three days ago in Seattle. I came up here and all this shit hit the fan. You know, I haven't even been in town, I got off, I got off the Western Airlines flight that gets here at nine something or ten something, 9:55, and then all of a sudden, my girlfriend hits me with all of this, you know, asking questions about who I pay the lease to and all of that."

"Now see now here . . . Here's the thing that I'm getting a little concerned about is everybody . . ."

"I don't blame . . ." Junior interrupted.

". . . tying this damn thing to me," Mackay said, completing his thought.

"Well, Neil," Junior said, "it is tied to you. But it's only tied into you from me. I'm the only one that can put you down. Nobody else. All these people is doing is reading the newspaper and they're taking it from the newspaper."

"That's the only thing I'm getting it from," Mackay responded, "is from the newspaper too."

"Yeah, but, but they're saying that I did it for you."

"Well, you know that's not true."

"Neil," Gilbert shot back, his voice taking on a tone of exasperation. His anger—his feigned anger—was rising. "Don't try to bullshit me," Pauole cried, his voice starting to break. Neil Mackay insisted he wasn't. That denial brought the full force of Junior's ire.

"You know, don't bullshit me," Junior repeated, angrily. "You know, you're just as involved as I am, you know. I did this favor for you and . . . you know, I just took . . . all I wanted to do is, you know, just something nice for you because you were so nice to me . . . You know I wasn't even around the place when it happened, you know, I didn't want to be around the place, you know. You told me that you wanted the guy hurt and these guys here told me that they could do it and you gave them the money and that was it. Now those are the only people that can implicate me, OK, and the only people that can implicate you is . . . Me. And I'm not going to implicate you, so please . . . don't bullshit me on the telephone, OK, you know."

"Now, Junior, now," Mackay stuttered, trying to calm the thundering beast.

"Oh, Neil! Don't do that, OK?"

"Junior, I'm not doing anything. I'm trying to figure out what the hell to do."

"You know, help me," Junior begged. "That's what you gotta do is help me, you know."

"Well," Mackay replied, "I'm not here to help anybody."

Junior immediately played the guilt card. Reminded Mackay that he'd wanted some help for his son, for Scotty, because Robert Pfeil was squandering his inheritance. Then segued into the predicament he found himself in, with no place to go, no place to hide. Told him about the police questioning his girlfriend, Amy Shotwell. Asking her if she'd ever heard of Neil Mackay and Amy responding she never heard of Neil Mackay. "I am in deep fuckin' shit," Junior declared, and "you sound like you don't want to help me. If I go, you gonna go, you know."

"No," Mackay said, staying with his cool voice, "the only thing I'm being quiet about is that you're saying too much."

The wheels seemed to be turning in Neil Mackay's brain. Junior suggested a payphone-to-payphone call. Mackay had an alternative thought. "Just a second," Mackay told him. "There's people all over the place here. Call 949-9810."

Junior said he didn't get the number. Mackay repeated it, number by number. "What do you want me to do?" Junior asked. Wait a few minutes, Mackay responded.

"OK, where's it at?"

"Close," Mackay replied. Their second phone call was at an end.

AT 5:10 A.M. PAUOLE CALLED THE SECOND NUMBER GIVEN him by Mackay. At this point, it was clear that Mackay had already begun to work out a plan to get Junior Pauole off his back. The plan was to "call the lady" in Anchorage, who would get Pauole some money. He was unwilling to say her name over the phone and referred to her as only as "the older lady." That older lady, it became clear from the emerging context, was Barbara

Homay, Neil Mackay's first wife and trusted associate. Even then, the paranoia crept in. Mackay mentioned that he was in the Ilikai lobby and noticed a "gal sittin' over there, takin' down notes."

Toward the end of the conversation, however, Mackay began to talk about a potential defense strategy. When Junior says he's not going to hold the bag for the shooting, Mackay says, "How could you, because you don't know anything about it." When Junior suggests that his cohorts are going to say he went to Hawaii and got the money from Neil Mackay, Mackay responds with, "That's what they want to believe."

Junior wouldn't let it rest. He came back with, "And I made a big mistake Neil, I made a big mistake you know, I told them I was gonna go to Hawaii and get the money you know, I made a big mistake, I told 'em that, I was gonna go to Hawaii and make, and get the money and that's how they figure it out, you know, they figure that it was from you."

"Yeah, but you didn't go to Hawaii. Uh, now . . . you haven't been back to Hawaii."

If there was a shift here, it was one in which Neil Mackay finally seemed confident he could take charge of the situation. He suddenly became the one asking the questions. These were not *la-dee-dah* questions. These were pointed questions. Questions that, after all this back and forth, told the listeners in Anchorage of his involvement in the plot to harm Robert Pfeil.

"Now let me ask you a question," Mackay blurted out, taking command of the conversation. "Uh, you mentioned something about a, ah, metal thing. Is it ground up?

"Hm, the car, you mean the car?"

"Yeah?" Mackay replied expectantly. Junior immediately sensed—knew—that Mackay was asking about Larry Gentry's Lincoln. The car they used in the shooting of Robert Pfeil. Neil Mackay did not contradict him.

"Well, the car, you know, the car," Junior replied, "uh, was given to a junk company, it was paid, it was paid by me, I paid the, I gave the, I gave one of the guys the money to get rid of the car because they, it's a long story, it has something to do with, something to do with him being accused of being a cop killer or something, you know, and now the guy, and now the guy that did this, they also got him on another, on another murder charge where he killed this Chinese lady or something, uptown somewhere, downtown . . ."

Yeah, what about . . . Well, what about the g-u-n?" Mackay didn't say the word. He spelled it out, letter by letter.

"I don't know nothing about that," Junior declared. "Those two guys got that, that uh, the g-u-n."

Neil Mackay immediately shifted gears. This business had to be concluded. He now had the answer to Junior's dilemma. He would help. "Uh, well the only way I can figure," Mackay said, "[is] get you uh . . . cash."

The cash would come from "the lady."

Their wired conversation came to an end as Neil Sutherland Mackay verified that Junior Pauole had the phone number for "the lady." He repeated it for him. 947-9544. Neil was in charge now. He even advised Pauole to calm down and insisted he would try to help. Junior was to call "the lady." Then he was to follow up with a call to Neil Mackay at noon the following day.

Anchorage woke up to the news of the overnight arrests. By early morning November 9, 1985, Neil Mackay had been charged with Attempted Murder in the First Degree. Gilbert Pauole and John Ian Arthur Bright were transported before the Honorable David Stewart, District Court Judge for the Third Judicial District in the State of Alaska. Their bail was fixed in the amount of $5,000,000 each, cash-only.

They were subsequently transferred to the Cook Inlet Pretrial Facility in Anchorage. Junior Pauole never got a chance to call "the lady."

That evening, Anchorage recorded its first snow of the season. Three days later, Junior Pauole made a jailhouse call to *Anchorage Times* reporter Earl Swift, admitting his role in the Pfeil shooting. According to their interview, Pauole claimed he was "drawn into the plot to kill Pfeil without knowing of the animosity between Mackay and Pfeil."

He also fingered Larry Gentry and John Bright.

"Yes, I did get the money from Neil Mackay," Pauole told Swift. "But Larry Gentry is the man who got the shooter for me. All I did was that (Mackay) asked me to do something for him, and this was about two years ago."

23

Anchorage, Alaska, December 1977

THE LITANY OF SUSPICIONS HOUNDING NEIL MACKAY might have been less convincing had he not tried to abduct his own son. He would, of course, claim otherwise. After all, he'd met each of Judge Roy Madsen's custody requirements. The no drugs mandate. The parenting classes. The acceptable governess. The acceptable home. By all rights, Scotty was his.

One man still stood in his way. Robert Wagstaff. Mackay was on a scorched earth campaign to be rid of him. He felt he had more than ample justification. There was no mistaking where Bob Wagstaff stood with respect to Mackay's quest:

"Neil S. Mackay has never had legal custody of the child since the child's birth," Wagstaff wrote in a March 27, 1977, trial brief. "The only relationship with Scotty has existed by way of severely limited visitation rights which require the presence of another adult. Scotty has had only one authorized overnight visit and another adult was then present. In short, there is no pre-existing relationship that can be looked to between Neil Mackay and Scotty Mackay for historical direction.

"With respect to Neil Mackay's ability to fulfill the role of a parent from the perspective of the best interests of the child, it is important to point out that Neil Mackay has no experience with children, suffers from uncontroverted brain damage, is 53 years old, lives alone, and does not presently have physical custody of Scotty. There is no demonstrated ability to satisfy or develop the moral, social, psychological, physical, religious or educational needs of a child. In this context, the placement of Scotty with Neil Mackay would represent a significant and major change in both of their lives. This fact alone is controlling to the selection of the appropriate [custody] test to be applied."

Neil Mackay thought he was home free when Judge Madsen removed Wagstaff from the case, calling him an impediment to settling the custody matter. There was not even a hearing. Just a precipitous decision by a judge who'd grown tired of this case. A move that the Alaska Supreme Court quickly quashed.

"It is our conclusion that the attorney representing N.P.M. (Scotty Mackay), Robert H. Wagstaf, should not have been removed unless good cause existed for his removal," the Alaska State Supreme Court ruled. "The nature of the cause should be specified by the Superior Court, and its conclusions should be supported by adequate findings of fact."

Bob Wagstaff was, once again, Scotty Mackay's attorney. Neil Mackay kept fighting by other means. He filed suit on behalf of Scotty, alleging that Robert H. Wagstaff, Theodore Pease Jr., Russellyn S. Carruth and Robert B. Pfeil had "wrongfully misappropriated Scotty's funds under circumstances amounting to fraud."[15] They were, in other words, stealing candy from a baby.

That wasn't all. After regaining custody of Scotty in the June debacle with his sister, Mackay filed a petition for permanent exclusive physical custody. He was ready to have it all decided by September 12, 1977. It didn't happen. Something about Mackay not having met all the court's conditions. He'd skipped the mandated drug test. Mackay wrote again in October, requesting—demanding?—that Madsen set the permanent custody hearing for "a day certain in November." Judge Madsen ruled instead that Mackay move for full custody by December 24, 1977, or, as Mackay put it, "forever hold my peace."

It was somewhat curious, then, that Neil Mackay wrote the judge again on November 8th. Not so much *that* he wrote, but *what* he wrote. For someone in such a hurry, he was suddenly begging to put things off.

---

15 Pease and Carruth were lawyers for Muriel Pfeil's estate. Pease was also Muriel's former divorce lawyer, having been replaced by Doug Baily only weeks before her murder.

"Under all the circumstances," Mackay declared, "I am writing at this time to request an understanding that no hearings will be scheduled in this case during the period of December 2, 1977, through March 19, 1978. Scotty has been invited to visit his 81-year-old great aunt who lives in Lakewood City, California, which is in easy distance of Disneyland; has been invited to spend some time on a ranch in Idaho; would like to spend some time on the beach at his home in Honolulu; and has a father who has had no vacation in over a year."

He got Dave Talbot to follow up that letter with a formal motion, submitted on December 8th. In it, he declared that he, Neil Mackay, no longer had mere rights of visitation, but "full care, custody and control since June 26, 1977." Talbot added that they were "just totally unaware of any fact or circumstance which would justify or require the limitation upon the normal rights of a father to travel with a son who will be five in March."

In parallel to all this sound and fury, Mackay went after Bob Wagstaff for having the temerity to request he submit to a laboratory drug screen, apparently in defiance of a court ruling to the contrary.[16] He demanded that Wagstaff be held in contempt and be "confined in an appropriate cell in the State of Alaska Correctional Annex . . . until such time as [he] purges himself of his contempt on the rulings of this court." It was, to say the least, a punishment at odds with the purported crime. Indeed, it seemed proof of what Wagstaff was alleging: that Neil Mackay was again abusing drugs.[17]

Then, on December 12th, Dave Talbot sent a letter to Robert Wagstaff.

Mr. Robert H. Wagstaff
Attorney at Law
912 West Sixth Avenue
Anchorage, Alaska 99501

---

16 Mackay voluntarily took the drug test on December 1, 1977, the day after Wagstaff's request. It came back positive for amphetamines. As a clear violation of the court's conditions, it put his custody fight in jeopardy. Mackay would later claim the result was a false-positive, an artifact of the drug screen protocol used.

17 The contempt allegation was an old Mackay trick. During his divorce from Muriel, he filed a motion to hold her in contempt and impose sanctions. That motion was denied by Judge Harold Butcher, who handed down his ruling just two days before Muriel's murder.

RE: Mackay vs. Pfeil, No. 76-7886
Dear Bob:

Neil had some urgent business requiring his presence in Hawaii and so he and Scotty flew to Honolulu Sunday night, December 11. Neil was lucky to get a reservation on such short notice and Western Airlines said it was either go Sunday night or not at all, until after New Year's. I know from the papers you filed last December that you are a strong believer that Scotty should spend some time in Hawaii, so I trust this development is OK with you.

We requested an order stating that the Court did not object to Scotty's going to Hawaii and California, but I understand from the Clerk of Court that Judge Madsen has declined to consider our application without giving you and Mr. Baily a chance to be heard. A copy of our application is enclosed.

As you know, the Court heard extensive testimony on November 29, 1977, from child psychologist Brent Davis, behavior therapist, Gin Bridwell, attorney Wayne A. Ross, Mrs. Virginia Zawacki and Mr. Mackay on the question you raised about the wisdom of Scotty's vacationing with his father. As I recall, the testimony was all to the effect that there is no reason to question Neil's right to do this—nor did you or Mr. Baily offer contrary evidence, or request time to do so.

I know that both you and Grandmother Pfeil have asked to see Scotty and I did my best to arrange that last week but, as you know, Alaska Treatment Center decided, and I suppose wisely so, that the Center must have a written request from the Court and also a written understanding with the parties and counsel as to just what it is the Treatment Center is being asked to do.

I now regret that you and Mrs. Pfeil did not take advantage of previous opportunities to visit with Scotty. As you know, Nell agreed months ago to Wayne Ross's proposal that Wayne take Scotty on visits to his Grandmother, but Mrs. Pfeil was not agreeable to that. Also, I now understand and that Scotty has been to your office on occasion, and I'm also sure the Willises would have arranged for you to see Scotty, even if Neil was reluctant to do so on account of the role you have assumed as Neil's adversary in this case.

Very truly yours,
Dave Talbot

What Talbot failed to mention in his friendly little missive was that Neil Mackay was supposed to notify the court before taking Scotty out of Alaska and that he was to post a $250,000 performance bond. He'd done neither. Now Scotty was gone. All hell was about to break loose.

24

Honolulu, Hawaii, February 22-27, 1978

THE 26TH FLOOR PENTHOUSE OF THE ILIKAI HOTEL & Condominiums is iconic. Its balcony is the backdrop for the swooping helicopter shot framing actor Jack Lord in the opening credits of the original *Hawaii Five O*. This time, the action was seventeen floors down, in Unit 929.

At the door of Unit 929 were Brook Hart, who'd been hired to represent Scotty in Hawaii, and Sheriff Raymond Ho. They were there to serve Neil Mackay a Temporary Restraining Order and Order to Show Cause, directing him to appear in a Honolulu courtroom and show why he should not be required to return Scotty to Alaska.

The Alaska authorities had given him plenty of chances.

Mackay hadn't shown up at the trial setting conference set for December 14, 1977, the hearing he had stridently demanded. Scotty wasn't there either. The court directed Dave Talbot to communicate that his client was defying the Orders of the Court. He was not, Judge Madsen said, "the child's custodian."

Mackay didn't show up—or call into—the January 16th final hearing. The one at which the Court vacated the September order that temporarily placed Scotty with his father. The one where Madsen ordered Scotty be returned to Carolina and Alfred Willis.

It took until January 18th for Talbot to report back to the judge. He'd spoken to his client, Talbot said, as directed. Neil Mackay, Talbot reported, was "adamant in his refusal to return Scotty to Alaska." Mackay said this even while knowing he was being fined $1,000 a day until he returned with his son.

By the time Brook Hart and Sheriff Ho showed up at Mackay's door, they knew something else. Neil Mackay had made inquiries about his son's birth certificate. Said he wanted his son to have a U.S. passport. Once they had the passport, he planned to leave for a foreign jurisdiction, possibly Hong Kong. That would put the pair even farther out of reach.

Expecting trouble, the Sheriff brought multiple police officers to the Ilikai. They pounded on the door and, when no one answered, they started to break it down. One of the people inside called security. His name was Charles Sullivan. Sullivan was there with his wife, Jean. The older couple—he was 67, she was 62—said they didn't know where Neil and Scotty were. Did not know where they could be reached. They believed, they said, that he was on the Island of Kauai, the westernmost major island in the Hawaiian chain.

But the Sullivan's were lying. The Kauai angle was a ruse, a long ball designed to take the cops off the scent.

Chuck and Jean Sullivan were friends of Mackay's, people who, like Neil, had lived in Alaska. He'd known them for more than two decades. They'd done business. At the moment, though, the Sullivan's were actively helping him stave off the process servers. In fact, while the police clustered like cockroaches at the Ilikai, Neil Mackay and Scotty were in hiding across the street at the Discovery Bay condominium. In a unit owned by the Sullivan's.

Neil Mackay had managed to sell the Sullivan's on the notion that people from Alaska were trying to kidnap Scotty. Chuck and Jean were just the folks to call. After having owned a hotel in Fairbanks, they had several addresses in Honolulu. One at the Ilikai, on the 20th floor. At least one at the Discovery Bay and another two units at the Villa at Eaton Square condominiums, near the Eaton Square shopping center.

During the next few days, Neil and Scotty shuffled between various Sullivan properties. They moved to a unit at the Villa. It was too small. They shifted to another, larger Sullivan apartment in the same building.

They were, in a way, hiding in plain sight and playing a game of cat and mouse. Their idyllic time in Hawaii was at an end. There would be no more glowing testimony from the likes of Virginia Zawacki, who wrote:

"I am informed and believe that since going to Hawaii with his father on December 10, 1977, Scotty has experienced the greatest period of growth, development, good health and happiness in his entire life to date. Scotty has been swimming, diving, surfing, sailing, enjoying long hours with his Dad, soaking up sunshine, eating fresh fruits and vegetables, and in general enjoying even greater freedom and happiness than he had in wintertime in Anchorage with his father. Scotty has also enjoyed traveling between islands, has made many new friends and has had many new educational experiences."

The first break for Alaska authorities came when a private investigator hired by Robert Wagstaff spotted Dave Talbot at the Ilikai, on February 27. Steve Goodenow was an experienced investigator. A former schoolteacher, he knew his way around people. He also knew his way around the Hawaiian Islands. It was tough duty, nonetheless.

For starters, according to Goodenow, Dave Talbot was extremely difficult to follow, because he didn't use a pattern. "Talbot would 'walk backwards,' to coin an investigative term. He would enter a building and go to several floors, walk around corners, and stop. We were forced to use at least three to four men to follow Talbot."

They had no choice. First, they had to locate Neil and Scotty Mackay through David Talbot, Jean, and Chuck Sullivan and/or their cohorts. Second, they had to prevent the movement of Neil and Scotty Mackay absent the knowledge of the investigative team. Finally, they had to apprehend the pair while supporting the Alaskan authorities who'd arrived in Hawaii.

The location of their targets, slipping through the thick warren of Honolulu's hotels and condos, didn't help. They had to surveil three separate buildings within a quarter of a mile of each other. At any given time, 2,000 people were at the Ilikai. There were approximately 692 apartments in two 42 story towers at Discovery Bay. The Villa housed at least 1,000 people and had the Eaton Square Shopping Complex attached. It was impossible to surveil just one building.

Even when they learned that Jean Sullivan and Dave Talbot were holding meetings at the Villa, the fact that both Sullivan and Talbot used pass keys complicated their surveillance efforts. The two of them could enter the building and then, once inside, be confident they weren't being followed.

With all the heat now making itself known—there was little question that Talbot and Sullivan knew they were being tailed—this cluster of allies seemed to be scurrying to figure out what came next. They had to get Scotty out of Oahu, at the very least. Court records indicate that talk had moved on to Singapore. Without a passport, that was a dead duck.

That Neil Mackay could even contemplate such far-flung moves was nevertheless a tribute to his financial prowess. A court ordered audit found he held accounts at four banks—two in Hawaii, one in Nevada and one in Alaska. Those four banks covered twenty-four separate account numbers. A financial statement presented in 1978 during the custody hearing pegged his worth at $10 million.[18] During that same period, he purchased five Certificates of Deposit worth a combined $500,000. That in itself spoke to his ready access to cash.

None of that represented a full accounting of his net worth. During his divorce from Muriel, he was accused of hiding some of his financial assets. When asked during his 1974 divorce proceedings whether he had any interest in the Mackay Building, Inc., he answered, "That's none of your goddamn business." Asked whether he owned stock in any corporation, he replied that he had "no present recollection."

His days as a banker had served him well.

It was Jean Sullivan who broke the Scotty stalemate. She was friends with a man who was the U.S. Consul for the Marshall Islands, part of the Micronesian archipelago deep in the South Pacific. According to court records, the Sullivan's had become acquainted with him because the man's father had a drinking problem and an apartment at the Villa. Sometimes they watched out for him. Maybe their friend Rodger could help their friend Neil.

He could. After bending Rodger Cotting's ear about Trust properties becoming available in Micronesia—they were soon to gain a measure of independence from the U.S.—Neil broached the subject of taking Scotty to Majuro, the island where Cotting was based. Mackay was coy about it, but Cotting already knew the broad outlines of the ask. In his own telling,

18 A number that Mackay would later dispute, saying it was too much by half, due to assets awarded to Muriel Pfeil during their divorce.

Mackay got Cotting to commit by saying nothing more than, "I told him I had some problems." When asked if he told him what the problems were, Mackay repeated the refrain. "I told him I had had some problems."

Cotting had children of his own. He was a devout Catholic. The idea that this child had lost his mother to a tragic murder and was now threatened with the imminent loss of his father, was tailor-made to wreak a powerful tug on his heart. Within two or three days, it was all worked out.

When Rodger Cotting flew back to Majuro—a long flight across the international dateline by way of Guam—he would take Scotty with him. Neil would not be on that flight. He wanted to make sure Scotty was safe. He would follow on the next available flight, three days later.

As Scotty Mackay arrived in Majuro, the flight manifest would list him as John Cotting. That's Rodger and John Cotting, father, and son. If you're keeping track, that's Scotty's seventh familial unit.[19] Neil Mackay would later deny that he'd ever heard his son called John Cotting.

Plausible deniability is a beautiful thing.

19 Scotty was briefly with Neil and Muriel, then Muriel alone, followed by Bob and Marianne Pfeil, followed by the Erwins, followed by Carolina and Alfred Willis. Followed by Neil Mackay alone. And now Rodger and Marie Cotting.

25

Majuro, Trust Territory of the Pacific Islands, March 1-7, 1978

SCOTTY MACKAY WASN'T THE ONLY ONE WHO ARRIVED in Majuro using an assumed name. On February 28, Neil Mackay boarded a Continental Airlines jet in Honolulu, his round-trip ticket to Majuro booked under the name Val Galleron. The Social Security card he carried bore the name Valentine Ralph Galleron. He had Galleron's Hawaiian National Bank card, his Master Charge card, his Chevron USA National Travel card. He even had Val Galleron's *Free Masons of Nevada* card.

When Mackay signed the Customs Declaration in Majuro the next day, March 1, 1978, he signed it as Galleron, Val R. He gave his address as 59-277 Ke Nui, Haleiwa, Hawaii 96712, an address on Oahu's north shore. Because Galleron was a U.S. citizen, no customs declaration was required. Because his new "friend" Rodger Cotting was at the Immigration desk, he slipped into the country unnoticed. Scotty was there to greet him, accompanied by Marie Cotting, Rodger's Filipina wife.

Valentine "Val" Galleron was a friend of Jean Sullivan. Galleron was also the business partner of another Mackay friend, a former Alaskan named Jack Guard. Guard and Galleron ran a heavy equipment company out on Sand Island Road, a dreary industrial area west of Honolulu. Guard and Company, Inc., sold new and used Caterpillar loaders, forklifts, tractor trucks and "many other machinery items." The man also had rental properties on Oahu.

Val Galleron was one of the door prizes in all those meetings between

Jean Sullivan and Dave Talbot at the Villa condominiums. He was in on the deception. When contacted later, Galleron was neither shocked nor surprised that Neil Mackay was using his credit cards. He'd signed up for this.

IN THEIR FIRST FEW DAYS ON THE ISLAND, Scotty and his father got to know both Majuro and their hosts, including the Cotting's four children. They may have been surprised by their landing spot. It was like Hawaii but it wasn't.

Majuro is a narrow buffer of coral between the Pacific Ocean and a gigantic inner lagoon, deep enough to anchor the Fifth Fleet during World War II. It features the longest road in Micronesia, all thirty miles of it, some of it just broader than a car axle. From the air, the island seems barely wider than that.

At the center of the atoll, every single inch seems to be crowded with buildings. Though it is surrounded by an ocean area the size of the continental United States, the island chain—the entire Trust Territory—holds only 535 square miles of land.

Fresh water is available once an hour. Honolulu is 2,300 miles away.

The island itself was cobbled together out of series of atolls by the U.S. Navy, using "muscle and mountains of coral," as one travel brochure described it. At its highest, Majuro rises twenty feet above sea level. Its inhabitants are crowded into a melting pot on the east side of the atoll, where Majuro's businesses are concentrated. In 1977 there were 5,000 souls on the island. Many of them, like Rodger Cotting, were U.S. government employees.

Part of the Trust Territory of the Pacific Islands, Majuro was, at that time, part of a vast protectorate, an artifact carved out by United States in the aftermath of World War II. Though there were changes afoot—the Trust Territories were poised to get their own Constitution—the heavy hand of the U.S. was never far from view.

The most famous real estate in the Marshalls, however, was Bikini Atoll, a coral reef of 23 islands that surrounded a vast central lagoon. After World War II, the atoll's residents were forced to leave their homes and relocate elsewhere. It was there, between 1946 and 1958, that the U.S. conducted 23 bomb tests. Nuclear bomb tests.

Three families were finally resettled on Bikini Atoll in 1970. Scientists soon found dangerously high levels of strontium-90 in their well water. A 1977 study revealed that the residents had abnormally high concentrations of caesium-137 in their bodies. Even as Neil Mackay and Scotty cavorted in Majuro, the Bikini Atoll controversy was once more rearing its ugly head.

By 1980, the few residents who'd resettled there were once more removed.

According to Trust Territory records, one of Neil Mackay's first ventures into the larger world of Majuro came on March 4th. He called on Jim Winn, the District Attorney of the Marshall Islands. It was not a social call. Accompanied by Rodger Cotting, they'd gone to Winn's home to ask about adoption procedures in the Trust Territory. Winn referred them to an attorney on the island, George Allen. Although they didn't explicitly tell Winn that the Cotting's intended to adopt Scotty, it soon became evident. Winn's wife saw Scotty and Marie Cotting on the street in Majuro. They weren't the only ones who saw them together.

Some weeks later, Rodger Cotting confided to Winn that they had seen George Allen about adopting Scotty. He also claimed he and his wife had changed their minds. For the time being.

The Cotting's weren't the only adoption candidates. When Chuck Sullivan arrived on the island some days later, bad heart and all, he too talked with Neil Mackay about adopting Scotty. Neil thought it would be a good idea. There were some clear advantages. The Sullivan's already knew Scotty. Spent a lot of time with him. They were "really close," to use Sullivan's phrase. Chuck was like a grandfather to the kid. They'd even gone so far as to pick out a new name for him. Scotty Mackay Sullivan.

"It would have worked out well," Sullivan later testified in court. "Neil would still be in the same building as us, but legally he would be mine." Eventually, they went to the courthouse in Majuro to complete the adoption papers. Those papers were never signed.

In the end, Charles Sullivan didn't know whether the whole adoption thing was a charade. Whether it was just a paper adoption. Whether it was just a game to keep the Sullivan's interested in helping Scotty. What he did remember was what Neil said. With an adoption, he insisted, there'd be no way the Pfeil's could get Scotty back.

Honolulu, March 10, 1978; Majuro, March 11, 1978

SCOTTY MACKAY, AKA JOHN P. COTTING, celebrated his fifth birthday on March 11th in Majuro, which Robert Lewis Stevenson once called "the pearl of the Pacific." There was a large party, with other children to help him celebrate. They were part of the Cotting's large Catholic faith community.

"He had a Spider Man cake . . . and we had apple dunking and sack races for the children," Mackay later told a Honolulu newspaper. He said several families also attended the party. "It's a custom here."

One wondered which part was a "custom." The apple dunking seemed particularly incongruous, given that the native fruit were more likely to be breadfruit. Still, it was a reminder that the Marshalls were, more than anything else, an outpost of the good old U.S.A. And the lagoon was deep enough to accommodate cargo ships from all corners of the Pacific.

For his part, Neil Mackay wasn't planning to stay much beyond the birthday party. There were court actions bubbling in Hawaii. He was, in fact, scheduled to leave Majuro on the next available flight. That flight was only three days away, on March 14. Scotty, who knew his father was leaving, demanded that he stay for his birthday.

"He told me, 'Dad, if you're not here for my birthday, it's not a birthday,'" Mackay told a reporter. Like a good father, he agreed.

That same day, a Saturday in Honolulu, Steve Goodenow managed to push an article onto the front page of the *Honolulu Advertiser*, Honolulu's morning newspaper. The article publicized the custody dispute. On page 4, there were two photos. One of Scotty Mackay and one of his father.

"Today is Scotty Mackay's fifth birthday," the story proclaimed, "but authorities hold out hope that this year's celebration will be a happy one. Scotty is missing. He was last seen here Feb. 20 and attorneys and investigators hired to look for him fear he may be in danger."

The seriousness of the situation was underscored near the article's conclusion. After talking about Muriel Pfeil's murder, and comparing the story to a television detective drama, the article called out steps being taken by the U.S. federal authorities.

"The U.S. State Department has also taken steps to see that Mackay does not add Scotty's name to his passport or take out a separate passport for the child."

With the temperature appropriately raised, the article offered a clincher. No use getting everyone riled up without giving them a way to react. "Anyone who might have seen Scotty," the article concluded, "is urged to call Steve Goodenow at 523-2408 or Detective Sergeant David Perry at the Honolulu Police Department immediately."

Goodenow got his first hit at 10:00 a.m. that very morning, March 11, 1978. It was then that a telephone call came in from Michael Fluetsch, branch manager of the Bank of America in Majuro, Marshall Islands, Trust Territories. Fluetsch, his wife and children had arrived in Honolulu at 6:30 a.m. that day from the Marshall Islands. On the way to the Ilikai Hotel—no irony there—Fluetsch read the morning paper and then showed it to his wife. There, on the front page, was a story about a father and his boy. A pair whom they knew to be in Majuro.

Apparently Fluetsch had last seen Scotty on Friday Honolulu time or Saturday Marshall Islands time. He had seen him in the company of his father Neil. In Majuro. After calling Guam and conferring with Brook Hart, Goodenow became convinced that Fluetsch was telling the truth.

They'd found Scotty.

26

Majuro, Trust Territories, March 1978

"It's now the 20th, I am stuck here on Ponape. How I got to Ponape is a very interesting story. I am sitting on the veranda type affair, there is a thatched roof over me which extends about 75 feet. I am overlooking several smaller islands, a rugged mountain range. It's about 4:30. It has to be one of the most beautiful settings I have ever seen. There are parrots, multi-colored birds, bananas, coconut trees, every kind of jungle vegetation imaginable within an easy reach of where I sit. Jean Sullivan and Mike Weight, her attorney, are sitting out in a separate viewing area that is detached from the main hut. It sticks out over a cliff-like arrangement and is on top of poles. Scotty Mackay, the subject of this entire investigation, is sitting with an older family who have come here as tourists. I wish I could say the same, but I didn't come here as a tourist, neither did Jean Sullivan, Mike Weight or Scotty Mackay. We came here as captives of the State, under house arrest for lack of a better word. We came here because we were forced off an Air Micronesia flight."

Steve Goodenow, The Village Hotel, Oegono Road, Ponape, Micronesia;

Trust Territory of the Pacific Islands Archives, Neil Scott (Scotty) Mackay Incident

Steve Goodenow initially arrived in Majuro on March 16, just after midnight. He was accompanied by attorney Ramon Villagomez, there to help him navigate Micronesia's justice system and whatever else might befall him. He already knew that Neil Mackay had been apprehended in Honolulu, having hurriedly left Majuro the day before. Knew that the father had arrived without his son. Knew that Neil Mackay had been uncooperative—wandering about the airport in a show of defiance until he was slapped with a warrant for Contempt of Court and booked into Honolulu's Halawa Jail. Surely news of Mackay's arrest had flown into Majuro before them. Surely, the locals were expecting them.

As Goodenow moved toward the Customs section, he was confronted by a person he described as "a rather large gentleman about 250 lbs., or more, 6'3" tall, with glasses."[20] This hulk positioned himself at the immigration counter. Then came a booming voice. "I want to see your passport," he demanded.

"Who are you?" Goodenow asked, turning to address the big man with the outsized voice.

"I'm the head American Consul in Majuro," the man answered, his voice aggressive, rough, not to be trifled with. "Rodger Cotting."

Goodenow showed Rodger Cotting the requisite court order from High Court Judge Robert A. Hefner in Saipan, hoping to placate the man. Cotting snatched it. Scoured it. Scanned the first page, turned quickly to the second. In the stilted language of the courtroom, the document read, "That Steve D. Goodenow of Honolulu, Hawaii, the petitioner herein, is hereby appointed as temporary custodian for the minor, Neil (Scotty) P. Mackay, until he has returned the child to Alaska."

"Do you know where Scotty Mackay is," Goodenow asked.

"Well, he's not here anymore," Cotting replied. "He went out on Air Naru."

The harassment continued. Cotting demanded that Goodenow's luggage be thoroughly searched. It went on like this for five or six minutes. Goodenow had had enough. He called over Ramon Villagomez. Introduced him as his lawyer. Ramon told Cotting to "lay off." Cotting demanded that Ramon show his passport. Told him he and Goodenow had to return to Guam because he knew why they'd come to Majuro. Villagomez was incensed. As soon they'd cleared customs they were hustled into the airport bar by Ramon's cousin, Majuro Police Chief Felix Cabrera.

---

20 It's notable that in some accounts, Goodenow describes the man as 6'1" not six-foot-three. He was, in either case, a big man.

Soon after seating themselves in the airport lounge, Goodenow and company spied Rodger Cotting again. He and one of the locals sat themselves in an adjoining booth. They repeated their comments that Scotty had gone out on Air Naru and was no longer there. Cotting was slurring his words and Felix observed that he'd been drinking before their encounter. Heard him disparaging the Marshallese. Like they were too simple—or too stupid—to be able to hide someone as important as Scotty Mackay.

To others who knew him, Cotting was the Budget and Program Officer for the Marshalls District. A U.S. Civil Service employee who, in fact, had been employed in the Trust Territory for approximately ten years. A man married to a local woman. A man with an unblemished record. Curiosity about this case, meanwhile, was starting to thread its way throughout the Trust Territories. The immediate question concerned Rodger Cotting and the possible kidnapping of Scotty Mackay.

One person in that loop was Lee Hoskins, Chief of the Micronesia Bureau of Investigation (MBI) in Saipan. A 27-year Army veteran, he'd retired as a Lt. Colonel working in Army Intelligence, then taken on the MBI role after retiring from the military. It was Hoskins who responded to the FBI inquiry about Neil Mackay.

"Subject is described as a prominent Anchorage attorney," the cable read, quoting Hoskins, "who is reputed to have organized crime connections . . . During a visit with his son, subject abducted and concealed him in Hawaii in defiance of Alaska court orders. Subject and son located in Hawaii but immediately fled to Micronesia."

Four days later, a corrective cable was sent from the FBI's Special Agent in Charge (SAC) in Anchorage.

"Anchorage files failed to reflect any information indicating NEIL S. MACKAY has organized crime connections. Investigator for State of Alaska, Attorney General's Office, confidentially stated that MACKAY has no organized crime ties to his knowledge.

"State records reflect a ROGER B. COTTING resides Box 271, Fairbanks, Alaska. (It is not known if ROGER COTTING as set forth above is identical with ROGER COTTING in referenced communication.)."

It wasn't the same person. The Majuro Cotting spelled his first name RODGER. His Alaska counterpart lacked the middle-D. He was ROGER.

Had the Alaska Cotting known about his Micronesian half-double, he might have been relieved they were not the same person.

The Micronesian Cotting was in way over his head. He wasn't the only one.

After filing their documents with the clerk of the court in Majuro, Goodenow and Villagomez made their way to the office of the District Attorney, Jim Winn. They told him they had been "met" by Rodger Cotting. Then they showed him the Court Order from Saipan, giving them authority to take Scotty into their custody. Winn suggested that they go to the Cotting home and see if Rodger would peacefully comply with the court order.

On the phone, Rodger Cotting's wife, Marie, told Winn that her husband was at the office of attorney George Allen. Accompanied by Jim Winn, the three of them went to Allen's office. Allen refused to see them. Said he was busy. Suggested they go to lunch instead. They were suspicious. Already knew Allen was working with Neil Mackay.

Goodenow was deep into a late brunch when George Allen finally showed up. He was sweating profusely, his clothes soaked clear through. There wasn't a dry spot on his red checkered shirt. In Goodenow's telling, "George Allen looks about as much at home in the Marshall Islands as snow in Honolulu." He handed Goodenow some papers. George Allen's ruse was now clear. He had stalled them. Had, in fact had, negotiated an Order which appointed Marie Cotting as Scotty's guardian. The language of local Judge Kabua Kabua related a sob story of the first order.[21]

"The Court finds the minor child, hereafter referred to as Scotty . . . was brought to the Marshall Islands under the care and custody of his natural father, Neil S. Mackay, who thereafter relinquished care and custody of Scotty to Petitioner . . . that Petitioner, a person known to the Court for more than seven years and the mother of four children, is a fit and proper person to serve as guardian . . . and that but for appointment of Petitioner as Guardian, Scotty would be an orphan without adequate protection or supervision."[22]

21 This is no typo. Kabua was both his first and last name.

22 Neil Mackay would later imply, in a Hawaii courtroom, that he'd given the Cottings a signed document handing them full custody of Scotty.

That wasn't the only Order issuing from Judge Kabua's bench. In a Protective Order accompanying the guardianship papers, the court literally called off the dogs, forbidding any action by Goodenow—or any other duly appointed officer of the law—to retrieve Scotty Mackay.

Confusion now reigned in Majuro. Goodenow and Villagomez beat a hasty retreat to the offices of Oscar deBrum, the Majuro District Administrator. His office was nothing more than a Quonset hut left over from World War II. Ramon and Goodenow found a spot in the hut and drafted a motion to set aside the guardianship. They wrote another to set aside the temporary restraining order that prohibited anyone from taking Scotty out of the jurisdiction.

George Allen decided to stall once more. It then became a war of attrition, with Allen testing who could hold out longer. Then came the wrench. To give proper notice, it was necessary to give 20 days' advanced notice. A real possibility loomed that no lower court hearing would be held for at least 20 days.

With their three-day tourist window, that would be too late for Scotty.

Then, suddenly, things began to shift. Goodenow and Villagomez filed their motion. Allen agreed to stipulate for an immediate hearing on the new motion, which avoided a 20-day notice provision in the Trust Territories code of civil procedure. All parties agreed to a hearing on the following morning, Saturday, May 18th.

After all this hustle-bustle, Jim Winn received a call from the District Administrator at about 8:00 that evening, asking him to come to his home. Judge Kabua was there. He was extremely agitated. Kabua told Winn that he had not been told about Judge Hefner's prior order when George Allen came to him for the Guardianship Order and the Order of Protective Custody.

They called Judge Hefner in Saipan. He told Winn to comply with his Order. The District Administrator, Judge Kabua and Attorney General Winn decided that Winn would prepare an Order for Judge Kabua's signature. It would be an Order Vacating all Prior Orders that Kabua had made concerning this case.

However, by the time Jim Winn finished, Judge Kabua had gone home to sleep.

Still, there were inklings of progress. Jim Winn heard a rumor that

Rodger Cotting was seen at the airport, down by the Tradition Air Transport Service hangar on Friday, the day before the Kabua hearing. That night he ran into the Australian who managed a plantation on Likiep Atoll and asked if he had just come into Majuro on Tradition's Grumman Goose.[23] He said he had but, when Winn asked if he had seen Rodger and/or a small, blonde boy of about five, the man evaded his inquiries.

Finally, he simply said that he could not answer Winn's questions.

Winn assumed that they had left on the Goose for Likiep when it went up to pick up the Australian. Winn asked the police on Friday night to try to locate either the pilot or Tradition's manager and part-owner of the Goose. They found the pilot on Saturday morning and brought him to the courthouse. He wouldn't tell Winn anything. Only on a witness stand under the penalty of perjury would he talk. Winn considered that possibility but thought he could get what he wanted from somebody else, specifically the plane's owner, who'd made the trip and had the airplane manifest, but the Goose's owner had disappeared. Winn learned he had literally gone fishing.

They kept looking for the Goose and the folks in Majuro who presumably knew Scotty's present whereabouts. Rodger Cotting had disappeared; Maria Cotting had disappeared. Steve Goodenow thought they were staying with the Allen's, with their car parked in Allen's closed garage.

He had good reason to think so. On Friday night—the night before the hearing—Goodenow learned from Brook Hart that Neil Mackay had capitulated. He and Villagomez went to the Cotting residence to share the news. It was Goodenow's understanding that a deal had been worked out for Jean Sullivan and Mackay lawyer Michael Weight to come to Majuro and straighten out this fiasco. Goodenow and Villagomez went to the Cotting residence. They knocked on the door, saw Chuck Sullivan come to the window for a brief moment and then close the curtain. There was no sign of the Cottings.

It was then that George Allen appeared. They talked to him through a crack in the door. Goodenow told him Mackay had relented and desired the return of Scotty to Alaska. The investigator then made several

23 First built during World War II, the Grumman Goose was a two-engine plane capable of landing on land or water. It was ideal for travel between the smaller Marshall Islands which had no airport or landing strip.

requests. “Basically,” Goodenow recalled, “I made it very clear to Allen that the matter had been resolved and that he was just stalling and wasting time for nothing.”

Before Goodenow left, he told Allen that he should contact him by 8:00 Saturday morning, since they were going to go into a hearing by 9:00 a.m. He also told Allen to get a hold of him so he could contact Honolulu with his response. When 8:00 o’clock came that Saturday morning, Goodenow still had no response from George Allen. In the courtroom, he had no response, and after the proceedings were through—and Goodenow was victorious—he still had no response.

George Allen remained noncommittal. He was not about to bite the hand that fed him.

27

Honolulu, Hawaii, March 14-17, 1978

A VISIBLY NERVOUS AND FATIGUED NEIL MACKAY arrived at Judge Paul Kokubun's Family Court on March 16th. He'd just spent two nights in the concrete nightmare of the Halawa Jail in Honolulu. Although he refused to talk to one reporter who asked him about Scotty's whereabouts, he was more voluble with another. Angry about news reports that he was an unfit father, drug user and alcoholic, Mackay lashed out, calling the charges "lies, complete lies." As to charges he'd used barbiturates, he said they "were a mistake" that he blamed on erroneous reports from the Veterans Administration.

What seemed to tweak him more, however, were the continuing legal battles and their attendant bickering. "Scotty has been tugged at, and tugged at, and tugged at," Mackay said. "He's been moved from place to place. I ask you, is this any way to treat a child? It's shameful."

A mirror in front of Neil Mackay's face would have been helpful at this point, but Mackay pivoted to his favorite topic. He was angry, he said, that more than $100,000 had been spent in the custody fight, money that was coming out of Scotty's inheritance. "All those lawyers want is that boy's money. They don't want Scotty, they just want his money," Mackay said. "I'm the only one who doesn't want my son's money because I don't need it."

In the courtroom, Mackay asked for bail so he could return to Alaska. Judge Kokubun refused. He was more interested in the return of Scotty from the Marshall Islands. Especially after Mackay repeatedly told the judge he "may have signed" a legal document giving Rodger Cotting full custody of Scotty.

Kokubun offered him a deal. Acknowledging Mackay's claim that he was "physically and emotionally exhausted," Kokubun offered to release him from the Halawa Jail and into a two-day commitment at the Straub Clinic and Hospital in Honolulu. The offer was conditioned on Mackay's willingness to revoke any legal authority he'd given the Cotting's "for the control, care or custody" of Scotty.

Mackay signed. His was an affidavit filled with weasel words: "I state that I unequivocally revoke, countermand, cancel and nullify any written or oral authority I may have published or distributed which may purport to authorize any other person to provide for the care, custody and control of my son, Neil P. (Scotty) Mackay."

After the hearing, Mackay was released to the Straub Clinic under guard by personnel from Hayes Guard. Personnel hired by Steven Goodenow. Two days later Mackay was released to house detention at his Ilikai condo. Judge Kokubun ordered that guards be posted there to ensure his compliance. Hayes Guard personnel were at it again, paid at Mackay's expense.

Neil Mackay wasn't going anywhere until Scotty was returned to protective custody.

The Judge hoped he'd taken care of that, too. It was he who'd ordered Jean Sullivan and Mackay representative Michael Weight to Majuro to "obtain physical custody and control of Scotty Mackay." He'd also made explicit the need for them to act with caution, "so as not to alarm, injure or create an atmosphere of fear in the mind of Scotty Mackay."

It was probably too late for that.

There were now orders issued for Scotty's return by the Alaska court, the Hawaii court, a court in the Pacific Trust Territories and in Guam. At least Mackay now admitted in Court that the last time he'd seen his son, he was staying with the Cotting family in Majuro. Rodger Cotting, contacted by phone in Kokubun's court, confirmed to the judge that Scotty was at his home. There was a technicality to Cotting's admission, though. He was at work. No direct contact was made with Scotty.

Marie Cotting wasn't much better. Brook Hart said he'd reached Marie

Cotting by phone, but whenever he asked about Scotty, "Mrs. Cotting said she couldn't hear."

It didn't much matter. In Majuro, it seemed that Scotty Mackay was almost in their grasp.

On Friday, March 17, at about 2:00 a.m., Steve Goodenow found himself at the Majuro Weather Station, his only communication link to the outside world, making a call to Hawaii. The hearing in Judge Kabua's courtroom was only a day away. What he overheard was a message from Kwajalein to the District Administrator. It was a request from the Grumman Goose aircraft to land and refuel and then take off and head back to Majuro. This was the only air transportation out of Majuro other than by scheduled airline. There was a good chance that Scotty was aboard that plane, but at the time Goodenow didn't grant it much substance.

Then the tips started to trickle in. Felix Cabrera sent one of his investigators to the Grumman Goose operations center. The maintenance man for the Goose plane told the investigator that the aircraft left to Likiep carrying a small Caucasian boy on Friday afternoon, March 17th.

District Attorney Jim Winn had also learned something of significance. He'd located the man who handled baggage and washed the Goose. As Winn put it, "he was apparently the only one who hadn't been 'bought.'" The maintenance man told Winn that he had helped a boy of Scotty's description get into the plane. No, he insisted, no one of Rodger Cotting's size and description was onboard.

Judge Kabua Kabua's courtroom, Majuro, March 18, 1978

Jim Winn called it a donnybrook. Steve Goodenow called it a farce. It was otherwise known as Judge Kabua Kabua's courtroom. In the Marshall Islands, the district court system was filled with many local judges who lacked legal training. They were, instead, powerful individuals within the community. Judge Kabua Kabua was both a chief lower court judge and one of the Marshall Islands' chiefs.

Joining Judge Kabua was the newly appointed Judge Bela Lalex, a former District Prosecutor. He was there as a distinguished guest. That should have been the first hint. Kabua Kabua was going to show the new man how things were done.

The courtroom was packed. Oscar deBrum, the District Administrator, was there. As was attorney George Allen, representing Rodger and Marie Cotting, who were not present. Tony deBrum, part of the Likiep deBrum family, and a trial assistant loyal to George Allen was present. So were Ramon Villagomez and Steve Goodenow, ostensibly representing Scotty Mackay. District Attorney Jim Winn was also in the courtroom, as was Felix Cabrera, one of his lieutenants, and four other police officers.

Because of their discussions with Judge Kabua the night before, Oscar deBrum and District Attorney Winn thought things were "wired." They were not. Judge Kabua permitted argument to go on for two hours.

Tony deBrum did most of the arguing, speaking on behalf of Marie Cotting. Tony DeBraum did not have a license to practice law but, in his capacity as a trial assistant, he could speak in front of the court, apparently representing clients. Tony was being used by George Allen to conduct the hearing.

Allen had filed his documents in Marshallese and Tony deBrum gave ninety percent of the testimony and made ninety percent of the arguments.[24] All in Marshallese. Jim Winn presumed this was done as a courtesy to the Court, because the Judge preferred to conduct matters in Marshallese. This pleased neither Winn nor Ramon Villagomez, who did not speak, much less understand, the language.

The hearing went along in what outsiders like Steve Goodenow described as an "unusual way." The matter was taped, although Goodenow wondered whether the tape recorder actually worked. The clerk gave a very limited translation of what was being said. Tony deBrum would talk for maybe three minutes, and the interpreter would provide a one-minute (or less) translation. Oscar deBrum, who also knew Marshallese, commented that not all the information was being translated.

Meanwhile they sat. More time was taken from the search for Scotty Mackay. After George Allen spoke up, in English, he and Winn got into a shouting match. Winn knew Allen's stalling tactics and demanded that the Court rule on his motion to vacate its prior orders. Finally, the judge ruled in Goodenow's favor.

24 Tony deBrum was just getting warmed up. Thirty-two years old at the time, he went on to become a Foreign Minister in the Marshalls, beloved for taking up the cause of nuclear reparations and an outspoken advocate of measures to fight climate change, which threatened low-lying islands like the Marshalls.

George Allen immediately disappeared, as did Tony deBrum.

After the Judge Kabua hearing, meanwhile, Goodenow and Villagomez questioned the pilot for the Goose, John Penny. Penny was evasive, although they did learn that the Goose had flown to the Island of Likiep. There were now three separate parties who were sure about Scotty's location. Goodenow and Villagomez tried to take it a step further, trying to find Marie and Rodger Cotting as well as Chuck Sullivan. They were nowhere to be found.

Then they got lucky. There's an old saying that success has many fathers, while failure is an orphan. This was clearly a case of many fathers.

Jim Winn claimed success. "I remembered that the Truk Islander was supposed to be in Likiep and that one of our detectives was aboard. We radioed the Truk Islander, the Detective went ashore, found Scotty and took him to the ship and on to Kwajalein the next day."

Felix Cabrera claimed success. "Having known that one of my Officers, Detective Eona Saimon, was aboard Truk Islander, a vessel assigned to the Northern Marshall Islands, myself, Steve Goodenow and Ramon proceeded [to the] communication station where I made inquiries about the present position for Truk Islander. One of the workers in communication stated the ship is in Likiep Atoll. I immediately contacted the Master of the vessel to tell him their position and instructed Detective Saimon, giving him the description of Scotty, to find him."

Steve Goodenow claimed success. "On Saturday, at about 5:00 o'clock, we decided that we would attempt to contact the Truk Islander, a tramp steamer that was operating in the area of Likiep. To our amazement, the Truk Islander was indeed at Likiep and aboard was a detective, one of Felix Cabrera's men. By radio, we requested the detective to go on to Likiep, and pick up Scotty Mackay should he be there."

Approximately thirty minutes after their first contact, the local investigators received a radio call from Officer Saimon. He had located the boy and had taken him to the tramp steamer. They were ready to depart for Ebeye. The island of Ebeye was located just off the Kwajalein Navy installation, a short taxi boat ride away.

Goodenow and Villagomez immediately made reservations to fly from Majuro to Guam, stopping at Kwajalein. Felix Cabrera telephoned the police on Kwajalein and requested their assistance in picking the boy up from Ebeye and then transporting him to the airport. Goodenow also called his friend Bob Cogswell, on the island of Ponape, asking for additional assistance.

Later that evening, at about 5:00 o'clock, Goodenow decided to call Brook Hart. It took him an hour and a half to connect. When Goodenow eventually got through, he found out that Mike Weight and Jean Sullivan had a court affidavit to take custody of Scotty. They were on their way.

28

Marshall Islands, March 19, 1978

THE FOLLOWING DAY, RAMON VILLAGOMEZ and Steve Goodenow were booked on a flight from Majuro via Air Micronesia to meet with Scotty, and his protective detail, at the Kwajalien airport. While at the Majuro airport, Goodenow spotted George Allen, seeing his wife off on an Air Naru flight bound for Naru and Ponape, two other waypoints in the vast archipelago of the Trust Territories. Allen made no mention of what lay ahead.

Jean Sullivan and Mike Weight arrived shortly thereafter from Honolulu and, at approximately 11:20 a.m., Steve Goodenow, Ramon Villagomez, Jean Sullivan, and Mike Weight boarded the outbound Air Micronesia flight, departing for Kwajalein and their pickup of Scotty Mackay. Also on that flight was Tony deBrum, Judge Kabua Kabua's functionary. deBrum told anyone who asked that he was simply travelling and perhaps going to Tokyo.

The real motive for Tony deBrum's trip was to be learned in Kwajalein.

On arrival at Kwajalein, Scotty's four-member rescue party got off the plane. Jean Sullivan thought she saw Scotty standing outside but he was actually inside, in the company of two police officers. It was at this point that Tony deBrum served Goodenow and Ramon Villagomez with High Court papers. The papers he handed over were unsigned and had not been filed with the court. In other words, deBrum's papers had no legal authority. Or so it seemed.

Realizing an attempt might nevertheless be made to stop them, Goodenow corralled Weight, Sullivan and Scotty and had them rush back toward the plane, avoiding security. Security saw them, but really couldn't do anything. All four clambered aboard.

Goodenow then got off the plane to see if anybody else might be attempting to pick up Scotty. This, of course, startled the crew. Finding no one, Goodenow attempted to reboard; Kwajalein security requested that Goodenow again check-in for the flight. At least they allowed Weight, Sullivan, Villagomez and Scotty to remain onboard without going through the formalities.

Safely back onboard the plane, Goodenow, along with Villagomez and Weight, plotted strategy as they flew toward Ponape, the next leg in their journey. In their favor were the orders from Judge Hefner's High Court, giving Goodenow custody of Scotty. They also surmised that a new series of papers would be issued when they arrived at Ponape. They just didn't know what they'd say. It was with some apprehension that they glided toward their next hop on the way home.

In Ponape, they got the surprise of their lives. Not only was Goodenow's friend Cogswell there, but Cogswell had arrived in force with the police chief from Truk and the Ponape Police Chief. The plane stopped and the boarding ramp came down, but no one was allowed off the plane. Goodenow tried to make his way to the terminal, but Cogswell intercepted him. Local judge Arvin Brown was waiting at the airport, he announced, and ordered Goodenow, as well as Scotty, off the plane. That was not all.

"If you don't get off the plane," Cogswell demanded, "I will force you off the plane. And if I have to be violent, I will be."

Friend or not, trying to make an argument with Cogswell seemed useless. He accompanied Goodenow back to where Scotty, Jean and Michael Weight were standing. Told Goodenow point blank that if he did not take Scotty and get off the plane, he would personally remove him from the aircraft. It soon became evident that the source of their troubles was George Allen. He'd called Judge Brown and asked him to sign a restraining order preventing Goodenow from taking Scotty out of the Trust Territories.

Inside the airport terminal, Brown reviewed all the papers. He was, Villagomez reported, "visibly shaking while conducting the airport hearing." After the judge read the order of Judge Hefner, deBrum showed him

Judge Kabua's Orders and said to Judge Brown, "Judge we have a later Order." At no time did Tony deBrum or anyone else say that Judge Kabua had vacated his prior Orders. Which, in fact, he had. Tony deBrum instead argued vociferously that Brown send all parties back to Majuro.

By some coincidence that was no coincidence, the Air Naru flight bearing Susan Allen, wife of George Allen, landed in Ponape shortly afterwards. Sue Allen apparently had more papers for Judge Brown to review. She joined the meeting in the Terminal building and Judge Brown quickly reached a conclusion. There should be a hearing. In Majuro, the next stop on Brown's regular calendar. The hearing would go ahead on Tuesday as scheduled. They were all to leave the plane and make their own reservations in Ponape.

In an after-report filed by Bob Cogswell, the Ponape police captain recalled a telephone conversation he had with Judge Brown later that evening. After thanking him for his assistance at the airport, Brown told Cogswell he had just spoken with Neil Mackay in Honolulu. Then Brown added, according to court documents, "The father was pleased with the turn of events in Ponape."

The Scotty Mackay rescue party, which came to call itself the Ponape 4, spent the night at the Village Hotel not knowing what would come next. The next morning Bob Cogswell showed up at their hotel. He looked to be in a state of shock. He sat down by Goodenow; looked him straight in the eye.

"Judge Brown is dead," Cogswell declared.

Goodenow and Weight sent telegrams to Honolulu and Guam. They were waiting for guidance. No word was forthcoming. During the two-and-a-half days they spent at the Village Hotel, Jean Sullivan slept with Scotty, while Mike Weight and Steve Goodenow shared a room. Through mutual agreement, they felt that since Jean had known Scotty the longest, it would be best for her to stay with Scotty but Jean was afraid. She immediately expressed her fear that someone would try to kidnap Scotty. Their fears regarding Scotty were expressed to Cogswell, who agreed to stay on top of things and keep watch. He was not alone.

Steve Goodenow also spent some evening hours on surveillance, keeping tabs on Scotty's room and checking out various hotel guests who showed interest in their situation. It was not all speculation. At one point, a radio call was overheard at the Village Hotel. The caller wanted to know if the "kidnappers" were there. Realizing that this attention was undesirable for Scotty, they tried to shield him from the general public.

To his relief, Goodenow eventually received a telegram from Associate Justice Robert A. Hefner. The High Court judge finally gave them clearance to head, with Scotty, directly to Honolulu on the next available flight. That evening, the Ponape 4 boarded an Air Micronesia flight from Ponape to Honolulu.

At about 12:30 a.m., Wednesday, the Ponape 4 arrived in Majuro. Scotty was asleep and stayed aboard the plane. Jean Sullivan and Michael Weight went into the airport. Jean was observed talking with her husband, Chuck, as well as Rodger and Maria Cotting. Ironically, Judge Hefner was aboard the plane, coming into Majuro from Saipan. The plane also carried the body of Judge Arvin Brown. It was taking him home to San Diego.

The rest of the flight was uneventful. Because they crossed the International Date Line, the Ponape 4 arrived in Honolulu at about 9:00 a.m., Tuesday, March 21, 1978. They were met by Goodenow's associates from Lawyer's Aid, Inc. and the Honolulu Police Department.

Ponape, Marianas Islands, March 21, 1978

JEAN MARIE SULLIVAN, SCOTTY MACKAY'S MATRONLY guardian, had no trouble finding time to give an impromptu interview to the *Micronesian Independent* before leaving Ponape. The newspaper headlined the article with the title, "*From Alaska to the Marianas: Poor Little Rich Boy In A Heartfelt Tragedy*." She had Scotty with her. She was unapologetic. Sullivan told the newspaper that the purpose of bringing "Scotty" to the Marshall Islands was to give the five-year old boy "piece of mind."

"This is something Scotty has not enjoyed since his mother met a violent death two years ago," she said. "The authorities are not thinking of Scotty's well-being. They are only interested in punishing his father for trying to protect him."

Sullivan told the *Independent* that the boy's mother was killed when her car exploded in an Anchorage parking lot two years previous. According to Sullivan, Scotty was named sole beneficiary to his mother's estate, worth about a million dollars, adding that the deceased wife's family was seeking custody of the boy in order to obtain the money. She went on to say that, after the death, the wife's family held the boy in Anchorage and refused to reveal his whereabouts for 30 days. Neil Mackay, she added, fled Alaska because he would "never get justice in Alaska for custody of his son."

"This whole affair has already been unfairly tried in the newspapers and on TV," Sullivan declared. "With all the sensationalism about the mother's death, the public and the courts have already made up their minds." In Honolulu, she claimed, it was even worse. The public was told that Scotty's life was in danger if he stayed with his father.

Scotty seemed to agree with Sullivan. "I want to live with my dad," he said on Ponape. "I love him very much."

This was, Sullivan said, the "crime of the century . . . The boy has been separated from his father," she proclaimed. "I know from personal experience of the loving relationship they have for each other."

Neil Mackay could not have hired a better mouthpiece.

29

Anchorage, Alaska, March 21-April 4, 1978

SCOTTY MACKAY'S PLANE FROM MAJURO ARRIVED in Honolulu at 6:45 a.m. on March 21. He had a busy day ahead of him. First, a visit to Kuakini Hospital. There, a pediatrician examined Scotty and pronounced him fit to continue his journey to Alaska. From there, it was a twelve-minute drive for a brief visit with his father, still under house arrest at the Ilikai. Steve Goodenow was there to supervise. Then he was off to the Family Court, where the adults in the room would once more make decisions for him.

The Family Court was in the *Ali'iolani Hale*, a historic structure first conceived as a Hawaiian palace. At front was a gilded sculpture of King Kamehameha, who sanctioned its construction. The first cornerstone was laid in 1872. The building had long since given up its royal heritage.

Scotty was perched on the hardwood benches outside the Family Court. He snacked on candy bars, yogurt, and Twinkies. Inside the courtroom a crowd of lawyers debated his fate. Lawyers representing his father conveyed Neil Mackay's wishes. Mackay said he would like to wait "for a day or so" to let Scotty "settle down," and then they'd return to Anchorage to resolve their legal problems. Lawyers representing Scotty, and the State of Alaska, argued otherwise.

By the end of the session, Judge Paul Kokubun decided to send Scotty on to Alaska. The five-year-old was whisked back to the Honolulu Airport and shuttled onto a Western Airlines jet bound for Anchorage. Steve

Goodenow was with him, still there to supervise. Jean Sullivan was also there, now a fixture of Scotty's entourage.

"The game is over," Brook Hart declared. "Scotty is on his way back."

Of course, the game wasn't over.

Scotty arrived in Anchorage the same day. His father, right behind him, arrived the following day. They would each go their separate ways.

Scotty, Goodenow and Sullivan were met by Bob Wagstaff's law partner, Collin Middleton. In Bob Wagstaff's temporary absence in Washington, D.C. on other matters, it was Middleton who presented the investigator with court papers handing over Scotty's custody to the Willis.'[25] Steve Goodenow quickly complied. Middleton drove them out to Eagle River for the handoff. With them was Jean Sullivan, who was to spend the night at the Willis home, bridging the gap between Scotty's disparate realities.

The Willis house was to be guarded around the clock, at Neil Mackay's expense, by Loomis Security. Carolina Willis, now more than ever, feared someone would try to kidnap the boy. She didn't rule out his father. Way out in Eagle River it took at least forty-five minutes for police to respond to an emergency call.

Back at his hotel, Steve Goodenow met Bob Pfeil for the first time. Robert Pfeil arrived in a separate car and Collin Middleton suggested the three of them go for a drink. Goodenow thought it was a good idea. At the very least it paid to be social with the boy's uncle, who'd worried about him the entire time he'd gone missing. The Pfeil family would later visit Scotty. Would find that he was "different" after returning from Majuro. More reserved. They also learned he had trouble sleeping.

Scotty's father arrived the following day, still facing contempt of court charges for removing Scotty from Alaska. Then there was the matter of the $500,000 bond Mackay was to post while he awaited his hearing. No visits with Scotty, his lawyer was told, until he posted that bond.

The trouble was, Mackay had told the Hawaii courts he was indigent. Doug Baily felt he might be concealing his assets.

Considering that, Baily moved to deny Mackay all custodial rights. The judge agreed. Judge Moody hammered home his point. Neil S. Mackay was prohibited from contacting Scotty or the Willis' unless he made an

25 This change in custody was Scotty's seventh.

application through the court. Mackay's agents were to turn over Scotty's clothing and property to his paternal aunt and uncle. The Willis' could also consult with a court-approved doctor, who'd further examine Scotty.

For his part, Mackay attorney David Talbot insisted that Neil Mackay had not violated the Court's orders. Hadn't violated the Hawaiian courts either. Mackay, he said, was a fit parent. Scotty had a Constitutional right to live with him. Talbot's arguments fell on deaf ears.

It only got worse. By the time Judge Madsen returned to the case, on March 28th, Bob Wagstaff was also back. "I don't trust Mr. Mackay," Wagstaff told the judge. "I don't trust Mr. Talbot. There's a current arrest warrant for Mr. Talbot in Hawaii for his contempt of the Hawaii court.[26] And Mr. Mackay will do anything to secure custody—legally, illegally—of Scotty. The Court has no choice but to take the strongest measures possible."

Talbot countered what the current security arrangements were sufficient and then added that the people guarding the Willis home were a danger to Scotty. "I have seen Scotty handling a Loomis Security guard's shotgun," he averred.

"Scotty was not playing with the shotgun of the Loomis guard," Wagstaff shot back. "That is an extremely misleading exaggeration to the Court."

So it went. Judge Madsen saw fit to order another drug screen for Neil Mackay, to be carried out that day. The lawyers continued to fight over the bond requirement imposed by the presiding judge. Madsen punted it back to the presiding judge who, on learning that Mackay had testified to assets of "several million dollars," ordered that Mackay post the $500,000 bond by April 3, 1978, or failing that, turn himself in to the jail at Sixth and C streets.

There were numerous orders of the court that Mackay had violated, Judge Carlson noted. "There are two ways to get him to comply. Incarceration or bond."

Talbot was in court April 3rd, asking yet another judge not to issue a bench warrant. Talbot maintained that no surety company would post a bond that large. Fine, Wagstaff countered, I will accept a real property bond. Mackay was given until 4:00 p.m. to show why the bond could not be written.

---

26 Talbot had beat a hasty retreat out of Hawaii when authorities sought to consult him as to Scotty's whereabouts.

He was a no show. Wagstaff declared that Mackay had no intention of complying. The judge ordered Neil Mackay's arrest, noting that Mackay "had the key to jail in his own hands."

Dave Talbot came back with a motion to preempt the judge, filed with the Alaska Supreme Court. The judge ignored him. Talbot's motion was not timely. Neil Mackay went to jail on the afternoon of April 4, 1978, his booking delayed only by a deposition scheduled for 2:05 p.m. in downtown Anchorage.

Neil Mackay was in the state jail annex for a week before making his $500,000 bond. Jail officials called him a "model prisoner." He slept a lot. Still unresolved was the contempt charge lodged against him—Madsen had assigned it to another judge. The unresolved custody case was also ahead of them.

The wheels were already turning. By the time Mackay got out of jail, Mackay was seriously thinking about changing his legal representation. The reality of his situation seemed to demand it.

"There are damn few attorneys in Alaska that are worth a damn," Mackay wrote to a friend in the ensuing years, "and they get fewer and fewer all the time . . . In Alaska, there is no way that any good attorney is going to go after another attorney. You can get attorneys there who will give you a big line of B.S. and take your money and with a lot of false hopes and promises, but when it actually comes time to fight the other attorneys, it will be settled behind your back . . . Sure you can find attorneys there that will want a large retainer and a lot of promises, but they simply will not do the job for you, and they will soon eat up the retainer because they have you 'stuck' and then you will receive monthly statements and the result will be the same—no action and you continue to pay."[27]

What Neil Mackay was looking for, in his own words, was a real "nutcracker." He would soon find one, a flashy divorce lawyer out of Beverly Hills by the name of Robert S. Kaufman. The man had represented Bob Dylan in a divorce action. Surely, he could faithfully represent Neil Sutherland Mackay.

So, there it was. David Talbot was no longer Neil Mackay's attorney of record. But David Talbot would get one more turn at the wheel of fortune. It would be a head-snapper.

27 That friend was an Alaska sourdough and entrepreneur named Jack Guard.

30

Honolulu, Hawaii, November 9-19, 1985

If Scotty Mackay—now calling himself Scott—had a life that seemed like a revolving wheel, that's because it was. Seven years after his dramatic return from the Marshall Islands, he was at it again. This time, his sleepover at Jim McGuire's condo ended just in time for him to witness his dad's November 9th arrest for attempted murder. Two Honolulu police detectives had shown up at 6:15 a.m., arrest warrant in hand. They'd been eyeing the condo all morning, awaiting the issuance of the Attempted Murder in the First-Degree warrant from Alaska.

Scott would slink back to McGuire's condo until Barbara Homay came to his rescue. Homay the ex-wife. Homay the "older lady," the one whom Mackay told Junior Pauole to contact for the $2,000 he needed to escape Alaska. Homay whose name was on many of Neil Mackay's corporations. Not too surprisingly, Barbara Homay had keys to the Ilikai condo. She'd stay with Scott for the duration. Scott would eventually learn she was his father's first wife, not just one of his female friends and business associates.

Scott's dad, meanwhile, was playing hardball. Although detectives said Mackay was arrested without incident, he refused to acknowledge that he was Neil S. Mackay, even as he was booked into a cellblock at Honolulu's police headquarters. He was, in a word, uncooperative. He willingly threw any obstacle he could at his pending extradition.

Anchorage District Attorney Victor Krumm flew to Hawaii on November 12, hoping to remove Mackay's roadblocks. Flying behind him via express mail was the paperwork and documentation that could positively identify the man held in Honolulu police custody. The packet contained certified copies of the arrest warrant, the state's complaint, as well as photographs and fingerprints of Neil S. Mackay.

Honolulu Deputy City Prosecutor Ed Kubo hoped the arrival of Alaska authorities would also let him introduce the taped telephone conversations between Mackay and Junior Pauole. Kubo had been unable to bring that into evidence because there were no Alaska law enforcement officials to verify the tapes' authenticity. Indeed, things picked up considerably once Alaska authorities arrived in Honolulu.

Anchorage Assistant District Attorney Eugene Murphy was there to emphasize that, among other things, Neil Mackay was a flight risk. At a November 19 hearing, Kubo was finally able to offer evidence of the phone call in which the murder of Pfeil was reported to Mackay by a man who phoned from Alaska. Kubo said Mackay told the caller, "Good," and hung up.

Mackay's defense attorney objected. "That may be a morbid and horrible thing to say, but it doesn't make him a murderer," John Edmunds told the judge. Honolulu Circuit Judge Robert Won Bae Chang said otherwise. He said the documents accused Mackay of arranging the murder. He ordered Mackay to stay behind bars pending his transfer to Alaska.

The urgency of the Hawaiian delivery was not lost on Alaskan prosecutors. Though jailed in Honolulu on an attempted first-degree murder charge, and a corresponding $10 million cash-only bail, Neil Mackay had nearly been released by that same Honolulu judge after a November 15 extradition hearing.

Judge Chang had initially ordered Mackay freed from jail because, in his view, Kubo had not shown probable cause for Mackay's arrest. In a *Honolulu Star-Bulletin* article published that same day, Kubo was said to be "shocked" by Chang's ruling and "too upset right now to be really objective" about the ruling. The difficulty, it seemed, was that Chang had little experience with extradition proceedings. According to Chang's reasoning, Mackay had lived in Hawaii since 1978 and was charged with arranging the contract killing from Honolulu. In Chang's view, therefore, Mackay had not committed a crime in one place, then escaped to another place—which was the classic description of a fugitive from justice.

Chang then ordered that Mackay be released and left the courtroom. Mackay also got up and prepared to leave, a free man for the time being. He was stopped by a burly officer from the Hawaiian sheriff's department. As he physically blocked Mackay's escape, he said, "I need a signed order from the judge before you can leave."

Mackay's attorney followed the judge into his chambers, demanding that signed order. Ed Kubo countered that he had he had just received the arrest warrant and "information" from Alaska. The evidence was on its way. Ed Kubo prevailed. Judge Chang was not inclined to release Mackay just yet. Chang instead reopened the hearing and ordered that Mackay continue to be held pending the arrival of the "governor's warrant" from Alaska.

Alaska authorities had dodged a disaster, but Chang's ruling—and the thought that Neil Mackay could have been released—brought back haunting memories of Mackay's Marshall Islands escapade. Neil Mackay was a known flight risk. They did not need a repeat performance.

31

Rochester, Minnesota, November 11, 1985;
Anchorage, Alaska, November 11-18, 1985

Robert Peter Pfeil died at 10:10 a.m. on November 11, 1985, at St. Mary's Hospital in Rochester, Minnesota. A blood clot had breached his lungs. The official cause of death was an "acute bilateral pulmonary embolism." His death was a homicide, said the death certificate, the result of "multiple gunshot wounds of hip and lower extremities."

His wife and children were not by his side.

He had last spoken to his wife, Marianne, the previous night by telephone. In that final conversation, she told him Neil Mackay had been charged with attempted murder in the shooting that felled him. "The first thing he said was, 'No kidding, no kidding,'" Mrs. Pfeil told *Anchorage Daily News* reporter Larry Campbell. "He just told me to tell the DAs to do a good job. At least he got that satisfaction.

"When I talked to Bob last night, he seemed in good spirits," she added. "He was eager to begin his therapy Monday morning. When I got up this morning, I just felt like I wanted to get on with life. I felt literally relieved, too. Like I could finally relax. We've all been a little jumpy around here. Never knowing who did it or why. Every time a car would pass the house more than once—it would bother me."

In hindsight, the Pfeil family had never been able to let their guard down. Even with an optimistic prognosis, they worried how the outdoorsman Robert Pfeil would survive life in a wheelchair. Because no matter their hopes, the doctors at the Mayo Clinic strongly suspected he was permanently paralyzed.

"That's something we had talked about, the children and me," Marianne Pfeil admitted. "He loved being out and hunting and fishing and working in the mountains. We would say sometimes that maybe it would be too hard for Daddy.

"Of course, we had always hoped, but maybe it wasn't meant to be."

Capt. Pfeil had, in fact, suffered a series of setbacks in his weeks at the Mayo Clinic. They started with severe fevers, which subsided after three days. He also suffered weakened motor function.

On October 31, 1985, he started to have a clotting emergency. A blood clot broke loose and traveled to his lungs. He lost consciousness, but doctors were able to revive him. A Greenfield filter was put in to break up the clots. After he stabilized, Pfeil chose to undergo surgery to remove the bullet in his spine. One doctor recommended it, while another advised against the operation. On November 6, the bullet was removed. It was risky, but if the bullet was not removed, he could become fully paralyzed. That was a dire outcome, compared to the less debilitating waist down paralysis he'd suffered in the immediate aftermath of the shooting.

The post-operative diagnosis was that the paralysis had not gotten better or worse.

On November 11, 1985, at 9:30 a.m., Robert Pfeil became pulseless. He lost consciousness. CPR was performed. An ultrasound was done. A blood clot was found in his heart and his lungs were filled. Doctors worked on him for forty minutes. It was fruitless.

The autopsy conducted at 1:00 p.m. that day confirmed that he would have been permanently paralyzed. It also found that the clots came from the gunshot wound in his right leg.

There was now a common thread that linked Bob's death to that of Muriel's. Like his sister, a motor vehicle was implicated. Even their father, Emil, had died in a conveyance of some kind.[28] It seemed a family curse, though it was far more than that.

Murders require a very particular kind of agency.

---

28 In Emil's case, it was a floatplane trying to take off in the fog. The pilot survived. Emil Pfeil was killed instantly.

While at Mayo, Bob came under the care of a West Point classmate, Dr. Thoralf Sundt, one of the top neurosurgeons in the world. In remembering that time, Sundt recalled that, "We spoke about our days at West Point, how much the institution meant to both of us, and how fortunate we had been to have the careers we had enjoyed—largely attributable in both of our minds to the training we received at West Point. I remember holding his hand and talking to him about his life before the injury."

Sundt went on to say, "His death struck me like the loss of no other patient I can recall. For the only time in my professional career, I completely lost my composure and literally sobbed by his bedside." Later, Sundt told the family, "Bob faced death like a true West Pointer. He remained dignified and composed throughout his entire hospitalization. I was so very proud of him."

Memorial services for Robert P. Pfeil were held at Central Lutheran Church in Anchorage on November 15th. Robert P. Pfeil was home.

Born May 16, 1930, in Anchorage, he was to be honored as a life-long Alaska resident and a senior pilot for Alaska Airlines. Aged 55 at his death, he'd learned to fly at age 16, and had a twenty-nine-year career as a professional pilot. He was survived, his obituary noted, by his wife, two daughters, his mother, a sister and "a nephew" who, unlike the other relatives mentioned, went unnamed. It was a small sign of the dark cloud of bitterness that still reigned over Bob Pfeil's death.

He was not a pauper. His net worth was $2.5 million at the time of his death but that's not for what he would be remembered .

No one could forget the time Bob rescued a 10-year-old boy from the freezing waters of Campbell Lake after he and a friend had fallen through the ice. His wife Marianne remembered him for his love of opera, adding, "he couldn't sing, but he could whistle." Childhood friends remembered a young man who spent many hours ice skating at a nearby park. And the 6-foot-4 All-Star center for his high school basketball team. His army buddies remembered how, back in Alaska, he rose to become aide-de-camp to Maj. Gen. James F Collins at Fort Richardson, lauded for his extensive knowledge of Alaska, a knowledge honed through many hunting and fishing excursions with his father on trips back home.

His mother, meanwhile, recalled how Bob stepped up and took over as the man in the family after his father's untimely death. That meant giving up his aspirations for medical school, even though he'd already been accepted at the University of Washington Medical School. That meant taking over his family's extensive real estate interests. In 1958, they sold a two-block parcel to the Anchorage School District, so they could build a new school. In 1959, he ran for the Anchorage City Council and lost.

"What can I say?" Marianne Pfeil told *Anchorage Daily Times* reporter Paul Fannig. "Bob was a good family man, a good husband and father who came home every night. He had a normal, happy, low-profile life. We had 21 good years of happy life, a good marriage. We were a happy family."

If there was one thing that said the most about Robert Pfeil, however, it was an exchange he had with a friend in the years after Muriel's murder, a murder that Pfeil pursued with unmatched vigor. The conversation, quoted in court documents, was at once a recognition of the danger inherent in his quest to find her killer—and the selflessness of that endeavor.

"Bob," the friend wondered, "aren't you ever going to give up seeing if Mackay killed your sister. You have—aren't you afraid for your own life?"

"Oh, I know that," Bob Pfeil replied.

"Well, you have also your wife and children to think about," his friend persisted.

"Oh, I have," Bob Pfeil replied. "But don't I have an obligation to my sister?"

IMMEDIATELY ON LEARNING OF ROBERT PFEIL'S DEATH, Steven Branchflower revised the charges he'd filed against the men who'd allegedly conspired to shoot him. On November 11, 1985, he filed an "Amended Information." Two days later, he announced that he would convene a grand jury to consider murder indictments against at least four of the men they'd identified in the Pfeil shooting. The grand jury would meet November 18th to consider evidence gathered in their month-long investigation.

Parallel to that move, a state District Court judge declined to lower bail of two of the five defendants in the now quickly moving case. Judge Michael White refused to reduce the $5 million cash-only bail of Larry R. Gentry, 33, and Robert A. Betts, 19, who were led into court with a handcuffed prisoner between them. They weren't going anywhere.

Betts, his right arm encased in a cast across which the words, "By The Power of God" had been written, said under oath that he had worked at a downtown gas station for the last three months and lacked money to hire a lawyer.

"How much money did you earn last year?" Judge White asked.

"I have no idea," Betts answered.

"Sir, give me some fairly close estimates so I can determine if the public should pay for your lawyer," the judge demanded.

"A thousand dollars," Betts replied. That was the same $1,000 that Betts was paid as the driver of the shooter's getaway car. The vehicle from which Robert Pfeil was shot.

The grand jury returned indictments just before 10:00 p.m. on November 18th. Branchflower described it as a marathon 12-hour session with "minimal breaks." Testifying were Sgt. Mike Grimes of the Anchorage Police Department; Gilbert Pauole, whose charges remained at attempted first-degree murder in a plea-bargain exchange for his first-person testimony; Dr. Paul Belau, the Mayo Clinic coroner who conducted Robert Pfeil's autopsy; Theresa "Sassy" Marshall, who spoke to John Bright's state of mind while he was on the run; and Russellyn Carruth, the estate attorney who recounted the abiding animosity between Neil Mackay and the Pfeil family.

Charged with first-degree murder were John Bright, Larry Gentry, and Robert Betts. Tyoga Closson was indicted on a charge of theft. A copy of the indictment was also delivered to a Western Airlines flight bound for Honolulu, where the charges pending against Neil Mackay would be increased to that of first-degree murder, his cash-only bail raised to $25 million.

32

Anchorage, Alaska, November 17, 1985

JUNIOR PAUOLE MADE A FULL CONFESSION nearly a week after his arrest. He spilled his truth over a five-hour interview with APD investigators and assistant D.A. Steve Branchflower. The topline revelation was simple. Neil Mackay had come to him with a proposition. "I had a problem with my wife," Pauole said, quoting Neil Mackay. "I took care of that. Now I'm having a problem with my brother-in-law. Can you help me with that?"

This was, if true, a calculated indirection on Mackay's part. It was a way of suggesting rather than requesting. Indirection is how Mafia dons prompt their subordinates without dirtying their hands. It's an acknowledged language that both parties understand. There's a reason for this nod, nod, wink, wink. It makes potential criminal conspiracy cases tauntingly difficult to prove.

It is worth pointing out, too, that it didn't take five hours to get those nineteen words out of Junior Pauole. Branchflower and the cops kept asking questions. They needed to build a case against Neil Mackay. They needed to cover every contingency. They needed to push Junior for details. Sometimes it seems, in retrospect, that he was too cooperative. Too willing to fill in the details. The trial judge would accuse him of embellishing. Especially when he implied that he'd directly asked Neil Mackay to divulge his exact intentions.[29]

---

29 One stark example came when Pauole was asked how he knew Mackay was asking for murder. "I just ask him: well, you know, will you be more precise, or will you tell

That said, what Junior Pauole admitted over those hours helped reveal the path that led to the allegations that Robert Pfeil was the victim of a contract killing. Neil Mackay didn't suddenly blurt out, 'I want you to kill this guy." Junior Pauole didn't immediately say, "I'll do it." There were stages. A seduction that looked like a seduction only after the fact.

First there was the introduction.

Junior first met Neil Mackay in about 1980, just after he arrived in Anchorage to manage Frank Colacurcio's strip clubs. The Wild Cherry, where Junior plopped himself, was in a Mackay-owned building. Neil Mackay showed up and wanted to know why the club was behind in its rent. Junior took care of the rent, but also talked to Frank Colacurcio about the man.

According to Junior, Frank told him, "It was important for me to get close to Neil Mackay." In that spirit, Junior agreed to pay a rent increase. He also asked his business associates at the Wild Cherry for more background on the man. "Norm Adams and Stanford Poll, who was in Alaska a long time, knew Mr. Mackay and [after] a conversation with them, I knew that Mr. Mackay had—had his wife killed or blown up."

There was also something else at play. As one Colacurcio associate pointed out, "Pauole kept his eye out for people who could advance him."

Junior immediately placed Neil Mackay in that category. "I knew him to be wealthy person," Junior admitted. "I don't know if he was a millionaire, but he was well to do. As time went on, I tried and became a good friend of his. I would ask him for legal advice."

There were other points of contact, which propelled them toward a position of trust. When he was in town, Neil Mackay got his hair cut across the street from the club and would drop in to talk—"usually social, nothing important," according to Pauole.

After a while, the casual conversations grew more personal. "I told him some things about the Colacurcio organization and how I felt about it and we got to know and trust one another pretty good."

Trusted one another enough for Mackay to ask for, and Junior to supply him with, some of the Wild Cherry dancers. "He told me he wanted somebody clean, somebody that's not gonna talk and that he would, he

---

me exactly what do you mean, or exactly what's on your mind?" That explicit back and forth violates the essential principles of indirection.

would pay for it and stuff. And I told him that I would find him some and I did. A number of times I got him girls."

Then came the subtle seduction.

Junior's willingness to open up about his underworld connections unlocked new layers in their relationship. Indeed, Mackay wrote letters to one of his friends—found in a search of the man's house[30]—revealing that he was already aware of the organized crime connection to the Wild Cherry. New levels of trust started to unwind. One involved the renter of a steakhouse known as the Porterhouse, on the ground floor of the Mackay Building. "Mackay wanted me to remove everything from the Porterhouse Restaurant—to hide it. He had problems with the person leasing it. I cleaned it out. I made $11,000.00 on it. Mackay didn't ask me for the money. It was mine."[31]

Equally revealing was where their conversations started to take place. "I spoke to Mackay at his condo in Anchorage," Junior revealed. "His apartment was real classy. Like what you'd see in a soap opera."

Neil Mackay, in Junior's telling, was starting to tell him about his obsessions. "Well, after a long time went by, we got to know one another pretty good," Junior told the cops. "And as time went on, he told me about his son, Scotty, and things that happened to him with Scotty and that he was having legal problems with Scotty's family. And he told me that his brother-in-law was—was suing him and was trying to get Scotty's estate."

"Neil told me that Robert Pfeil was not a nice guy," Junior added. "He felt it was wrong for Robert Pfeil to rape the estate of Scotty . . . He said he had to do something about it."

The time was ripe for a proposition.

At one point, in Pauole's telling, Neil Mackay finally felt confident enough in Junior to "open his kimono." Certainly, Mackay's relationship with Robert Pfeil was not improving. If anything, it was getting worse. It was then that the topline revelation burst out into the open.

"And after a long while and conversation went on like that for a long time," Junior confessed that, "right before—meaning months before he sold the Mackay building, he said that he was having a—he had a problem

30 Jack Guard again.

31 The money was from sales of restaurant furnishings.

with his wife, and he took care of it and that he's having a problem that—with his brother-in-law if I could help him take care of it."

Steve Branchflower and the cops were all over that one. "When he said that to you," Sgt. Grimes asked, "what did you think he meant when he said: 'I had problems with my wife, I took care of that'? Did that mean something to you?"

"Yes, I kind of knew what he was talking about because when I first met Mr. Mackay, I went and talked to some of the people that knew Mr. Mackay before l got there."

Junior already knew about Muriel Pfeil and the bombing. He had other thoughts. "Because I don't know if he was just being a mad old man, or he was just talking. You know, people that talked to me about him before says, you know, that—you know, he might be a little crazy or something, or he might—he—he used to drink a lot."

"I wasn't sure if I was going to help him and I wasn't sure exactly what I wanted to do, yet."

The uncertainty seemed to weigh on Junior. He even considered taking his dilemma to someone who'd surely know what to do, Frank Colacurcio. The man who'd more recently warned him he was getting too close to Neil Mackay.

"In my mind, I was trying to think. Should I bring it up to Frank? Should I ask Frank, or should I try to handle it myself or—and that's what I was thinking for a while."

If Junior Pauole tended to ramble, his confession tumbling out of his mouth in near stream-of-consciousness, investigators were at the ready to direct him back to the beginning. Every good story needs a precipitating incident, a time, and a place. A when and a where.

"It was at the end of 1984 when Mackay first asked me to help him," Junior told them. "He was getting ready to sell the Mackay building and this was the last—one of the few last times that I saw him up in the Mackay Building. And he told me that the problem with his brother-in-law was getting serious and that if I could help him out with the problem."

"How did you react to that?" they asked.

"I knew that he was serious. I could see that he was serious. But I wasn't sure that if I could—I wasn't sure if I could find somebody. But I told him that I would try. But I knew that he—but I knew what he wanted was serious."

"Where was Mackay living at the time?" they asked.

"Well, he was living in Hawaii, and he had a penthouse at the Mackay Building on Fourth Avenue. So, his time was kind of divided. But when he was in Anchorage, he lived in this penthouse in the Mackay Building."

With the approximate timeline now coursing in their minds, the investigators asked the logical follow up. A court case needs structure. Needs a chronology. Directing Pauole was like herding cats.

"Just approximately how long before Robert Pfeil was actually killed was this initial conversation where Mackay asked you to help out," one of them asked. "To have his brother-in-law killed?"

"I'm not sure but it was quite a while," Pauole answered. "A long while. Maybe a year. Maybe—I'm not sure."

The starkness of Mackay's request, seemingly out of the blue, was particularly striking to the investigators. Where, they asked themselves, was the context? They wondered aloud whether there had been other times, other conversations, leading up to the point. Had he mentioned the problem on other occasions before that, the problem that he was having with his brother-in-law and the monies in his son's estate?

"Yes," Junior answered.

"On how many occasions had he just brought it up when he told you about it," they asked. "Not an exact number; but one occasion, a lot of times, what?"

"More than I can count. That's a lot of occasions. It wasn't—we had a lot of conversations about it. Even to the point where he took me and showed me where he owned, and his ex-wife owned, some of the buildings and property around Anchorage and he had said to me, in the conversation as we was riding around, that his brother-in-law had won the buildings, or won the decision or the court had awarded him the building on the corner and that he didn't feel that he should have that—that it belongs to Scotty, which is his son."

Pauole had specific examples.

One night, Pauole said, Mackay was in Anchorage on a visit, perhaps as long ago as 1983. The two men went for a ride. Following Mackay's directions, Pauole drove along Gambell Street near 15th Avenue, then to the Park Strip and down by Bootlegger Cove. He said Mackay told him, "You know, I used to own this over here and I used to own that over here, and my brother-in-law got all of this. He stole it from Scotty."

Beginning in 1984, meanwhile, Pauole's own situation at the strip club started to change. "I started to have problems with the Wild Cherry from the ABC Board. We would average two—three thousand a day, five or six thousand dollars a day on weekends. Neil told me I should just get away from Colacurcio. He said Frank was just using me. Neil leased the building to me, not to Frank. Between me and Lake Bluff, Inc. Mackay used that to hide his assets from his brother-in-law."

Soon, Neil Mackay was acting as Junior's unofficial attorney. When Pauole wanted to change his contract with the dancers in 1985, he went to Mackay. "I showed it to Neil, gave him a copy to go over, check it out for me.

The two were close enough that police found a copy of Scotty's report card in Pauole's strip club office, with a handwritten note about the boy's good grades. The paper, still attached to Pauole's empty office wall, included the typed message: "A proud Dad!"

The one thing that Pauole stressed in his confession was that no matter what else happened, Neil Mackay couldn't seem to put the Robert Pfeil matter out of mind. "He said he had to do something about it," Pauole said.

"In March 1985," Pauole told the investigators, "I had found someone to do the job for me. That was Larry Gentry. He used to work for me. He was friends with John Bright. They were real good friends.

"I had plans to go to Hawaii to see Neil and for a family reunion," Junior continued. Pauole remembered it as July of 1985. "I told Larry. He knew who Mackay was. We had lost the license to the Booby Trap. I opened up the Good Times Lounge. I closed the bar just before I went to Hawaii. I took $100,000.00 that belonged to Colacurcio, for the 17 ½ percent that he never paid me. I started wearing a bulletproof vest, had someone with me who carried a gun. I planned on opening a bar in Hawaii. I had some phone calls threatening me.

"I told Mackay I found the guys who would do the job for him. He questioned me about them. He said he didn't want the guy to come back. I understood that Mackay wanted his brother-in-law dead. [That] statement was made several times. I had him believe that the guys were from Hawaii. He told me all about his brother-in-law, his daily schedule.

"I told Mackay it would be $10,000.00. He asked if I needed more. I said no. I said I would use my own money until the job was done. I only wanted to do the favor for Mackay and not be involved in anything else. I thought that's the way it would be. I ran into a friend, Sam Keliinoi, while we were out. I introduced Sam to Neil. I called Larry from Hawaii; told him everything was approved. I understood that John Bright would do the actual shooting. Gentry was my buffer in the whole thing."

Pauole said he made a second trip to Hawaii in August and got the $10,000 from Mackay. It was in a white envelope, he said. During this visit, according to Pauole, Mackay talked about Pfeil "raping his estate" and said he wanted Pauole to make sure Pfeil "doesn't come back."

Junior insisted that he again led Mackay to believe the hit man he hired was from Hawaii. "He hinted around that he didn't want anybody from Alaska."

When Pauole returned from his second Hawaii trip, he called Gentry and Bright and asked them to come down to his place. When they arrived, Pauole told investigators that he pulled out the envelope and showed it to Bright, asking him "Does this look like $10,000?" Pauole then had Bright feel the envelope to verify its contents.

By September, Pauole was getting impatient. He told police he began to think Bright was bent on taking his money with no intention of delivering. He called Bright. "I told him, 'Well, the homework is done,' you know and all this. At that point all I was doing after that was waiting. OK, then I got scared . . . and I told him that if it's not gonna be done, forget it . . . and I also told Larry Gentry that, forget it. Don't do it because it was taking too long, and I felt that John Bright was having mixed feelings about doing it.

"I was starting to feel pressured by Mackay," Pauole added, "in his subtle way that he does to put pressure on you, you know."

Things dragged on, according to Pauole. Then, one day in early October, Bright "sprung" a driver on him. "He says, 'Oh, by the way, I had to hire a driver. I need $1,000.'"

"I gave him the $1,000 . . . and I questioned him about the driver and at that point I knew I made a mistake . . . I just knew it inside me . . . because there was another person involved that I didn't know."

THERE WAS MUCH TO UNPACK ABOUT JUNIOR'S CONFESSION. As time went on, some of the details got a little hazy. The dates and times, the details. Especially the details about the money transfer. It was hand carried, he said at one point. No, it was mailed, he said at another. These were the kinds of inconsistencies that could come back at him. Maybe—just maybe—they were intentional. He'd protected Frank Colacurcio in the past. He knew how these things worked.

There *was* a letter confirming Junior's interest in opening that bar in Hawaii. He wasn't all bullshit. It was a reference letter with a date, no less. The name of the bar was the Rodeo Room in Waikiki. The letter writer was Virginia Zawacki. Yes, that Virginia.

33

Anchorage, Alaska, April 4, 1978;
Fairbanks, Alaska, Summer, 1957; Summer, 1976

If there was ever a clear inkling that Neil Mackay was involved in Muriel's murder, other than the firm convictions of the Anchorage police, it first came to light on April 4, 1978. Neil Mackay was giving a deposition in a bland conference room, only blocks from Anchorage's industrial core. He hadn't seen his kid since Honolulu. To see him again, he'd have to pony up a half-million-dollar bond. He'd do anything to see Scotty. Even if it meant talking to people he'd otherwise not deign to acknowledge.

It was nobody's idea of fun.

There were four lawyers in the room, two of them representing Neil Mackay. It was Dave Talbot's last hurrah as Neil Mackay's counselor—and Bob Wagstaff who led the questioning. Since Wagstaff had hired Steve Goodenow, he was the one who knew what questions to ask. He inquired about whom Mackay had met when he plotted Scotty's abduction. Asked about his drug use. Asked about the alias he used to travel to Majuro.

"Who is Val Galeron," Wagstaff asked early on.

"Fifth Amendment," Dave Talbot snapped. "Mr. Mackay respectfully declines to answer that on the grounds that his answer might incriminate him. Just for the record, I don't want to involve Mr. Mackay in any beef with immigration or something like that."

"Why were you using his name?" Wagstaff persisted.

More objections. Finally, Dave Talbot had to stipulate. "Well, I heard a rumor, Mr. Wagstaff, that Mr. Mackay, uh, somebody laid this on me, that

Mr. Mackay had flown into Honolulu under an assumed name, and this might get him in some trouble with immigration. I don't believe there's any claim that Scotty was with him, so I'd rather not go into that."

Then came the heartbeat question from Wagstaff. Actually, there were two. Two heartbeat questions. The first involved Rodger Cotting, the man implicated in helping transport Scotty to Majuro and then keeping him one step ahead of the authorities.

"What was the purpose of his taking Scotty to Micronesia?" Wagstaff asked.

"I told him I had some problems," Mackay answered, blandly.

"Did you tell him what the problems were?" Wagstaff wondered.

"I told him I had some problems," Mackay replied, noncommittally. "I don't remember what specifics I went into, but I told him I did want to come over and that he agreed to take Scotty."

Then came the next heartbeat. The one that Wagstaff had been saving. He was patient. Saved it until the deposition was nearly at an end. Strung it on to a series of questions about people and associations Mackay had in Hawaii.

"What kind of people does Jean Sullivan associate with," he finally asked. There was no lead up. No preface. It was meant to catch Mackay off guard.

"Well, it's pretty hard to describe how other people associate themselves with other people," Mackay replied, eliding the deeper meaning of the question. Wagstaff wasn't letting him wriggle off the hook.

"Well, I, I appreciate that Mr. Mackay," Wagstaff continued. "Let me ask the question a little bit more specifically, this, has Jean Sullivan, to your knowledge ever associated with persons who have been convicted of crimes?"

"I can't . . . she, she operated a hotel there in Fairbanks for many years. Association with everybody, from every walk of life, I'm sure."

There was chatter and cross chatter, but Bob Wagstaff kept digging.

"To your knowledge has she ever associated with or been associated with a person who's been convicted of a crime?"

"I have no specific knowledge, but I venture to say that she has from operating a hotel, being, living in Fairbanks and Alaska as long as she did," Mackay answered, staying generic. "I know nothing about her personal friends. She and I are friends, I have friends, she has friends. Her, her particular taste for what she might consider a friend, wouldn't necessarily meet my taste. But I wouldn't criticize her friends and I'm sure she wouldn't criticize mine."

Jean Marie Sullivan had, in fact, associated with someone convicted of a crime. It seemed like ancient history to some, but in 1957, Jean Sullivan befriended a man named Bernard G. "Johnny" House. Johnny House was a murderer. A convicted murderer. A convicted murderer who'd served time at Alcatraz.

Robert Wagstaff had long been searching for the man who'd assassinated Muriel Pfeil. All this time, he'd needed a connection between Neil S. Mackay and a hired killer. All guesses now seemed to lead him to Jean Marie Sullivan.

ON MAY 21, 1957, BERNARD G. "JOHNNY" HOUSE shot down Jack Perry, a 32-year-old bartender at the Esquire Club on the Richardson highway near Fairbanks. House was arraigned on a charge of assault with a deadly weapon and freed on a $3,000 bond.[32] When Perry died five days later, murder charges were filed. On June 7, 1958, House was sentenced to life imprisonment for first degree murder. An appeal bond was approved, however, and House was released on $25,000 bond.

A motion to allow House to go to the Lower 48 while he appealed his first-degree murder conviction was granted by Judge Vernon D. Forbes on June 20, 1958. House's attorney, Robert A. Parrish, said he would submit a written order for the judge's signature. It included permission to drive through Canada. House was freed.

His $25,000 bond was posted by Mrs. Jean M. Sullivan and Jack Fricke, who both approved House's move to the Lower 48.

In House's written motion, the attorney prosecuting his appeal was listed as Edward Boyko of San Francisco. Boyko would later move to Alaska, take an appointment as State Attorney General and then, as an attorney in private practice, represent Neil S. Mackay.[33]

---

32 It is worth noting that Alaska was a Territory and not yet a State. As such, crimes such as murder were appealed through federal authorities: Alaska did not then have an appellate court system.

33 Boyko believed that a trial should be a performance. He wore a pinstripe suit, a

Johnny House moved out of Alaska and set up his new home near Tacoma, Washington, as he awaited his appeal. The AP reported on December 29, 1959, that House was ordered held in the State of Washington for grand jury action on a charge of transporting a woman across a state line for purposes of prostitution. That case dated from May 1956. At the time of the order, according to the FBI, House was living in Vail, Washington, under the name of John Hampton.

Upon learning this, Alaska Judge Forbes ordered bondsmen to produce Bernard G. (Johnny) House within 10 days. Unless House was produced by Feb. 1, 1960, Jean M. Sullivan and Jack Fricke would forfeit the $25,000 they put up when House appealed his first-degree murder conviction.

On his return to Fairbanks, House was involved in a brawl at the Gold Rush Saloon. He was charged with three counts of disorderly conduct under state law, and later with two more disorderly conduct, and four assault and battery charges by the city. His bond totaled $2,900 and was posted by Jean Sullivan and Savannah Brown. The two women were now holding the $25,000 bond for House's murder appeal.

Johnny House's appeal on the murder charge failed. He was initially sent to the U.S. Penitentiary in Marion, Illinois, a medium security federal prison. In 1960, he was transferred to Alcatraz, where he spent two and a half years. Alcatraz was not a medium security prison. Neither was Hazelton, a high security prison in West Virginia, where House was transferred in 1963.

On May 9, 1968, Bernard G. "Johnny" House finally caught a break. He was pardoned by Alaska Governor Walter J. Hickel. Hickel was only months away from reluctantly resigning the governorship to become President Richard M. Nixon's Interior Secretary.

Johnny House returned to Alaska and seemed to lead a quiet life. There was one report in 1973. A news article in the *Fairbanks Daily News-Miner* that Bernard House, age 61, had sustained minor injuries to his leg and arm in an accident on Geraghty Avenue, across from a *Mark & Save* grocery store. The account had him living at the Sullivan Hotel. The same Sullivan Hotel that was owned by Jean and Charles Sullivan.

---

vest and gold jewelry, and in later years added a cane during jury trials. He was also known to use astrology during jury selection.

The big story about Bernard "Johnny" House, however, broke in December of 1975, in an investigative series by the *Anchorage Daily News* about criminal elements infiltrating a major Trans-Alaska pipeline supply warehouse in Fairbanks.

"Surrounded by a chain-link fence and a cloud of mystery, the central pipeline supply warehouse at North Star Terminals in Fairbanks provides an illustrative—if murky—view of the Alaska Teamster empire in operation," the December 18, 1975, story started.

"Organized and run as a tight-fisted Teamster fiefdom, the operation involves a collection of convicted criminals—including the union's top man on the job—and has raised serious questions in the minds of Fairbanks, state and federal law enforcement authorities familiar with the facility."

The Fairbanks warehouse was a major distribution and staging center for Alaska's Trans-Alaska pipeline. It held everything from paper clips to bulldozers to explosives.[34] Among its leadership were a rogue's gallery of criminals.

Fred Dominic Figone, known to underworld associates as "Freddy the Fix," was convicted and sentenced to a year on probation by California authorities in the early 1950s. He was also arrested in Alaska in 1966 on charges of being an accessory after the fact to a felony. Bernard "Johnny" House, the No. 3 man on the roster, was sentenced to life in prison in 1957 on conviction for first-degree murder. Insiders at North Star Terminals said House operated as Figone's right-hand man in administering the facility.

Jack "Red" Martin, the No. 4 man on the roster, also had felony convictions. His record revealed a 1962 federal conviction in Seattle for violation of the Mann Act, regarding his involvement in interstate prostitution, and numerous lesser charges as recent as the 1970s.

There were others at the Teamster-controlled warehouse that sported criminal convictions. Peter Rosario Buonamassa, listed on the roster as the No. 1 yard crew employee at North Star, was convicted of murder in 1957. He'd received a governor's pardon from former Alaska Gov. William A. Egan.

---

34 C4, the plastic explosive associated with Muriel Pfeil's murder, is often used for oil and gas exploration, although dynamite is more common because it is cheaper. With Ft. Richardson nearby, C4 would not have been difficult for the North Star crew to obtain in any case. And ten years later, John Bright could get C4 with apparent ease.

There was also Cliff "The Galloper" Judd, who had served time on narcotics convictions and had been arrested for gambling, intimidating a government witness and tax violations. Then there was the yard crewman named Jack Jeffery McCracken. He was convicted on a 1969 intent to kill shooting involving an Anchorage bartender and a waitress.

The Fairbanks warehouse was, in short, a rogue's gallery of former convicts. By 1976, they provided unequivocal proof of their propensities.

THE SUMMER OF 1976 FOUND THE NORTH STAR TEAMSTER'S crew entwined with a series of murders and suspicious disappearances. That was the same year Muriel Pfeil's orange Volvo station wagon was blown up. The killings overlapped in uncanny ways.

Teamster job steward Jack "Red" Martin, the Teamster job steward at the warehouse, was the first one to get hit. He disappeared mysteriously from his Fairbanks home on July 18. His body was found a week later with two bullet wounds in the head. Harry Pettus, a foreman and listed as No. 2 Teamster in command, was last seen at his Fairbanks home on July 26. His apartment door was open, and he left behind personal effects, according to police investigators.

Then there was Jack Jeffry McCracken, a Teamster pipeline warehouseman who made the news in September of 1976. McCracken, who'd been previously convicted of multiple felonies—including assault with intent to kill—was arrested on a felony firearm charge. Top Teamster warehouseman Bernard "Johnny" House was among the courtroom spectators at his bail hearing. House was seen patting McCracken's shoulder and overheard saying, "Keep your spirits up."

McCracken's arrest came when he got caught up in the ongoing homicide investigation of Jack Martin and Harry Pettus. He, along with many others at the warehouse, was questioned in connection with the homicide. All denied involvement.

It was a year before Harry Pettus' body was found. The corpse was so badly decomposed that authorities had to use X-rays, taken in Seattle during Pettus' medical treatment two years previous, to compare with those taken at his autopsy.

Investigators consistently told news sources that they were making "good progress" in the Martin-Pettus murder cases. Neither murder was ever solved. Not in 1976, not ever. Muriel Pfeil was not the only person in Alaska killed in 1976 under mysterious circumstances. She was merely one in a series.

Still, the question remained: were these murders related or mere coincidence? Hard to say. If one needed someone to kill his wife, the Fairbanks crew was there to serve. If someone needed an introduction to these folks, Jean Marie Sullivan was just the person. She didn't even have to be an active participant.

Bernard "Johnny" House lived at her hotel. She knew him. Sometimes all it takes is proximity. These things can be arranged.

That was not enough, of course, to convict Neil Mackay of Muriel's murder. Or Bernard House, for that matter. These were just allegations. The Teamsters were notoriously tight-lipped. The cops couldn't even solve the known Fairbanks murders that lingered in their backyard.

34

Anchorage, Alaska, April – May, 1977; Honolulu, Hawaii, May 3, 1978

Given Neil Mackay's history, it was a wonder he ever got custody of his son. The Micronesia abduction was reason enough to look askance at his demands. Not just because he disregarded the provisions and rulings of the Alaska court—reason enough to disqualify him—but for his parallel disregard of Scotty's safety.

It may have helped that Neil Mackay apologized to the court for his Pacific escapade. In a March 27 letter to Judge Madsen, he made an admission. "I realize that my actions from December 15, 1977, to March 22, 1978, have created an atmosphere of apprehension and concern with this court that will be difficult to dispel."

That's about as far as he got. The bulk of his apologia was a justification, a rationalization, a *mea culpa* without the *culpa*.

"I have behaved toward my son in such a way as to reflect my love and concern for my boy . . . I love my son and believe I am a good parent . . . My motives were those of a father whose love for his son overcame other considerations for a time."

He did pledge to cooperate with the court, which was the very least he could do. Even that was hedged. Mackay said that he would "accept any reasonable demands requested by the court to convince it of my sincerity." The emphasis was on "reasonable."

No matter, he was still under the gun of the various fitness tests imposed by Judge Madsen. No drugs, show parenting skills, have a governess for

Scotty. If he could check them off, he had a chance, despite his egregious transgressions.

The governess checkpoint had turned into an unmitigated disaster. First off, the governess *du jour*, Margaret Venable, went off to see her mother in Kansas instead of following Mackay to Hawaii. The story only got worse. In anticipation of moving to Hawaii, Venable dropped her son at her ex-husband's house for "the weekend." Then didn't bother to pick him up.

John Venable tracked her to Kansas, but she refused to talk to him. Called into court to testify, the U.S. Air Force veteran had much to say about his ex-wife. "When I met her, she had her own massage parlor in Topeka," John Venable testified. "She carried on business in our house. I would hear things like, 'No, I am expecting my husband home.' I saw her zip up her smock. She wore nothing underneath. I then made her quit entirely."

"I believe it was Marge's massage parlor," Venable continued. "Her primary trade was truck drivers." Then an admission: "I knew about it before I married it."

Neil Mackay already had a string of bad governess decisions. There was Barbara Kimpton, the fifty-two-year-old nursing administrator. Neil Mackay liked her because she paid her rent on time. They spoke for a half-hour about the job. They didn't discuss her salary. Kimpton admitted she hadn't cooked in a long time. She was 52 years old. She seemed perfect. Until she abruptly left town.

Her predecessors were worse. One of them, Lillian White, had dated a man involved in at least two Anchorage burglaries. Lillian White lasted less than a month. She was followed in short order by Monique Dutarte, of whom Mackay would later say, "A French girl, I don't remember her last name." He hired her as a housekeeper, in desperation, through a mutual friend. Monique lived in his apartment for a week and a half. Then she got an urgent phone call from her parents in France. She had to leave.

Margaret Venable had seemed to be the proper fit, age 39 not 52—and not "a French girl." She had been evaluated by the Department of Health and Social Services in July 1977. They found her perfectly acceptable. That bit about Marge's Massage was a little much. Courthouse wags wondered what Neil Mackay really knew about Margaret Venable.

Still, things seemed to be going better on other fronts. Neil and Scotty were now certified enrollees in the Alaska Treatment Center's Parent

Effectiveness Training Program. Everything was coming up roses. They ultimately lauded Neil Mackay's emerging parenting skills. They wrote:

"Although Mr. Mackay has little background experience working with children, he has made a tremendous effort to learn various methods and techniques of child-rearing . . . Mr. Mackay has progressed from the anxious, spoiling father, afraid of being rejected by his son, to a confident, rather skilled father able to discipline by non-physical means."

Of course, all that meant nothing if Scotty was still a flying mess of neuroses, night terrors and uncertainty. In the way of all miracle cures, he was showing tremendous progress. This was, they inferred, no longer the child over which Carolina Willis had presided.

"I found Scotty to be an extremely happy, well nurtured child both physically and emotionally," wrote David Dunay, his casework supervisor. "He enjoys being with his father and actively seeks his attention and approval. There is close physical contact where Scotty will sit close to his father or on his lap. The relationship between this father and his son appears to be genuinely strong and mutually supportive in terms of cooperation and affection. Some examples of his work indicate Scotty to be intellectually equal to or ahead of other youngsters his age."

If there was some snark in their report, it came indirectly, through their description of Scotty's home environment. This was not Alfred and Carolina Wills' low-rent apartment complex scattered along the gravel roads of Eagle River. This was money talking.

"The Mackay residence is an upper income penthouse-type apartment. It's well furnished, seven rooms include 4 bedrooms, living room, kitchen, and playroom. In addition, there is a large, heated garage and another storage/playroom in the basement. It adjoins Mr. Mackay's Law Offices on the same floor. This gives Scotty ready access to his father almost anytime throughout the day."

In summarizing the situation for the court, David Dumay offered his unqualified approval. His sign-off was, moreover, seconded by Staff Manager Martha Morgan. Dunay's view was further supported by Behavioral Therapist Virginia "Gin" Birdwell, who made eleven observational visits across a thirteen-week span, running from July to October

1977. She scheduled them at various times of the day, hoping to ensure a reliable sample of their daily experiences.

Birdwell taught Neil Mackay about "contingency management skills." Only when Scotty complied with cooperative behavior—stopping aggressive behavior with a toy or ceasing to tease his dog with a loud toy gun—would he receive hugs, praise, or special privileges. If Scotty ignored his father's command by trying to redirect his attention to the television, Mackay was taught to turn off the television until Scotty complied. The core behavior she wanted to correct was Scotty's bossiness.

Eventually, said Birdwell, "the rate of Scotty's bossiness has almost extinguished." To prove that Birdwell provided five graphs of Scotty's behavior across several dimensions. There was a chart for Scotty's noncompliance. A chart for his bossiness. A chart for social reinforcement. A chart for contingent discipline and a chart for extinction, which she clarified to mean "contingent ignoring of negative behavior."

The charts were not exactly exemplars of high science. There was lots of counting, but this was anything but a longitudinal study. There were only five charts and only five data points on each chart. For a total of twenty-five data points.

It was a vast expanse of sparsity. A skeptic would suggest that a trained seal could pass these tests. Scotty Mackay was not a trained seal. He was a bright, observant boy who wanted, more than anything, to please his father. Passing those tests was one more step toward helping his father gain custody.

A MORE ABIDING REASON FOR NEIL MACKAY'S VICTORY was Robert S. Kaufman, attorney at law. He unstintingly proved himself to be the nutcracker Mackay wanted. One of Kaufman's first targets was Steve Goodenow, a private investigator. On May 3, 1978, a claque of lawyers gathered at the Dillingham Transportation Building, a landmark building just a short walk from Honolulu harbor. The ostensible reason for being there was for Kaufman to question the expenses Goodenow incurred while chasing down Scotty. There was an underlying theme here, as old as dusty law books.

Neil Mackay, through Kaufman, wanted to jam Steve Goodenow over the money he was owed. Or thought he was owed. Sometimes—more often than not—the money game leads participants to bow out. They can no longer afford to go forward, no matter how righteous their cause.

Goodenow's attorney registered his first objection only seconds into Kaufman's examination, as his client stumbled when the Mackay attorney asked, "Do you do business under a fictitious name?" Then a series of more piercing questions, all garbed in the mundane. Kaufman asked if his business associates were licensed private investigators. "No, they are not," Goodenow answered. Did those associates "work on the Scotty Mackay matter in any way whatsoever?" Kaufman asked. "Some of them, yes," Goodenow replied.

One could see where he was going but Kaufman had bigger fish to grill.

"Do you have records which show how much time they specifically spent on this case?" Kaufman asked, his voice polished gravel.

"Without reviewing my records totally, I cannot definitively answer that question," Goodenow muttered. When asked whether employees made out timecards, there was a bit of waffling too. Sometimes, Goodenow admitted, investigation time was kept on case notes. Kaufman wanted to see billing statements. Goodenow showed him two. They totaled just over $3,000.00. A fraction of the amount owed. None of it paid.

Kaufman immediately meandered down the path of legal technicalities. Did other officers and directors do investigative work on this case? Yes. How about independent investigators? Yes, Goodenow said, we used them on the outer islands, on Maui and Kauai. They were off-duty police officers.

"Did you register anyone working on the Scotty Mackay case with the Department of Regulatory Agency's Professional Licensing Division?" Kaufman wanted to know. "Do you have knowledge of the rules of the Department of Regulatory Agency's Professional Licensing Division with regard to the requirement that anyone acting by or for or on your behalf as an investigator be registered with that department within seven days after their being hired by you? Steve, we've reviewed the records of the Professional Licensing Division, and we found during the year 1977 that no one other than yourself was registered with them. Is that correct?"

Goodenow's attorney, James E. Duffy of Honolulu, was about to issue another in what would become a protracted string of objections. He instructed Goodenow not to answer. It would be a long afternoon.

Kaufman kept at Goodenow, chip, chip, chipping away at him, and his team, and his story. Mackay's attorney had done some digging. Some background digging. As Steve Goodenow related how they finally found Scotty, onboard an inter-island ship, Kaufman paused to ask about a quote in Goodenow's narrative. One that referred to "a detective, one of Felix Cabrera's best men."

"How do you know that detective was one of Cabrera's best men," Kaufman demanded. "Do you have an answer to that question?"

Goodenow's attorney was once more forced to intervene. Goodenow stammered, "The police chief of Majuro told me that."

"Did he tell you that this man, one of these detectives that you indicated as one of his best men, spent one year in the Majuro jail?"

Goodenow's attorney jumped in. "Let me object. I think you're being argumentative."

"No. I'm asking if he was told that," Kaufman responded blandly. "I'm not being argumentative."

"That's irrelevant, Counsel," Goodenow's counsel shot back.

"It's only irrelevant if you don't like the question," said Kaufman, the barb on his hook starting to shine.

Goodenow's lawyer had heard enough. "Come on, Counsel," he snarked, glaring at Kaufman. "You may get away with this in Los Angeles. This is different here."

Bob Kaufman's local co-counsel, Bob Hogan, jumped in trying to soothe the room. "Counsel, cut it out."

"You cut it out, too, Bob," snapped Steve Goodenow's lawyer.

Kaufman obsessions were now on full display. First, he wanted to put Goodenow's apparently sloppy business practices under the microscope. That was a way to finesse the monetary charges. Second, he wanted all of Goodenow's investigative documents, whether his attorney's objected or not. Finally, he wanted to know what Goodenow was pursuing in his current investigations. Both bore directly on Neil Mackay's ability to gain full custody of Scotty.

"Are you doing any continuing investigation at this time into the fitness of Mr. Mackay to be the custodial parent of Scotty?" Kaufman demanded. "Have you done any investigatory work regarding the death of Muriel Pfeil?"

That's a secret, Goodenow's attorneys responded. Attorney-client privilege. Kaufman vowed to go to Court and get a more robust Order for those materials but it turned out he had a secret weapon. When Kaufman asked Goodenow what he'd received in terms of payment, the investigator had a one-word reply.

"Nothing," Goodenow admitted.

"Have you received . . ."

"Not a damn thing."

Months later, Kaufman armed himself with a *subpoena duces tecum* aimed at securing all of Goodenow's records related to the Scotty Mackay case. Kaufman was not required to serve it. To use the words of MBI Chief Lee Hoskins, in a memorandum to Majuro's acting attorney general, "Goodenow rolled over and surrendered everything *en masse*. Reason: Goodenow apparently has some $50,000 + invested in expenses in this proceeding and has some hopes of collecting it through cooperation."

Hoskins' source? According to court documents in the Trust Territories, it was Neil S. Mackay.

ROBERT KAUFMAN WAS EQUALLY AGGRESSIVE in Judge Madsen's courtroom. It was show time. The final stretch toward Nell Mackay's ultimate goal. No one was more important than the defense psychiatrist hired to reexamine Neil Mackay and his son. The game was simple: put a fresh spin on all the negative psychological reviews trailing his client.

The defense psychiatrist's name was Dr. Dean Ralph Ackley. After gentle questioning by Kaufman, Robert Wagstaff got the first bite of the apple.

"Why did Mr. Mackay go to Hawaii," Wagstaff inquired.

"He said real estate transactions," Ackley replied. "He thought he had the permission of the Court."

"Objection," Kaufman interjected. "Foundation."

"Sustained," Judge Madsen declared.

So, it went. In his opening testimony, Ackley made it clear that Kaufman "wanted me to form an opinion of Mackay's fitness as a parent." In preparation for that task, he talked to other doctors, and had some of them examine Neil Mackay. "I also went to the atoll in the Marshall Islands," Ackley testified. "Provisions for Scotty's care there were crucial issues. I wanted to talk to people who had no bias. I talked with Rodger and Marie

Cotting. I spoke with Father Donahue. Father Hacker. I spoke with the McEvoy family."

It was Robert Wagstaff's turn to complain. Objection. Hearsay. Kaufman was on it like a falcon on prey.

"Perhaps Mr. Wagstaff feels I neglected to lay foundation," Kaufman replied, his voice butter on bread. "Experts may give an opinion even if it's based on hearsay. I'm happy to ask if his opinion as to fitness is based upon what he learned in the Marshall Islands. An expert can testify as to hearsay. Horn Book Law," he smirked.

Judge Madsen recognized Wagstaff's hearsay objection. Kaufman was undaunted. "I ask to my present case to the court." Ackley was allowed to continue, his opinions free to flow.

"I based my opinion in part of what I learned in Marshall Islands," Ackley pronounced. "I wanted to know the acquaintance of people there. Wanted to know how Scotty related to the people he was with. Wanted to know the circumstances surrounding transfer to the atoll. How he adjusted. I inquired of Mr. and Mrs. Cotting. The Cottings were warm, emotionally responsive people, highly intelligent. Cotting is an American citizen. His wife is from Guam."

"They have four children. Their home is a modern house. Located in the principal population area. They have two dogs and a cat."

Another objection from Robert Wagstaff. Robert Kaufman was still in tailored suit mode. "I'd like to ask Mr. Wagstaff to let me present my case. I like to present cases that experts can testify as to hearsay. The only way to learn about Scotty is hearsay."

Judge Madsen ruled in Kaufman's favor. Ackley started to sing his unstinting praise of his subject. "Scotty was outgoing," Ackley insisted. "Able to associate with other children. He was affectionate to his father and responsive to his father's admonitions. He was also free of emotional disturbances during my time there. His social skills were well-developed. He was talkative, able to play well. There was an absence of disturbance or impairment—his language skills are well developed. And Mr. Mackay recognized and met Scotty's need for security."

Dr. Ackley also addressed the psychological weights pressing in on the boy. "Scotty experienced no disturbance," Ackley insisted. "He enjoyed island hopping. But he feared returning to Alaska. Scotty developed, over the trip back to Alaska, increasing disturbance. Severe anxiety. He had a frantic desire to return to his father."

Well done, Dr. Ackley. Put a bow on it.

In what could be seen as a purely defensive move, Ackley laid it on thick about the high character of the Cottings. He even got an endorsement from their parish priest. Not once did he mention that the Cottings were facing potential contempt of court charges in Majuro.

As Scotty was being transported back to Alaska, questions emerged about the role—and liability—of the Cottings in the Scotty Mackay affair. According to court records, Steve Goodenow, for one, believed Rodger Cotting may have committed a criminal offense. That view hinged on the March 11, 1978, court order from Judge Hefner in Saipan. It read, in part:

"Any person who shall interfere or prevent Mr. Goodenow from taking custody of the minor Scotty, is subject to contempt of this Court."

It was Ramon Villagomez who took the further step of writing the High Commissioner of the Trust Territory. As a Saipanese, Villagomez took personal umbrage at what Rodger Cotting had done. He was explicit in his complaint that Cotting interfered in their attempts to return Scotty Mackay to Alaska. Villagomez wanted the Cottings to pay a price. He was joined by Majuro Police Lt. Andrik Isaac, who also wrote the High Commissioner about the Cotting's apparent contempt of court. Even Captain Cogswell in Ponape wrote that "Rodger Cotting appears to be involved in this."

People in the Trust Territory were forced to pay attention. Marie and Rodger Cotting were served with an Order signed by Associate Justice Robert A. Hefner. The Cottings were to appear in the Majuro Courthouse and show cause why they were not guilty of contempt.

An eight-point list of allegations supported Hefner's order, among them, "Marie Cotting and Rodger Cotting knew of the High Court Order of March 16, 1978, and attempted to circumvent the Order by filing a Petition for Custody in the Marshall Islands District Court."

They faced a maximum sentence of 6 months in jail or a $100.00 fine.

35

Anchorage, Alaska, June 30, 1978

THEY'D FOUGHT AND FOUGHT AND FOUGHT. Scotty Mackay had now gone two years without his mother, two years of flitting from parent to temporary custodian and back again. Getting Robert Wagstaff out of the way was the last hurdle. Sometimes it's the deep pockets who win. Robert Wagstaff was not one of them. He had not been paid since August of 1977. He could not afford to stay in the game much longer.

There were other considerations. Judge Madsen would admit, many years later, that there was an abiding sense Neil Mackay had killed his wife.[35] The problem was, as Madsen put it, they couldn't prove it. Lacking that, Madsen felt the child should go with his father.

Neil Mackay now had an ally in the courtroom. Wayne Anthony Ross, who'd conveniently taken over as the guardian of Scott Mackay's estate, was now positioned to keep Robert Wagstaff away from Scotty's money. That seemed a first step in eliminating Wagstaff entirely, but it wasn't getting them any closer to resolution.

So it was that In March of 1978, while Scott was still in Majuro, Wayne Ross—who often shortened his name to the initials "W.A.R."—suggested a novel solution. "I am willing," Ross wrote to Judge Madsen, "my wife is willing, and my boys are willing to have Scotty Mackay and his father, or Scotty Mackay himself alone, placed in our house upon his return to the

35 University of Alaska Fairbanks, Judge Roy Madsen, Project Jukebox interview with Arthur Snowden, October 25, 2006.

State of Alaska. This placement can continue indefinitely, at least, until this Court can review the matter of his placement at a formal hearing with all parties present and with full argument as to what placement is best for the boy.

"We have plenty of room," Ross added, "and have three sons, Gregory, age 7, Brian, age 5, and Timothy, age 2, for Scotty to play with. Scotty has played with my sons in the past and I believe that placement at our home is a suitable alternative for the Court to consider. We would, of course, see to it that the Court's Order with regard to visitation of Scotty with his grandmother Muriel Pfeil is carried out."

WAR's "true" intentions were already on the record. When Ross was interviewed by Investigator Goodenow in Hawaii, Ross told him that he hoped his efforts to find Scotty Mackay were unsuccessful. His March 24, 1978, memorandum was but a continuation of that theme.

"He apparently remains of the opinion that Scotty Mackay should not have been returned to Alaska at all," Wagstaff noted, "which may explain his position that such costs and expenses incurred therein are unnecessary and unreasonable.

It wasn't legal arguments that won the day. More than anything, all sides were completely exhausted. In that exhaustion came a belated realization. Somehow, in all their ardor, they'd come to neglect the person at the center of their attention. Finally, all sides came together. Reached an agreement. Acknowledged it in court.

Robert Kaufman went first.

"I want counsel to acknowledge that we have the best interests of our client in mind and have a recommendation to enter this agreement," Kaufman intoned. "Mr. Mackay has the read decree. I've signed it with his consent."

"Mr. Kaufman is correct," Wagstaff said, concurring. "The Consent decree is a reflection of the stated will of all parties. The parties have determined it is in the best interests of the child. The child has been harmed. The settlement is in his best interests. I express my best wishes."

Robert Pfeil's attorney was up next. "I concur," Doug Baily said. "I have consulted with Robert Pfeil. I am authorized to sign it. As to Marianne Pfeil, I haven't represented her—there's no question but that she will comply with the agreement."

Only one voice remained. Wayne Anthony Ross, the interlocutor and *guardian ad litem* for Scotty's estate. Ross, too, was on board not surprisingly. He'd long supported Neil Mackay's quest. "I commend counsel," he proclaimed. "As GAL of the Estate, the settlement is in the best interests of the Estate."

With those formalities out of the way, Kaufman said, "I would like Mr. Wagstaff to deliver Scotty in accordance with the Order."

"I will do everything," Wagstaff replied. "The Willises have said the order will be complied with. If there's a problem, I need only call Mr. Kaufman."

"Yes," Kaufman noted. "Scotty is to be delivered to Mr. Mackay at 12 noon tomorrow."

Alfred and Carolina Willis delivered Scotty to Neil Mackay on Saturday, July 1, 1978. Robert and Marianne Pfeil forever withdrew any claims to the custody of Scotty Mackay. In a concession, Grandmother Muriel C. Pfeil was given "reasonable visitation" with Scotty, on or before their birthdays and at Christmas. All parties agreed not to harass, annoy, or place each other under surveillance.

A week later, the pair arrived in Honolulu where, with the court's approval, they would now reside. "We're happy to be back," Mackay told reporters and friends waiting at the Honolulu International Airport arrival gate. "It's very emotional."

"Sometimes people have to stand up and fight for what they think is right," Mackay added. "Scotty and I decided the best thing was to fight this thing through."

A little more than a month later, Neil Mackay was saying almost the same things again. This time in Majuro. He told reporter Cisco Uludong, of the *Gannett News Service*, that Majuro would be a good place for his son to grow up. That, by tracing where they went the previous April while attempting to evade authorities, Scotty might forget the entire ordeal.

"The father, who said he had legal custody over Scotty all along, said he ran away with Scotty 'to protect my son,'" Uludong reported. In the article, also carried by the *Honolulu Star-Bulletin*, Uludong pulled several direct quotes from Neil Mackay.

"There is no doubt I made some mistakes along the way, but in evaluation of what I did, I did it to protect my son and not to hurt him," Mackay declared. "I venture to say that in some areas, if I face the same problems, I might have done it differently, but my intentions and motivations would be precisely the same."

Mackay also told Uludong that news reports portraying him as a drunk and drug addled were "misrepresentations calculated to sway other people so they could achieve some given end."

"There was a lot of misleading, false and manufactured information and all this was done for a monetary gain by the people who were doing it," Mackay concluded.

36

Honolulu, Hawaii, January 1979

BACK IN HAWAII, ONE OF NEIL MACKAY'S FIRST TASKS was to choose a school for Scotty. He was under court orders to do so. The one he chose was the Kaimuki Christian School. Housed in a residential neighborhood lodged between the mountains and the sea, Kaimuki school was strategically removed from the hubbub of nearby Waikiki. An extension of the Kaimuki Christian Church, it traced its roots to the Restoration Movement, an early 19th century religious reform effort that stressed an unencumbered Christianity, based solely on the Bible. There were no central headquarters, councils, or other organizational structure above the local church level.

Scotty started Kaimuki in the fall of 1978. It was then that he first came into contact with his elementary school teacher, Mrs. Pat Moody.[36] It didn't take long for Mrs. Moody to sense that things were not quite right with the young man. One of her first hints came when Scotty told her that everything was kept in boxes, "because they may have to leave suddenly." She later learned why: Neil Mackay confided that they were going to live in Hong Kong and then, at another time, that they were moving to Australia.

There was also a not-so-subtle air of protectiveness about them. Neil Mackay was adamant that Moody not allow Scotty to go home with anyone she didn't know. Eventually Scotty revealed the deeper truth. The boy

36 Mrs. Moody's observations are taken directly from a January 28, 1987, interview conducted by Inv. Joe Austin.

told her he had to be where there was security. That sense of security was shattered in January 1979, although recollections vary widely.

One thing everyone agreed upon was that Robert Pfeil had visited Hawaii on vacation, with wife Marianne and their children. While there, Bob met up with a friend from Alaska, who was living on Oahu at the time. Together, John Johnson and Bob Pfeil ventured over to Scotty's school. It was, they said later, a spur-of-the-moment decision. An unplanned excursion. Johnson knew where the school was. They drove there. As the two of them stood at the side of the track, Bob spotted Scotty through the fence. He called out to his nephew, who was only months from his sixth birthday.

"The boy had a look of fright and horror on his face," Johnson recalled. "He ran. We left."

The incident soon took on the outlines of myth. When Neil Mackay learned of it, he immediately went to Charles Sullivan. "Neil ran down to tell me about it," Sullivan recalled. "He said Bob Pfeil tried to kidnap Scotty. Scotty ran and hid under the teacher's desk. Scotty said, 'that bad man' was there." Later, the story morphed into two or three visits by Bob Pfeil. Each of them, Mackay was convinced, were "part of a kidnapping plan."

Pat Moody heard about it too. Moody said that she received a telephone call from Mackay, who was upset because Scotty told him that he had seen his uncle. She said that when Mackay called her, the incident had allegedly taken place two days earlier and that when Scotty saw his uncle, Scotty ran and hid under her desk. The problem was, Pat Moody did not recall any incident where Scotty hid under her desk. That much she could confirm. She added that Neil Mackay told her that, during the incident, the man waved at Scotty and said to him, "come here."

Bob Pfeil had an entirely different memory. He told Marianne afterwards that "Scotty appeared 'sad' and 'different' from the other children when he saw him on the school yard." Grandma Pfeil also saw things somewhat differently. She was quick to clarify that "Bob did not go into the school to see Scotty—he only saw him through the fence." But Grandma Pfeil was not there.

According to Jean Sullivan, Neil Mackay already had fears that Bob Pfeil would kidnap Scotty. "The incident at the school made him believe it more," Sullivan said. "Neil said Scotty had the wits scared out of him."

Charles Sullivan concurred. "Neil was mad, hurt, shaken when he found out that Bob was at Scotty's school," Sullivan insisted. "Sometimes he would shake when he spoke of Bob Pfeil. Bob Pfeil was a dirty name to him. I saw him shake more than a couple of times. He would really shake when he spoke of the possible kidnapping of Scotty."

Three months later, Grandma Pfeil decided to go to Hawaii herself. As the only Pfeil with visitation rights, she was determined to exercise them. There was one stipulation: she had to give a three-week notice. After the events at Scotty's school, Neil Mackay was less than welcoming.

"I wrote a letter to Neil," Grandma Pfeil noted. "It was returned to me. I contacted Neil's attorney. He said he would contact Neil for me. Neil said I could have two hours with Scotty. Neil said he would be present also. The trip to Hawaii was only for me to see Scotty for two hours. I was alone."

"Neil told me where to sit, told me if I said anything he didn't like, he would ask me to leave. Scotty said he didn't have a bedroom, said he slept with his daddy. I stayed the full two hours."

"I didn't get to hold him at any time," she said later. Mackay remained between her and her grandson, even taking him out of the room for a while, apparently hoping she would give up and go away. "I wanted to talk like we always did," she said, but Mackay "put his legs out so the child could not get past."

When she left the condo and waited for the elevator, Scotty ran down the hall, kissed her quickly on the cheek and then raced away. Mackay said, "I told him to do that.'"

Grandma Pfeil's response was immediate. "Neil," she exclaimed, "you couldn't even let me leave thinking that little boy gave me that kiss without being told to." That was the last and only time she'd seen her grandson since her son's assassination.

On October 11, 1979, Neil Sutherland Mackay took another step toward putting the past behind them. He filed a petition with Jean King, Lieutenant Governor of Hawaii. King granted his petition and issued a Decree. From that point forward the name NEIL PFEIL MACKAY was changed to NEIL SUTHERLAND MACKAY, JR.

"Just had to get rid of that name Pfeil," he wrote a friend at the time. "This is just another step forward for Scotty with the change of name."

Later, Grandma Pfeil received an envelope containing a change of name notice. It said her grandson's name was now Neil Sutherland Mackay, Jr.

37

Honolulu, Hawaii, November 26-27, 1985

WHAT THE PROSECUTION NEEDED WAS EVIDENCE—CONCRETE evidence—that linked Neil Mackay to Junior Pauole. They trusted they'd find that evidence at Mackay's Waikiki condo. Their decision put Sgt. Mike Grimes in Honolulu, requesting the assistance of Investigator David Sommers of the Organized Crime Strike Force of the City and County of Honolulu. Grimes wanted—more than anything—letters, correspondence, photographs, or any other records that corroborated Pauole's statement that Neil Mackay paid him $10,000 for the murder of Robert Pfeil.

When they arrived early one Wednesday morning, investigators quickly realized that Mackay's condo enjoyed a sweeping view of palm-tree-lined Ala Moana Boulevard. It was here that the thoroughfare made its final meander toward Kalakaua Avenue and Waikiki's main drag. Here, that a sweep of high-rise beach hotels beckoned visitors from around the globe. This was a haven that promised balmy winters and azure-blue surf. A light rain that cleansed the morning air.

The green oasis of Ft. DeRussy Park glimmered in the near distance. The Hawaiian sun and street sounds trickled through the window blinds. The investigators did not linger on the view.

They instead shooed Barbara Homay and Scotty out of the premises. There was more than five hours' worth of work ahead of them. Although Homay had taken steps to clean up her former husband's clutter—and opened the drapes to purge the darkness he preferred—there was a mess of papers and books, creeping into every available nook and corner. Neil S. Mackay was a highly litigious soul. This was the detritus of his obsessions.

In the twelve years preceding Robert Pfeil's shooting, Neil Mackay was involved in six distinct lawsuits—and their appellate offspring—that pitted him against one or more members of the Pfeil family. The first was the divorce suit, *Muriel Adele Mackay v. Neil S. Mackay*, filed in August 1973. The second major lawsuit began shortly after Muriel Pfeil's death, when Robert Pfeil filed his petition to adopt Scotty Mackay.

The third major lawsuit involved Muriel Pfeil's estate. Although the estate was probated in October of 1976, the litigation was ongoing at the time of Robert Pfeil's shooting. Then there were the costs associated with returning Scotty to Alaska after his Marshall Islands misadventure. During the course of the custody and estate litigation, yet another suit was filed—this one by Scotty Mackay against Robert Pfeil and four lawyers, alleging that Pfeil had fraudulently and illegally made estate payments to Wagstaff and Baily of $85,000.

The last lawsuit was *Neil S. Mackay Jr. v. Robert Pfeil*. Here Mackay sought to wiggle out of an Alaska order directing him to repay Scotty's estate for the Marshall Islands fiasco. For prosecutors, that legal action seemed to be the final straw. Mackay not only lost, but Judge Holland awarded the defendants full costs and attorney's fees, finding that the suit was "transparent and flimsy," "a last-ditch attempt," and brought "in bad faith" and "for the purpose of harassing the defendants.'"

It was no coincidence, they thought, that the decision came down in late August of 1985. Only months before Robert Pfeil was shot.

IT TOOK A COORDINATED ASSAULT ON THE BOXES and stacks to find what they were looking for. Neil Mackay was a hoarder. One of their first finds, however, was a treasure. A one-page letter from Virginia Zawacki to Neil Mackay, dated 2 July 1984, that read in part: "As I advised you this a.m., Junior called me last Saturday and yesterday afternoon I gave him an envelope to him [sic] to be hand carried to you."

Another letter, also by Virginia Zawacki, was sent on Junior's behalf to Jeanne Rolles, Property Manager of the Outrigger Hotel, where Junior sought to open a bar. Dated August 19, 1985, Zawacki wrote:

> Mr. Pauoli [sic] is an excellent tenant, e.g., pays rent on time, has taken care of miscellaneous problems (plumbing, electrical, etc.} without calling upon the undersigned for assistance, and promptly secures required insurance on the premises. The undersigned has had no problems with Mr. Pauoli.

Then they found a three-page letter, dated June 23, 1984, sent by Mackay to Jean Sullivan. In that missive, Mackay tells Sullivan:

> As for Scotty's estate, things are pretty bad . . . Mr. Pfeil just thinks that I have been avoiding the matter, which I just wish I could, but things have gone on too long and enough is enough. Hell, I can understand the human mind, and we all have a little stealing in us, but when you steal, it should be kept in moderation, and when caught don't blame it on someone else.

There was another, this one to attorney Lance Speigel, who handled the Marshall Islands settlement with the Pfeils. In a four-page letter dated October 8, 1984, Mackay revealed the depth of his contempt for Robert Pfeil. The upshot: Robert Pfeil was out for his own interests—a persistent theme. As for Scotty, Mackay asked, what has he received?

"NOTHING so much as a Xmas card."

Mackay was not finished, sending another letter to Speigel on April 20, 1985. In it, he rejected his attorney's advice to settle the Marshall Islands matter, despite the fact that accrued interest had ballooned the $175,000 to almost a quarter of a million dollars.

They also came across an "entertainment" contract that Mackay had written for Junior, one that changed the terms of his financial relationship with the dancers at his clubs. Hounded by the state for failing to make unemployment insurance contributions, he had Mackay change the terms of their employment. They were no longer employees. They were entertainers. He would no longer have to pay their Workman's Compensation insurance.

Of equal—and perhaps greater—interest were detailed revelations about Neil Mackay's financial holdings. Financial reports for five separate corporate entities—entities where he might be hiding assets. An exhaustive list of bank accounts—in both his name and Scotty's—in Hawaii, Alaska, and Nevada. Tantalizingly, a list of Mackay's safety deposit boxes. In other evidence, there were letters regarding various Certificates of Deposit. The letters were addressed to Barbara Homay and Virginia Zawacki as well as Mackay himself.

They also found a bound appointment book with all of Neil Mackay's private numbers. Numbers that corresponded with the phone lines he directed Junior to call on the night of his arrest. Numbers that were also found in Junior's phone book. Yeah, these numbers said, these two were more than casual acquaintances.

They had hit the jackpot. One more to go.

Anchorage, Alaska, December 18-20, 1985

BY 1984, NEIL MACKAY WAS GONE FROM THE MACKAY BUILDING. The State of Alaska, which at one time housed 300 state employees there, was after him. Mackay had neglected—or refused—to correct fire code violations. No one was supposed to be in the building. But Neil Mackay had fashioned a workaround.

He had all the locks changed and rewired the elevators, he confessed to friend, "so rather than the City having control of the bldg., they don't. Those elevators will only work with the use of certain keys. You can only board same from the basement and it works out real good and keeps the bastards out."

His ruse could not stand. The city shut him down. So, he purchased a home in Rogers Park, an Anchorage neighborhood only blocks from Lake Otis. Virginia Zawacki, three years divorced from her husband, would lease the house and live upstairs. The basement would house Mackay's new office, gathering all the documents and artifacts once held in the Mackay Building. From there, Virginia would continue to manage Mackay's business interests in Alaska.

The cops figured it was another treasure trove.

On December 18, Sgt. Grimes presented affidavits to Judge David Stewart, seeking a search warrant on the premises. The scope of the search took them as far back as 1976, the year Muriel was killed. On December 20, the Homicide Division served the warrant on the downstairs portion of 1634 Stanford Drive. The initial party of five APD officers eventually grew to six, plus one FBI agent.

Entering the downstairs portion of the residence, they found two separate areas. The larger of the two contained office equipment and supplies, with a desk located along one wall and office credenzas along another. A smaller area held a desk and was filled with filling cabinets adjacent to a storage room stacked with cardboard boxes. They quickly learned that some of the boxes featured the initials NSM—Neil S. Mackay—others had the name "Mackay" written on them.

This was not a treasure trove. It was the mother lode. They would divide and conquer, with the caveat that they always worked in pairs. They always photographed the evidence as it was found. They always marked the evidence as they seized it. Preserving the chain of custody was paramount.

Sgt. Grimes and Larry Arend focused on the smaller office and storage areas, with Arend snapping evidence photos as he went. The other pairs fanned out to cover the main office. FBI Agent Roger Lee, meanwhile, took on the collection of evidence tags. Uniformed cops kept Virginia Zawacki out of their way.

They would be there for three and a half hours. It would take nine pages of police department evidence forms to summarize the contents. The items gathered ranged from personal matters to legal documents, from business acquaintances to newspaper clippings. They couldn't help but note the bit of doggerel attached to one wall.

"First there was a father, then a son, neither wore kilts, but both had fun. They romped and they stomped it is to be said and the son became as father, so the Bible read. Mackays, they were a proud Scot line, a bond formed between them that was just fine. As a seedling, the father took the boy in tow and shall all remember now with God's help, we all watched Scottie grow."

Beyond that, there were old family photographs and special events calendars from Our Redeemer Lutheran School. A business card from private investigator David G. Fechheimer, address 1808 Laguna St., San Francisco, California. A copy of a letter regarding the Municipality of Anchorage and State of Alaska lawsuit against the Mackay Building, Inc. A typed memo dated June 12, 1984, referencing Muriel Pfeil. A photostat copy of a *Honolulu Star Bulletin* dated Monday, March 27, 1978, headlined

"Boy's Transpacific Saga Appears to Be at an End." And a photostat of a newspaper clipping from the Seattle Times dated Sunday, November 7, 1976, headlined "Alaska travel agent slain by gangsters?"

The latter news article held a tantalizing—if ultimately false—premise. "Was an Anchorage travel agent murdered in an underworld move to take over her agency," wrote veteran *Times* reporter Stanton H. Patty. "Police sources told the Seattle Times the slaying could be tied in with nationwide efforts by organized crime to gain control of travel agencies."

Among the forty-two items of greatest interest, however, was a typed letter Mackay wrote about Scotty. There was also a March 1, 1982, check issued by the Wild Cherry to Neil Mackay. A letter and attachment to Mr. Scott Bass of the Wild Cherry at 145 East 4th Avenue, referencing the property of the Wild Cherry. An envelope photocopied attached from PAUOLI Inc. at 145 East 4th, to Lake Bluff Inc., one of Mackay's corporate entities.

Digging further, they found a power of attorney granted by Mackay to Virginia Zawacki, dated December 9, 1977. An assignment by Barbara Homay to Lake Bluff, Inc., dated September 27, 1982. A list of corporations and bank accounts, dating from September 10, 1985. A register of bank accounts dated September 20, 1979. A November 1982 list of Mackay's active corporations. And a certified copy of a corporate resolution for signing and endorsing checks regarding Melrah, Inc. authorizing Barbara Homay and Virginia V. Zawacki as signatories.

When they followed the money, these were the trails they'd take.

38

Anchorage, Alaska, December 5 – January 14, 1986

It took until December 5 for acting Hawaiian Governor John Waihee to authorize the extradition warrant sent by Alaska Governor Bill Sheffield.[37] It didn't resolve anything. Neil Mackay was not giving up. At the December 6 extradition hearing, Mackay's attorney said he would oppose extradition on the grounds Mackay should be tried in Hawaii. His assertion was based on the flimsy premise that Mackay was alleged to have ordered the Alaska murder by telephone from Hawaii, not Alaska. It was, he argued, a jurisdictional issue.

The Neil Mackay who appeared in court, meanwhile, was a man transformed. His white beard shaved off, his hair cut, and his mustache neatly trimmed, Mackay wore a blue and white aloha shirt and grey slacks. There was a felt animosity in the courtroom. Mackay prompted a sharp exchange when a state sheriff refused to allow him to stray more than a few feet away for a private consultation with Hawaiian attorney John Edmunds.

In Anchorage, District Attorney Victor Krumm blasted Edmunds' assertions about the perceived lack of jurisdiction as "preposterous." Mackay, he said, "could conceivably face Hawaii charges for conspiracy to commit murder in addition to the Alaska charge. But to the extent there was a homicide, the homicide was in Alaska."

Edmunds was unmoved. He vowed to challenge every detail of the

37 Hawaii had only recently elected George Ariyoshi their new governor, so Waihee was the only person then authorized to sign the warrant.

case, including the reliability of government witnesses who had been granted immunity from prosecution. He questioned whether Mackay could receive a fair trial in Alaska. He also protested Mackay's bail requirement as "excessive and ludicrous." Judge Chang responded by revoking Mackay's bail. Deputy Attorney General John Campbell Jr., citing rulings in other states, successfully argued that people arrested on governor's warrants for extradition should be held without bail. That ruling was ultimately upheld by the Hawaii Supreme Court. Neil Mackay, they said, was not entitled to bail.

The end was near. On Monday, January 6, 1986, Mackay attorney John Edmunds notified Judge Chang that, while Mackay still believed he had a legal basis to challenge his extradition, he realized the Hawaii courts were not likely to agree with him. Edmunds added that Mackay "intends to enter a plea of not guilty and vigorously contest all charges against him." In a hearing before Judge Chang, Mackay consented to the transfer, which was scheduled for the end of the week.

"I am in full agreement with my attorney," Mackay told Judge Chang. "I waive extradition."

Neil S. Mackay arrived in Anchorage on a commercial flight early Tuesday morning, January 14th, his delay occasioned by the need to finalize Scotty's living arrangements with Barbara Homay in Hawaii. Anchorage journalists were at the airport when his plane arrived.

Kim Rich of the *Daily News* noted that "After the other passengers had deplaned, Mackay was taken off the plane and escorted down a stairway from the plane to the ground outside the terminal building, where he was placed in an unmarked car and driven from the airport." He was taken straight to the 6th and C street jail, in anticipation of his imminent arraignment.

Even as that was happening, Gilbert Pauole was secreted out of Alaska for security reasons. He was taken to a jail in the Lower 48, under an assumed name. The man they called "Junior" was now in the federal witness protection program. So was his erstwhile girlfriend, Amy Shotwell. What a beautiful pair they made.

BY THE TIME NEIL MACKAY WAS BOOKED INTO the Sixth Avenue Jail Annex on January 14, 1986, the police were less than a month away from deserting the building. The jail was all that remained of a once actively functioning facility. By that time, the jail held only women and juvenile offenders. Mackay was booked into a solitary confinement area, which looked prescient when, the next day, police received a tip about a possible jailbreak at the nearby Cook Inlet jail. That jail held Mackay's co-defendants, as well as two murderers and a rapist. Armed security now patrolled Cook Inlet around the clock.

In early February, Mackay was moved to the maximum-security section of the Sixth Avenue Annex; that area had only two cells and was effectively separated from the rest of the jailhouse population. It was as private as could be expected, though cramped, with a steel bed, an open toilet, and a small opening—four by ten inches—through which food or a telephone receiver could be passed. Wire mesh covered the steel bars.

Neil Mackay was nevertheless allowed to transform that space into a jailhouse law office. In a move of unexpected generosity, a desk was wedged into his cell, upon which sat an electric typewriter. He'd had the same setup in his previous cell; both required that his cell be rewired. His lawyers, meanwhile, delivered case file after case file, the bulk of its materials from the Robert Pfeil murder investigation, taken directly from Anchorage police and prosecutors. He was now in the facsimile of a Neil Mackay heaven; he was confined, of course, but able to take an active role in his own defense.

On March 18, 1986, at 10:30 a.m., a new inmate was moved into Cell #2, the sole cell adjacent to Neil Mackay. His name was Paul Dennis Newsom; he was ostensibly there as a temporary measure before being transferred to a jail in Minnesota. He needed to be in a secure area, away from the general population. Newsom had good reason to fear for his safety. He was a known informant, credited with breaking up a jailhouse drug ring, and his cover was blown. He had been raped and stabbed while in a federal prison and had been threatened repeatedly by prisoners in Alaska jails, including threats from a convicted contract murderer.

In fact, Newsom had already proven useful in the present case, having engaged John Bright in incriminating conversations at the Cook Inlet facility. He was, it seemed, on an indirect path from Cook Inlet to the Sixth Avenue Annex, interrupted only by a brief stop at the Bethel Jail, 399 miles due west. The Sixth Avenue Annex staff insisted that, while they knew he was an informant, they didn't know Newsom had already assisted police on the Pfeil killing. The cell next to Mackay, they insisted, was the only one which met the designations for protective custody and maximum security that Newsom required.

Upon learning that the adjacent cell was occupied by one Neil Sutherland Mackay, however, Paul Newsom immediately set out to help police "have Mr. Mackay."

Although they couldn't see each other, Newsom could tell Mackay was at his typewriter. During a lull, Newsom asked his neighbor an innocent sounding question. It all started with coffee.

"Actual start of our conversation verbatim," Newsom later told APD officers Hoffbeck and Austin, "went 'hey, Cell 1, do they give out coffee here?' It was me talking to Mackay. He said, 'what?' I said, you know, do they give out coffee, sell it on commissary, whatever. He said 'no, but I'll give you some, it's the decaffeinated kind.' I said anything will do right now; I sure appreciate it. He said, 'what's your name.' I said Paul, he said, 'mine's Mackay' and then he spelled it out for me. Then he passed over ten packets of High Point decaffeinated coffee."

They talked about food, Newsom said, with Mackay telling him the food was good and that, most of all, he was glad he didn't have to be bothered by the noise and interruptions, because he could get his work done. Newsom claimed Mackay told him he was getting transcripts from the other trials—and Newsom had the temerity to ask, "I wonder why those guys are informing on you." Newsom quoted the answer, "He said they got religion. He said they walk into court with a Bible and think it will get them off."

As Newsom described it, Mackay would talk a little, then stop and resume typing, at work on his case. In those interludes, Newsom used a Flair pen to write what he'd heard on a 9 x 6 ruled sheet of Mead paper that he'd brought over from the Bethel jail. Unlike Mackay, he lacked a desk. He used his bed instead.

The topics were wide-ranging.

According to Newsom's notes, all the co-conspirators save Junior were paid in cocaine. In the informant's way of speaking, that came out as Mackay saying, "I'm the only guy dealing in cash dollars." Newsom added that the killing "was done to stop the rape of Scotty's Trust Fund and to gain control of the Trust." Newsom segued from talking about the series of phone calls from Junior on the night of his arrest, to allegations that Mackay had talked about Colombian drug dealers. "He said at any one time they can have a half a million dollars cash in their pockets." Then, in a near stream of consciousness ramble, Newsom moved on to Larry Gentry, and how Mackay was angry because the Gentry's of the world weren't able to keep their mouths shut.

"I asked him, I said, 'you're the bad, the big bad killer, huh?' And he said yeah, and see . . . He said, uh, I told him that I felt real bad for him, and he said that 'a man's gotta do what a man's gotta do.' Referring, we were talking about the cash transaction with Junior and the drug dealing with the rest of the people and that a man's gotta do what a man's gotta do is the killing of the airline pilot. Or the shooting and his subsequent death."

Hoffbeck interjected at this point, declaring that, "I glean what you're saying there, in order to protect the estate of Scotty . . ."

"Yeah, see, he," Newsom interrupted, "This man is a smart man, OK? He's no dummy, and he's not coming out saying I killed or contracted to kill. He's saying little things like, uh, a man's gotta do what a man's gotta do, you know, he's talking about Scotty's estate and trying to get control of Scotty's estate and that a man's gotta do, and you know we're talking about the death of the contract killing, the death of the airline pilot. Ask yourself—what is he talking about, you know? We're talking about $10,000 cash being prepaid to Junior and cocaine being given to the rest of these people . . . [to] kill someone. Then he says a man's gotta do what a man's gotta do. What are we talking about?"

That was the problem. Newsom had read the newspapers—although he demurred and said the only newspaper available in Bethel was the *Tundra Times*, which didn't carry much news about the Pfeil murder. But he admitted he'd read the part where "they had just got done arresting the people," which said more than perhaps he intended. Those articles invariably carried a recap of the entire case, start to finish. And by the time of the arrests, the police—and reporters—knew a great deal.

There was, in other words, a lot for Paul Dennis Newsom to build upon.

39

Anchorage, Alaska, April 1985 – March 1986

One thing was certain. There was going to be a trial. Although a Judge had been chosen—Judge Mary "Meg" Greene—her selection had not been a foregone conclusion. Four judges were picked before her. Four judges were rejected through preemptory challenges or recusal—some had past associations with the people involved. The rest were eliminated by virtue of judicial calendars that projected out at least a year. Greene was the only one left.

Greene was green, at least as a judge. She'd been on the Fairbanks bench for all of one year, having been appointed in January 1985. She was the second least senior Superior Court judge in the state. Almost immediately, the prosecution filed a five-page request for Greene to give the "complex, lengthy and important" case to someone with more experience.

Maybe they were discounting her hardscrabble Wyoming upbringing, her father lost to an industrial accident at age three. Her mother scrimping by as a telephone operator. The Harvard Law degree she earned despite that humble start. The 80 cases she'd handled before the Alaska Supreme Court and the Court of Appeals during a single three-year period. Her public defender works in remote villages throughout the vast Alaskan wilderness.

The Mackay case was her trial by fire. She was immediately thrust into the internecine warfare expected of a high-profile murder case. Even mundane issues took on an ominous cast. Across that distance, her hair would go from brown to white.

In one example, Neil Mackay's legal team abruptly changed its tune about conditions in the Sixth Avenue Annex. Mackay, it seemed, had lost his privileged status. In an April 1985 bail hearing before Judge Greene, Mackay attorney Bill Bryson complained mightily but bail was not utmost in his mind.

"Our ability to represent Mr. Mackay is becoming very difficult," he told the judge. "His hand is in a sling, the typewriter and desk have been removed from his cell, and the telephone in his wing has been taken out. He did have use of a conference room, but when we reserve the room—we go down and they tell us they need the room even though it is empty. He's hard of hearing so we have to speak loudly. Everyone can hear. They have also cut back on his library time."

Prosecutor Timothy Petumenos smirked. "Mr. Mackay," he said, "is asking for special treatment. The general population does not get desks or typewriters in their cells. He is permitted one hour each day in the library, as is everyone. He has turned down the opportunity to be in the library when it's available. The contact room is also available to other inmates with their family."

Judge Greene turned to Chester Chiara, who was superintendent of the 6th & C Jail, and there to answer her questions. "It's a suitable facility for Mr. Mackay," he declared, before adding that Mackay was a high security individual. "Any movement of him, everything comes to a complete stop."

As for the desk and typewriter, Chiara pointed out that if Mackay had them, other inmates would demand the same. The electric typewriter, he said, was a security risk. Tape recorders were not allowed unless special permission was given. He didn't have a problem with Mackay's counsel bringing a tape recorder—as long as it was battery operated. As for Neil Mackay's use of a phone? During his time at the Sixth Avenue Jail, Mackay had submitted only one request for a phone call.

In her ruling from the bench, Judge Greene said, "I believe we have a special situation because of the masses of court material, his hearing, and his hand. Until he is able to write, I order that Mr. Mackay be given a typewriter in his cell or another room. The availability is on 24 hours' notice and subject to the availability of the conference room. He is not to have the typewriter more than two hours, twice a week. I deny Mr. Mackay's request for a table or a phone. Mr. Bryson, will you please prepare the Order."

Judge Greene did not address the bail question but it was not going away.

BY JANUARY OF 1986, THERE WERE NINE ATTORNEYS arrayed before Judge Greene. All of them men. Most of them impatient.

Seven were defense attorneys assigned to the various suspects accused of Robert Pfeil's murder. The most famous among them was Neil Mackay's attorney, James Shellow. Shellow was best known for representing unpopular political defendants, having made his mark going to bat for American Indian Movement activists at Wounded Knee, Vietnam war protesters, all manner of accused murderers and even alleged organized crime figures. Something of an academic—with a Phi Beta Kappa from the University of Chicago in physics and mathematics, a doctorate in experimental psychology, a CPA, and a law degree—Shellow was used to being the smartest man in the room. Such was his reputation that Alaska attorneys flocked to the courtroom, just to see him practice.

The other two were prosecutors. The State of Alaska had elected to go to its deep bench. They lured former Anchorage Assistant District Attorney Peter Gruenstein out of semi-retirement. Gruenstein had notched a series of victories in high profile murder cases, among them the conviction of Charles Meach, who killed four teenagers in 1982; Donald "Cowboy" Stumpf, convicted of killing a Korean tailor; and three teenagers convicted of killing an elderly real estate saleswoman before stealing her car and going on a drug-induced joyride.

Joining Gruenstein was former Assistant Attorney General Tim Petumenos who, after convicting a former state legislator of bribery, had gone into private practice. Gruenstein had specifically asked Petumenos to join his team, "because my feeling and the feeling of other people in the office is that the best legal talent is required for this case."

Rounding out the menagerie were five of the co-defendants—only Gilbert Pauole was missing, having waived his right to be present. He was "Outside"—Alaskan vernacular for the Lower 48—his attorney said.

In the Federal Witness Protection Program. Even with Junior Pauole out of the picture, there were extraordinary security measures in place. They'd all been scanned by a metal detector. There were uniformed and plainclothes guards stationed at every corner and, seemingly, on every precipice.

Two of the defendants—Tyoga Closson and Robert Betts—were under the impression they'd be joining Junior Pauole in the Witness Protection Program. That, in fact, they would be given immunity deals. That they, too, were part of the security protocols.

Fred Dewey, who represented Betts, had an issue just being there. "Frankly, I don't think my client will be going to trial," he announced. Throughout the hearing, he stressed that the prosecution had reneged on a deal to give Betts immunity in exchange for statements to police. That wasn't his only beef. The first words out of Dewey's mouth were a call to banish news cameras from the courtroom. That was, he said, the only way to protect his client's identity.

That brought a chorus of affirmation. Me too, said Rex Butler, attorney for Tyoga Closson. Mackay's attorney, Jim Shellow, was already there, having been part of that chorus from the get-go. Two weeks earlier, during his first appearance on behalf of Mackay, he asked Judge Karl Johnstone to exclude electronic media. There was already too much media attention to this case, he warned. Now, before Judge Greene, Shellow was complaining about a State press conference where various allegations were made and the "swirl of publicity." His client, he claimed vociferously, could not get a fair trial.

The battle lines were drawn. Judge Greene would soon rule that photos not be taken of Closson or Betts. That, moreover, none of the defendants were to be shown in the handcuffs that bound their wrists. A single, resolute attorney representing the news media—John McKay—rose to counter that prevailing notion. We already have photos of Robert Betts, he said. Taken this morning, outside the courtroom. It's unconstitutional to ban photos we already have. The judge ruled otherwise.

John McKay knew he had a fight on his hands. Determined to win full media coverage, he filed a motion opposing Mackay's preemptive move to prohibit electronic media coverage. He'd seen it coming. Had already put the court on notice, requesting "reasonable notice and opportunity to be heard before any restrictions are imposed on coverage by print or electronic media in this case."[38]

Then, on January 31, 1986—the day of the Status Hearing—McKay took the next step, filing a motion to intervene on behalf of multiple Alaska media organizations. He noted that television stations already had file footage of trial participants. That led to his next assertion. Noting the already substantial coverage of the case, McKay asserted what seemed to him obvious. "Defendant Mackay cannot show a substantial effect resulting from audio and camera coverage of the trial that is substantially and prejudicially different and separable."

As one critique duly noted, "Keeping the media informed was clearly a low priority for the parties."[39] That said, the print press ultimately saw very few restrictions. The Anchorage newspapers seemed to be full speed ahead. Maybe too much so.

On Sunday, January 26, 1986, the *Anchorage Daily News* ran a front-page story that drew heavily on the conversations between Gilbert Pauole and Neil Mackay, recorded on the night of Pauole's arrest. Featuring a Dee Boyles illustration that took up the bulk of the upper fold, it was a scoop of the first magnitude. *Mackay tapes tell mixed story*, the headline declared over a Sheila Toomey by-line. There was no denying this story was sourced from APD tapes. Tapes leaked to the *Anchorage Daily News*, which promptly published them. That was a problem.

Unauthorized disclosure of police reports was prohibited under Alaska Law. The State wanted somebody to answer for the breach. They pointed to the defense attorneys. The defense attorneys pointed elsewhere. Wanted a judge to start questioning their colleagues under oath. Nasty stuff. Judge Serdahely, whose job it was to make that determination, denied the request. Serdahely punted.

He sent the matter to the Alaska State Bar association.

Then there was the near fiasco of Earl Swift. The prosecution pursued him relentlessly. Pursued him because he had taken jailhouse calls from John Bright, Amy Shotwell, and Junior Pauole. He seemed to have inside knowledge. He was a journalist for the *Anchorage Daily Times*. In their zeal

38 Letter from D. John McKay to Judge Karl S. Johnstone (January 21, 1986).

39 "News Cameras in the Alaska Courts: Assessing the Impact," Alaska Judicial Council, January 1988

to get Neil Mackay, the prosecution seemed more than willing to pursue the man, even as he made a cross-country trip in the lower-48. Eventually, they abandoned their goose chase, largely because his superiors at the *Times* took steps to protect him.

Judge Greene, meanwhile, had other concerns. January 31 was also the day she turned away the State's request that she recuse herself. "I have looked deeply into my own soul and see no reason why I am not competent in this matter," Greene proclaimed. Her voice was flat and matter of fact. The Wyoming in her would brook no retreat.

"Now that we have a judge," Shellow responded, hardly skipping a beat, "I will be filing for severance." With that, there was another chorus of agreement, all the attorneys save one falling over each other to distance themselves from their co-defendants. Only Mitch Schapira, who represented Larry Gentry, had a divergent take.

"I do not join in the motion to sever," Schapira declared. "I am very concerned. I have an innocent client in jail. I do not want to lose his right to a speedy trial. I don't want to join anyone else."

From that point on, there was a clamoring. Hands waving. Demands articulated. The first order of business would be the Motion to Ban Electronic Media. Judge Greene scheduled it for two weeks out. That would give the disputants time to file their motions. Luckily for her, that matter belonged to Judge Johnstone.

Mackay's attorneys had more pressing matters before them. They wanted their client released on bail. The State, having already experienced Mackay's history of impulsive behavior, wanted to make it more difficult for the man to leave the jailhouse. They proposed that Mackay's bail be set at $25 million cash only bail, rather than its current $10 million.

That, in turn, shifted the focus to Mackay's two investigators, David Fechheimer and Steve Goodenow. At the upcoming bail hearing, the State dearly wanted to depose Steve Goodenow about Neil Mackay's propensity for escape. David Fechheimer was equally intriguing. Beyond the fact that cops found his business card at Mackay's condo, Fechheimer had previously worked for Robert Pfeil, who hired him to investigate the circumstances of Muriel Pfeil's murder. Fechheimer did a substantial amount of work on that case, over a period of many months. He doubtless had insights into her demise.

It was about to get interesting, really interesting. Shellow had someone he wanted to depose. One Gilbert Kapualoha Pauole, Jr. And the State was not giving him up. Were, indeed, fighting to keep Junior off the deposition raceway. He was, after all, in the Federal Witness Protection Program. It was not a trivial matter to produce him. Shellow waited for his moment.

"I don't own these people," Shellow insisted, referring to Fechheimer and Goodenow. "If he wants them," he added, addressing Peter Gruenstein, "he can call me on the phone and ask."

Gruenstein did not take Shellow's response lightly. Addressing the judge, he snapped, "either he can speak to the spectators, or he can reply to the motion."

"If he'll produce Pauole, I will give him the two investigators," Shellow said after Gruenstein waded into his trap. Maybe Shellow owned the two investigators after all.

Steve Goodenow did, in fact, show up for the March 6, 1986, bail hearing. He would only address a circumscribed set of questions, everything about Majuro and nothing about anything else. Gruenstein got him to testify about Mackay's use of a false identity when he left Hawaii for the Marshall Islands. How he was using credit cards belonging to Val Galleron. How Neil Mackay got friend Jean Sullivan to stay mum on Scotty's whereabouts.

"Those," said Gruenstein, "are examples of Mr. Mackay's ability to get law-abiding people to disobey the law." When Mackay returned to Honolulu from the Marshalls, Gruenstein pointed out, he was using Val Galleron's ID.

From the witness stand, Goodenow went down the list of people who had helped hide Scotty. Goodenow testified, there was no evidence that Mackay was in contact with any of them, notwithstanding contrary evidence from the Marshall Islands. Asked when he first met Neil Mackay, court records quote Goodenow as saying, "I first met Mr. Mackay when he returned to Hawaii." Then he said something decidedly supportive of his new client.

"Mr. Mackay took Scotty to the Marshall Islands to free him from publicity," Goodenow testified. It wasn't the first time someone had sung that tune. He added, "I only spoke with Mr. Mackay briefly. He was under house arrest. He remained there. He gave us no trouble. He didn't interfere with our attempts to obtain Scotty."

Goodenow went on. "I believe Jean Sullivan was lying [about Mackay's role]. There was no evidence that Mackay put her up to it." Instead, Goodenow said, "I believed Sullivan and Cotting were hiding Scotty. I became very confused. I felt they were violating court orders. Then I found out that Jean Sullivan was 'on her way to help me.'"

At the end of the bail hearing, Peter Gruenstein argued that Mackay was "an extraordinary flight risk" because he has "more money to flee with than anyone I have ever prosecuted."

Shellow countered that the $10 million bail was double the net worth reported in Mackay's then 10-year-old financial statement. Shellow added that facts surrounding Mackay's flight with Scotty in 1978 had been misrepresented and that Mackay was preparing to return voluntarily to Alaska when he was arrested in Hawaii for contempt of court.

Shellow further argued that the state's case against Mackay for Robert Pfeil's murder was weak and unlikely to result in his client's conviction. The chief prosecution witness, Gilbert Pauole, he insisted, had committed perjury at least four times in the past. The grand jury that charged Mackay was not told about these previous perjuries.

"If Pauole was here, the Court could see his demeanor," Shellow insisted. "This Court could believe he was lying. He would appear to the court that he was lying." The defense attorney was not finished. "Had the grand jury known factors concerning Mr. Pauole's credibility, the grand jury might not have indicted."

By the end of the bail hearing, Judge Greene only agreed to take the matter of Neil Mackay's bail under advisement. Then, on March 14, 1986, she released her decision. It was not a win for the State. Nor was it a complete win for Neil Mackay. But a win it was.

If Mackay could find a 24-hour custodian, post $700,000 cash and a secure bonding for $6.3 million, he could leave the Sixth Avenue Jail. Neil Mackay did not post bail. It would be a long time before he did.

40

Honolulu, Hawaii; Seattle, Washington; December – July 1986

THE BUSIEST MAN IN THE HOMICIDE DIVISION, by air miles flown, was the chain-smoking, Rolaids guzzling, coffee swizzling Inv. Joseph B. Austin. An eight-and-a-half-year veteran of the force, he'd been named Police Officer of the Month in 1979 for his "consistent high standard of performance as a patrol officer." By 1986, he'd made Homicide Sergeant. A father of one, widowed at 41, he'd remarried and then divorced. Fellow officers knew the 45-year-old by his bushy white moustache.

The son of an electronics engineer in the U.S. Civil Service, he grew up moving from country to country and state to state. He'd learned to make friends quickly. It was a skill that came in handy.

His first flight was on January 22, 1986. To Honolulu.

When Austin and Grimes arrived at the Ilikai Hotel on January 23rd, they were after the current resident of Unit #709. Her name had surfaced multiple times, across both the Ilikai and Stanford Drive searches. Mrs. Phyllis B. Forman agreed to meet them in the lobby. Her first words came by way of a denial. Asked by Sgt. Grimes if she had a phone number at the Ilikai she replied, "I have a phone number there, but it's not listed, and I don't want to give it out. It's not my phone to give out, it's not my privilege to . . ."

"Were you aware that you're listed as a corporate officer on several of Neil Mackay's businesses?" Grimes broke in.

"I signed some paper or something, but I don't know what, I don't know what it was I really don't, it was something, didn't mean anything to me," she replied blandly. "Papers like that don't mean anything to me, absolutely nothing, in my position it means nothing . . . I was working as a salesclerk or something at the time, didn't really matter to me."

She was, in fact, listed as a corporate officer on several Mackay businesses. Listed on the Board of Directors. Listed as a secretary. She'd signed a Power of Attorney document for one corporation, handing control back to Neil Mackay. Her name was on deposit slips made out to Honolulu Federal Savings. Phyllis Forman was entrenched.

She'd known Neil Mackay, she said, for fourteen years. She was "a friend, just a friend." A friend who didn't seem to know anyone in Mackay's circle. She didn't know Muriel. Met Barbara Homay once. Didn't know Barbara's brother, Frank. Didn't know Virginia Zawacki. Didn't know Gilbert Pauole. Did know Jean Sullivan but didn't know where she was. The last she saw Neil Mackay, she told them, was in the lobby. The day he was arrested.

"OK, did you have any conversation with him?" Austin wondered.

"No," she insisted. "Only but I was frantic 'cause I was trying to get an apartment over there, and only just on my way that I was trying to get an apartment at the Tradewinds, and I didn't know if I could."

She also admitted to watching over Scotty when he was in the fifth grade. Talked about him with his father. Said she visited Mackay while he was in jail. Admitted, after being shown a list, that she'd seen some of the corporate names on files "up there in the apartment."

As the hour stretched toward 10 a.m. the cops were running out of questions. Forman was evasive. Noncommittal. A blank. Grimes hit her with one last dart.

"OK," he asked, "do you know if Scotty was ever aware that his mother had been murdered?"

"That was never discussed, never discussed," Forman shuddered. "No, nothing was ever discussed in that. What a cruel thing to say."

IN MARCH, JOE AUSTIN GOT A CALL FROM SEATTLE. A call from Junior Pauole's estranged wife. Over Thanksgiving, Melanie Pauole had gone into her recipe box, looking for a holiday recipe. There, on the top shelf, was something unexpected. A note. A typed note. She'd worried over it. Then worried some more. Now, she was calling to tell Austin what she'd found.

At the top of a torn sheet of notebook paper were two typed lines, Melanie told him. The first said, "Robt. P. Pfeil." The second said, "3706 North Point Dr." Five lines below that were two more phrases, also typed. "Mrs. Muriel Pfeil" on the first line, "618 I (eye) street" on the second. The typist skipped another two lines and then typed, "P.O. Box 1664—main post office downtown."

Just below that were three handwritten lines. Age 57. 6'6. 180. Melanie told Austin something else. She was being followed. There were incidents with a car that seemed to shadow her. Subtly threatened her. No, she said, she had no idea how the note got into her recipe box.

Sgt. Austin directed her to send it to him, at once.

The provenance of that note depended on Gilbert Kapualoha Pauole, Jr. It was no easy feat to contact the man. He was subject to the whims of the Federal Witness Protection Program. Requests had to be made. Permissions had to be granted. Arrangements had to be negotiated. Finally, after much back and forth, they were able to talk.

"Gilbert Pauole, Jr. told me," Austin ultimately wrote, "that the document which includes the typed name and address of Robert Pfeil, was given to him in Honolulu, Hawaii by Neil S. Mackay sometime prior to the summer of 1985 for the purpose of facilitating the homicide of Robert Pfeil."

That's not all they had. There was another document, one seized in the search on Stanford Drive. A typed letter about Scotty. An unsigned letter, apparently typed by Neil Mackay, with a cryptic first line that read, "Encl the orig of ltr to Scotty from Mrs Murphy." Austin sent both letters to Jan Beck, "Examiner of Questioned Documents," in Seattle.

Beck examined the two documents. Said that both appeared to have been typed by a Smith Corona typewriter and looked to have been typed on the same machine. On June 9, 1986, Austin met with Beck in Seattle, at his fifth-floor office in the historic Arctic Building.[40] Showed him a photograph from their first search of the Mackay's Ilikai residence. It showed a blue typewriter. Beck told Austin that the typewriter in the photograph appeared to be a Smith Corona Electric, possibly Model Number 315.

He was that kind of expert.

---

40 In 1936, a politician had used that same fifth floor to jump from his campaign office. His body struck the pavement directly in front of a car occupied by his wife.

Honolulu, Hawaii, July 15-18, 1986

THE NEXT TIME JOE AUSTIN LANDED in Honolulu was July 15, 1986. He picked up Phyllis Forman at her place of employment, within shouting distance of the Ala Wai golf course, and drove straight to the Ilikai. In the lobby he showed her that same photo, the one with a two-tone blue portable typewriter, sitting on the dining room table of #709. Asked if the typewriter was hers, she said "No, it is Neil Mackay's." Yes, she added, it was still in the apartment. He wanted to seize it, but that required a search warrant. He would wait.

The next morning, Austin paid a visit to a man named Bill "Jo-Jo" Reuter. A friend of Junior's, he was a logical person to ask about rumors of a second murder plot. Which was why Austin asked Reuter about an alleged conversation in the summer of 1985. One in which another associate was claimed to have lined up a hit job for Gilbert Pauole in Seattle or the Portland, Oregon, area. Reuter said it was possible but could not recall specifically discussing the subject.

Austin also asked Reuter if he had been involved in any illegal activities outside of transporting drugs to Alaska. Reuter insisted that he had not. Jo-Jo did admit that, in June or July of 1985, he borrowed $200 from Neil Mackay. To put that in context, Reuter added that he'd asked Mackay for advice in setting up his security company—based on Reuter's ranking as a martial arts expert. Said that he also talked to Mackay about teaching Scotty self-defense. Part of that conversation hinged on what Reuter described as Neil Mackay's abiding fear that Robert Pfeil was still trying to kidnap his son.

At first glance, it looked like another attempt to butter up to a man with well-known obsessions. If that was extortion, it was extortion lite. In the end, Jo-Jo Reuter was not much help one way or the other.

It took another day to get the search warrant. At least there were some perks. Austin was at the Waikiki Village Hotel, just a half block from the beach. It featured the Underwater View Bar and was a just a five-minute walk from the Ilikai.

When Sgt. Austin finally arrived at Neil Mackay's condo on July 17th, he was accompanied by Investigators David Sommers and Richard Lee of the Honolulu Organized Crime Strike Force. The time was 4:36 p.m. Phyllis

Forman answered the door, but she was not alone. Scotty Mackay, now 13, was there. So was his temporary guardian, Barbara Homay. Scotty slunk away; Homay kept her eye on their every move. Inv. Sommers ignored Homay. Presented Forman with a certified copy of the search warrant. Phyllis Forman pointed to a living room table and the typewriter, covered by a white piece of plastic. Investigator Lee took multiple photos, then seized the machine.

Joe Austin was not finished. He turned to Barbara Homay. Told her he wanted to talk to her. Wanted to take a statement. Then watched as she cloaked herself in avoidance. Homay told him she would have to talk to her attorney first. Told Austin he would have to submit a list of questions. Said she would consider answering them. Homay promised to call him before noon the following day. Promised she'd give him her answer. Hers was a boilerplate response with Neil Mackay's fingerprints all over them.

The next morning, Joe Austin dawdled into the Kaimuki Typewriter Service in Honolulu. Mackay's typewriter contained a service tag from the shop. Austin figured he'd ask shop owner Richard Sugano to check his service records. He wanted to know if there'd been any recent work on the machine. Sugano found none.

With that, Austin packaged Neil Mackay's typewriter and air freighted it to Jan Beck in Seattle. Then, on the afternoon of July 18, 1986, he caught a return flight to Anchorage. Barbara Homay never called him back.

41

Anchorage, Alaska, 1950s

NEIL S. MACKAY'S CLAIM THAT HE COULD NOT get a fair trial in Alaska had a long, tortuous history. Casual observers could point to his fractious divorce from Muriel Pfeil. That one cost him three-quarters of a million dollars. Or the convoluted court labyrinth he navigated to wrest control of Scotty from Robert and Marianne Pfeil. That cost him another half million. Or the persistent rumors that he'd killed his wife. Neil Mackay's antipathy toward Alaska's criminal justice system had a much longer history.

It went back, in fact, to the mid-1950s. It was his Rosebud moment. Or, since Neil S. Mackay rarely did anything halfway, his Rosebud moments.

When Neil Mackay arrived in Alaska in 1951, he had a metal plate in his head and twenty-eight years of tribulations. "He always missed his father," Dave Talbot told journalist Sheila Toomey. His stepfather, a railroad boss whom his mother married several years after his father's untimely death, "was not kind to him," Talbot added. "Let's say the discipline was brutal."

"Neil told me one time that's how he learned how to swim, by getting baptized so often," Talbot continued. "Neil's mother would have him baptized in this little fundamentalist church . . . but Neil would backslide, and Neil's stepfather would give him a whipping and Neil's mother would take and get him baptized again."

In high school, Mackay helped support the family by driving an ambulance for the local undertaker. The survivors went to the hospital; the remainder went to the mortuary. When World War II came crashing into Yermo, California's reality, Mackay tried to enlist. His Canadian citizenship was a barrier. He joined the Navy, which shifted him to a training position in the Marines. He never saw combat; his metal plate resulted from a jeep accident on base.

When he arrived in Anchorage with wife Barbara and a law degree from Southwestern Law School, he was intent on leaving all that behind. He did not immediately pursue a law career, instead taking a job at the First National Bank of Anchorage. As a Vice President in charge of the loan portfolio. It was there that he learned the ins and outs of foreclosures and how to land buildings at cut-rate prices from stressed investors. He became an aggressive real estate speculator.

It wasn't until the mid-50s that Mackay decided to take the Alaska State Bar Exam. Like other budding lawyers, he traveled to Juneau to take the test. At the conclusion of the exam, all the would-be lawyers gathered for food and drinks. It was then that the Attorney General, J. Gerald Williams, joined them. There was conversation and anticipation—at that time, the AG had the power to pass or fail each applicant.

According to an APD interview with long-time banker and attorney Gordon Hartlieb, who was among the individuals who'd taken the Bar Exam that year, it was during this convocation that Neil Mackay approached then-AG Williams. Their conversation did not go well. The two started fighting and had to be separated by other attendees. It was Hartlieb's belief, according to court records, that Neil Mackay failed the Bar Exam that year.

It was an inauspicious debut into Alaska's fledgling legal culture. Alaska was still a territory. Statehood was a half-decade away.[41] The rules were still half-formed.

Undeterred—and just plain stubborn—Mackay took the bar exam again in 1954. He quit his job at the bank, purchased a building on Fourth Avenue in Anchorage and opened an undertaking business. Admitted to the bar in 1955, he opened a law office in the same building.

---

41 Much of the historical information covered here is based on Pamela Cravez's landmark research into Alaska's territorial legal culture. Her book, The Biggest Damn Hat, is required reading for anyone interested in the development of Alaska's post-statehood legal institutions.

He was headed for trouble.

One of Mackay's contacts from his banking days was a woman named Mary Hill. A sixty-eight-year-old Finn, with no schooling, limited English language skills and sparse business sense, she was widely known as a spendthrift; in the first few years of their acquaintance, Mary and her husband, a Finnish miner named John Hill, managed to squander a cash fund of $80,000.[42] She was more than willing to sign promissory notes for friends and acquaintances, a practice Mackay urged her to abandon.

When John Hill died in 1956, it was Neil Mackay who took care of the funeral arrangements. He also took on the role of Mary's financial and legal counselor. Not one to go through life alone, by March 1957 Mary had married Herman Keno, another Finnish miner she had known since 1940. Neil Mackay considered Keno highly unpredictable; seven or eight times he had to bail him out of jail and pay his fines. Mary herself apparently came to agree, filing for divorce from Keno in November 1960.

But not before she and Herman had gone to Neil Mackay and made a business deal. Mary had acquired several properties near downtown Anchorage, and she asked Neil Mackay to sell one of them. She felt it was worth $40,000. Neil and Barbara agreed to pay her $1,000 up front and $150 a month for life. They signed the deal in 1957 and, within months, the Mackays sold the lot to the National Bank of Alaska for $25,000.

By 1959 Mary and her new husband came to Mackay's office and said they wanted a cash settlement. Up to that point, Mackay had paid them $4,950. He agreed to buy them out for $10,000 cash if they would throw in a mortgage note they held on another property, worth about $4,000. They agreed. Neil Mackay would ultimately make $7,500 on the deal.

Some time prior to these negotiations, Mackay began having "problems with the Grievance Committee" of the bar association. Someone had filed a complaint against him concerning the Mary Hill Keno transaction of January 9, 1957. The charge before him was misconduct "by cheating or over-reaching a client." The recommendation then went to the full board, which rejected the committee's decision. There would be no disbarment.

---

42 John Hill's given name was Johan Korkeamoti, which loosely translates to High Moth in Finnish. $80,000 in 1956 was equivalent to $800,000 in 2021.

The matter sat until the Alaska Supreme Court, in a fight with the nascent Alaska State Bar Association, seized the Bar Association's assets and records, including the Mackay file. On September 24, 1959, Mackay, represented by attorneys Wendell Kay and Dave Talbot, appeared before the Supreme Court for a hearing on the old disciplinary case. On examining the matter, the Supreme Court reached an entirely different conclusion about Mackay's disbarment.

"We are of the firm opinion that the respondent, Neil S. Mackay, has manifested by his conduct in his dealings with his client, Mary Hill Keno, complete lack of comprehension or appreciation of the duties and responsibilities resting upon one in his position and as a member of the legal profession. We find him unfit to continue as a member of the profession and as an officer of the courts of Alaska. The facts being as they were in this case, we feel that the six-month suspension recommended by the trial committee is entirely inadequate and that the misconduct of the respondent calls for his disbarment.

"We, therefore, order that he be disbarred and that his name be stricken from the roll of attorneys of the State of Alaska, effective thirty days after the filing of this opinion." As Pamela Cravez trenchantly notes, "Neil Mackay was probably one of the wealthiest lawyers in Anchorage."[43] The Alaska Supreme Court's decision was, in this context, unsparing.

If there was a silver lining, the federal court continued to allow Neil Mackay to practice before its bench. Eventually, the state court issued a revised version of the Mackay case, reversing its original decision. Neil Mackay was reinstated, with one proviso. That proviso was birthed by an inquiry about Mary Hill Keno, who was then a resident of the Woodhaven Rest Home.[44]

August 6, 1964

Mr. Ernest Rehbock Trustee for the Alaska Bar Association 941 Fourth Avenue Anchorage, Alaska Re: Mary Hill Keno

---

43 Ibid, Pamela Cravez, *The Biggest Damn Hat*

44 Mary Hill Keno died less than a year after the complaint, at age 76. Herman Keno died in Hope, Alaska, in 1970, at the age of 72. Mary's obituary listed Herman as her survivor and husband.

Dear Mr. Rehbock:

We are presently attempting to obtain satisfaction of the State of Alaska's claim against Mary Hill Keno. Mrs. Keno is presently a recipient of state aid. Over six thousand dollars ($6,000) in assistance has already been granted her.

Our investigation in this case indicates that the attorney who represented Mrs. Keno on matters involving her property may have taken advantage of his relationship with Mrs. Keno and may have defrauded her of an unknown amount of property. Mrs. Keno is known to have been wealthy at one time. Our investigation discloses that the attorney involved was prosecuted by the Alaska Bar Association in 1959 for his actions in connection with the property of Mrs. Keno.

We would like to obtain the records of the proceedings before the Alaska Bar Association in order to determine whether the state may have an action to set aside a fraudulent conveyance of Mrs. Keno's property. Our files indicate that Mr. Neil Mackay was Mrs. Keno's attorney in this case.

Very truly yours,
WARREN C. COLVER ATTORNEY GENERAL

Neil Mackay's reinstatement turned on a $7,500 repayment to Mary Hill Keno. That decision was itself soon suspended, as Mackay appealed to the U.S. Supreme Court. Ultimately a newly formed Alaska State Supreme Court agreed that his suspension was excessive and cleared Mackay's name.

It was too late.

As Mackay's friend, lawyer, and former State Attorney General Edgar Paul Boyko told *Alaska Daily News* reporter Sheila Toomey, the Alaska Supreme Court had "ruthlessly, brutally" targeted Mackay. "It's a black stain on Alaskan justice," Boyko opined. "I think that kind of started Neil on a spiral down and he's never been quite right since."

42

Anchorage & Fairbanks, Alaska, March 1986 – August 1987

WITH A JUDGE, PROSECUTORS AND A BEVY of defense lawyers lined up, the trials for Robert Pfeil's alleged assassins could finally begin. It was a three-tiered cake, each with its own demographic. This was the American criminal justice system in microcosm.

At the lowest level were the four co-defendants with no resources. Tyoga Closson. Larry Gentry. Robert Betts. John Bright. Of necessity, they were represented by a rough combination of public defenders and private attorneys. Their lawyers were all seasoned professionals, who would strenuously argue for their clients. They were also up against terrible odds, in part because several of them, taking steps to save their own skin, had worn wires and provided damning evidence against their co-conspirators.

At the middle tier was Gilbert "Junior" Pauole. His one piece of luck was that he had an experienced attorney at the earliest stages, one who'd served as an assistant U.S. Attorney. Richard Kibby helped draft a cooperation agreement that promised to hold up against the exigencies of a contract murder case. The charges and negotiated sentence that Junior faced had not, in fact, changed when Bob Pfeil died. Junior Pauole continued to be held on charges of attempted first-degree murder. The continued viability of that deal made Junior the focus of many a defense argument.

And then there was Neil S. Mackay. The accused ringleader had done well for himself. James Shellow's first comments about the case were a shot across the prosecution's bow. "From what I've learned so far," he proclaimed, “there are serious, serious inequities involved here.” Ever the shrewd strategist, he declined to elaborate on his complaints. No matter. Mackay’s team had already made an auspicious debut, thanks to their success in getting Judge Greene to grant their client continued jailhouse access to a typewriter and tape recorder.

There was a sense, too, that James Shellow had a healthy view of his own courtroom prowess. At a Canadian hearing, the Milwaukeean was asked his views about electronic media in the courtroom. His reply?

“I like it there. Why? Because I can manipulate it. I can manipulate witnesses. I can manipulate jurors. I can manipulate the judge. I can manipulate the prosecutor. I’ve been in a courtroom a long, long time and every time a variable is introduced, whether it’s the camera or whether it’s an automobile or whether it’s 200 pounds of cocaine on the table, anything that provides another variable can be manipulated by someone who’s had experience in the courtroom and I’m usually in a courtroom with persons who have had less experience than I.”

The demands of the Mackay case were daunting. Travel from Shellow’s home base in Wisconsin was no picnic. The complexities of the case were worse, with a decade’s worth of animosity and bad faith between Neil Mackay and the Pfeil family. By August 1986, Shellow added trial and appellate attorney James McComas to Mackay’s defense team. A Harvard Law graduate, McComas had risen to Chief of the Trial Division at the Public Defender Service in Washington, D.C., before returning to Milwaukee and private practice in 1986. An imposing but affable presence in the courtroom, his posture always perfect, it didn’t hurt that, with his full beard and wire-framed classes, he looked like a perfect fit for the Alaskan legal community.[45]

ONE OF THE FIRST TASKS OF NEIL MACKAY’S DEFENSE TEAM was to swat away the persistent rumors that he’d killed Muriel Pfeil. That was one of the reasons they’d hired Fechheimer and Goodenow. These two brought an immediate advantage. First, as members of the defense team, they could not be forced to testify against Neil Mackay. There were two added benefits. Goodenow’s knowledge of Hawaiian crime figures was unparalleled.

45 Indeed, after the Mackay case, McComas and his wife moved to Alaska, where McComas successfully practiced criminal law for a number of years.

David Fechheimer, in working Muriel's case, had befriended Anchorage detectives. He did, in fact, know a few things. In combination, their efforts served to rebuff any effort to introduce Muriel Pfeil's murder into the Robert Pfeil trial.

"The police investigation was thorough," the defense declared knowingly. "Mr. Mackay was interviewed on numerous occasions by police investigators. At least seventeen different suspects are referred to in the portion of the police reports which have been made available to the defense through state-initiated discovery.

"While some of these seventeen individuals or entities conceivably could have been working at the at the behest of another, Mr. Mackay was not the only individual or entity identified by the police as potentially responsible for the death of Muriel Pfeil."

Mackay's defense went through the litany of other targets or perpetrators. Judge Karl Johnstone. Joachim Peiper. Louis Edward Dickinson—or his wife. The mysterious $15,000 in cash transaction at an Anchorage restaurant within six days of Muriel Pfeil's death. The two mentally ill men who gave false confessions. The bar owner of the Baronof Lounge. There was also the notion that the bomb that killed Muriel Pfeil was meant for a female reporter investigating corruption in the Fairbanks Teamsters organization. Even Robert Pfeil came under their microscope.

"Robert Pfeil initiated a private investigation in an effort to establish what he repeatedly said he believed: that Mr. Mackay was responsible for Muriel's death," defense attorneys noted. "Robert Pfeil's investigation resulted in no evidence connecting Mr. Mackay to the death of Muriel Pfeil.

Indeed, on the last occasion that Pfeil met with Fechheimer, the investigator reported that there was no evidence that he could find connecting Mackay to the murder. Pfeil then asked Fechheimer whether or not he had any theories as to who might be responsible for his sister's death, and Fechheimer replied that he did have such a theory. He told Robert Pfeil that he believed Pfeil had arranged the death of his sister.

"Robert Pfeil's response was 'I was wondering when you'd get around to that.'" the defense affidavit continued. "Robert Pfeil did not use Mr. Fechheimer's services after this meeting."

Robert Pfeil fired the guy. The State's response was terse.

"Mackay has misstated the evidence that exists," they said in rejoinder. "For example, Joachim Peiper, the notorious SS commander, sold Muriel Pfeil a car. Muriel's own sister was closer to him than Muriel was. With the sole exception of Mackay, the police never turned up anyone with a convincing motive to kill Muriel. Karl Johnson did not assert that the bomb was intended for him. The news reporter does not now think that the bomb was intended for her; she had a different color Volvo of a much older vintage, and she would park all around the parking lot, while Muriel parked in one particular spot."

The battle for truth—always at a premium—was now at full throttle. Shellow's approach was well-documented. His strategy at Wounded Knee was to put the state on the defensive. In taking on the FBI, he once got copies of FBI license plates and reported them to the newspapers and police as suspicious. He held a barely restrained contempt for the press, once testifying in a Canadian case that he "would certainly not be offended" if news organizations never came into court and never reported anything. "The danger of having trials reported," he contended, "is the danger that they are reported selectively."

43

Anchorage & Fairbanks, Alaska, March 1986 – August 1987

With trials set to begin, Neil Mackay's defense team went into hyperdrive. Mackay's money filled their pockets, and they were digging deep into the past. They unearthed Junior Pauole's testimony in the Frank Colacurcio racketeering trial. Scooped his testimony before the Alcoholic Beverage Control board while he ran Colacurcio's Anchorage clubs. Of course, they perused the full range of his criminal activities, starting in Hawaii: the stickups, burglaries, heroin.

They soon learned that Junior had never really stopped dealing drugs. It wasn't heroin this time. It was marijuana—most of it imported from Hawaii—and, as the 80s dawned in America, cocaine. The early 80s were, in some ways, the heyday of cocaine. With the growing sophistication of South American cartels, no place was immune from its allure. Finding Junior's drug dealing partners suddenly took on a new urgency.

Make no mistake. Mackay's defense team never wavered from their obsession with Junior Pauole. Drug dealers are easily demolished before a jury. Drug dealers who conspire in murder plots? Easier still. They would do anything and everything to repudiate Junior Pauole's very breath.

Part of that repudiation would focus on Junior's testimony in the trials to come. The best way to destroy a liar is to catch him in the act. Anything Junior said during the trials of his co-conspirators would be recorded, transcribed, and held up to scrutiny.

TYOGA CLOSSON'S MARCH 4, 1986, TRIAL FOR GUN THEFT was first on the docket. Although Closson had supplied the murder weapon for the low, low cost of a $75 rental fee, he thought his cooperation with authorities would pay off. After two days of testimony, it took the jury seven hours to convict him. Judge Greene sentenced him to an 18-month sentence. Even so, Closson's case took some strange twists.

Despite a tape-recorded confession in which Closson admitted taking the .45 pistol from the home of a local attorney, despite testimony from two eyewitnesses who saw that gun in Closson's bedroom, despite testimony from three witnesses who heard Closson admit he'd stolen the gun . . . Closson claimed he was lying when he made that confession.

He insisted he was instead trying to protect his girlfriend, Joanne Harris, whom he claimed had actually stolen the gun. He went further. Closson told jurors that it was Harris who wanted him to trade the weapon for the half gram of cocaine. He insisted he had innocently accepted the gun from Harris and put it in his car after showing it to co-defendant Robert Betts. Then, Closson claimed, the gun "came up missing."

"Call him a fool in love," defense attorney Rex Butler told the jury as he backed up Closson's tall tale. "Maybe that's the crime he committed, but he did not steal the gun."

It got worse. Asked to explain these discrepancies, Closson said that Assistant D.A. Steven Branchflower had coached him to lie during an omnibus hearing for a search warrant. Mr. Closson, all of 18-years old, would soon face perjury charges.[46]

NEXT UP WAS 33-YEAR-OLD LARRY GENTRY WHO, like Tyoga Closson, thought his cooperation with investigators would spare him criminal charges. He was, in fact, the last conspirator to be charged. It took Robert Pfeil's death to turn the screw on Mr. Gentry. The prosecution could not let that pass.

Gentry's trial began a little more than two weeks after Tyoga Closson's conviction. Special prosecutor Peter Gruenstein began by reading a letter from co-defendant Robert Betts claiming Gentry and John Bright agreed to shoot Bob Pfeil to pay off cocaine debts. Gentry had received, the prosecution alleged, $3,000—all of which went to pay off his drug debt to Junior Pauole.

46 Closson was found guilty and sentenced to two-years on the perjury charge.

"That's what Robert Pfeil's life was worth to Larry Gentry," Gruenstein proclaimed.

Gentry's defense attorney countered that, while his client may have known something was amiss, he never intended for the assassination to occur. With Gilbert Pauole a witness in waiting, attorney Mitch Schapira made sure the jury knew the real culprit. It was not his client. It was not Larry Gentry.

"Gilbert Pauole is a pimp who has spent his life manipulating people," Schapira maintained, claiming he suckered people into doing things they would not do normally. Schapira piled on with colorful images. By bringing Junior Pauole to the stand, Schapira said, the prosecution "is going to take us on a glass-bottom boat ride through the sewers of Anchorage."

Three days later all eyes were on the man who'd caused so many whispers.

There were two things about Junior Pauole on the witness stand. First was the unmistakable presence of the armed U.S. Marshall at his side, his eyes swiveling like a hawk. Second was Pauole himself. He was a balding, bearded presence, slightly paunchy, smaller than his outsized reputation. When he spoke, his voice had the lilt of Hawaiian pidgin, but it was emotionless, always emotionless.

Gilbert Pauole testified over several days. Gruenstein began by having him describe how this plot came into being. "I want to ask you," Gruenstein asked, "about the time that Mr. Mackay asked you specifically to help with his problems he was having."

"At the Mackay Building," Junior said matter-of-factly, "we had a meeting in the evening there, and he asked me—he told me that he had a problem, and he took care of it, and he has a problem now, and if I could take care of it. And I asked exactly what did he mean, and I already had a feeling what he meant. And he told me that he wanted to get rid of his brother-in-law."

As the days wore on, Larry Gentry was moved closer to the center, a position he—and his attorney—disdained. "He was always part of it," Gilbert Pauole insisted of Larry Gentry's role in the plot to kill Robert Pfeil. "I always kept contact with Larry through this whole thing to see what was becoming of it."

Nothing that Pauole said illustrated this more clearly, according to the prosecution, than when John Bright—frustrated by his difficulty pinning down Robert Pfeil's schedule—turned to sleeping all day. Exasperated that Bright wasn't stalking his quarry, Pauole nagged Larry Gentry. Larry nagged John Bright. The ambush happened only days later.

Just before Junior left the stand, though, there was a rare touch of levity. Mitch Schapira was taking a side road, trying to suggest why Gilbert Pauole was so willing to throw his longtime friend and colleague under the bus. Wasn't it because Gilbert Pauole was jailed and facing 20 years in prison because of Larry Gentry? "Vengeance is enough of a motive for you to want to get back at someone," Schapira insinuated.

"I'm not a vengeful man," Pauole responded, deadpan.

"Not a tiny, little, itsy, bitsy bit?" Schapira wondered.

"I don't hate him," Junior replied. "If I never see Larry again it will be too soon. But, no, I don't hate him."

The jurors laughed. It was spontaneous. Almost nervous. Quickly suppressed. Gilbert Pauole bulldozed their mirth. "He was just as involved as I was," Pauole told Schapira. "We both put this contract together."

After a month-long trial, Larry Gentry's fate was bound over to the jury. They found Larry Gentry guilty of first-degree murder. It took them a grand total of six hours to reach their decision. Larry Gentry would lose more than his freedom. His wife Susan announced she was seeking a divorce, saying at a hearing for co-defendant Robert Betts that, "I need to go on with my life."

Two months later, after much deliberation, Judge Greene sentenced the schlubby 33-year-old carpenter cum bartender to 40 years in jail, with 15 years suspended. Greene noted that Gentry had cooperated with police and had a supportive family, which "bodes well for rehabilitation."

His family vowed to appeal. They seemed to have an ace-in-the-hole. One of the jurors told his mother, Norma Gentry, that he felt uncomfortable about his guilty vote. Said he felt pressured when he was the only one still arguing for a second-degree murder charge. Gentry's attorneys were poised to ask for an acquittal or new trial, based on juror misconduct.

It was a longshot.

Now twenty-years-old, Robert Betts had, perhaps, the cleverest defense of all. He would claim, as he always had, that when he signed on to be John Bright's driver, he had no clue as to Bright's true intentions. Even in his initial statements to police, Betts claimed that his co-defendant had, according to court documents, "been hired to rough-up or scare Robert Pfeil."

In pre-trial hearings his attorney, Fred Dewey—who had once represented convicted serial killer Robert Hansen—argued that his client should not be tried in the first place, owing to an alleged immunity agreement offered for his cooperation. According to Dewey, the police had even intimated promises of reward money and a new identity. Betts, Dewey said, was nothing more than a naïve pawn in a deadly game played by people far more sophisticated than he.

"You will hear from Betts that—while in the car—the intention was not to kill, but to assist Bright to intimidate Pfeil by order of a union boss by shooting into the car engine," Dewey claimed during his opening argument. "All that really matters is what Mr. Betts intended to do."

In Dewey's telling, Robert Betts was just the "guy from the pool hall." Betts did his best to look the part. He sat impassive, occasionally pursing his lips. Sometimes he rested a closed right hand thoughtfully on his chin. The long hair he sported at the beginning of the trial soon evolved into a more business-like cut. He did not testify in his own defense.

The problem was, once more, those pesky police recordings. That, and Betts' own words to police investigators. There were juicy quotes.

"You knew exactly what I was going to do with the gun," he told Ty Closson. When police asked if he knew Bright was going to shoot Robert Pfeil, Betts replied. "I had an idea he was going to." At another point during that same interview, Betts claimed he knew maybe four minutes before the shooting that Bright intended to kill their intended victim. The prosecution claimed otherwise.

"He may not have known the motive, but he did know the purpose," Gruenstein said of Betts. "He did it for money and excitement."

There was another kind of excitement when Gilbert Pauole took the stand. There were few spectators—save defense attorneys—to hear it, but in the spectator box sat Grandma Pfeil. She had come to see these men who had decided it was okay to shoot and kill her son.

Wearing a stylish glen-plaid business suit, her white hair swept upwards, the matriarch of the Pfeil clan walked slowly to the front of the courtroom and took a seat in the first row behind the prosecution table. Marianne Pfeil, and her two daughters, filed into a nearby row.

Junior Pauole, predictably, testified about Neil Mackay and, of course, the murder plot. Gruenstein asked him how many times they'd discussed the contract on Robert Pfeil's life. "And I don't mean an exact number," Gruenstein said, "but one occasion, a lot of times, what?"

"More than I can count," Pauole maintained, his voice soft, steady, hovering on boredom.

Grandma Pfeil would notice. At the close of the day's testimony, she relayed her impressions *to Anchorage Daily News r*eporter Sheila Toomey, telling her it was unlikely she would return. "I get sick just thinking about it," the elder Pfeil said. "To see him (Pauole) for the first time, and to see that boy (Betts). He didn't seem to have any feeling. He just sat there and rocked. No, I don't want to see them at all."

Robert Betts was in a chair next to the jury box as closing arguments began. He seemed relaxed as Peter Gruenstein said he was not very smart, that he was cold-blooded and without remorse for what he'd done, showing not a whit of sympathy for his victim. "This is not the world's greatest execution," Gruenstein said. "This is not going to make the annals of organized crime."

The jury began deliberations the next day. It took them six hours to reach a verdict. Robert Betts was guilty as charged. First-degree murder. They used his own words against him. Judge Greene sentenced him to 50 years.

Robert Betts, too, would appeal his conviction. Once more, there was that pesky issue of immunity agreements, real or implied. Betts contended the validity of any immunity agreement was for a jury to determine. Judge Greene ruled otherwise. The Alaska Court of Appeals would have to decide.[47]

HAD GILBERT PAUOLE NOT REACHED AN AGREEMENT with the State, he would have been the next-to-the-last conspirator to be tried. The honor of going last was reserved for Neil S. Mackay. John Ian Arthur Bright, the

47 The Court of Appeals ruled against Betts. His sentence stood.

alleged triggerman, was still awaiting his turn. Even as the Robert Betts trial began, Bright's attorney, Public Defender John Salemi, had successfully argued for a change of venue. There was too much pretrial publicity in Anchorage, Salemi argued.

Some of that pretrial publicity had come from none other than John Bright himself. There was, to begin with, his bizarre December 1985 handwritten letter to Earl Swift of *The Anchorage Times*, in which Bright claimed to have warned Robert Pfeil of the assassination plot prior to the hit.

In March 1986, Bright sued the Cook Inlet Pre-trial facility for violating his rights. It, too, got prominent press placement. "I am a pretrial detainee," he wrote, "and being subjected to the same treatment as those inmates placed were [sic] I am placed and/or housed for punishment. I have did nothing to be punished for and there was no court orders requiring me to be placed within restrictions of segregation and/or isolation."

The *coup de grace*, though, was a series of twitchy telephone conversations with Earl Swift of *The Anchorage Times*, beginning in May of 1986. They were front-page news. In them, Bright unwaveringly denied murdering Robert Pfeil. Called efforts to implicate him the product of "police ineptitude." Bright did not expect a fair trial, Swift reported. "You've got four different points of plea bargaining, is what it comes down to, or you're guilty," Bright said of criminal defenses. He ignominiously dubbed his attorney, public defender John Salemi, a "public pretender."

Bright also told Swift he was familiar with violence. "When I shoot people," he told the reporter, before catching himself. "I guess I should say, '*If* I were to shoot people,' they'd know it."

"You know when you get laid for the first time, how you really get into it and want to do it again," he added. "Well, I know this sounds incriminating, but it's like that with killing somebody, or beating them up."

"Once you get started on something like this," he admitted to Swift, "it's like drugs. You get them all animated, and then you turn off their lights. And it's kind of exciting, getting ready for it."

John Bright's trial began September 29, 1986, in Fairbanks. It took three days to seat a jury. Not because of juror prejudice but became many of the folks in the jury pool said they couldn't afford to serve the month or so the trial was expected to last. Somewhat predictably, the two sides presented diametrically opposing views of John Ian Arthur Bright. The prosecution portrayed him as a cold-blooded assassin. Defense attorney Salemi portrayed him as an innocent fall guy.

Gilbert Pauole was the inevitable villain. Salemi warned jurors that not all witnesses testifying on behalf of the state would be telling the truth. "Many have reasons to lie, covering their own involvement," he said. "Some lied because it's just natural for them to lie." Salemi added that other witnesses were testifying out of fear, threats, greed, or intimidation. One man was the cause of it all. Junior Pauole.

"He fell in with the wrong crowd," Salemi said of Bright. "But he's not a murderer."

After two weeks of testimony and twelve hours of deliberation the jury reached its decision. Escorted into the Fairbanks courtroom by three Alaska State Troopers, Bright joked as they removed his handcuffs and leg shackles. "I was kind of getting attached to them," he grinned. He also laughed and said he was "getting used to a trooper escort." He showed no surprise when the verdict was read and immediately huddled in animated conversation with defense attorney John Salemi.

John Ian Arthur Bright was guilty of murder in the first-degree. It wasn't a difficult task.

Ten months later, John Bright was back in judge Greene's courtroom. On the morning of Friday, July 31, 1987—the day of his sentencing hearing—he faced Judge Greene as a jailhouse regular, his hair long, a sleeveless sweatshirt and vest showing off his biker tattoos. In the morning, he was the biker of his dreams, his head cocked in subtle defiance, only a whisper of a grin on his face. When he returned to face the court that afternoon, he'd shorn and brushed his hair. He'd put on a dress shirt and jacket.

That's not all that had changed. John Salemi was gone, the victim of Bright's disdain and the long slog it took to get from conviction to sentencing. It was now up to Phillip Benson to plead for mercy after the prosecution's expected savaging of his client.

Give Phillip Benson credit. He was colorful in Bright's defense. He told Judge Greene that she should "consider Mr. Bright just another of the youthful punks of this maggot, Junior Pauole," enjoining her to give Bright an opportunity he'd never had. He should, Benson said, be treated like his fellow accomplices, who received less than maximum sentences. It was

"Junior Pauole that murdered Robert Pfeil . . . no matter who pulled the trigger," the defense lawyer insisted.

Judge Greene sentenced John Ian Arthur Bright to 99 years in jail. She also restricted his parole eligibility for 40 years. That meant the 23-year-old would be in his 60s before he could apply for release.

Marianne Pfeil was in the Fairbanks courtroom when Bright's sentencing came down. Asked by reporters how she felt about the result, she declared herself satisfied with the sentence. "I think justice was done. I only wish it was the last one."

"One more to go," she said. "One more to go."[48]

---

48 Many thanks to reporters Kris Capps, Rosanne Pagano, Earl Swift, Larry Campbell, Kim Rich and Sheila Toomey for their superb onsite reporting throughout the four trials revisited here. Court reporters are great; journalists add color and flair.

44

Anchorage & Fairbanks, Alaska, Fall 1987

By this point, Neil Mackay's defense team was sure they had Gilbert Kapualoha Paoule, Jr. pegged.

Junior's accusations, they noted, were the only condemnatory evidence against Neil Mackay. There was not one scintilla more. Neil Mackay's indictment, they said, "was returned upon the uncorroborated testimony of a known drug dealer, convicted felon and an acknowledged perjurer." They added that the grand jury might not have indicted their client had they known the sordid details of Junior Pauole's "work" history. What a history it was. It read like a veritable perp walk by a guy who ended up carrying a gun and wearing a bulletproof vest out of fear of his organized crime contacts. His was a résumé that screamed, "you can't trust this guy."

Pauole, they noted, committed perjury before a federal grand jury in Washington State. Committed perjury in a federal trial in Portland, Oregon, which resulted from the Washington indictment. Lied to investigators employed by the Alaska Alcohol Beverage Control (ABC) Board. Committed perjury at a hearing conducted by the Alaska Alcohol Control Board.

As the manager of Colacurcio's clubs, and erstwhile protector of the dancers, there was something unsavory about Gilbert Pauole's outlook on life. A certain coziness with the violence that accompanied that milieu. A certain casual acceptance of its realities.

Junior Pauole was a problem they could solve. That wasn't the only issue they faced. The search of Mackay's law office, for example, had turned up unmistakable signs of his relationship with Junior Pauole. The entertainment contract drafted by Mackay controlling the terms of employment for the dancers at the Good Times, one of the Colacurcio clubs that Junior managed. The check issued by the Wild Cherry to Neil Mackay. The calendar book belonging to Mackay that contained, among other things, Junior's phone numbers and, listed in Junior's personal phone diary, Neil Mackay's phone numbers. Including his private phone number—a closely guarded secret.

They could fix that, too. Call it an illegal search and seizure. Keep it out of evidence.

What they needed, though, was information that separated Mackay from Pauole. The Union angle was a start. A thorough scouring of the discovery materials from the state turned up several additional items of interest. It looked like a treasure trove. A "bingo."

The biggest "aha" came from Larry Gentry, who testified on November 2, 1985—after he decided to cooperate with police—about that planned hit in Portland, Oregon. A hit, it was alleged, that was ostensibly for the benefit of Frank Colacurcio. In Gentry's telling, Pauole told him about an informer who had helped convict Colacurcio of tax evasion, and that there were plans under way to murder the snitch.

The defense was outraged. In his grand jury testimony, they alleged, Sgt. Grimes had "deliberately omitted . . . that this was something Pauole intended to do on his own and that the putative 'beneficiary,' Colacurcio, knew nothing about it."[49]

The state already knew what it was up against. "The Defendant has resources far greater than the State," Peter Gruenstein told the court in August of 1986. "Virtually everywhere we went we discovered that the defense had been there before."

Prosecutors found other defense advantages lying in the reeds. "It is the

49 The state asserted otherwise, noting that, in his November 2 search warrant application, "Sgt. Grimes did inform Judge Stewart of this planned murder in Portland. Actually, Judge Stewart had been apprised a week earlier, through the testimony of Sgt. Grimes on October 27th, of a possible murder to be committed in Portland."

state's understanding," they wrote in response to an early defense memorandum, "that the defense resources have permitted transcripts to be prepared of many of the previous proceedings in this and the related cases involving Closson, Gentry, Betts and Bright, including in at least one case daily transcripts of trial proceedings."

With a man like private investigator Steve Goodenow on board, moreover, the defense team was able to scour Hawaii and cement Gilbert Pauole's links to organized crime. They didn't have to go far. A man named Charles Russell shared a business office with Junior's drug-running friend, Jo-Jo Reuter. Then they found Charles Stevens. These two men, Mackay's team would argue, were inexorably linked to Junior Pauole and organized crime interests in Hawaii.

The defense had everything it needed. In early August, they daylighted a "pattern of state misconduct." That was Defense 101. Later in the month, they took things to the next level. They unblinkingly argued "that Pauole arranged for the murder of Robert Pfeil as a 'favor' to Mackay or as a predicate for a later extortion attempt upon Mackay."

Where the state saw a ladder, the defense saw a stepstool.

With extortion as the exculpatory hook for Neil Mackay's defense, Charles Russell became the perfect point man. The March 30, 1978, *Honolulu Star-Bulletin* screamed the headline. *5 Mauians Arraigned on Extortion Charges.* Russell was prominently mentioned among the alleged extortionists and held by the U.S. Federal magistrate on $100,000 bail. His bail reflected the fact that he'd been convicted of armed robbery, car theft and credit card fraud in 1967 at age 21.[50]

The "good news" for the defense was that Russell—and his four co-defendants—were acquitted on the extortion charges by a local jury. It apparently made him available for the alleged Mackay extortion plot. If that wasn't enough, there was the other Charles. Charles Stevens.

In 1983, Stevens was named by the Nevada Gaming Control Board as one of three "unsavory associates" of a Las Vegas casino official indicted on federal racketeering charges. The official, Frederick Pandolfo, was charged with a skimming operation at the Stardust Hotel casino. Charles Stevens was no lightweight. He had convictions for burglary, possession of

50 Sentenced to a 40-year sentence, he was pardoned in 1970 after serving three years.

a sawed-off shotgun and federal parole violations. He'd also been named as an organized crime figure by the Honolulu City Prosecutor.

More to the point, Stevens was accused of the 1978 murder of an Oahu couple whose dismembered remains were found in a shallow grave. Convicted in 1981, the jury verdict was "mysteriously" overturned by a corrupt judge who later killed himself in a Las Vegas hotel room. Stevens was a free man. Free and presumably able to assist in the alleged Neil Mackay extortion plot.[51]

If Mackay's team wanted to develop the Union angle, just for an added flourish, there was no one better than Hawaiian gangster and convicted murderer, Henry Huihui. A former organizer for the Building Trades Council, Huihui was accused—by the president of the Hawaii State Federation of Labor, no less—of being the muscle behind organized crime attempts to take over key construction unions in the islands.

"I expect to be a target for Henry Huihui," labor president Walter H. Kapua told the *Honolulu Advertiser* on May 18, 1977. "I'll protect myself if I have to." Government authorities thought he was responsible for as many as eight killings.

The list of Hawaiian gangsters with at least a filigree of a connection to Junior's world didn't stop there.

One was a man named Ronnie Ching, who "made his bones" at the tender age of 16 and admitted to committing 20 murders. One of those murders, carried out in 1978, had Ching dragging an alleged informant from a Waikiki club and then burying him alive on a Waianae Coast beach. Ching, who weighed upwards of three hundred pounds, was just the man for the job: he sat on the burial pit until the man struggled no more.

Described as an "emotionless killing machine," he was finally arrested and confessed to a long string of murders in 1984. Court documents indicate Neil Mackay knew all about Ronnie Ching. He told Junior that Ching, "got what was coming to him . . . he played the game; he paid the price."

Then there was Charlie "Fat" Kaohu. Junior told Neil Mackay that he'd gone to prison for that man. Charlie "Fat" was among the men arrested in the massive 1969 drug raid that sent Gilbert Pauole to federal prison on federal drug charges. Charlie "Fat" was up for the same rap: authorities had him on four counts of selling heroin. Kaohu was also known as an

51 It took authorities until 1988 to rearrest Charles Stevens, albeit on drug charges.

escape artist, having once escaped the Hawaii County jail and making it as far as Maui and, on another occasion, briefly escaping the Oahu Prison.

Charlie "Fat's" brother, Alvin Kaohu, was the more infamous of the two. A reputed organized crime figure, Alvin had been charged and convicted of hiring several men to kill a Hilo, Hawaii, gambler in 1977. Alvin made the news in 1984 for unexpectedly gaining parole before completing his minimum sentence.

His parole, according to the *Honolulu Star Bulletin*, was to be served at a dairy farm run by accused murderer Gertrude Kapiolani Toledo. She'd allegedly shot her husband.

So, there it was, in all its glory. Gilbert K. Pauole was a man close to crime boss Frank Colacurcio, an organized crime figure who, according to court documents, was himself implicated in the murder of at least five associates who'd crossed him. Junior was also a man who bragged about knowing gangland figures in Hawaii. A man who'd demonstrated a brand of loyalty hardly known outside criminal circles.

The defense now had its own theory on the origins of the Robert Pfeil contract. It was all about Junior.

Nor were these the only coups delivered by defense investigators. Early in 1986, they visited a man named Loren Schaeffer. Schaeffer happened to be an Assistant Manager at the Great Alaskan Bush company, one of the many topless/bottomless strip clubs in Anchorage and a drug associate of Junior Pauole. The investigators asked him to come to their office for an interview. Schaeffer agreed. According to court documents, they talked about Gilbert Pauole. From that meeting came some explosive charges. Charges of witness intimidation by Anchorage police. Here's how Neil Mackay's defense team presented the matter in court documents:

> Loren Schaeffer [has been] subpoenaed to provide testimony for the defense in the trial of Larry Gentry. Upon learning of Schaeffer's having been subpoenaed, Investigator Michael Grimes, the lead detective on this case, threatened Schaeffer with prosecution if Schaeffer remained in Alaska and testified for the defense. Schaeffer fled.

With the union story, the extortion story and now the police intimidation story, Mackay's team had a potent mix. They were on the verge of creating an alternate reality. One in which Mackay was, indeed, only a patsy. Theirs was money well spent.

If there was a problem with any of this, though, it was that Schaeffer told authorities—in a sworn affidavit—that the Mackay's defense had it backwards. It was defense investigators who tried to intimidate him.

"I am not sure of the exact date, but sometime during February or March of 1986," Schaeffer swore in his affidavit, "I received a visit from two gentlemen, who identified themselves as investigating the Robert Pfeil murder on the side of Neil Mackay. They asked me at that time to come to their offices to give a statement. I agreed to do so.

"Within days of this first meeting, I went to their offices . . . At that time, I was asked questions about what I knew about Junior Pauole . . . Later I was confronted in my truck by the clean-shaven gentleman who had previously taken my statement at this office. At this time, he was very aggressive, intimidating and accused me of illegal conduct in a threatening fashion."

So began the charges and countercharges. For the defense, it was a criminal attempt at witness intimidation. For the prosecution, a reckless and unfounded accusation. There were, however, additional considerations.

At the top of the list were all those newspaper articles Mackay sent Junior. Articles featuring the very gangsters his defense was calling out as exculpatory. The front page of one proclaimed "Huihui associates found guilty." Another detailed the testimony of Ronnie Ching in the murder of Charles Marsland III, son of Honolulu City Prosecutor Charles Marsland Jr.

What was Mackay's fascination here? Why did he send them to Junior? For the State, at least, it was evidence of ulterior motives.

There was also the fact that Junior hadn't lived in Hawaii since 1970, when he was carted off to the McNeil Island Federal Penitentiary in Washington State. While there was no shortage of Hawaiians at McNeil, Junior had thrown in with the Italians. With Frank Colacurcio. In criminal terms, he had irrevocably switched allegiances. In Junior's telling, he was shunned by Hawaiian crime figures simply because of his Colacurcio ties. Hawaiian gangsters were fierce guardians of their turf.

That wasn't the whole cloth. Junior routinely visited Hawaii. He had friends there. His mother's tavern to visit. Larry Gentry told police that

Junior had once gone to Hawaii for a month. Gilbert Pauole readily admitted that he knew Charley "Fat."

Which was, presumably, more than enough to tar Pauole with the sins of his acquaintances. Birds of a feather and all that.

Muriel Pfeil in 1973, five months after giving birth to her son and three years before her murder. (Anchorage Daily Times photo, courtesy Anchorage Daily News)

Robert Pfeil (left), Chief Pilot, Alaska Airlines. (Anchorage Daily Times photo, courtesy Anchorage Daily News)

Device Was Located In Engine Area, Anchorage Daily Times, October 1, 1976.
(Anchorage Daily Times photo, courtesy Anchorage Daily News)

Neil Mackay, left, listens to his attorney, James Shellow, during an Anchorage court hearing in February 1986. (Copyright Anchorage Daily News; photo credit: Jim Lavrakas)

Robert Pfeil on his back porch after rescuing two boys from Campbell Lake's thin ice.
(Courtesy Anchorage Daily News; photo credit: Jim Lavrakas)

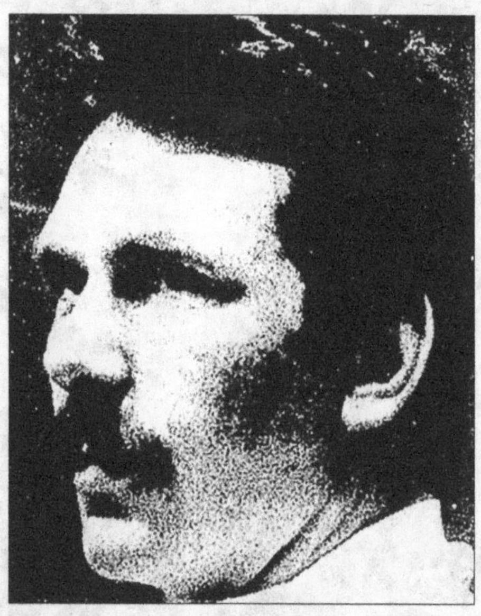

Left: Gilbert "Junior" Pauole in a Fairbanks courtroom for the Neil Mackay murder trial, guarded by a U.S. Marshall. (Courtesy Anchorage Daily News; photo: Bob Hallinen)
Right: John Bright, convicted killer of Robert Pfeil.
(Anchorage Daily Times file photo, courtesy Anchorage Daily News)

Steve Goodenow, Scotty Mackay, and Jean Sullivan in Honolulu after Scotty's rescue in Micronesia. (Courtesy Honolulu Star-Advertiser; photo credit: Ron Jett)

today is food day

• Best buys, SECTION F

• Executive dining room recipes, page F-1

The Honolulu Advertiser

Home Edition

Aloha!

Hawaii

The Nation

Washington

The World

People

Money Matters

Sports

The Index

Death bill all but dead now

Here's Scotty but wherever does it end?

Their role here is small — so far

yakuza in Hawaii

Alaska State Trooper Jeff Willis stands ready with a shotgun as he guards a car taking Gilbert Pauole from Superior Court in Fairbanks. Pauole lies on the floor in the back seat of the car. (Copyright Anchorage Daily News; photo credit: Jim Lavrakas)

45

Honolulu, Hawaii; Chino Valley, Arizona; Indio, California; Palm Desert, California, Ironwood Estates, Arizona; November 1986 – January 1987

When Jan Beck wrote Sgt. Joe Austin in late 1986, he said the note found in Melanie Pauole's recipe box was "very probably typed" on a Smith-Corona typewriter. Not just any Smith-Corona. Neil Mackay's Smith-Corona.

"My conclusion(s)," he wrote, "are based on the following features of the typewriting being the same in the questioned and known samples: typestyle, spacing, damaged characters, misaligned characters, and unevenly printed characters. There are no significant differences between the samples in these features.

"In addition, I have examined the actual typefaces on the machine in question and confirmed that the damages to the typefaces found in the questioned and known samples are also present on the machine itself."

One letter—that torn sheet of notebook paper from Melanie Pauole—irrevocably tied Neil Mackay to Junior and, ultimately, to Robert Pfeil.

Mackay's defense team was already on it, having submitted a 159-page consolidated motion to suppress evidence as far back as September of '86. In it, they argued that every item seized at both the Ilikai and Stanford Drive locations should be tossed. They needed it all to go. They needed to break the ties—any and every tie—between the two men.

Sgt. Austin, meanwhile, was soon off on round two of his odyssey. First stop, Hawaii. It was while snooping around at the Ilikai that Austin came across a man who happened to know Charles Sullivan. This man told him

Charles Sullivan made some startling assertions shortly after Mackay's arrest in the Pfeil shooting. He said Sullivan appeared to be "scared to death." Sullivan was, the witness said, hiding from Inv. Austin and had returned to the Ilikai only because he thought Austin had left town. Then this new witness said some things that piqued Austin's interest.

Sullivan had told him, according to this source, that Neil Mackay was involved in a $20,000 cash transaction that Sullivan facilitated with a third man—about two months before Robert Pfeil's murder. Ten thousand dollars, the source added, went to the third man. The rest went to Neil Mackay. But, the source added, Sullivan did not want to get involved in the matter.

"He did not want a free trip to Alaska," the witness said, quoting Sullivan, "because Neil Mackay can get rough." Another person at the Ilikai, the witness added, had warned Sullivan that he better "zip his lip if he knew what was good for him."

Thanks to this witness, Joe Austin was able to find Charles Sullivan at home that same evening. He brought David Sommers of the Honolulu Prosecutor's Office with him. It was Jean Sullivan who met them at the door. She stalled them, saying her husband was in bed with a bad leg. He would have difficulty walking. They sent her to fetch him. He was a long time coming and, when he finally arrived, Charles Sullivan claimed that he hadn't seen Mackay since the late seventies. There was also a hint of animosity. Sullivan said he "had known Mackay for thirty-five to forty years but didn't like him or the way he did business."

Two days later, Jean Sullivan called Joe Austin and said she wanted to talk. Austin spoke to her at their condo, while Charles waited in an adjacent room. She provided the details about the Neil Mackay cash transfer. Austin—and others—had been scouring Mackay's records to find that cash. Now, perhaps, they were finally on the brink of a breakthrough. Austin was struck, however, by the date Jean Sullivan was giving. It was 1978, she insisted. In Palm Desert, California. To Austin, that seemed wrong or, at the very least, inconvenient.[52]

Sensing that Jean Sullivan was still nervous about telling the complete truth, Austin suggested she wait until she was ready to be completely forthright. It was then that Charles Sullivan joined them. Austin emphasized the importance of telling the complete truth and urged them to think it

52 Sullivan had the correct date.

over. There was no need to think about it, Jean Sullivan insisted. She knew who was there. Jack Guard and Neil Mackay.

"No matter if Mackay goes in for a thousand years," she added, "that doesn't mean we're safe."

Jean Sullivan remembered a conversation they'd had, one that took place after Muriel's death. Mackay confided he'd handed Muriel a check during their last encounter. Said his final words were, "I hope you live long enough to cash this."

Their fear had a name.

THAT WASN'T ALL. WHILE IN HONOLULU, Austin also met with Toni Goss, a woman who had dated Mackay in 1981. Goss noted that, even after they stopped seeing each other, Mackay would still call her when he was lonely. During their dinners together, Mackay would talk of his divorce, becoming upset and yelling. From Mackay's remarks and emotional outbursts, Goss thought he was speaking of a recent divorce. Mackay was, however, speaking of his divorce years before, from a woman long dead. In late 1981 or 1982, Mackay told Goss that Muriel "got what she deserved." He also told her he was hiding his assets and had investments overseas.

According to Cathy Kaneshige, an officer for the Bank of Hawaii, Mackay had Scotty perform much of Mackay's banking. Mackay prepared the paperwork, and then Scotty delivered it to the bank. What was strange, though, were Mackay's instructions to never discuss Muriel Pfeil's death with Scotty. Jean Sullivan, the wife of Charles Sullivan, corroborated this; said that Mackay did not want Scotty to know anything about his mother. He was not even to have a picture of his her in their house.

Then there was Mary Robbins, a banker employed by the Kapiolani Branch of the First Hawaiian Bank. Mackay spoke to her about opening accounts in the names of two ladies. Talked about wiring funds, said he was involved in many different corporations. Mentioned his overseas investments.

Austin also met with an Oahu real estate agent who handled Junior Pauole's attempt to purchase a house in the summer of 1985. The date was crucial—Junior had spoken about a critical meeting in Hawaii with Mackay during that same time period, one that he claimed led directly to the assassination of Robert Pfeil. During the course of her dealings with Pauole, Mickey Patterson said, Neil Mackay called her and posed as Pauole's lawyer. Said he "forcefully complained to her on Pauole's behalf with respect to the transaction." Neil Mackay's fingerprints were turning up everywhere.

As December 1986 turned to January 1987, Joe Austin found himself hucking his air-logged body to the American southwest. Neil Mackay's trial was a month away. There were ends to be wrapped. He found himself in Phoenix, at the Attorney General's office. He wanted—needed—a search warrant for the residence of Jack Guard.

Described by a Hawaii witness as "an old Alaskan, a sourdough, who was stooped over," Jack Guard had a long history with Neil Mackay. For the cops, there were multiple red flags. One was that $20,000 cash transaction in the desert. The transaction that, cops felt, was a possible source of the cash paid Junior Pauole for the life of Robert Pfeil. According to court records, moreover, Mackay and Guard had been close friends for a long time; Guard had a criminal record, having been charged with bringing illegal gambling devices into Alaska.[53] According to court records, Guard was also investigated, along with Mackay, as a possible suspect in the homicide of Muriel Pfeil.

Jack Guard and his wife Ruth lived in Chino Valley, Arizona, two hours northwest of Phoenix. Austin arrived at a cluster of wood-frame buildings snugged into the scrub. With him were agents from the Arizona Attorney General's office and Alaska special prosecutor Tim Petumenos. They served the search warrant on Mrs. Ruth Guard shortly after 5 p.m. It was another half hour before her husband joined them.

Jack Guard was not inclined to be helpful. He was a gremlin of a man, with white hair and a gritty voice that vanished down his throat when he was asked questions he didn't like. He said he thought he met with Neil Mackay and Sullivan in Las Vegas but was emphatic that Sullivan did not take them to a bank to cash a check. Asked if he had paid any monies to Neil Mackay, he scoffed, "it would be my business." Guard also denied cashing a $20,000 check and giving the money to Mackay. He added that Neil Mackay was "a damn sight more honest than most people."

53 Guard got wrapped up in a racketeering investigation involving the interstate transportation of pinball machines, on the premise they were gambling devices. It was a thin case, based on the "free plays" users earned with high scores. It didn't get far.

Things continued in that vein for the next hour.

Even as they chatted, the search of Guard's property was ongoing and relentless. They went through everything. His house, a barn, a white storage shed, two fifth-wheel camper-trailers, a cargo van, a truck (cab and box), and his 1976 Ford pickup. They seized a veritable bounty.

They took his typewriter/adding machine ribbon. Multiple checkbooks and check registers. Bank and phone records. An envelope containing a letter from the Showboat Hotel. Eight envelopes containing letters from Neil Mackay to Jack Guard—letters that went to Neil Mackay's fraught mental state, his complaints, his obsessions.

In a February 20, 1983, letter to Jack Guard, Mackay wrote:

> Scotty's Estate, by Mr. Pfeil, are now suing Barbara and myself and for fraud . . . The Pfeil family?????? With their absolute greed for money, they simply are miserable people, but this is of their own doing, not only now, but in the past. This Bob Pfeil—well, I have no comment on him because you pretty well know the story on this man without going any further.

In a follow up letter, dated February 21, 1983, Mackay added:

> You mentioned as to how things were going as between me and my brother-in-law? I simply can't answer this, because as I see it the matter will never end so long as he has control of Scotty's money. They have stole [sic] so much of Scotty's money—oh hell no need to go into this, but in answer to your question the situation is no better and has progressed "mo badder" since I had to return to this damn state of Alaska and came within its jurisdiction.

The cops also found a brown manila envelope with miscellaneous documents labeled "Mackay." A hospital bill for Scotty Mackay. An envelope postmarked February 6, 1986, with a letter and newspaper clippings regarding the Pfeil murder trial.

One precious envelope, one that contained photocopies of the suspect cashier's check. The one for $20,000. The one payable to Neil S. Mackay.

Just after 6:30 p.m., Jack Guard changed his tune. Joe Austin showed him the check. "He got real fidgety," Austin recalled. Suddenly, Jack Guard remembered. Yes, he admitted, he was with Neil Mackay, in Las Vegas, in 1979. He also admitted to being in Las Vegas in 1985, for a bar owner's convention but, he insisted, he saw neither Neil Mackay nor Charles Sullivan at that time. Later, he would claim he didn't remember what he told police while at his Arizona home.

"You asked me so many questions," he declared. "You come down there like John Wayne."

Austin and Petumenos, meanwhile, had more immediate concerns: the money. Follow the money. While Petumenos returned to Alaska and kicked off an assessment of Mackay's assets by accounting firm Coopers & Lybrand, Joe Austin continued his improvisational tour of the Southwest.

In Indio, California, he tried to track down the bank manager who'd approved the $20,000 cash transaction between Mackay and Guard. Austin tracked down the man, but he couldn't recall any such transaction. Did not recognize the name or physical description of Charles Sullivan. A meeting in Palm Desert, at the golf course home of a former airline pilot, failed to turn up anything save the pilot's disdain for Neil Mackay.

A call to Frank Hayes on January 5, 1987, was equally frustrating. His sister was Barbara Hayes, AKA Barbara Mackay, AKA Barbara Homay. Frank's wife told Austin they hadn't seen Neil in "over thirty years." Said that Neil and Barbara had trouble in their marriage because Mackay was a heavy drinker. Added that, by the time of their divorce, the two of them hadn't had a real marriage for a long time.

When Frank Hayes came on the line, he said Barbara was his only living relative. Said that he and Barbara "think differently." Asked by Austin about signing corporate papers, Frank said he had done so at his sister's request, that he was just a figurehead and had subsequently signed over the Power of Attorney to Barbara.

Hayes did add some background detail. He said that his mother and Mackay's mother were close friends. That Neil was the president of their high school student body and that everyone looked up to him; he was hard working and wanted to get ahead. Hayes also noted that Neil and Barbara were going together in their senior year. That Mackay had lived in Yermo, California, thirteen miles east of Barstow, where they went to high school.

Then Frank Hayes admitted he had been out of touch with his sister for the last two years.

Austin's last foray was to the Ironwood Estates, just outside of Phoenix. He wanted to track down Jean and Charles Sullivan's current neighbors at their suburban condo. One neighbor refused to talk. Another neighbor said that Neil and Scotty had stayed at the Sullivan house for several months by themselves. That they left the house a mess and damaged the Sullivan car on a trip to Yermo, where Neil showed Scotty his childhood home. The neighbors added that Neil Mackay neither told the Sullivan's about the vehicle incident nor offered to pay for the damages.

So, it was clear. Neil Mackay could be an utter ass. There are lots of asses in the world. Most of them don't solicit murder contracts.

46

Kaimuki Christian School, Kaimuki, Oahu, Hawaii, January 29, 1987

On the night of Robert Pfeil's shooting, Junior told cops that he'd called his benefactor. "The job is done," Pauole told him. Mackay, he asserted, responded with, "Good, I was just getting ready to fight him in court." But there was a wrinkle. Mackay's defense was insisting that Scotty Mackay answered the phone and handed it to his father. One last trip to Hawaii was now in order. Once more, it was Joe Austin who drew the tough duty. This time, the reason was Neil Mackay's relationship with his son. Prosecutors planned on calling the young man at his father's trial. They needed to know how he'd do.

Austin found himself at the Kaimuki Christian School, speaking to Pat Moody, Scotty's longtime teacher and part-time guardian. Her answers seemed to ramble as she grabbed her memories, but there was a thread, a through-line, that was compelling. She told Austin that Scotty "will only believe what his dad tells him and if his dad said it was the truth." In that vein, she said, Scotty once asked her if mothers and dads tell the truth. Then proudly announced that he always told the truth.

Not surprisingly, she described Scotty as "being afraid of something" and that he didn't have a regular home life. She confirmed Grandma Pfeil's assertion that Scotty slept in the same bed as his father.

There was, Moody added, a persistent obsession with things maternal. At one time Scotty asked Moody if she would be his mother. She added that Scotty had grown very dependent on her. Added that she didn't think

Scotty knew anything about his mother. The thought was confirmed when Moody asked him if he had a picture of his mom. Scotty told her he wasn't allowed to have a picture of her. Moody said that Mackay also told her Scotty was not allowed to see his grandmother.

The elementary teacher added that if anyone started getting close to Scotty, Neil Mackay would pull him back. Moody said their father-son relationship was not normal. With Mackay, it was like the two of them were the only two people that existed. One time, Scotty told her he wasn't allowed to play with other kids. When he told his father he wanted to move into the Kaimuki neighborhood—which was crawling with children—Neil Mackay said there was no way.

There was something else she noticed. Neil Mackay's affectations. She said Mackay was always trying to impress people with who he was. She remarked that Neil Mackay used to tell Scotty that he flew with famed airman Chuck Yeager. (He hadn't.) And then, out of nowhere, Mackay told her that he'd twice tried for the Hawaii bar and flunked.

There were other oddities. Moody said that the two times she was in Mackay's apartment it was dark, dingy, and dirty. That the man kept the drapes closed. That he wouldn't let Scotty keep the things he'd made in school. Scotty's schoolteacher said she started to realize that Scotty lived like an old man and didn't have a childhood.

While his father wanted everything perfect for Scotty, and wanted him to have a regular life, there were glaring inconsistencies. For example, Scotty stayed with her for nearly six months off and on, while Mackay made trips back and forth to Alaska. Why didn't he leave Scotty with relatives during those periods? Why hadn't he told Scotty that Barbara Homay was more than his dad's friend? Why hadn't she told him she was his first wife?

Pat Moody readily conceded the moments of unfettered generosity. Neil Mackay sent money for Scotty's care and also gave her his Mastercharge card so she could purchase clothing for the growing boy. But he had no medical plan for the kid. One time she had to take Scotty to the Kaiser Hospital to treat a broken arm. She had to put Scotty on her own program. Mackay later blamed her because, he alleged, Scotty's arm "had not healed right."

For all of that, Pat Moody said that a lot of people helped Scotty so that he could lead a normal life.

When Mackay's aunt died, Neil called Moody and told her he did not want her to tell Scotty. Moody disagreed with him. He got upset with her. A short time later, Mackay called back and said, "I want Scotty home now." All of a sudden, he took Scotty away. This was during the 4th grade, Moody recalled. She hadn't seen him since.

What Inv. Austin finally wanted to know, above all, was how Scotty Mackay would handle the witness stand during his father's upcoming murder trial. Pat Moody said that Scotty would only be able to tell what his dad told him to say. She added that Scotty was a good boy.

His problem was his dad.

47

Anchorage, Alaska, November 10, 1986 – January 6, 1987

On August 11, 1986, Mackay's defense team filed a motion to dismiss his murder indictment with prejudice. It's a time-honored trope for defense attorneys to attack the state. Not just the state's *case*, but the state as an entity. As in, "The State." As in, The State has overstepped. As in, The State has loosed its immense powers against a hapless plaintiff. As in, The State has manufactured or failed to disclose information important to the accused's defense.

This was where the superior resources available to Neil Mackay made their presence known. They had, in fact, dug deeply into the discovery record—the very one they contended was inadequate. This was where they believed the state's case should take a well-deserved hit.

The object of their derision was the prosecution's Statement of the Case, which the prosecution had offered as a "helpful reference point . . . in which salient portions of the record describe the investigation from beginning to end." It was an invitation that Mackay's defense contemptuously declined. They reserved their deepest scorn for Sgt. Mike Grimes, the lead detective on the case. The man who, in detective Joe Austin's testimony, "assigned probably 300 officers in the first days of the investigation."

For Jim Shellow and his newly added co-counsel, Jim McComas, "the state's brief describes less the investigation as it actually occurred 'from beginning to end' and more the state's *post-hoc* rationalization of the reasons to excuse the violations of Mr. Mackay's rights." There were, they said, many omissions, inconsistencies, and incorrect assertions. Mackay's team chronicled twenty-eight of them in a mere fifteen pages.

Omitted, they said, was the fact that Robert Pfeil was asked at the hospital—after his shooting—if he had any evidence or information implicating Mackay; "Pfeil acknowledged that he did not know if Mr. Mackay was involved." Omitted, they said, "are the facts that Sergeant Grimes has acknowledged forming the opinion that Mr. Mackay was behind the Robert Pfeil shooting as soon as he learned that Robert Pfeil was the victim."

Omitted from these representations, averred the defense, was "the fact that there was no direct police involvement or effort to investigate the possibility of a union connection to Robert Pfeil's killing." Omitted "from the state's general assertion," they declared, "is the crucial fact that Sergeant Grimes identified for Pauole and his counsel that the state's desire was to make a case against Mr. Mackay *before* any negotiations were undertaken and before any deal was concluded."

Nowhere in the prosecution's statement of facts, concluded the defense, "do they purport to identify either the 'several admissions' Grimes swore Mackay made during the second phone call or the 'several references and admissions by Mackay that he had in fact hired and paid $10,000.'"

In their view, Mackay's attorneys had unearthed a litany of errors. They were inclined, moreover, to believe the worst. These omissions, they argued, were grounds for dismissal

"The defense firmly believes that no remedy short of dismissal with prejudice even begins to address the seriousness of the pattern of misconduct in this case. Nor would any other relief the defense urges even begin to remedy the actual prejudice suffered by Mr. Mackay."

Which, in lay terms, meant they wanted Judge Greene to toss *all charges* lodged against Neil Mackay and *forever foreclose any attempt to retry him*.

JUDGE GREENE COULD BE FORGIVEN FOR NOT GOING straight at the motion to dismiss with prejudice. In complex cases, with top dollar attorneys, there was always somebody clamoring. For Greene, it was a gimme, gimme, gimme of motions filed and decisions to be made. Every matter was pressing to at least one party.

The news media intervenors, for example, took umbrage at a November 12, 1986, order to exclude the press and public from a pretrial hearing. Only later did Judge Greene reveal the reason. "The filings and exhibits," she noted, "contain verbatim transcripts which, if publicly revealed, could severely prejudice the accused's right to a fair trial."[54]

Then there was the matter of Gilbert K. Pauole's long-awaited deposition. It didn't begin until November 18, 1986, when he was to be delivered by the U.S. Marshal's Service to Anchorage. Even as Judge Greene ordered it to go forward, she plucked multiple feathers out of the defense's wish list. Mackay's boundless collage of leading questions was now significantly clipped.

Gone were questions about preparation for depositions—a favorite of defense lawyers seeking to discredit a witness's testimony ("they told you what to say; they coached you"). Gone were questions about Pauole's alleged illegal activities in Hawaii during the summer of 1985. Gone were questions about money from persons who might be involved in organized crime in Hawaii. Gone were probing questions about Pauole's involvement in the Federal Witness Protection program. Gone were questions about his testimony before federal grand juries. Gone were questions about Pauole's potential exposure for other crimes.

There was still plenty they could ask.

They could ask about Pauole's access to $10,000 in the fall of 1985. They could ask about Pauole's union connections—but only those of Pauole himself or of his friends and associates. They could ask about his activities in Hawaii, but only as they touched upon his attempts to buy or lease a club there or with respect to his Hawaiian friend, William "Jo-Jo" Reuter. They could also ask about his collection of newspaper clips about the murders

54 To address explosive revelations from jailhouse informant Paul Newsom, Judge Greene agreed to close the proceedings to the public and seal the associated records. That move prompted an outraged response from the Media Intervenors. D. John McKay filed an anticipatory objection on November 9, 1986. In it he asked, "What is going on in the secret trial of Neil Mackay, and why must it remain secret?" He continued in that vein, wondering "Is the state using improper methods, fabricated evidence, and perjured testimony? Is it interfering with Mr. Mackay's constitutional right to counsel? Or is it defense counsel attempting to utilize a combination of secret pleadings and selective public disclosure to undermine public confidence in the proceedings and elicit sympathy for his client's cause?" It was none of the above.

of Muriel and Robert Pfeil, as well as union activities at Alaska Airlines.

They could ask about Pauole's plans for a second murder but only as it related to John Bright.

Representing the defense at Pauole's deposition was James McComas, who by this point had taken over much of the day-to-day work on the case. McComas made no attempt to hide the underlying rationale for his questions.

Why, McComas wondered, did the state have him agree to a second plea deal? Were they removing certain items? Were they making promises that couldn't be written down? Had they promised, more specifically, that he wouldn't be prosecuted for a host of unrelated activities?

Pauole's answers were as good as the questions, in great part because he didn't dispute their underlying premise. No, he said, he didn't think he'd be criminally prosecuted for hiring underage girls as dancers in his clubs. No, he didn't think he'd be criminally prosecuted for providing false ID to underaged employees. No, he didn't think he'd be criminally prosecuted for possessing firearms as a convicted felon. No, he insisted, he didn't think he'd be criminally prosecuted for possession of cocaine with intent to distribute or sell. He also said "No" to thoughts he'd be prosecuted for soliciting a murder in Oregon.

Then came the clincher, if only because it was a question that reeked of Alaska: Do you think you'll be criminally prosecuted for involvement, or aiding and abetting the theft of fish?

No, Junior Pauole replied. Nothing was said about being charged for fish theft.[55]

WHILE BOTH PARTIES WERE DISTRACTED BY THE Pauole deposition, Judge Greene got to work in earnest.

Even before the Pauole deposition, she ordered Mackay to submit to an expert to ascertain the existence and extent of any claimed speech and/or language disabilities. His defense team was claiming that the seeming admissions he'd made in the Pauole tape—about the "G.U.N." and the

55 Such crimes are not unheard of in Alaska. Due to its prominent commercial fishery, thefts ranged from 100-pound fish boxes from seafood wholesalers; to fish taken out of season and sold off-market; to purloined hatchery fish sold in the underground economy.

"metal thing"—were the artifacts of his ongoing battle with aphasia. This was, Mackay said, a condition that caused him to struggle to find words and sometimes speak inappropriately.

Then, in the last week of December, Judge Greene issued four crucial decisions in quick succession. The first one dealt with the wildcard in the pack, the state's chatty informant, Paul Newsom. After hearing a week of evidence, Greene felt she had enough information to split the baby. If a good decision was one where no one was happy, this one qualified.

Greene found no evidence that the police had deliberately placed Newsom in the cell adjacent to Neil Mackay. It was, by all accounts, "an unplanned and fortuitous event," predicated on the need to keep a vulnerable inmate—Newsom—away from the general population at the 6th Avenue Jail. As to the assertion that Mackay's statements were involuntary, the judge found the defense arguments flimsy.

"Mackay is not an unsophisticated defendant; he is an attorney," Greene wrote. "He is of at least average intelligence and suffers from no major mental illnesses. Newsom's 'interrogation' of Mackay could not possibly have lasted more than several hours and were intermittent. Mackay was not reluctant to speak to Newsom even at the beginning of Newsom's discussions with him."

Next up were decisions about the legality of searches at Mackay's two properties. The trickiest one turned out to be the house at 1634 Stanford Drive in Anchorage. The house at that address, owned by Neil Mackay, was leased to Virginia Zawacki. Carved out within that building was an office space devoted to Mackay's business—he'd essentially transferred his office holdings to the Stanford Drive address when he left the Mackay Building and moved to Hawaii.

The police seized 43 items from Stanford Drive. Judge Greene ruled every single one of them inadmissible. Not only did she suppress that evidence, but she also ordered it returned to Neil Mackay. The search warrant was overbroad, the time span so expansive as to become a fishing expedition.

Judge Greene's ruling on the Ilikai search at Mackay's Hawaii condo was almost entirely the opposite. She didn't find Mackay's claims that the warrant was based on "material misstatements" convincing. Greene found that they were, at best, exaggerated—as in when Grimes characterized the Pauole-Mackay conversations as clear and repeated admissions by Mackay that he'd provided the $10,000 for the shooting of Robert Pfeil. The Hawaiian judge, after all, had the transcripts of those conversations. He could check their veracity.

Nor did the judge find the Ilikai search warrant overbroad or lacking in probable cause. The fruits of the Ilikai search, she said, could stay. Suppression of that evidence was denied. All of this was meaningless if Judge Greene ruled to dismiss the charges against Neil S. Mackay with prejudice. She did not.

There were problems with the police investigation, to be sure but, in the court's mind, none of them rose above the level of negligence. There was no showing, she said, that the police failures were intentional or reckless misrepresentations or calculated omissions. Mackay's motion to suppress and dismiss, based on the taped conversation between him and Pauole, was tossed. Mackay's motion to dismiss on the basis of the State's "unconscionable plea agreement" with Pauole was also tossed. Mackay's motion to dismiss based on alleged improprieties at the Grand Jury? Tossed.

Waiting in the wings were two more Mackay motions to dismiss. One related to misconduct during the investigation. Tossed. Another focused on "unconstitutional interference with Mackay's right to present a defense." This one went back to allegations that the state had interfered with witnesses during the Gentry trial. Tossed. "Mackay," ruled Judge Greene, "has failed to prove any intimidation of witnesses on the part of the State."

There was one more motion to lay bare. Mackay had long argued that the facts "reveal[ed] a persistent and pervasive pattern of State misconduct." That conduct, he said, started during the initial investigation, stretched into the grand jury proceedings, and then careened across the post-indictment phase. There was only one remedy to Mackay's mind. Dismissal with prejudice.

That was, in Judge Greene's view, an "extraordinary" remedy.

"The court," she wrote, "has considered the cumulative effect of all improprieties which the court has found and detailed in other decisions on these pre-trial motions. The court finds that Mackay has not suffered irreparable prejudice. Where errors have occurred, the taint of those errors may be removed, and Mackay may be given a fair trial. Dismissal with prejudice is unwarranted."

The trial of Neil S. Mackay for the first-degree murder of Robert Pfeil could finally begin, with restrictions.

During the pre-trial phase, Judge Greene approved dozens of protective orders restricting the scope of what could—and could not—be presented to the jury. She sought a delicate balance between probative evidence—vital information that helped the jury make informed decisions—and prejudicial evidence—information that could inflame passions and move the jury to emotional or irrational decisions. It was a legal tightrope. There were always close calls, where only a few points separated the probative from the prejudicial. Neither side was particularly happy with the outcome.

The state appealed at least one of Greene's rulings. The one that forbade them from linking Neil Mackay to Muriel's death. They also wanted to overturn her ban on evidence that Pauole provided prostitutes for Mackay, the latter as means of placing Mackay in the same gutter where Junior crawled. The judge granted a one-day delay, so the state could argue before the Court of Appeals. She was skeptical of the outcome. She was right. The appeals court rejected the state's appeal without comment. They fared no better before the Alaska Supreme Court.

At the end of the day, no mention was to be made of Neil Mackay's alleged statement inducing Pauole to kill Robert Pfeil. No mention that Junior Pauole procured women for Mackay. No quotation from Charles Sullivan saying Mackay told him, "he was convinced Robert Pfeil was going to keep after him until Pfeil proved that he killed Pfeil's sister." Discussion of the vast litigation history between Pfeil and Mackay? Limited. The divorce? Dates and times only. The dispute over who had to pay for finding Scotty in Micronesia? Another summary. The collections action in Federal court? A summary. The custody litigation? Summary. Summary. Summary.

That was just the start. In subsequent rulings, Greene banned use of the word "accomplice." Said there was to be no referral to the "fraud" allegations raised in letters between Mackay and Jack Guard. No use of language that Robert Pfeil was "sabotaging the father/son relationship." No reference to Robert Pfeil as "Captain" Pfeil. There were, in total, sixty plus protective orders. Some of them were multi-part bans.

Hands would be tied. Words would be corralled. What Neil Mackay was—and might have done—at age fifty-three was irrelevant to what he was—or might have done—at age sixty-two. The search for the truth has its limits.

48

Fairbanks, Alaska, February 10-11, 1987

Marianne Pfeil flew to Fairbanks every day of Neil Mackay's trial. Up at 6:30 am for the ten-minute drive to the airport. The sun not rising until she hit Fairbanks, after eight o'clock, fashionably dressed and clutching several morning newspapers. Thankfully, the folks at Alaska Airlines, her late husband's employer, had generously given her a free pass.

Even getting out of the courtroom by 1:30, she'd do well to catch the four o'clock plane back to Anchorage. By five, she was at her two-hour aerobics class in the Captain Cook hotel, then headed straight for the Jacuzzi. She was home by 8:30, trying to get to bed by eleven. Just so she could start all over again the following day.[56]

It was the in-betweens that absorbed her. The cramped courtroom, the tendentious legal patter, her family's dirty laundry on display. Her usual perch was the front row of the spectator section, behind the prosecution table. That put her less than ten feet away from Neil Mackay, stationed on the other side of the courtroom, at the defense table. She would remember him smiling at her, just once, a wan smile of forced familiarity. She did not return the gesture.

The prosecution's opening statement was February 10, a Tuesday. As was her custom in the previous trials, Marianne wanted to be there with

56 Many thanks to Sheila Toomey of the *Anchorage Daily News* for her insightful piece on Marianne Pfeil, from which this profile is derived.

Bob's mother, Grandma Pfeil, for the opening statements. This time it was different. Judge Greene, following the strict rules for criminal cases, would not allow either of the women into the courtroom for the openings. They were witnesses. They were not to be prejudiced by what they saw or heard. Marianne would have to wait until she'd finished her own testimony, directly after the defense opening the following day.

What Marianne didn't hear was prosecutor Peter Gruenstein's grim tale of her family's nearly two-decade feud with Neil Mackay. Not that she needed to be reminded of Bob's misgivings about his sister's marriage to Neil Mackay. Of the bitter, seemingly endless divorce proceedings between Neil and Muriel, with their spats sometimes trickling into the public domain with tales of physical abuse. Of the child at the center of it, the only spawn of their brief marriage. Of Muriel's death in a car bombing. Of the custody battle that cast her and her late husband into a pitched battle with the child's father. A child whose custody and name seemed to change with the seasons, a puppet to be played by his wise elders. A child variously known as Neil Pfeil Mackay. Scotty Mackay. N. Scott Mackay.

"He was so obsessed, he couldn't even stand that Scotty's middle name was Pfeil," Gruenstein said to a packed courtroom. So, he changed it again, to Neil Sutherland Mackay, Jr., his vanity project nearly at its crescendo. Except, the prosecutor pointed out, "That didn't end the bitterness and hatred between them. That was just getting going."

More old news. It was part of Marianne's story, regurgitated for the jury. Even with Scotty's custody settled, and Bob giving up the fight, the chaos and animosity still snarled around them. In Gruenstein's telling, that peaked in 1985, when Mackay's lawsuits over Muriel's estate were crumbling in courtroom after courtroom. That's when he turned to Gilbert Pauole, claimed Gruenstein. It was a fatal decision supported by tidbits and almost overlooked details.

Marianne missed the tidbit about a piece of paper with the Pfeil's Lake Campbell address typed on it. A scrap of evidence found in Pauole's Seattle home; its Elite typeface linked to Neil Mackay's Smith-Corona typewriter. She also missed the teased prospect of an informer who'd heard Mackay confide the motive for Bob Pfeil's murder firsthand. It was all about the rape of Scotty's estate, Gruenstein insisted.

Marianne didn't see the prosecutor's oversized poster, crammed with photos of the erstwhile co-conspirators. Nor did she see Gruenstein's slightly rumpled presence, dutifully pointing to each photo in turn, laying the outlines of the conspiracy with nothing more than a conductor's baton.

On one side of the poster, a photo of Neil Mackay, an arrow pointing toward Junior Pauole. Another arrow connected Pauole to his murder crew, Tyoga Closson, John Bright, Robert Betts, and Larry Gentry. All were attached to a timeline that stretched to the top of the poster. That pointed to Robert Pfeil. Their victim.

Of the lot of them, Gruenstein could only murmur, "Mackay thought he was buying a professional job. Instead, he got the Alaska gang that couldn't shoot straight."

Marianne would also miss the day's final drama, after Mackay's attorney, Jim McComas, rose twice to object to Gruenstein's assertions. She also did not hear him complain, more loudly, with the jury out of the room. Once about allegations the prosecution hadn't removed a line in their chart referring to Mackay's assertion that Pfeil was "sabotaging the father-son relationship." Another about a prosecution statement that McComas had found "extremely prejudicial to the defense."

The offending quote? The one where Mackay reportedly said of Robert Pfeil, "I'm having a problem with my brother-in-law. Can you help me with that?"

Instead of granting the mistrial McComas wanted, Judge Greene provided remedial instructions to the jury. They were to forget things they'd heard. As if they could unhear them.

UNFORTUNATELY FOR MARIANNE PFEIL, SHE WOULD also miss the defense opening, though she was in Fairbanks, awaiting her turn on the stand. She would not see the dozen or so local lawyers in attendance, drawn to the magic that Jim McComas was said to possess. She would not hear—not this day—McComas' stentorian tone, his lips caressing every syllable. Would not hear the voice that one wag said he played "like an oboe." Would not lay eyes on a man who, in person, looked the part of the preacher, perching on his lectern in a beard that fell just short of biblical.

McComas wasted no time getting to the urgency of his plea,[57] spreading

57 The so-called "Golden Moment" in an opening statement occurs within the first

sympathy across a wide avenue, then turning his glare on a single man.

"In overview of the case," McComas declared, "I would like to say, ladies and gentlemen, that there is nothing funny about this case. This is not an amusing story about some Alaskan gang that couldn't shoot straight, led by a notorious but lovable ringleader, Gilbert Pauole.

"When the children of Robert Pfeil ran into the Pfeil household on October 12th, 1985, and told their mother that daddy had been shot there wasn't anything funny about that. When the police, about a month later, arrested Mr. Mackay in Hawaii and took him from his home and his son on a false accusation that he was involved in this, there wasn't anything funny about that either.

"This is real. And what is real here is that a man was killed, and the man died, and an innocent man, Neil Mackay, is being falsely accused of being involved in that crime. And both of those wrong acts, the killing and the false accusation go back to the same source. Gilbert Junior Pauole."

Lest anyone doubt it, McComas was drawing a picture that tied two antagonists together, then reassigned blame to a third. Gilbert Kapualoha Pauole, Jr. was suddenly the man on trial during this biting cold 14-degree day. It was a trick as old as the law itself. Ladies and gentlemen, says the defense, the wrong man is on trial.

McComas was even kind enough to gift the jury his explanatory word of the day. "The word is extortion, ladies and gentlemen," he declared.

The defense attorney had his own oversized poster. The photo was of Neil Mackay and Scotty, bedecked in leis after the latter's "triumphant" reunion with his dad in Hawaii. The accompanying text quoted a taped conversation between Junior Pauole and Larry Gentry, in which Pauole shifted the blame for Mackay's shooting to a union that wanted Neil Mackay as the patsy. The juxtaposition was almost perfect.[58] How could this beaming man, the poster suggested—his arm draped lovingly across his beatific son's shoulder—how could he be responsible for shooting Robert Pfeil? That, McComas said, was a risk Neil Mackay would never take.

Then, in a mesmerizing series of linguistic tricks, James McComas became, as it were, Neil Mackay's alter-ego. Or his ventriloquist. The words

---

thirty-seconds, when the presenter has the jury's undivided attention.

58 Almost perfect because the full conversation added, "It was Neil Mackay went and killed that guy's sister."

were not his own. The jury was to believe he was channeling the thoughts and utterances of Neil Mackay. At one point, early on, there was a dialog where McComas reproduced an alleged Pauole request for financial assistance. A request that included Pauole's erstwhile friend, William "Jo-Jo" Reuter. "[Neil Mackay] was asked if he could loan them some money," McComas said. "He refused. He was asked if he could help establish letters of credit at a bank and he refused. He was asked if he could give them any financial help and ultimately, he refused."

McComas loved that story so much, he told it again less than an hour later. This time with gusto.

"You will learn that during the first trip Pauole made to Hawaii between approximately July 7th and August 18th, that whole time he was in Hawaii he was going around trying to figure out how to pull off the financing of both his house and the club he wanted to open," McComas told the jury, once more channeling his client. "During that period of time, he and Reuter singly or together made requests of Mr. Mackay to join them as a partner in the business. Denied. Made requests to loan them money. Get serious. Made requests to put some money in a bank so they could get letters of credit. No way. The final request, well, at least guarantee the lease. If we can get a lease for our club, will you guarantee the first year for us; that will help us get a lease.

"And Mr. Mackay, because of the constant nagging by Pauole and because Pauole is an amiable guy who knows how to manipulate people, said all right, he would consider that . . . And so, Mr. Mackay drafts something up and puts it in an envelope and sends it with Pauole to be hand delivered . . . Pauole doesn't literally deliver the mail."

McComas was doubling down. No money changed hands between the two men, he declared. The murder money did not come from Neil Mackay, he repeated.

"What you will learn is that Junior Pauole didn't need $10,000.00 from Neil Mackay to have Robert Pfeil killed," McComas told them. That part rang true. Slowly, slowly, the defense attorney was separating his client from culpability. The narrative was unfolding in compelling fashion, the jury entranced.

That alleged phone call from Junior, telling Mackay the job was done? No, McComas said, that didn't happen. You will learn, he told the jury, that

Mackay first heard of the shooting from friends in Anchorage, who'd seen an article in the paper. Had seen an article, in fact, that misspelled Pfeil's name, making it P-h-e-i-l instead of P-f-e-i-l. "It was a ridiculous hope on his part," McComas acknowledged, "but as they will communicate to you, that maybe it wasn't the Robert Pfeil he knew."

They. The mysterious, unnamed "they."

From there, McComas took off on a series of assertions that, ultimately, would be unsupported by any evidence presented at trial by the defense.[59] Evidence that was not supported in the next few days, in the next few months, in the entire course of the trial. The jury didn't know it, but they'd just been ghosted.

Mackay's defense would cling to the extortion angle, hanging it on the top rung. There was also an anecdote, telling of how Neil Mackay was called by a stranger after Muriel's murder, a man who said, according to Mackay-McComas, "remember you sent me down to the Kenai to pick up a clock to do the bombing?" The guy's story was off enough, McComas said, that Mackay figured the man was just trying to extort money from him. So, he told the would-be extortionist to "just come on over and, of course," McComas triumphantly proclaimed, "in the presence of a witness nobody ever shows up."

Too bad. A witness would have helped.

By the end of trial, there would be over one hundred unsupported defense assertions. Assertions made but left dangling. Assertions made but never confirmed, either by witness testimony or defense evidence. For those few hours, on day two of the trial, Jim McComas held his captive audience spellbound. All the world's a theater.

Marianne Pfeil would ultimately see it for what it was. She had it nailed when, two months into the trial, she said, "This is my life on stage up there. My family. I have to finish it."

---

59 During an anteroom conference Gruenstein complained about the unsupported assertions. "The defense is arguing facts that can't be verified, unless Mackay takes the stand and says he did say that." McComas countered that his assertions "point out Mackay's state of mind." The judge let it go.

49

Fairbanks, Alaska, February 19 - 20, 1987

GILBERT PAUOLE ARRIVED AT THE BARNETTE Courthouse flat on the floor of an unmarked Chevrolet sedan. Three gray-suited U.S. Marshals surrounded him. A bevy of Alaska State Troopers stationed themselves outside the salmon-toned sheet cake that called itself a court building. Their shotguns were at the ready.

Pauole's every move was carefully choreographed. A cluster of officers hustled their charge through a back entrance, surrounding him like a pack of not so friendly wolves. Took him upstairs to Judge Mary Greene's cramped second-floor courtroom. Marianne Pfeil was in her usual and accustomed place, behind the prosecution desk, when Junior was led into the courtroom. She recognized him from the previous trials, a medium-tall, sallow-skinned man with black thinning hair, a mustache, and a beard.

As Pauole moved toward the witness stand, the coterie of five Marshals and Troopers spread to the four corners of Courtroom D. A sixth marshal sat directly behind Pauole, a calm but ever-vigilant presence. Judge Greene advised the jurors to take no notice of Pauole's security detail. Don't hold it against him, she admonished.

It was impossible to un-see them.

With three trials to his credit, Junior seemed like the most relaxed person in the room. His demeanor exuded an eerie calm, born of his natural deportment and months—years—of courtroom appearances. During the previous Pfeil trials, he managed to frustrate the most relentless questioning by calmly agreeing to the details of his unsavory life. He openly admitted his criminal record, his ongoing efforts to defraud the IRS, his long record of lying under oath. He seemed unperturbable.

The same could not be said of the U.S. Marshals. They immediately objected to the presence of a news photographer, who thrust his camera in Pauole's direction. One of them rose to intercept the cameraman. No photos, he demanded. Judge Greene overruled him. The years long battle over media access had come to a new resolution. They could take photos during the Mackay trial.

With that formality out of the way, prosecutor Tim Petumenos got to work. There were no lingering introductions. He asked Pauole who had directed the murder of Robert Pfeil.

"Neil Mackay asked me to have Robert Pfeil killed," Pauole answered, his voice flat and emotionless. Then he ID'd Mackay, pointing to him at the defense table.

Petumenos stayed direct and deliberate. It was all about establishing Junior's *bona fides*, a slow dance designed to entangle Neil Mackay in Junior's unsavory life but first, the jury had to get to know the witness before them. They started with Hawaii and Junior Pauole's knowledge of the players in that state's organized crime entities. Then moved to his association with racketeer Frank Colacurcio in federal prison.

"Frank liked me," Pauole said. "I gave him a parka. He was a VIP."

The goal was to inexorably tie Neil Mackay to Junior Pauole's little corner of the world. To the pimps and the dancers, as well as the bouncers and the patrons and how that led Mackay to develop, in Pauole's telling, a confessional relationship with the ex-con from Hawaii.

This was no causal relationship, this back and forth between Neil Mackay and Junior Pauole. "I told Mr. Mackay that I was involved in organized crime," Junior testified, adding that the Colacurcio organization covered fourteen states. "I was very comfortable with Mr. Mackay. He wouldn't put me down. Mr. Mackay would send me newspaper clippings from Hawaii, about crimes there."

The prosecution moved copies of two such newspaper clippings into evidence. The rest seemed *pro forma*, with testimony about late-night phone calls between the two men. About Junior helping him deal with a troublesome tenant by cleaning out the Porterhouse Restaurant and pocketing the $11,000 he made selling off its contents. About visits to Mackay in Hawaii and his Anchorage condo.

All this so Junior could drop the bomb. A bomb he had dropped at his confession and every previous trial.

"Mr. Mackay asked me to help with his brother-in-law," Junior said in a quiet lilt that betrayed no emotion. It was a variation of what he'd said so many times before. "He wanted him killed or hurt. It was in his apartment, right before he sold the Mackay Building."

Jim Shellow objected. Judge Greene overruled. Gilbert Pauole continued. "[Mr. Mackay] said he was sure it was what he wanted. I said I would look into it—I was not sure I could find someone to do it. The subject came up from time to time. I kept putting him off. I made him believe I was looking for someone from Hawaii to do it." It was duck and weave, the binding of Neil Mackay to Junior Pauole slowly growing more tightly entwined.

The prosecution introduced Scotty's report card, the one found in Pauole's office at the Wild Cherry. Introduced the entertainer contract Mackay drafted to rejigger Pauole's relationship to his dancers. Introduced that typed note that bore Robert Pfeil's address. Introduced a business card from the Outrigger hotel, where Pauole had planned to open a bar. Introduced that letter of recommendation written for Pauole by Virginia Zawacki. Introduced Junior's July 8, 1985, plane ticket from Alaska to Hawaii.

The real outburst, however, was still on standby. It started when Petumenos slid back into the VIP theme, first introduced to mark Frank Colacurcio's status in federal prison. How were you to treat Neil Mackay, he asked Pauole. Were you instructed that "Mr. MacKay should receive VIP treatment when he came into the Club and be handled so that he wasn't disturbed by anybody?"

"Yes," Pauole answered. That question and answer took them, in a meander that lasted two hours, to John Bright. Pauole said he saw Bright was a sidewalk commando. A loose cannon who routinely took on the pimps trying to seduce dancers out of his club and into the streets of Anchorage. Pauole even managed to keep a straight face as he admitted that, "sometimes I would use my dancers as prostitutes for VIPs."

That line of questioning would soon lead to trouble. Among the banned lines of inquiry were any hints that Junior Pauole procured women for Neil Mackay. That's exactly where they were headed. When Petumenos asked whether Junior provided women as a favor to VIPs and Junior said, "Yes," he'd gone one bridge too far.

"I object Your Honor," Jim Shellow snarled at the mere mention of how VIPs were treated.[60] During the ensuing recess, Mackay's defense team strutted into a full-throated attack. There were multiple violations of court orders, they insisted. They had learned, they alleged, that the state had withheld police tapes made on the night of Pauole's arrest. The state claimed otherwise, but no matter. There was only one cure for these blatant violations, McComas pronounced gravely. He moved for a mistrial and then rubbed salt in the wound. "The State attorneys should step out of this case," McComas insisted, "if they feel it is too hard to comply with Court orders."

It was an ignominious start. Judge Greene delayed the trial for a day, so that the defense could review the "missing" tape. She took the mistrial motion under advisement and then brought the jury back in long enough for Pauole to make a damning declaration.

"I told Mr. Mackay I found the guys who would do the job for him," Pauole testified. "He questioned me about them. He said he didn't want the guy to come back. I understood that Mr. Mackay wanted his brother-in-law dead . . . I told Mackay it would be $10,000.00. He asked if I needed more. I said no."

ON DAY TWO OF THE STATE'S CASE, JUDGE GREENE denied the defense mistrial motion. Petumenos asked for a new judge for his sanction hearing. Also denied. The trial resumed, with tidbits slipping in like pockets of song. The 30.06 rifle intended for the Pfeil shooting came in, as did the sawed-off Mossberg shotgun. The state introduced two more Pauole plane tickets from Alaska to Hawaii, one for September 21, 1985, another for October 7, 1985.

---

60 Notably, more than two hours elapsed—with two jury absences from the courtroom—between the comment that Mackay was to receive VIP treatment, and the second VIP reference. It was the latter reference that precipitated the defense objection.

Amy Shotwell testified that she met Junior at the airport on October 7, 1985. Said he was upset and moody. "He had a manila envelope that Neil wanted him to deliver. I saw a white, legal-size envelope at home. It had lots of money in it, $100.00 bills." Amy had, of course, seen Junior with lots of money before. He used to carry large sums of money down to Seattle—club money. Skimmed money. But she said she'd never seen him carry money in envelopes before. Robert Pfeil's October 12 shooting, the jury was to note, was just around the corner.

Then there was Junior, talking about his late-night call to Neil Mackay on the night of his arrest. "I provided Mackay's phone number to the police. I placed a call to him; I was to get Mackay to talk to me—try to get him to send me some money."

Jim McComas objected to the transcripts of Pauole's post-arrest conversation with Neil Mackay. The taped versions were played instead. Pauole stared vacantly into space as he listened to the three telephone conversations between himself and Mackay. Occasionally, he glanced toward the defense table and the white-haired defendant he once described as a friend.

Before the day was up, the state introduced Pauole's phone book into evidence. The one that had all of Neil Mackay's phone numbers. Had, in fact, all of Mackay's closely guarded, private phone numbers. The message was clear. Neil Mackay knew Junior Pauole—and his underworld connections—well enough to contract him to kill his brother-in-law.

With the jury excused, all that was left for Junior Pauole was to face Jim Shellow as he prepared for cross examination. There was a hint as to what he'd face when the defense attorney took him through the details of a prior conviction. It was just a bar fight, Pauole insisted. "I was to stay out of bar fights for a year."

The reality of Junior Pauole was not lost on Peter Gruenstein. He would soon admit that, "Mr. Pauole has got to be one of the most cross-examinable, impeachable witnesses that has come before any court in this state."

50

Fairbanks, Alaska, February 23 - 25; March 2 - 9, 1987

EIGHT DAYS, EIGHT BRUTAL DAYS, EACH designed to make the state's case implode. To make Gilbert Pauole fall apart. Gilbert Kapualoha Pauole, Jr. made it too easy. His lies and half-lies, many of them in defense of his overlords, had come back with a haughty smile. In skilled hands, these deceptions could haunt him mercilessly. Actually, it didn't take that much. There was an abundance to draw from, stretching back to Frank Colacurcio and then fast-forwarding to everything Pauole said at the trials of his co-conspirators.

That wasn't all. None of Pauole's co-conspirators were testifying at Mackay's trial. The four of them, having been convicted, were appealing their verdicts. They couldn't risk saying something untoward in yet another courtroom. The table had been cleared.

Shellow started his assault on the Pauole's credibility the second he began his cross-examination. He attacked early and often. Plied his best professorial voice, with its reedy sweeps in tone and volume, always finding a way to end with a sneer. One of the journalists in attendance described the approach as "being nibbled to death by ducks." It was an apt description.

The only risk to Shellow's approach was tedium. He tended to bore into the details, in the hope he'd be able to spring an "aha" moment later on. There was another problem, already discovered in Pauole's past trial appearances. As one attorney noted, "Pauole is so willing to admit past sins that he takes the fun out of cross-examination."

On day one of his slow-burn assault on Pauole's credibility, for example, Shellow got Junior to admit that he lied when the told a Portland, Oregon, federal jury that he could read. "It was to protect Frank Colacurcio," he admitted. "I just guessed at answers." Shellow wanted to take him deeper. Pulled out the transcripts of the Larry Gentry trial. Accused Pauole of being a habitual liar. Junior denied it. Shellow pulled out Pauole's testimony in the John Bright trial. Forced Junior into a trickle of admissions.

"In the past lying was a habit," Junior conceded. "I have lied under oath before. I lied to protect people, to conceal things . . . I don't think I lied convincingly. I have never broke down. I never broke down and say I was lying. The pitch in my voice is just the way I am. My answers were carefully rehearsed with Frank Colacurcio. Sometimes I just distort things."

The defense seemed determined to pile on the details. There were more unflattering utterances where the first one came from. So many more that the state was forced to request a halt, so they could refer to the court documents the defense was citing. James McComas responded that they were identifying the documents by date and tape; said that's all they were required to do. Greene disagreed. The defense was to let the State have a brief opportunity to find the items to which Shellow was referring but the deluge was on.

Sometimes, Junior was able to skate through on a technicality. As when Shellow asked him about lying to the Alaska Beverage Control board about Frank Colacurcio's interest in the strip clubs that Pauole managed. "The question wasn't asked, so the answer wasn't given," Junior maintained, then admitted, "Colacurcio did have an interest in Anchorage clubs."

Then there were questions about other people in the Colacurcio organization. Or their associates. One was a man named Samuel Finke, who Pauole said invested money for people. "Did you tell the ABC investigator that Mr. Finke asked you to put out a murder contract?" Shellow asked.

"I told investigators all they wanted to know at the time," Junior responded. "I did not tell them that Finke asked me to put out a murder contract on someone."

And so it went. Shellow named names and called out Junior as a guide to the malign workings of the criminal underground. Two Colacurcio rivals were mentioned. People wanted them hurt, Pauole admitted.

Shellow kept pushing. More lies revealed. Lie after lie. Yes, Junior admitted, he lied when he told police a friend of his was not a drug dealer. That was a problem. It wasn't some past-tense lie. It was a lie he committed just after his post-arrest deal to tell the truth. Shellow would soon get Junior to admit to another lie he told police after he signed his deal with the State of Alaska.

This one involved the source of $100,000 they'd found after Pauole's arrest. Money that ultimately went to his wife, Melanie. Junior claimed to have taken it from his Wild Cherry "construction account" after breaking with Frank Colacurcio. That was partially true; the original source of the funds was Colacurcio, who wanted it invested in an Anchorage club. Junior got it from a Colacurcio associate who didn't want to give it back. So, Junior admitted, he torched the man's Mercedes; and then, Junior said, "he did give me the money, $100,000.00 in $100.00 bills."

Yes, he admitted, he was being vindictive when he torched the man's car. Said he used gasoline in plastic bags, but did not send him a dead fish, courtesy of Frank Colacurcio. Yes, Pauole confessed, "There was a construction account with my name on it. It was a bogus account." Junior also admitted that he told a "white lie" about the origins of the hundred-grand. "I think I had intentions of hiding the money."

Now, he added, it was gone. Shellow provoked the first genuine laugh from the jury—and spectators—when he asked Pauole how he squandered the money. With a sigh and a twist of body language signaling deep regret, Pauole said, "I gave it to my wife."

Shellow placed the construction company's bank statement into evidence and moved on. There were weightier things on his mind. He began showing up for court each morning with a smile and a transcript of the previous day's session. He searched it methodically, looking for any discrepancy with which to taunt Junior Pauole. Shellow's cross-examination technique was an attack of a thousand cuts.

The defense attorney zeroed in on a white envelope full of money, mentioned in the Portland, Oregon, trial, where Pauole lied to protect Colacurcio at a federal tax evasion trial. In that case, the white envelope held the nightly take from a Washington state restaurant and was delivered each evening to Colacurcio.

Then for four days, Shellow tediously dragged Pauole through eight or nine previous versions of his testimony. Many of the discrepancies unveiled by Shellow involved trivialities. Did Pauole call a friend the night he was arrested? One day he said he did. On another day, he said maybe it was a few days after his arrest. Shellow bobbed and weaved, coming at one point to phone calls made and phone calls answered. As part of that, he asked that all of Pauole's phone calls be produced, especially those from the Cook Inlet jail. Judge Greene ordered that they be produced and "read without theatrics."

While he was waiting for those records, Shellow asked Junior who he was talking to the day his girlfriend came home and found all the doors locked. An innocent enough question. Junior said he thought it was Neil Mackay. Maybe.

"I do not recall receiving any calls from Neil Mackay between October 12 and November 1, 1985," Junior added, hedging. "I do not recall telling Amy that I was talking to Neil Mackay. I could have been talking to my wife. I didn't want to hurt Amy's feelings. I would lie to her so she wouldn't know I was talking to Melanie. I have learned to be tactical with people."

He'd just been set up. On day two, a Tuesday, Shellow produced a poster-sized blow-up of Pauole's telephone bill for the period in question. Showed him that no calls were made to either Neil Mackay or Melanie Pauole.

That same day the jury learned that Pauole also had trouble remembering the note with Robert Pfeil's name typed at the top. Pauole had never told police about this incriminating note. It wasn't until four months after his arrest that police laid it in front of him. Only then did he acknowledge its existence. This snatch of paper, they told him, was found in Melanie's recipe box. Pauole was at a loss to explain how it got there.

In court, he was still at a loss. Pauole said he'd forgotten about it. Insisted that nothing since his arrest had jarred his memory about its existence.

Then Shellow thrust out the transcript of Pauole's testimony at the trial of one of his accomplices. He read a series of questions by prosecutor Peter Gruenstein, with answers that had Pauole agreeing the paper was mailed to him by Mackay and then, several questions later, that Mackay gave it to him in person.

Pauole's credibility was shriveling before his very own eyes.

"Within one short page, you went along with two diametrically opposite versions that were suggested to you by Mr. Gruenstein," Shellow said. "Why, why would you go along with whatever Mr. Gruenstein suggested?"\

"Maybe at that time I was confused," Pauole replied.

"The other possibility is that you're lying," Shellow suggested.

"No," Pauole countered.

"What happened to it would be enormously important, you can see that, can't you?" Shellow asked the question with the smirk he reserved for Junior Pauole.

By Tuesday's end, the Court was dealing with more mundane issues. Those being the proposed sanctions against Timothy Petumenos for violating the court's ban on any discussion that Junior Pauole procured sex workers for Neil Mackay.

Anchorage attorney Hal Horton, who represented Petumenos at the hearing, told the Judge "Mr. Petumenos was trying to steer the witness around the topic of prostitutes. It was done in good faith. No special emphasis was placed on the use of the word VIP. Mr. Petumenos had a script he was attempting to follow. Outlined in yellow were the areas to stay away from."

He showed Judge Greene the script. Said things went off track when Junior Pauole started talking about befriending the dancers in an effort to keep them way from pimps and prostitution. That was "the Sir Galahad problem," Horton said, and Petumenos felt he had to steer things in a different direction.

It was a clear violation of the order, Judge Greene ruled. "It was reckless, and some sanction is needed. I am entering a $50.00 sanction. Payable now."

Judge Greene also called it "a very minor sanction" intended to ensure compliance with her court orders, "at a very high level," by all the lawyers in the case. She was, she added, trying to head off any more major complaints by one side against the other.

"We have what has turned out to be a very contentious trial," she said. "Unfortunately."

On day three, Shellow got Junior to talk about the alleged Portland, Oregon, murder contract—to be carried out after the Pfeil murder—which

Junior described as a "bullshit story" designed to suck in John Bright and Larry Gentry, "to hurry them up" in the contract on Robert Pfeil. Then, in the next breath, Junior admitted that, "If the Pfeil murder worked out, maybe we would have gone on to do the Portland contract." Shellow pushed Pauole to reveal some of the folks on the Colacurcio organization hit list. A guy known at "Gaspipe." A man named Richard Hansen. He also got Pauole to admit he knew a "Mr. McQuade."

"I had an idea of what he did for a living," Junior said of McQuade. "He never came out and said, 'I kill people. You want someone taken care of?'"

It didn't seem to help when Junior said that he never said "let's feed him to the pigs" of a potential murder victim. Or that Frank Colacurcio never asked him to murder anyone. The attack on Pauole's "truth" was taking a toll. Junior was no longer the good-natured strip club guru who'd been pushed into a murder he didn't want to commit.

In a break for the prosecution, Judge Greene let Junior address remarks he'd made to *Anchorage Times* reporter Earl Swift. It was a mixed bag, designed to overcome what the state contended were misleading questions—and accusations—elicited by the defense.[61] Before he could tell the truth, however, Junior had to admit he'd lied. Neil Mackay was not the beneficiary of those lies—what emerged instead was something of Pauole's habitual deference to authority figures.

"I told Mr. Swift I did not know of the animosity [between Mackay and Pfeil]," Pauole told Shellow. "I *did* know of it for many years. I also know of the death of Muriel Pfeil and that Mackay was a public suspect in the matter. The statements I made to Mr. Swift was [sic] false. I was afraid of Mr. Mackay."

It was only Wednesday. James Shellow was just getting started. On a smoke break outside the jury room, members of the jury were approached by what Judge Greene called a "media representative." They were "asked questions about the case." By Monday, March 2, Judge Greene had issued

61 The defense, the state said, had offered to ask only three questions of Pauole about Earl Swift. Shellow could not contain himself; he kept going. The result was an accusation that Pauole had perjured himself when he said he hadn't implicated Mackay in his Swift interview. He had. But, the state insisted, he had a reason. *Fear of Neil Mackay*.

a response to *All Media Representatives Involved in the Coverage of State v. Neil Mackay.*

"You are ordered to have no contact with members of this jury until the conclusion of this case, i.e., until after a verdict is received or a mistrial declared. Failure to comply with this order could result in contempt of court and/or suspension of your media privileges."

The question was: how did the media representative get that close to those jurors in the first place?

IF THERE WAS A SIGN OF HOW THINGS WERE GOING, a sure one came that same Wednesday. It was so jaw-dropping that Judge Greene released the jury at 10:45 a.m. Bid them to not return until the following day. The cause of this consternation? The state had just filed a letter they called a "Truth Agreement."

Under that new agreement, they would cut ten years off Pauole's sentence if he testified that Neil Mackay was innocent. Contingent, of course, on that being the truth. The prosecution was willing to bet that Pauole wasn't lying about Neil Mackay's involvement and that he wouldn't take the deal, however attractive.

Judge Greene said that the timing of the new deal, in the middle of Gilbert Pauole's testimony, was "not only novel, but unheard of. It raises a significant question of fairness."

Jim McComas was even more blunt. "The State is trying to make a farce out of this trial," he declaimed, "It's a bogus offer to Pauole."

"They're trying to pollute the jury," he added. "Mackay's personal reaction is to have the jury decide. The conduct of the State has gone beyond reckless. The Court should dismiss the prosecution of this case. For 15 months Pauole has given statements, he has been programmed and rehearsed in what he should say. Pauole knows if he recants the State won't believe him. Pauole knows he cannot recant because there is no incentive for him. It's only a paper offer. The deal has not been offered to him prior to this trial, only after cross . . . The court should put an end to this charade."

"We agree these issues should go before the jury," Tim Petumenos responded. "Mr. Pauole is everything Mr. McComas has said. He is an admitted perjurer, a gangster and everything else. The offer is a gamble.

Mr. Kibby was surprised to hear the defense didn't accept the agreement—we called him on the break.[62] A change in Pauole's testimony now would not affect his Federal Witness Program. The agreement is not meant to be fiction . . . God-knows, he brings in more baggage to this courtroom than a Greyhound bus."

Judge Greene said she would consider the matter overnight and decide the following morning whether to allow the state to proceed. There was little left for surprise in her courtroom. Except perhaps that Pauole's attorney, Richard Kibby, told reporters he *was* surprised by the prosecution's offer. He added he would fly to Fairbanks and confer with his client.

It wouldn't be necessary. "I will not allow the State's introduction of the letter," Judge Greene ruled the following day. "And I deny the defense motion to dismiss." In other words, they were stuck with each other.

BY DAY SIX, JUNIOR SEEMED MORE PREPARED for the onslaught. His talk about the union, he said, was deliberately misleading. "I just used 'union' to say something to Larry, because I recalled that Neil Mackay told me that Mr. Pfeil was involved with a union." "I made up the union story. I never said Anchorage Union. I only said union." "I have never known any union gangsters, nor have I had experience with them."

He did know at least two Hawaiian gangsters, he admitted to Shellow. One was Charles Stevens, whom he'd known "for years," and admitted was "pretty high up in organized crime list." He also mentioned Charles Russell, the alleged enforcer, and Big Junior, who once brought marijuana to him. Plus, a man named Harold Alonzo in Hawaii.

"Mr. Alonzo was my connection for marijuana and cocaine," Junior revealed. "I paid him in cash, in a white envelope."

There it was again. That damned white envelope. Maybe it wasn't as unique as Pauole claimed it to be.

By the end of the week Shellow's torturously slow pace, and deliberate attempt to dismember Junior Pauole, had taken its toll. The master tactician had drifted into tedium. Day by day the local lawyers, so anxious to see a master at work, slowly drifted away. They had better things to do. Gilbert Pauole, meanwhile, was forced to back down, to retreat, to explain

62 Richard Kibby was Pauole's long-standing attorney of record.

himself defensively, by resorting to a constant refrain that had him muttering, "What I meant was . . ."

Then there was the hit on Neil Mackay's pocketbook. All those transcripts from the trials of his co-defendants, and from the previous day's testimony, did not appear in James Shellow's hands as if by magic. Although a court recorder took notes, the word-for-word versions were on tape. Only on tape. Somebody had to meticulously transcribe those tapes. Hour after hour, day after day, sitting at a typewriter with a reel-to-reel tape recorder.

That person was Georgi Haynes of H & M Court Reporting. She'd started her business some thirty years previous, with the help of none other than Neil S. Mackay. He'd even called her as a character witness during his successful attempt to regain custody of Scotty. By May of 1989, Georgi was forced to sue James Shellow, Neil Mackay, and Shellow's law firm to recover $95,000 in costs, interest, and attorney fees. She won, but that fight told the tale.

James Shellow was a spare-no-expense type of lawyer. With a client who pinched every penny.

51

Fairbanks, Alaska, March 5 - 9, 1987

THE STATE HAD A DAY AND A HALF TO REHABILITATE Junior Pauole. They decided to start with some of his greatest vulnerabilities: the times he'd lied in the days and weeks *after* agreeing to tell the truth. Tim Petumenos pulled up a series of charts, listing all of Junior's past statements. They were to go through them one by one.

Junior's answers belied the fact that he had a fair amount of experience within the criminal justice system.

"I didn't fully understand what it meant to 'turn' State's evidence," he revealed. "I didn't think I would have to say anything about my friends in drug deals. I thought it would only be about people involved in the Pfeil murder . . . Amy had a drug problem . . . I did not think I would have to talk about Amy's drug problem."

Pauole's take on these matters was, quite simply, formed of the notion that police investigators are often willing to overlook "petty" matters when they have more important crimes to investigate. Like murder. Getting caught up in Pauole's drug deals represented a distraction from the bigger fish the cops (and prosecutors) needed to fry. There was another technicality that Pauole was also not shy about.

Under Petumenos' re-direct, Pauole had an "out" for his lies about two other matters of importance. "All statements about the Portland matter were not under oath," he declared. In the code of the underworld, some lying was a necessary part of survival. "In my drug dealing I had to lie, I had to keep a straight face," Junior added. "On my one-to-one basis with friends, I wouldn't have to lie. No need to."[63]

Petumenos swept in for the kill. Or, at least, grabbed for it. He wanted to know if Junior felt he was a successful liar. Like, for instance, at Frank Colacurcio's trial. "I don't think I was a successful liar at the Colacurcio trial," Junior replied, deadpan. "He went to prison."

Then this: "I have never been charged with perjury as a result of the Colacurcio trial."

Almost every question Petumenos asked required a bench conference, one where Mackay's team raised issues with the way the questioning was being conducted. When that wasn't happening, Shellow was objecting. Petumenos was asking leading questions of Junior, he complained and coaching the witness. Or, he said, he was violating one of the Judge Greene's rules of evidence. The one that said, "You cannot do with witnesses what you cannot do with documents." Put differently, Petumenos was asking questions that led to statements not supported by other evidence.

Things like, Junior didn't want Frank Colacurcio to know he couldn't read because "maybe he would think I wasn't competent for the job." Or assertions that the Finke's wanted one of Colacurcio's associates "beat up." Or that threats were made to another Colacurcio associate. Or chatter about "gangster talk" and Pauole's memories of statements about "dead fish."

"I never actually sent dead fish to anyone," Junior insisted. "That's Frank's way of trying to rattle someone." Shellow objected. Sustained. Put another one in the defense column.

By midday, Jim McComas was asking for judicial relief. "I ask for a mistrial or dismissal because of repeated violations by the State. This Court has found reckless violations by the State and has not given us any relief."

In his defense, Petumenos responded that he was "not coaching the witness."

Judge Greene had, by now, developed a stock refrain. There was a clear violation, she said. She would not grant a mistrial. She would not dismiss the case either. "You are stuck with Pauole's answers," she proclaimed.

The state, meanwhile, didn't need to be reminded that Mackay's team was not exactly comprised of choirboys. In one particularly egregious

63 That was not what his soon-to-be ex-wife thought. For Melanie Pauole, the mere existence of Amy Shotwell was a lie that Junior lived on a daily basis.

example, from November of '86, they'd issued at least two *subpoena duces tecum* on officials of the Alaska State Department of Corrections, and at least one private doctor who worked with prisoners. Their ploy worked. They were able to access confidential information that they were not otherwise allowed to see. Things like privileged psychological examinations. Their target? Mackay informant Paul Newsom.

There had been, moreover, something deceptive about their approach. Gruenstein and Petumenos noted that "the people who received these subpoenas were not told that the subpoena merely obligated them to appear in court and did not obligate them to give the attorney immediate access to the records described in the subpoena." Mackay's team was, they said, circumventing the law.

As the day ended, Petumenos managed to get a little payback. It came in the form of a long rebuttal answer from the man they were stuck with.

"I never asked Mr. Mackay for money for a bar," Junior declared. "I had my own. I sold my triplex for $151,000.00. I did not want a partner in my bar. It would have been a turn-key operation. All set up. I have never extorted Neil Mackay. It never crossed my mind to extort him. Neil Mackay and I were friends."

As ever, Gilbert K. Pauole was quiet-spoken and polite. It was the best he could do. He was pretty much the same the next day. Under Petumenos' questioning, he remained calm and non-plussed, exuding a vague sort of island vibe. They asked and answered questions designed to reveal Neil Mackay's "extralegal" side.

There was an airline Mackay had told him about, Junior testified, called South Pacific Air. It didn't land at a regular airport, Mackay told him. He could use an alias. When he moved equipment out of the Porterhouse restaurant, Pauole said Mackay required it be done on the weekend, so no "legal people would see me." Junior also revealed that Mackay told him he had to hide what he owned from Robert Pfeil—so he had Junior instead write his rental checks to Lake Bluff, Inc., one of his many corporations.

Then Petumenos turned things to questions about Scotty. "Mackay told me his son got into his first school fight, he was kinda proud of it, but he was concerned, too." What about allegations that you planned to kidnap him, Petumenos asked.

"I have never said I had plans to kidnap Scotty. I knew him. Mackay made him a part of my life."

There was one more doubt they had to remove: all that talk about the union as the actual source of the contract on Robert Pfeil's life. They played the tapes. Junior's eyes glassed over. One of them was the crackly, almost unintelligible tape, made at Junior's triplex, of a conversation with the wired-up Larry Gentry. The defense loved this one, treasured it as a definitive assertion of the truth. Yeah, it's the one where Pauole said the money to assassinate Robert Pfeil "did not come from Mackay . . . it came from town here . . . the union doesn't want Pfeil as the head of the union no more."

Then they played the next tape in the sequence. The one where Pauole pointed to Neil Mackay as the source of the contract, albeit obliquely ("you were right the first time"). "Why did you change your story, Petumenos asked. "Larry started to panic," Pauole replied. "I had to try and calm him down."

Then, "I had to leave because I was losing control over Gentry." The final two tapes with Larry Gentry were played. Junior put his rapidly deteriorating life into perspective. "About three minutes after I left my house, I was arrested."

In a follow-up anteroom conference, Judge Greene refused to let Junior talk about his feelings of remorse for what had happened. His last words before James Shellow put him back on the rack were instead addressed to his deal with the State of Alaska.

"My understanding is I won't have a deal if I lied," Junior muttered.

52

Fairbanks, Alaska, February 8; March 13, 1987; April 13, 1987

The emotional highs of Neil Mackay's trial traced a three-humped curve, with each apex one month apart. The first was Muriel C. Pfeil, the matriarch of the Pfeil clan. Born in 1899 to a Swedish immigrant mother, Muriel C. Pfeil was a woman from a previous century. A square-jawed matriarch who was most comfortable in a house dress. A former schoolteacher who still looked the part, though she had retired many years before. Anchorage had grown up around her and she still lived in the same modest home where she and her husband raised three children. Her dahlias were famous, a gawk-stop when they were in full bloom, though she could not explain why they were so big or so beautiful.

But Grandmother Pfeil was no bumpkin. She was a social presence in Anchorage, had gone to her share of balls, fundraisers, and premiers. In that role, she favored short-brimmed hats, knee length dresses and fur stoles. It was that woman who arrived in Fairbanks. Stylish in a business suit that belied her years, her white hair swept up into a knot, Grandmother Pfeil moved slowly as she took her place on the witness stand.

No one really knew what to expect. There were rules in place to contain her. Just in case. The subject of Muriel's death was to be mentioned only in passing, a shadow that became a specter in the courtroom. She was also to park her personal opinions and speculations about Neil Mackay. Even as she took her seat, however, she was forming an impression of the man on trial in Courtroom D.

"I looked at him two or three times," she said later. "He just sat there. I felt he had no feeling, no remorse."

Even so, she started out saying she'd met Neil Mackay in the early 60's, before this marriage to her daughter, and "got along with him fine." Gruenstein quickly segued to Muriel's divorce and her growing bond with her grandson during that stressful time. "I needed Scotty and Scotty needed his grandmother," she said.

Questions about Muriel's death came next. She related the visit from Marianne and Bob, bearers of bad news. "Muriel's car was towed right past my house," she added.

The personal recollections kept coming. She spoke of telling her son that they had to find out who put the bomb in Muriel's car. "I felt Neil Mackay was responsible," she revealed. There was her memory of perching at Bob's hospital bed, the night he was shot. How Bob looked her in the eyes and said, "I am going to die." It was when she was asked about her grandson that her anger started to leak out.

She heard things that disturbed her. Like Scotty saying he didn't have a bedroom. That he "slept with his daddy." She tried to see Scotty again, she testified, but never got any responses from Neil Mackay.

"The last time I saw him was on his sixth birthday," she added. At Neil Mackay's apartment. In Hawaii. Her grandson was now a teenager.

Grandmother Pfeil's anger, already bubbling, hitched up a notch when Jim McComas took over. She interrupted his questions, refused to give him the one-word answers he preferred, contradicted him at every turn. "Bob did not go into the school to see Scotty," she seethed, after McComas asked about an incident that sparked fear in a young Scotty Mackay. "He saw him through the fence. Bob said Scotty ran from him."

It got worse. McComas stumbled into her personal beehive when he questioned Grandma Pfeil about statements she'd allegedly made about how Muriel died. Grandma Pfeil had had enough. "I never made statements on how Muriel died," she seethed. "That's absolutely a lie you are making."

Judge Greene admonished her. At eighty-seven years old, she'd seemingly lost all fear of authority. "Your Honor," she replied, "I'm a human being too."

The judge sent the jury out of the courtroom. "I just want to answer things I recall," she told Judge Greene. Then she editorialized and made a comparison to a past judge, Judge Madson, who'd presided over Scotty's custody hearing. "I told Judge Madson of my concerns of Neil having custody of Scotty." This was her personal mantra. Neil Mackay should never have been given custody of Scotty.

She was not finished. With the jury back in the courtroom, she was asked what would have helped the situation, given that Neil Mackay got custody anyway. She told the judge, "I thought Mackay would have a housekeeper for Scotty."

McComas objected. Overruled. Gruenstein asked a follow-up about Grandmother Pfeil's Hawaiian visit with her grandson. "What were your thoughts when you left Mr. Mackay's apartment after your visit with Scotty?"

"When I left, I thought to myself, 'How could Neil be so cruel.'"

The court struck her answer. It was to be as if she'd never said it. Even so, Judge Greene could hardly extinguish Grandmother Pfeil. Her words were firm as she said, in closing, "I don't think Scotty knew he had a grandmother. I don't think Neil told him . . . Neil never allowed a display of affection between Scotty and me."

With the jury dismissed, Jim McComas declared that Grandmother Pfeil was "a powder keg." She was, he added, a mistrial waiting to happen.

Excused from her grim duty, and out of the courtroom, Muriel C. Pfeil told the assembled journalists that she would rather have asked the questions than answered them. All her questions would have been directed at Neil Mackay. All of them would have been about Scotty.

"I would ask him how the boy's getting along . . . Has he matured to a teenager in the right way? I would ask, does he have good morals?"

Her thoughts soon drifted to her two dead children and her lost grandson. It's "fate, destiny," she pronounced as she rested on a bench outside the courtroom. "You have to accept things," she said.

"Yesterdays are gone. You can't relive them . . . Tomorrow is promised to no one."

NEXT UP WAS NEIL MACKAY'S SISTER, CAROLINA WILLIS. The two of them hadn't spoken in nine years. They looked at each other tentatively as she took the stand. She wept, but they still did not speak. Her testimony was to be restricted. Nothing about the murder of Muriel Pfeil was to cross her lips. She could only address her custody of Scotty Mackay.

Of course, she was more than that. She was an elemental link to the love that glowed and the hate that glowered at the center of this case. Dressed in a lavender blue suit and blouse, her blonde, curly hair made her look younger than her sixty years. Still slender and attractive, she spoke quietly, deliberately. Her husband Alfred, and their two children, sat in the front spectator row, providing moral support.

Under gentle questioning, she said, "I'm the younger sister of Neil. I worked for him at the time of his divorce." Minutes later the judge was forced to address Muriel Pfeil and her murder. Carolina had taken them there with her quiet recitation of the circumstances that led her to gain custody of her nephew. It was all about the divorce. The bitter divorce and the seemingly inevitable progression toward Muriel's death.

Then, just as quickly, the questions swung to the seesaw that found Scotty gone with his father to the South Pacific, then back with her again. "The Pfeil's would visit three or four afternoons a week," after Scotty's return, she said. "There were times that Scotty would spend nights at the Pfeil's. There was a very loving relationship between the Pfeil's and Scotty.

There were grim memories too, particularly when she recalled relinquishing Scotty to Neil for the final time. "I had prepared him for what would happen," Willis told the jury. She said she sent Scotty to stay with the Pfeils the night before she turned him over. She wanted to pack up the boy's belongings, she murmured. "It wasn't something that he needed to witness again, seeing all his things bundled up . . . again."

It was in that moment her emotions started to overflow.

"I had a picture of Scotty and his mother, to be given to him," she recalled. "We got to the Mackay Building . . . he kept asking if we were going to stay with him. We said no, but we would always be there."

At Mackay's penthouse apartment, Carolina Willis said she handed Scotty through the door, to one of Mackay's lawyers, and never saw him or Mackay again. "The last time I saw my brother was just through the crack in the door that day," she said. Then added, "that was the last day I ever saw my brother until today."

Her testimony at an end, the defense moved to strike everything she had said from the record. "This witness, your honor, contributed nothing to this case," said attorney James McComas. He insinuated that she was brought into court just to stir up feelings. Superior Court Judge Meg Greene let her testimony stand.

Later, outside court, Willis said she didn't know whether she'd reunite with Mackay before leaving Fairbanks. "That has to be up to him, doesn't it?"

There was another question. It was brutal, but Willis fielded it with aplomb. Did she think her brother killed Bob Pfeil?

"Oh, I don't know," she replied. "I pray to God he didn't . . . It's sad," she said. "It's all so sad."

The final hump in the emotional curve was Scotty Mackay. He was in Fairbanks as a defense witness, there to dispute a critical phone call that Junior Pauole claimed to have made in the hours after the shooting of Robert Pfeil. The two sides fought over him. Peter Gruenstein wanted to know if he understood the oath he was to take. The one about telling the truth. Jim McComas was curt in response. "He's fourteen. He's bright.

The cramped Fairbanks courtroom now hosted a reunion of sorts. Neil Mackay hadn't seen Scotty since his Hawaii arrest. More than a year had passed. They were allowed to embrace for a brief, emotional moment before Scotty took the stand. He was asked the usual small stuff, the establishing questions, the legitimizing answers. His blond hair had darkened to light brown and at fourteen he was tall for his age. He resembled the Pfeil side of the family, long legged and rawboned.

He said his favorite subjects in school were science and algebra. He said he belonged to a military strategy club and wanted to be a military pilot and a lawyer when he grew up, "just like my father." He added that he understood that his father was charged with a very serious crime, but said he wouldn't lie to save him, "'cause my father always raised me in an environment where honesty is the best policy."

After drawing a diagram of their Ilikai condo, Scotty quickly said what he was there to say. The time in question was October 12, 1985, about an hour after Robert Pfeil was shot.

"At About 5-5:30 pm, Mr. McGuire came over with some dinner," Scotty said, his poise unassailable. "He gave it to us about 6 pm. My father went to bed. Just me and Mr. McGuire stayed in the living room to watch

TV. A phone call came in about 7 or 8. I answered it. I said hello . . . There was no answer. I hung up. There was only muffled static. I was scared. I woke up my father."

Soon after that, Scotty claimed, another call came in. Scotty said his father answered it. "The second phone call rang only 4 or 5 times before he answered. I slightly ran for my dad when second call came in, on the first ring. I was next to him. He said, 'Hello . . . how are you.' Then he said, 'as soon as he gets back, I'll send him over.' Dad went back to bed. I watched TV."

Under questioning from Jim McComas, Scotty insisted that, "I never heard my dad say, 'Good, I was going to take him to court.'"

If there was a discrepancy, it was that phone company records showed a one-minute call from Pauole's Anchorage home to Mackay's Honolulu condominium. A call made that very night. At that very time. The other discrepancy, if it could be called that, was that "The lawyers asked me in January of '87 to recall what happened in November of '85. I remembered it all pretty well," Scotty claimed.

Special prosecutor Peter Gruenstein kept his voice soft and his questions friendly but asked Scotty to explain how a boy his age could possibly remember something so minor more than a year later. Scotty said the call was unusual and left him "fearful."

"Was that the most unusual thing that happened to you, a boy of twelve at the time, . . . receiving this short phone call?" Gruenstein asked.

"Yes," said Scotty.

The young man was unable to remember other details from that night. What a neighbor brought over for dinner, what he was watching on television when the phone rang, what anyone was wearing. Except that Mr. McGuire, he said, wore shorts, no shirt, and had bare feet. The phone call stood out in his memory so many months later, he said, because nothing like that had ever happened to him before.

At a quick bench conference, Gruenstein insisted it was important to ask Scotty about his Grandma Pfeil. Thought his father had undue influence on him. His answers about Grandma Pfeil could open a window on those feelings. Judge Greene toed a narrow line. Gruenstein could examine around areas of contact with his relatives, but that was all. The next exchange took the air out of the room.

Peter Gruenstein asked Scotty if he saw any of his relatives in the room. "I don't see any relatives in the courtroom," he replied.

Gruenstein pointed out his aunt, Marianne Pfeil, sitting in her usual perch behind the prosecution. She listened grimly. Gruenstein asked her to stand. He asked Scotty if he recognized her. Scotty said no.

"Do you have bad feelings about her?'

"I have no feelings good or bad about my Aunt Marianne. I was happy being with my father. I remember my uncle Bob. I did not want to see him . . . I don't remember Caroline Pfeil . . . I remember the Willis's," then added, "I have not wanted to see the Willis's."

Not once was Muriel Pfeil's name mentioned during these rueful exchanges and Scotty never referred to his mother. The defense stayed away from the subject and stridently objected when Gruenstein butted in with his persistent questions. When asked on cross about the Pfeils, Scotty said he had no interest in getting to know them. He said he hadn't seen any of them since he moved to Hawaii with his father except for a single visit from his grandmother shortly after that. He said he didn't know if his grandmother Pfeil was alive or dead.

"Is that because you haven't wanted any contact with them?" asked Gruenstein. Yes, Scotty said, adding that it was his decision. That he hadn't been influenced by his father. When asked why he didn't want to know his mother's family, Scotty said, "Because I was happy living with my father."

Gruenstein closed by asking Scotty if his testimony was "the God honest truth."

"The God honest truth," Scotty insisted.

When Scotty was excused, Marianne asked for, and got, defense permission to talk to him. They met in the hallway outside the courtroom, with reporters at the ready. Scotty was plainly unenthused, having to be prodded to acknowledge her presence.

"I'm your Aunt Marianne," Scotty Mackay's aunt said, softly. "I just wanted to meet you. Your grandmother, she is still alive. She is 87 years old. She says hello."

Scotty acknowledged his aunt but squirmed awkwardly. Marianne Pfeil pushed him. "Do you have a greeting for her?" she asked.

"Just say hello," Scotty said. Then he moved away quickly, as if her mere proximity could infect him.

"This has been a sad morning," Marianne said later. "I'm glad grandma wasn't here. She would have been so hurt. Muriel's son . . ." Her voice trailed off into an expression of infinite sadness.[64]

If the prosecution seemed skeptical of Scotty Mackay's credibility, they had good reason. The usual conditions applied, of course. Scotty was a child defending a parent upon whom he depended but they had more than that. They had Pat Moody from the Kaimuki Christian School in Oahu, Scotty's schoolteacher, and sometime guardian, waiting in the wings.

Except for one thing.

The State was ultimately thwarted in their effort to bring Pat Moody to Fairbanks. Blocked in their attempt to use her testimony to impeach Scotty Mackay. The culprit was Judge Robert Won Bae of Oahu. The same judge who had earlier obstructed attempts to extradite Neil Mackay on the murder charge.

Judge Chang ruled that traveling to Alaska for the trial would be an undue personal and financial hardship for Ms. Moody. His ruling was also informed by his *finding of fact* that she denied having said what she told Joe Austin. Because of those denials, he said, Moody was not the "material and necessary witness" that Alaska authorities claimed she would be.

Such was her turnaround that one could be forgiven for thinking someone had gotten to her.

64 Many thanks to the clutch of Anchorage news reporters who captured this poignant scene.

53

Fairbanks, Alaska, April 1987

As the trial wound down, the Mackay defense team announced that Neil Sutherland Mackay would not testify on his own behalf. A defense speech expert, who could explain Mackay's unusual—and perhaps incriminating—answers in the Pauole phone call, would also not appear. Not surprising. Mackay was constitutionally protected from testifying and prosecutors could not use his failure to do so against him. The defense could call as many or as few witnesses as they desired.

The prosecution took exception. They'd been blindsided. Not only because McComas had told jurors in his opening remarks that an expert would appear and explain the eccentricities of Mackay's speech. (It was, they claimed, aphasia.) More because Jim McComas had "impersonated" Neil Mackay in his opening by channeling his client's inner thoughts. Had used words that spoke of what Mr. Mackay "knew," was "concerned" about, "understood," "believed." Had talked about conversations between Mackay and Pauole that suggested that Mackay himself would tell his side of the story, in person.

Then cavalierly failed to offer any supporting evidence at trial. Failed because the only person who could speak to those things was . . . Neil S. Mackay. There were over one hundred of these unsupported "things." Tantalizing, inculpatory insinuations left suspended, to be lodged in the back of jurors' minds. It was no surprise that the prosecution took the matter up with Judge Greene.

"Mr. McComas gave every reason for us to believe that Mr. Mackay would take the stand," Peter Gruenstein complained. "We cannot cure the prejudice now, but I would still almost ask for a defense-induced mistrial—these issues are ones I cannot deal with."

McComas' response bordered on the absurd.

"It was our initial intent to have Mr. Mackay take the stand," the defense attorney claimed. "The defense action was because of the State. They went on and on, called numerous witnesses on cumulative matters. The jury got tired. They asked us to move on. If we put Mackay on, the trial would have been extended even longer. We had to, for the sake of length, not to call Mackay."

The state's case had, in fact, constituted an extensive parade of witnesses. Of their original plan to call 100 witnesses, they'd called closer to half that. Fifty-eight in all. Still generous compared to the seven called by the defense but enough to leave Gruenstein room to express his righteous indignation.

"Mr. McComas's reasons are incredible to believe," Gruenstein complained. "We reserve the right of the State to ask for a mistrial."

The gangly defense lawyer was circumspect in response, promising not to violate court rules by reiterating the one-hundred unproven claims during his closing arguments. Well, Gruenstein countered, the trouble is that the defense statements are already embedded in the juror's minds. "The defense only has to imply them, and the jurors will fill in the gaps."

"Jurors will not remember what was said in opening statements," McComas countered. As if he had not been drilling those ideas into their heads the entire trial.

Judge Greene once again split the baby. Said Gruenstein could tell the jurors that opening statements are not evidence. Could, furthermore, attack the defense case but he could not, under any circumstances, fault the defense for not coming through on its broken promises. Beyond that, there was plenty of stupid to go around and at least one genuine dud.

Stupid was putting Paul Newsom on the stand. All Mackay's defense had to do was get him to account for his assault, rape and kidnapping convictions and he was forever stained. (Though the defense was worried enough that they took pains to impeach Newsom over multiple days.) Stupid was putting a phalanx of Pauole's less-than-innocent friends and acquaintances on the stand. Amy Shotwell could speak authoritatively about Junior's relationship with Neil Mackay, but she had conveniently destroyed Pauole's book of drug debts before the cops could get their hands on it.

Stupid was using Tim Todd to deny allegations of the so-called Oregon murder plot. Todd had also partnered with Junior in running kilos of cocaine. Or Matthew Vickers, who could speak to Junior's desire to hire him as a bodyguard for Neil Mackay—and could put the finest details on John Bright's role in the assassination. Vickers had once been jailed for assaulting a police officer. Was, at the time of his testimony, in prison on drug charges. It was hard for him to refute the former, although he protested vigorously. On the stand Vickers testified that Junior paid him to break the bones of pimps who were hounding his dancers. Price? Two-hundred dollars a bone. Vickers was proof of Pauole's malignancy. As if they needed more.

Which left room for the defense to bring on their own version of stupid. First up was Lance Speigel, whom Mackay had hired in his federal lawsuit against the Pfeils. There was a settlement proposal made, Speigel testified. "I suggested that Mr. Mackay pay the judgment. He rejected my recommendation." Later, Speigel added, "Mr. Mackay did not want to follow my advice. He objected strongly."

This was a Neil Mackay who steered closer to the prosecution's description. Stubborn. Head strong. Arrogant.

The next questionable call was named Lucian Dancaescu. Whatever he knew—and there *was* that $100,000 grand he gave Junior Pauole under duress in 1985—his less than stellar reputation was a problem. On the witness stand, he admitted he'd visited Frank Colacurcio in prison. Had, in fact, held money for Colacurcio. The same money that went to Junior. Then had the temerity to claim he only knew of Colacurcio's "reputation from the newspapers." Oh and, yes, he admitted, he was outside the bank when his wife withdrew a half-million dollars. In cash.

It takes more than the questionable calls, though. Those stupidities were soon outdone by a dud. The one that seemed central to the defense case. Until it didn't look as good as it should have.

The Union theory propounded by the defense was to be the end-all-be-all explanation for Robert Pfeil's assassination. Over the course of several weeks, a parade of Alaska Airlines employees took the stand to push back on the defense theory. They included the former and current chairman of the Alaska Master Executive Council of the Airline Pilots Association. The Chief Pilot for Alaska Airlines. An Alaska Airlines security specialist.

When Alaska Airlines security chief Carl Sanders took the stand for the prosecution, he stuck a pin in the theory that Robert Pfeil's murder was a union-financed hit. Sanders started by recalling a call from Grimes and Branchflower on October 30, 1985, asking him to research the name McKenzie. "I did not find any McKenzie in Anchorage," Sanders testified. "I found two out of Seattle, one female, one male. The male had been terminated in 1984. I relayed that info to Mr. Grimes's office." Sanders also found another name, close to McKenzie. "Mr. McKerney was terminated in January of 85."

It was a dead end.

It didn't get any better when the state called Daryl Eygabroad, chairman of the Machinists Union in Seattle. Eygabroad talked about the union strike of 1985, the purported reason for the vendetta against Robert Pfeil. "The employees ran that strike," Eygabroad said. "There was very little problem. Picket lines were peaceful . . . There was no violence. No threats toward any pilots."

A squad of Alaska Airlines pilots added another layer of shade to the union theory. One Alaska pilot, who knew Robert Pfeil, said that he "was never aware of threats toward any pilot." Another said, "As pilots, we did not honor picket lines. I was not aware of any threats or violence toward pilots. Maybe some name calling . . . I had no concerns for the safety of our pilots."

The state even called in one of Alaska Airlines' corporate attorneys. Geraldine P. Carolan testified that, during the 1985 strike, "There was no acts of violence toward any pilot at all."

On cross, Jim Shellow went after Carolan, attorney-to-attorney. Carolan stood her ground. She was not about to be intimidated.

"I'm not under subpoena for the State," she declared on cross-examination. "I would have resisted a subpoena by the defense. There were some threats—death and bomb threats. I recall that [Alaska Airlines CEO] Bruce Kennedy had a cross put on his lawn. There was one person who had a horse poisoned."

On re-direct, Peter Gruenstein let Carolan pull out the rug.

Carolan testified that two employees were terminated for their actions. A man who crossed the picket line to go to work, she added, "had nothing whatsoever to do with Mr. Pfeil. There was no pilot threatened whatsoever. No deaths. The most serious incident was one punch thrown. The strike was not a big deal after the first couple of weeks."

Peter Gruenstein took a little more than three hours to make the state's final case against Neil Sutherland Mackay. Thirty-five words said it all. "There was one long, dark shadow over Bob Pfeil's otherwise sunshine-filled life," Gruenstein. "Robert Pfeil had but one mortal enemy in the world and he sits before you, awaiting the justice he deserves."

Gruenstein said more, of course. Nothing was more important than solving the problem of Junior Pauole. He reminded the jurors not to believe Junior "because he's a fine human being," but because other evidence corroborated his testimony.

"The defense is trying to put Pauole on trial in place of their client," Gruenstein reminded them. "Neil Mackay is the issue in this trial and all the evidence points in one direction. It points to Neil Mackay."

The next day, James McComas countered that, "efforts to blame Mackay for the death of his brother-in-law, Robert Pfeil, should end with rejection of the gangster's lies and a not-guilty verdict."

The union theory, however, had become a shadow of its former self. "Was a union involved in the killing of Robert Pfeil?" McComas wondered. "Again, that's something that the defense can't prove one way or the other for sure." Then he quickly pivoted to the patsy theory. Took pains to remind everyone within earshot that Robert Pfeil was killed only because Junior Pauole was setting the stage for a major extortion attempt. Mentioned a million-dollar prize that gleamed in Junior's eyes. Suggested that, if Mackay was worried about custody of his son and their relationship, he would not endanger either by starting a plan to kill Robert Pfeil.

"Would he risk his greatest gift?"

Not being able to discuss his client's thoughts didn't seem to thwart McComas' argument. The lanky lawyer from Milwaukee chatted up the jury for nearly six hours with only glancing references to the notes and charts at his fingertips. His best prop was a life-sized photo of Gilbert Pauole. He addressed that prop animatedly. As if the man in the photo were present and alive in the courtroom.

On rebuttal, Gruenstein spewed acid on the defense case. Called their extortion plot "a story out of the mouth of a lawyer." Called it an "absurd, ridiculous, crazy theory." Then walked them through an imaginary conversation.

"Neil, this is Junior," Gruenstein said as he dropped into his most dramatic range, with ridicule and sarcasm fighting for control. "I want to tell you something . . . I arranged for the killing of Bob Pfeil . . . Everybody's going to think you're behind it . . . I want a hundred thousand dollars or two hundred thousand dollars to start this bar . . . Now, I want you to give me this money or I'm going to tell the police you did it."

The defense theory, he added, makes Junior Pauole into "this evil genius," Gruenstein told them. "A sophisticated member of organized crime." This was the same man who bought a getaway ticket and put it in his own name, because . . . Junior Pauole wanted the frequent flier mileage. "This is not a genius."

Finally, after months of a trial filled with anger and recriminations, it was all over. The fate of Neil S. Mackay slipped into the hands of nine women and three men. They would be sequestered in a Travelers Inn motel until they reached their verdict or declared an impasse. No one wanted the latter.

54

Fairbanks, Alaska, April 1987

THE JURY'S WORST DAYS WERE SPENT IN THE SMALL, stuffy jury room of the outdated courthouse. Beyond that room, one floor down, the attorneys were arguing over what the jury could see during their deliberations. They argued a lot, argued over every assertion, every nuance, every speck of evidence. There was a lot to consider.

Photos of the crime scene, including aerial shots. Four bullets. The car door. Autopsy photos of Robert Pfeil's lungs and spinal cord. A piece of plywood used by John Bright to surveil the Pfeil house. Photos from inside Mackay's condo. Photos of his Smith-Corona typewriter. Photos of the pay phones where he deliberately moved his ongoing conversation with Junior. A list of phone numbers and phone calls, plus the personal letters and tapes. Reels and reels of tapes.

The jury got the case on a Friday. Their first request was for tapes and transcripts from several witnesses, including Paul Newsom and Charles Sullivan. Judge Greene responded the next day. It was less than they expected.

MEMBERS OF THE JURY:

We cannot provide tapes of the testimony to you. However, you may request a playback of all or any portion of the testimony of all or any witness. Playbacks are done in open court.

The transcripts of the testimony which you have requested will be provided to you at various times today as they become available. By the end of the day today, you should have transcripts of testimony of the four witnesses you have requested.

Mary E. Greene
Superior Court Judge

Even the request for transcripts proved contentious. Mackay's team said they'd provide them. Redacted, of course. Gruenstein said they couldn't just take selective transcripts from the defense. "We strongly oppose transcripts," he insisted. Judge Greene thought otherwise. They'd provide transcripts. Allow playbacks.

The jury, meanwhile, sent confusing requests to the judge, first listing several items, then leaving some off their follow-up note. Perhaps it didn't matter. By April 26th, they were firmly focused on Junior Pauole. They wanted tapes, lots of tapes. Two days of his direct testimony. Three days of his cross-examination. Two days of his redirect. Twenty hours of tapes in all.

Perhaps curiously, they wanted to go through the transcripts of Chester Chiara, superintendent of the 6th Avenue Jail. Paul Newsom had reentered the conversation, albeit obliquely. The nature of their request told court-watchers the jury was considering Newsom's reliability and trustworthiness. It was evident they trusted Chester Chiara more than they trusted Paul Newsom.

The worst day for the jurors came only three days into their deliberations. Having worked through the weekend, they sent a note to Judge Greene on Monday, April 27. It was signed by the jury foreman, Dave Snodgrass.

27 April 87

A question about the evidence has come up. It seems as though there is possibility that certain documents (Jack Guard interviews by Austin and Hoffbeck) have come in our possession that have no EXHIBIT #'s.

We would like to know if we should have these. Several of the juror members have read these already.

Thank you,
Dave Snodgrass

Now everyone knew. There was evidence in the jurors' hands that shouldn't be there. It was not just any old information.

The one-and-a-half-inch stack of annotated documents focused on two Jack Guard police interviews. Interviews in which he made dozens of references to other crimes and murders. Crimes that implicated Neil Mackay and connected him to a raft of old Alaska criminals. One reference stood out. It was Mackay's bitter bar association fight in the 60s, with Chief Justice Buell Nesbitt. Intimations that Neil Mackay had hatched a murder plot against Justice Nesbitt. This was serious stuff. By the end of the day, Judge Greene had addressed a painful missive to the jury.

April 27, 1987
5:40 p.m.
MEMBERS OF THE JURY

Thank you for providing the materials to me; these items were not admitted into evidence and should not have been provided to you. You should not discuss the information that was contained in the documents and those of you who have read them should not tell others what was contained in the documents. Those of you who have read the information must disregard it and not consider the information in your deliberations.

Mary E. Greene
SUPERIOR COURT JUDGE

Everything was now in limbo. Lawyers and staff on all sides of the case, the judge and even the in-court deputy looked grim and tired at the emergency hearing convened late Monday afternoon. The question swarming around them was a shattered beehive that hummed with dread. They fought the notion that a mistrial was in their future. Jim McComas suggested they find out "who read all or portions of the material, who discussed it, heard about it—their reactions." It was a start.

He added, he wanted that done outside of counsel's presence. He claimed it would be too intimidating for attorneys to be present and he encouraged the judge to ask Gruenstein to waive his right to be present. Gruenstein was pissed. "It's outrageous to ask Counsel in a lawsuit to not be present during *voir dire*. I am not going to waive my presence."

Cooler heads prevailed. Judge Greene said she wouldn't question the jurors without having a motion before her and said they'd resume the next morning. Jurors, who were not told of the *brouhaha*, continued deliberating in another part of the courthouse until 8 p.m. and then retired to the Travelers Inn for their fourth night in exile.

Superior Court Judge Meg Greene set the mistrial hearing for the following morning at 8:05 a.m.

Bright and early the next day, with Fairbanks ready to enjoy sixteen hours of daylight, defense attorney James McComas told reporters that the documents were "unbelievably, horribly prejudicial material." McComas admitted that the interviews "make reference to untold other crimes alleged to involve Mackay," including murders. Gruenstein said the material also contained matters prejudicial to the state and averred he might not oppose a motion for a mistrial if one was made.

It took eight miserable hours to reach a decision. The arguments were endless. The jury, meanwhile. stood at the window of the jury room and "told cars where to park," said juror Denise Rivera. They mocked the quirks of lawyers and witnesses alike. Played pickup sticks with pencils. According to juror Gina Murrow, "we looked out the window and made-up stories about people on the street."

"Sequestering was miserable," she said. "It's like being in jail," with no privacy except in the bathroom and Kentucky Fried Chicken every day.

By Tuesday evening, Judge Greene declared a mistrial. The jury, she concluded, was incurably tainted. Indeed, seven jurors had been exposed to the materials. Some had found them particularly illuminating. "I find there is prejudice here that cannot be undone," Greene declared, a pronounced quaver in her normally uninflected voice. "I find manifest necessity and declare a mistrial."

Slumped in their chairs, periodically rubbing their eyes, the attorneys stoically waited for the jury to file in. "I have some good news and bad news," Greene told the nine-woman, three-man panel. "The good news is you get to see your families tonight. The bad news is I have declared a mistrial."

"It's not your fault," she told the jury. "In fact, it was nobody's fault . . . Life sometimes throws us a curve and this was our curve."

The recriminations would ring across Alaska, a clarion call taken up by even the least cynical among them. A three-and-a-half-month trial, estimated to have cost several million dollars, was now nothing more than a speck of dust. What were these people thinking? What new levels of incompetence had they reached?

Heads would roll. Well, at least, that's what some enraged citizens demanded. The kind who write letters to the Editor.

55

Fairbanks, Alaska, April 30, 1987

MARIANNE PFEIL HAD A FRONT ROW SEAT TO the bizarre. She'd come to Judge Greene's cramped courtroom to see if Neil Mackay made bail in the wake of the sudden mistrial. His attorneys wanted him declared indigent and bound over to the custody of his sister. A woman he hadn't seen for nine years, save her brief testimony in that very courtroom. Mackay had been in secure custody for eighteen months, his attorneys whimpered. He's unable to meet the terms of his release.

The cost of Mackay's defense, they told the judge, included expenses and fees for the trial and trial preparation of about $750,000 in cash plus three pieces of property, bringing the total to slightly over $1 million. Mackay "has now expended not only all of his money, but tens of thousands of dollars of his lawyers' money," cried Jim McComas. Jim Shellow added that his firm was $86,000 in the hole.

"Mr. Mackay has been broken by this prosecution financially," McComas insisted. He pointed to Mackay's property transfers to his defense team as proof. James Shellow got the building that once housed the Wild Cherry. Steve Goodenow got some property in Eagle River and Mackay's Ilikai condo.

"He would never have given up the Ilikai apartment as payment to Steve Goodenow if he had a choice, McComas added. "That's Scotty's home."

"What hasn't changed is Mr. Mackay's danger to the community or his risk to flee," Peter Gruenstein countered. "Mr. Mackay is a demonstrated flight risk," the prosecutor insisted, referring to Mackay's Micronesia misadventure for what seemed like the millionth time. Gruenstein added that Mackay had a history of hiding assets. That he'd only recently reported his net worth at about $10 million.

"To say the prosecution has broken him is perhaps oversimplistic," the prosecutor emphasized.

Greene also expressed skepticism about Mackay's claim of poverty. In an earlier bail order, she'd concluded that, based on the best information available, "Mr. Mackay's net worth is between six and eight million dollars." The judge lowered his bail from $7 million to $1 million. She said she would not consider releasing him on personal recognizance until she saw some "cold, hard facts about his financial worth. That's as far as I'm willing to go," she insisted.

The resulting financial reports would only muddy the waters. Coopers & Lybrand found a maze of corporate holdings and bank accounts. His Money Market accounts had been closed. His First Hawaiian Bank accounts? Closed. His First Interstate Bank of Nevada accounts? Unable to verify. His First National Bank of Anchorage accounts? Closed or no longer in Neil Mackay's name. His tax statements? Inconclusive. Coopers & Lybrand did find that there were some unusual transactions, however, and that it seemed likely "Mr. Mackay had access to additional sources of funds in Hawaii which are unknown to us."

Then came the James Shellow report, with Neil Mackay's attorney acting in his capacity as a Certified Public Accountant. Shellow did what he could with what he had, including the Coopers & Lybrand report and records seized from various Mackay properties. "I believe based on the foregoing," he solemnly declared, "that Mr. Mackay has a negative net worth."

Then there was a display of truly bizarre proportions.

It started with five of the mistrial jurors, who showed up to support the defense request that Mackay be released from jail. They were among seven votes for acquittal, as against three for conviction and two undecideds. At least two of them said they had volunteered to work as support staff for the defense team, free of charge, during Mackay's retrial. Defense attorney James Shellow seemed amazed, although very pleased, at the jurors' offer.

When the hearing ended, the jurors and the defense attorneys hugged each other and wished each other well. Shellow could be heard inviting everyone to visit him in Milwaukee, where he lived. "Nothing like this has ever happened to me before," he said, basking in the temporary glow.

Asked by jurors to rate the trial participants, the former jurors praised Judge Greene, whom they described as fair and considerate. They expressed cautious support for the lawyers on both sides. Lest anyone think a trial is not a popularity contest, at least one juror revealed that defense attorney James McComas was terrific.

"He has a big heart I think," said former juror Gina Murrow, "compassion for humankind in general." Shortly thereafter, three of the jurors went to the defense attorney's office in the courthouse to hammer out the details of their support.

Other spectators, including local prosecutors and defense attorneys, appeared astonished and bemused at the public display of affection. Kris Capps, the *Fairbanks News-Miner's* veteran court reporter, was seated in a back row of the courtroom next to Harry Davis, the Fairbanks district attorney. After watching the courtroom antics for a while, Capps leaned over and said, "tell me the truth, Harry. Have you ever hugged a juror?"

The prosecutor's "snarl could be heard two rows away," reported fellow journalist Sheila Toomey. Neil Mackay, meanwhile, thanked several of the women for their support and then was whisked away by his Trooper escort. Marianne Pfeil, who happened to be seated in the middle of the former jurors, had an entirely different reaction.

She was stunned.

NEIL MACKAY, WHO SEEMED GENETICALLY PREDISPOSED to a morose fatalism, seemed positively ebullient once he got to the Judicial Service vehicle stationed outside the courtroom. Ensconced in the front seat, next to Trooper Stephen J. Foster, he started chatting him up. It was not unusual. The two of them had chatted many times since the trial began. Transporting Neil Mackay was Foster's full-time assignment. Their destination was the Fairbanks Correctional Center, a mere six minutes from the courthouse.

Mackay probably said too much. Trooper Foster reported the conversation to his supervisor. And wrote it up that very same day. After setting the stage with the minute details of what was to be a routine matter, Foster related that:

"Mr. McKay [sic] stated that he was surprised and yet pleased that the jury members had shown up to speak on his behalf and also to give him praise and what he called 'encouragement.' He made the comment that it made him feel good and humble that they had shown their feelings even after such a long trial.

"After finishing that comment McKay stated that he knew what the outcome was gonna be of the trial and that there would have been an acquittal if not a hung jury. He went on to state that he knew the jury was 10 to 2 at the time of the mistrial. I mentioned to him that I was skeptical of his figures and that I thought the point was moot.

"McKay further stated that he and his attorneys were quite sure of the outcome and had no doubt of it. Again, I looked skeptically at him, and he related that his attorneys had spoke to all of the jury members and that they had conducted interviews which gave him that figure."

Once Neil Mackay got talking, it was hard to stop him. There was much in his soliloquy that matched his letters to Jack Guard. Inside that trooper transport, he was a philosopher king.

"Mr. McKay went on to state that he felt that he was in a good position. He felt confident and that he was very pleased with the judge that he had received. He felt that she had made all the right decisions and had done the best job he had ever seen a judge perform and he went on to state that he was impressed with Judge Greene's abilities.

"While pulling into the back gate of Correctional Center, he specifically went on to state that he wanted to talk to me about economics. I said go ahead. He says you know that when you have money, people see it and it causes problems, and as long as they see it the problems will continue.

"But when it's gone and they don't see it anymore, the problem will go away. I replied in the affirmative. He said well I got my bail reduced to a million dollars. That's good. He leaned over to me, and he said what would you do with a million dollars? I said I wouldn't know what to do with a million dollars. I hesitated and then said I wouldn't know what to do with $10,000. He said $10,000? I said yeah. He said shit, I've got that. That's pocket change, and then he snickered. He says yeah, I've got a million dollars."

An interesting series of comments from a man who'd just pled poverty. His attorneys were forced to file papers claiming his remarks "constitute a sort of 'black humor.'" They were compelled to say considerably more. "The state's suggestion—that Mr. Mackay, having the keys to his cell in the form of $1,000,000.00, elected to inform a state trooper instead of opening the lock—is absurd."

Except, of course, Neil Mackay was notoriously tight-fisted. Even the men who knew him best did not spare him in that regard. These were men who'd known him for decades. All were quoted in a Page 1 story by Sheila Toomey for the *Anchorage Daily News*.

"He was tight with money unless he decided to be generous," said Dave Talbot. "The more profit you made, the more skillfully you did it, that was the mark of success."

"He was obsessed with money," added a former drinking buddy who later became a judge. "There was something wrong with the man. It seemed like money was all he ever thought about."

"He's a Scotsman and he liked money for money," concluded friend and former Alaska State Attorney General Edgar Paul Boyko.

THE INVESTIGATION INTO THE JURY ROOM FIASCO would not be kind. Accusations were scalpels, slashing in every direction. Some of them pointed to one of the defense investigators. Officer Joe Hoffbeck said Greene handed over the documents not meant for the jury to defense investigator Steve Goodenow, who then left the courtroom to make copies that were to be distributed to the defense and prosecution. Hoffbeck added that, after the documents were discovered and Greene was questioning the jurors individually, Goodenow was sworn in as an honorary bailiff and allowed to handle the tapes of Greene's questioning.

Sergeant Joe Austin added that Superior Court Judge Mary E. Greene gave the defense team her keys so they could more easily get to their temporary offices—on the same floor—by walking through an anteroom adjacent to the back of the courtroom.

It was more complex than that. Some exhibits in the Mackay trial *were* carried from the courtroom, two flights upstairs to the jury room, when Goodenow helped a court clerk carry four boxes of evidence to the jury room. The defense investigator knew a back way into the chambers of trial Judge Meg Greene. On the other hand, some material may have been left standing unattended in the hall outside the room. Control of keys to the courthouse was lax, moreover, and when the jury retired each night, trial exhibits were left in a room that could be opened with a courthouse master key.

An Alaska State Trooper report also found that documents presented to the judge during the trial were stored in a small, wooden cabinet behind Greene's chair. Both admissible and inadmissible evidence was kept there, it said, and sorted out later. Trooper Sgt. James McCann, who wrote the report, compared the system to "storing the dynamite with the matches."

Whatever the verdict, the clerk broke court system rules by allowing someone other than a court worker to handle exhibits.

"You could call that a breach of security," presiding Judge Jay Hodges declared, after reviewing the Alaska State Trooper report.

In a statement issued by phone from their Milwaukee law offices, defense attorneys Jim McComas and Jim Shellow said no one connected with the defense "had any knowledge of or participation in providing the jury with these police reports, which were prejudicial to our client." In a telephone interview from his Honolulu office, Steve Goodenow also rejected allegations that he had back-door knowledge of the Fairbanks courthouse or that he was alone when delivering exhibits to jurors.

"I had absolutely nothing to do with those documents getting in front of the jury," Goodenow said. "I have no knowledge as to how they got there."

The person who really mattered—Judge Hodges—took issue with McCann's report. He had his doubts about Sgt. McCann. "It does not appear that the report is really objective," Hodges said, "and I take issue with the personal feelings and innuendoes injected in the report by the investigator."

By June of 1987, the Alaska Court System reached an official conclusion about the misbegotten materials found in the Mackay jury room. They concluded that the trial judge, the attorneys, and the in-court clerk were equally responsible for letting documents not in evidence make their way into the jury room. The supervisor for the in-court clerks in Fairbanks conducted her own investigation and determined that "clerical error," not lax security, led to the mistrial.

"In categorizing this as clerical error, I am not placing the blame on the in-court clerk alone," the supervisor said in a memo. "It is the duty of the trial judge, the attorney for the state and the attorney of the defense as well as the in-court clerk, to carefully go through the exhibits prior to the exhibits going into the jury room at the time of deliberation.

"Therefore, the trial judge, the attorneys of record and the in-court clerk must bear the burden of this mistrial equally."

Judge Greene rejected the conclusion. "She does not feel that it is a judge's responsibility to go through the exhibits prior to them going to the jury room," she was quoted in a news account, "but rather is the responsibility of the attorneys for both sides in concert with the in-court clerk."

In the wake of the mistrial, Judge Greene scheduled Neil Mackay's retrial for August 17th, even though a trial judge had not been assigned. It didn't take long. On May 18, 1987, Greene wrote to all concerned that, "This is to advise you that Chief Justice Rabinowitz has determined that I should continue as the judge assigned to this case." Indeed, the Chief Justice had Greene's' back and, in fact, encouraged other jurists to close ranks behind her.

In a June 6, 1987, luncheon before the Alaska Bar Association, the chief justice praised Greene as "enthusiastic and bright."

"The Anchorage papers say Judge Greene is ill-equipped to try that case," Rabinowitz said, referring to Mackay's second trial. He didn't agree. He described her as "typical of the new wave of judges." He added that her judicial enthusiasm matched that of other new judges. Rabinowitz also praised Greene's research ability and her integrity. He said everyone would be pleased with the court system if all judges put in as many hours as Greene did.

The Chief Justice's comments were greeted with extended applause from the audience.

Only the day before, Judge Greene had rejected a request by Mackay that the state provide funds to offset some of his defense costs. "I do not believe evidence presented that Mackay is indigent," Greene said. "I find he is not. I do not believe he doesn't have assets to pay for his attorneys and costs," she added. "At the least, he has a sizeable debt owed to him. There is no evidence that is not a collectable debt."

There would, however, be at least one change at Mackay's second trial. It was no secret to courtwatchers that considerable friction prevailed between Judge Greene and Peter Gruenstein. Fairbanks district attorney Harry Davis was taking over the lead prosecutor role.[65] A case could be made that it should have been his in the first place.

Colorfully known by defense lawyers as "Mad Dog," Davis was respected as a great trial lawyer. Anchorage attorney Doug Pope, who'd tried cases against him, considered him a handful. He wasn't alone. A news article, noting his accession to the Mackay case, noted that Davis was "variously described as a hardnose, cantankerous, tenacious, and bullheaded. And that's just what Harry Davis' friends say about him."

He once told the *Fairbanks Daily News Miner* that losing made him "physically ill."

In a telling biographical sketch, Anchorage journalist Sheila Toomey revealed that the then forty-year-old Davis was the youngest district attorney in the state when he was appointed in 1975. Born in Texas, raised in Florida, he came to Alaska when his stepfather served as a territorial judge.

Davis was controversial from the day he took office. One of his first actions was to ban plea bargaining. The system was "too lenient with criminals," Davis insisted. "No one was going to jail. Ninety-six percent of all cases were sentence bargained."

Davis was appointed during the oil pipeline boom. Fairbanks was going through what seemed like a crime wave. Davis saw a plea ban as a deterrent. "What I said was, we're going to play it hardnose," he told Toomey. "We're not going to bargain."

Suddenly, prosecutors and defense lawyers had to go to trial. The police had to bring cases that would satisfy a jury. Judges had to preside over trials and decide on sentences. Everybody in the system hated it, according to Davis.

"The first war I had was with the police," he said, then with "the entire

65 Also new to the case were Assistant Anchorage D.A. Mike McLaughlin, an attorney experienced with high profile criminal cases, and David Mannheimer, of the State Office of Special Prosecutions and Appeals. McLaughlin would examine many of the key prosecution witnesses, including Gilbert Pauole, Amy Shotwell and Marianne Pfeil. Mannheimer would help craft the State's effort to reframe the evidentiary boundaries of the case. Key to that change was introducing evidence related to the death of Muriel Pfeil. Mackay's defense would demand—and win—the right to question Mannheimer about that tactical shift.

defense bar and a good percent of the judiciary." That didn't leave Davis with a whole lot of fans, Toomey found.

It didn't matter. Even Davis' critics agreed on one thing. They thought he was a good choice to prosecute the Mackay case.

Former Fairbanks Chief Prosecutor Dan Hickey enumerated the reasons. Hickey described Davis as practical, methodical and a genuine threat to the high-powered defense team that proved so popular with at least half the jury in the first trial. "Harry's a good trial lawyer because Harry's always prepared," said Hickey, a sentiment echoed by opposing attorneys.

Davis generally prosecuted high-profile murder cases, so he had plenty of experience. He was also considered a killer on cross-examination, both merciless and relentless. An investigator in his office once described the Davis technique to the *News Miner* as follows: "When he pokes a hole and draws blood, he wants to sink his fangs in and hang on."

Mad Dog, indeed.

56

Fairbanks, Alaska, November – December, 1986

It was a wounded Harry Davis, his shoulder broken from a slip on the Fairbanks ice, that went before Judge Greene. One of his first moves was to ask her to reconsider decisions that barred "a substantial amount" of evidence. If admitted, Davis argued, that evidence "could change the complexion of the case." His fellow prosecutor David Mannheimer, also new to the case, would go farther. "Previous prosecutors made a lot of mistakes," he insisted.

One of them was their failure to get Mackay to a timely examination of his alleged aphasia. The defense had used that gap in the record to dampen the effect of Mackay's incriminating statements to Junior Pauole. The ones where Mackay spelled out "G-U-N" and asked Pauole what happened to the "metal thing."

Judge Greene fixed that one, again ordering that Mackay "submit to examination" by an expert. It was a small victory. There was another decision, a bigger one by a long stretch, waiting in the wings. In an omnibus hearing before Judge Greene, Davis revealed that, in an interview with Jean Sullivan she'd revealed that "she'd discussed the Muriel Pfeil bombing with Mackay." And heard evidence of a murder plot.

Bringing in evidence that Neil Mackay had plotted Muriel Pfeil's murder now played a central role in reimagining the prosecution case. The defense, Davis claimed, wanted the jury to think there was no evidence as to who murdered Muriel Mackay. "That was a lie," he argued, "based on a lie, and forced upon the jury. We can prove the truth. On September 30, 1976, Muriel Pfeil was killed by Neil Mackay. Robert Pfeil knew that, and we are going to prove it. Is it acting in bad faith to try to get the truth to the jury?"

Asked to back up his assertions, Davis was resolute.

"We can produce evidence of the first murder," he told Judge Greene. "The evidence will show that the motive arose out of a bitter divorce. Mackay settled for over a million and had to pay. The murder occurred out of bitterness and hatred. The battle continued over visitation rights. When we interviewed Jean Sullivan, she told us she'd discussed the bombing with Neil Mackay. He said he'd told Muriel he 'hoped she'd enjoy and live long enough to enjoy the $750,000 check he gave her.'[66] When Jean Sullivan heard that statement, she thought Muriel would be killed."

"As to the bombing," Davis continued, "it was done by a professional assassin. The location, the place point to that. It was done in the window of time between 12:30 and 2:00 pm, so as not to expose Scotty Mackay. It exposed the assassin to great risk. It was a workday, a Thursday afternoon, in downtown Anchorage. He had to unlock the vehicle, open the hood, connect the bomb to the coil. That gives us strong circumstantial evidence. Mackay knew her schedule. Anyone following her would know. Mackay knew when Scotty was at the babysitters."

The importance of the Muriel Pfeil murder was greater than it may have appeared. It wasn't simply a matter of proving that one crime begat another. It also went to the heart of the defense argument. At the defense closing in the first trial, Jim McComas asked the rhetorical motherload question. "Would Neil Mackay have killed Robert Pfeil and risk losing Scotty?"

A reasonable person would answer, "No."

There was another rhetorical question wrapped inside that one. "Would Neil Mackay have killed Muriel Pfeil to *get* Scotty?" Here's what Jim McComas said in his closing statement at the first trial. "Ladies and gentlemen, as Mr. Mackay knew, anything he did to hurt Robert Pfeil was going to risk separating this which he had just spent two years trying to get. The custody of his son. That's what mattered."

---

66 Court records note the settlement was actually paid in ten installments. Still, $75,000 wasn't chicken feed.

"Look through the eyes of a guilty man," Davis countered. "The motive lies between the two murders. They're intertwined. The murder plot goes on."

What else did Harry Davis want to revisit? Or, better said, *need* to revisit?

He wanted to knock down—once and for all—the Mackay team's "alternate explanations" for Muriel's murder. Like the Nazi guy whom she'd befriended, the one the defense claimed had died when his house was bombed. "Wrong," said Davis. Joachim Peiper's house was torched with him in it. The theories that Robert Pfeil was the actual target of the car bomb? Rubbish. The other targets? They now had second thoughts. Their car didn't match Muriel's. They parked their cars all over the lot.

Then, Davis asserted, Mackay had made inquiries to Anchorage entrepreneur Peter Zamarello, asking him for references to a hit man—two or three months before Muriel's death.[67] Had told Charles Sullivan that Pfeil would eventually prove Mackay guilty of Muriel Pfeil's murder. There was Mackay's statement to Paul Newsom as to why Robert Pfeil was killed. It was the money. Robert Pfeil was robbing Scotty's estate.

Harry Davis would also fight to have the transcript of the fistfight between Robert Pfeil and Neil Mackay introduced into evidence. They didn't have to prove animosity with that one. It was there in plain old body english. While he was at it, what about letting in evidence that Junior Pauole provided prostitutes to Neil Mackay? It was more probative than prejudicial, he argued, because it went to the level of trust between the two men. Went to how Neil Mackay relied on Junior to indulge his penchant for things just outside polite society.

There was one more, equally important to reimagining the case against Neil Mackay. Judge Greene had sided with the defense in agreeing that only one of Junior Pauole's statements about the source of the contract money was admissible. That was the one pointing to the Union.

That kept the jury from considering Pauole's statement that it wasn't

---

67 According to court records, it was an allegation Zamarello later recanted, at least in a March 1986 interview with Mackay's defense attorneys. Those same court records indicate that after the Muriel Pfeil killing, Zamarello told APD Capt. Christianson he believed Virginia Zawacki "set up the entire situation and that Mackay had an alibi for the day of Muriel's death."

the union, but Mackay who was responsible. That argument fell apart, Davis reasoned, under close scrutiny.

"Mackay asserts that Pauole planned to set him up as a patsy and an extortion victim. If so, then clearly this motive would have been just as active on November 7, 1985, as it was on November 8th. This purported motive does not explain why Pauole would tell Gentry in October that Mackay had instigated Robert Pfeil's murder, then tell Gentry on November 7th that this was false, and that Mackay was a 'patsy,' and then confess to Gentry, during their emotional confrontation on November 8th, that it had been Mackay all along."

It was a good argument. If, that is, Davis could get Judge Greene to change her mind.

The defense had one Ace up its sleeve—their reckoning that Judge Greene had no reason to repudiate her rulings from the first trial. Indeed, to help her along, Mackay's team provided a handy list of every single protective order she'd enforced during the first trial. The defense was wrong. Instead, Judge Greene found that she had the "discretion to reach or not reach the merits of any motion that seeks to relitigate matters previously decided."

In the end, Greene changed little. She left in place the fifty-some Protective Orders from the first trial, most of them favorable to Neil Mackay. Her opinion was more juridical than literary. "While it is certainly true that matters may develop differently in a second trial," Greene noted, "it is also true that . . . a prior ruling should stand unless there is good reason to relitigate it."

Once a judge starts second-guessing herself, in other words, the game is over.

The game *was* over, hurtling toward a final determination or at least what looked like one. It didn't happen all at once. Even before Harry Davis showed up in his shoulder sling, Neil Mackay had been released on a $100,000.00 bond to his business associate and fellow attorney, Frank Nosek. Total out of pocket cost to Neil Mackay? Ten grand. There were photos of him leaving the courthouse in sunglasses, in the company of Bill Bryson, his always stylish local counsel. Bryson, in his Armani suit, had his swagger down to a tee.

Then Judge Greene started peeling away at the state's second bite of the apple.

What about the new stuff? Like the motion to introduce evidence that Neil Mackay arranged the murder of Muriel Pfeil? Denied. Davis did not have sufficient proof to bring in evidence on a criminal charge that was never charged. "Most importantly," Judge Greene wrote, "the court does not believe Mr. Pauole's statement" that Neil Mackay acknowledged his role in the murder. "The court believes this to be embellishment."

There was more where that came from.

The motion to introduce the November 8, 1985, wire where Pauole claimed Neil Mackay was the true source of the Robert Pfeil contract? Denied. The motion to bring in statements attributed to John Bright by Sassy Marshall, Matt Vickers, and Larry Gentry—among them the recorded conversation where Bright told Larry Gentry that Mackay was behind the shooting? It couldn't come in. The state hadn't met the prerequisites for admission. What about the Bright assertion that the money came from Hawaii? Same result.

That was just the start of the problems with John Ian Arthur Bright. He wouldn't agree to testify except through a grant of transactional immunity. Because, you know, he didn't want to mess up his sentencing by muttering some inconvenient inanity at Neil Mackay's trial.

If the state could take any comfort, the judge's second trial rulings were not all in one direction. Greene was more flexible than some of her critics averred. The defendant's latest motion to dismiss the case? Denied. The defendant's motion to prevent an expert examination to determine the existence and extent of Mackay's alleged speech disorders? Denied. The defendant's motion to exclude Mackay's speculation that Robert Pfeil was the intended victim of the car bombing that killed his ex-wife? Denied. The motion for a change of venue? Denied.

One tantalizing change was Greene's ruling to override the exclusion of banker Gordon Hartlieb's 1987 interview with the APD. The one where he recalled a visit to Mackay's Ilikai penthouse in the early 70s. While there, Mackay told him that he did not trust banks and took Hartlieb into his den. He then opened a desk drawer where he showed his visitor stacks upon stacks of U.S. currency. Mackay told the banker that he held approximately $450,000 in cash there. He called it his Mad Money.

The struggle to identify the source of the $10,000 paid to Junior Pauole for the contract killing appeared over. The defendant, it seemed, reveled in having a hefty supply of cash. Ten thousand dollars was nothing.

And what tranche of rulings would be complete without at least one mixed bag decision from hell? The attempt to suppress Mackay's statements to Trooper Foster were granted in part and denied in part. Mackay's right to counsel was not violated, the court held. Nor was there any Fifth Amendment violation until, that is, Foster said "I wouldn't know that to do with $10,000." That was too close to soliciting an incriminating response from Neil Mackay. Ten-thousand dollars was, after all, *the* magic number. The number marked "contract murder."

In the end, it hardly mattered. The state decided not to introduce Trooper Foster's statement. Or, for that matter, Trooper Foster.

But . . . There was one seeming prize. The judge allowed three of the four excised excerpts of the Mackay-Pauole wires back into evidence. She had reevaluated her decision. Changed her mind. It was a dog bone.

NOT ALL THE IMPORTANT DEVELOPMENTS WERE CONFINED to the Fairbanks courtroom. Just before the second trial began, Neil Mackay was sued by the Pfeil estate to the tune of $6 million. The suit alleged that Robert Pfeil was "shot by agents employed and instigated" by Mackay.

"As a result of the wrongful death of Robert Pfeil," the filing continued, "his dependents have suffered injury, including but not limited to loss of support, other pecuniary losses, loss of assistance and services, loss of consortium, loss of prospective training and education, mental anguish, medical and funeral expenses."

That wasn't all. The suit, filed by Rainier Bank Alaska on behalf of the Pfeil estate, asserted that the "wrongful action in deliberately causing the injury and death of Robert Pfeil was so outrageous as to warrant the imposition of punitive damages."

A few months earlier, meanwhile, police were called to the Bootlegger Cove home of Frank Nosek. There were reports of a man with a gun, lingering outside the house, knocking on a bedroom window at 2 a.m. The witness was Nosek's 18-year-old son, who said he saw the man standing about two feet from the house. The man said he was going to shoot the young man.

The junior Nosek told police he jumped back from the window and saw a flash and then heard something hit the house. Officers found a small crack in the window, but a K-9 tracking dog was unable to pick up a scent. Neil Mackay was there, pending his retrial. It was too close for comfort.

The second trial got off to a rollicking start. In a move that smacked of putting cheerleaders in the laps of jurors, McComas placed the first trial's "Mr. Mackay is innocent" jurors at the defense table. Davis objected. McComas promised he wouldn't identify them as former jurors. Judge Greene told Denise Rivers and Dolly Edwin to sit in the back.

Jury selection, always a challenge, was also highly illuminating. One jury candidate openly wondered "how a millionaire could have no money for bail. I would want to hear Mr. Mackay tell me that he's innocent. I need one-on-one contact." Another opined that Mackay wouldn't get a fair trial in Fairbanks. He was followed by a juror who felt that it was the defense attorney who "put the stuff in the juror's room." Jim McComas called an anteroom conference. Complained to the judge, "I'm very upset that people believe I put the stuff in the jury room."

Judge Greene took pains to explain that the "documents went to the jury by a mistake of the Court clerk."

It was, however, prospective juror Charles Williams who took the door prize. "I have read and heard about this case," he admitted. "Most people think he's guilty. I kinda lean toward guilty. I read of the mistrial. I thought it was all kinda stupid."

Ultimately Fairbanks was bored with Neil Mackay, Round Two. Once jury selection was finished, few spectators bothered to drop into the courthouse. Lawyers who were transfixed during the first trial now wandered in only sporadically, leaving almost as soon as they arrived. The trial itself, once ambitiously scheduled for August, had been moved three months out to accommodate the new prosecutors.

57

Fairbanks, Alaska, January 2 – February 9, 1988

As the second trial began, Judge Greene noticed one of the jurors speaking to the media and spectators. She admonished everyone on the jury not to do so. In that vein, she also admonished both the state and the defense. Control your witnesses. That one was squarely aimed at Muriel C. Pfeil, whom both sides recognized was out of hand at the first trial. Grandmother Pfeil wasn't the only violator, though, and Judge Greene didn't need another circus.

There were other hiccups. The attorneys fought over words. "Admitted perjurer" was out. "Gangster" was out. Note taking was in. So was use of the word "evil." McComas felt it was prejudicial. Co-prosecutor McLaughlin noted that "Robert Pfeil felt that Mr. Mackay was evil. He used that term. The word 'evil' conveys the intense feeling he had." Judge Greene denied that it was prejudicial.

"It won't be a shock to the jurors," she proclaimed.

Greene's biggest challenge was to rein in the testosterone of the opposing sides. It started with the first witness, Marianne Pfeil. Jim McComas, ever touchy, accused Harry Davis of violating the myriad protective orders in effect and renewed his motion to dismiss the case.

"We are acting in good faith," Davis shot back. "We have many protective orders to watch for. The defense is trying to set up the prosecution for a mistrial."

"I have not violated the Court order," McComas responded testily.

"I did not ask for a mistrial. I asked for the dismissal of charges." With the slightest of sighs, Judge Greene answered, "The motion to dismiss is denied." Then wearily added, "Court orders are to be followed."

She would be forced to deny the motion to dismiss over, and over, and over. Even the testimony of the medical examiner who performed the autopsy of Robert Pfeil raised the ire of Jim McComas. "This is the fourth violation of the protective order," he bellowed as he moved to dismiss. The violation? Dr. Belau continually referred to the victim as "Captain Pfeil."

There was at least one change noticeable in Jim McComas. He allowed numerous prosecution witnesses to testify without subjecting them to cross-examination. Get them on, get them off. Witness excused. The variation was to strike the witness' testimony. He clearly didn't have time for some of these people. Unless, of course, they were affiliated with the Anchorage Police Department, were one of Junior's underworld associates, or had the name Gilbert Kapualoha Pauole.

The latter was his usual talkative self. His story consistent, never wavering. His past lies still ripe for the taking. Though not quite as adept at confrontation as Jim Shellow, McComas held his own in forcing Junior to refer to prior statements—statements that tended to undercut what he'd just said on the witness stand. Having gone through this once before, there was the added opportunity that Pauole would slip up on his past slip ups. Which, in fact, he rarely did. Not that anyone was counting.

For the most part, McComas was content to take Junior through the litany of his prior perjurious statements. When it was his turn to put on defense witnesses, he had shrunk it down to just four people. Last up was a man who'd worked for Junior Pauole, a man who'd been his bodyguard.

Matthew Vickers spoke of his role in keeping Frank Colacurcio out of the Wild Cherry. Of being paid for the strong-arm work of breaking bones. Then he spoke of the job he wouldn't take. The one that Junior said would pay him at least $7,000.

"I did not accept the job," Vickers said. "I did not trust Mr. Pauole. I quit my job. I know John Bright. He borrowed a pair of boots from me, and also some dark clothing. Bright gave me a package. I put it in my refrigerator. I later found out it had explosives in it. I had the package gotten rid of."

Vickers was preceded by Scotty Mackay. By Jean Rolles, the Honolulu property manager who'd met Junior during his ill-conceived attempt to rent the Rodeo Bar in Waikiki and by Lance Spiegel, one in a long line of Neil Mackay's attorneys.

They were all in and out in a snap. One day was all it took. Only one day total for the entire defense case. On January 28, 1988, Day 37 of the trial, the defense rested. In retrospect, their case seemed perfunctory. James McComas was chomping at the bit to get this thing into the jury room. There was always the chance that going on too long could do more harm than good.

McComas' closing statement, on the other hand, was anything but perfunctory.

"The case rests on Gilbert Pauole," McComas suggested, his moves animated, confident, even showy. Most of his argument focused on Pauole Pauole's history of lying under oath. On Pauole's deal with the state that rescued him from a probable 99-year jail sentence. On Pauole's insistence that he got $10,000 in hundred-dollar bills from Mackay during a visit to Mackay's Honolulu condominium. On those three emotionally charged phone calls he made to Neil Mackay. Under, he stressed, police supervision.

"Was Gilbert Pauole the biggest liar you have ever seen in your whole life?" McComas asked. To discover the top man in the Pfeil murder conspiracy, he suggested that jurors need look no further than this "spontaneous and effective liar," he said. The only evidence the state has against Mackay, he railed, is the unsupported word of an admitted perjurer, a semiliterate gangster who lacks a high school diploma but "has a doctorate in dishonesty."

Gone was the suggestion, made during Mackay's first trial, that Pauole acted on a contract from an airline union which was upset with Pfeil and wanted him out as a leader. In its place came the theory that Pauole had hatched a "harebrained idea of getting money out of Mackay." Pauole set up Pfeil's murder on his own initiative, McComas insisted.

For much of the time, propped on a stand next to McComas, was a huge poster of Pauole, smiling at the jury from behind his nightclub bar. Periodically McComas turned to the poster and demanded an answer: "What's the truth Mr. Pauole?" he shouted to the poster at one point. "What you say in court or what the facts turn out to be?"

Remember Pauole's testimony, McComas told the jury with a grand gesture, "and you have a flood of doubts." Mr. Mackay has been falsely accused, he thundered. "You are the only people who can end it."

The jury was out for deliberations by 12:22 pm, on Wednesday, February 4, 1988. In a single motion, Judge Greene thanked and excused the four alternate jurors. Five minutes later, the alternates spoke to an awaiting press contingent. One man and two of the women said they would not have convicted Neil Mackay of Robert Pfeil's 1985 murder. The one man who would have voted guilty suggested that Pfeil's murder might have been "justifiable homicide," adding that it was "obvious the Pfeils' were going after Mr. Mackay's sanity."

Not that the alternates were convinced of Mackay's innocence.

"I don't think he's no squeaky-clean type of guy," said Don LaRoe, a Fairbanks electrician. If "a man is that intelligent, does he go ahead and hire a pinhead like (Pauole)?"

And that was the problem. None of them believed Gilbert Pauole. Even the sole guilty vote had trouble with Pauole. "He puts a price on someone's head," noted power system operator Kevin Dunham. "He even would have done it for nothing."

The actual jury, though, was having difficulties. One of them, apparently, was bringing up perceptions that were not in evidence. Was discussing "outside issues." When it was called to the court's attention, there was a sense that one of the jurors was "misbehaving." Saying things like "If you knew what I know, you would realize some of the witnesses are lying." Jurors had to be reminded that the only evidence they could consider was that presented in the courtroom.

All sides agreed, however, that it would do more harm than good to take it any further.

Indeed, the jury seemed to hit its stride the next day, asking to see transcripts of Gilbert Pauole's testimony and then transcripts from Sgt. Grimes and Investigator Austin. It was illusory. The day after that—day three of deliberations—they sent out a note saying they were deadlocked. Actually, they sent two notes. Judge Greene brought them in and read them *Jury Instruction Number 44*:

"As jurors you have the duty to consult with one another and

> to deliberate with a view to reaching an agreement, if that can be done without violence to individual judgment . . . No juror should surrender an honest conviction as to the weight or effect of the evidence solely because of the opinion of the other jurors, or for the mere purpose of returning a verdict."

On Sunday morning, February 7th, at 9:38 a.m., jury foreman Robert Blake sent a cryptic note to Judge Greene. In a slightly indecisive hand, he wrote:

> The Jury has Reached ~~AN UNAN~~ Their Decision. Robert Blake.

The jurors filed into the shabby second floor courtroom by 10:30 a.m. They handed the blue verdict form to Judge Greene. Reporter Sheila Toomey noted that Neil Mackay's hands were shaking. That James McComas was hunched over the hefty wooden defense table, clasping, and unclasping his hands, his knuckles gone white. Judge Greene read slowly, solemnly, in a resonant contralto.

"We, the jury, duly impaneled and sworn to try the above-entitled case, do find the defendant, Neil S. Mackay, NOT GUILTY of the crime of Murder in the First Degree."

"I wasn't guilty and I'm thankful the jury found me not guilty," Mackay said afterward, making a mostly unsuccessful effort to curb his emotions. His voice cracked as he added, "I want to get back to my son."

"Neil's going home to his son and I'm going home to my sons," McComas added, after Mackay refused to speak further. "We're both very happy," McComas said, acknowledging he was "scared to death" as the jury entered the courtroom.

Jury foreman Robert Blake, a supervisor for the Federal Aviation Administration, was equally effusive. He told reporters that the jury was trending toward acquittal from the very start. Their first vote, taken 15 minutes after deliberations began, showed two jurors for "guilty," six for "not guilty" and four undecideds. As additional votes were taken, Blake said, the undecideds steadily drifted toward "not guilty."

Mirroring the views of the alternates, their biggest problem, Blake said, was Gilbert Pauole. "If the truth were a bulldog and bit him on the nose, he wouldn't recognize it . . . Even those that were for 'guilty' didn't believe Pauole." The jurors didn't spend much energy debating Pauole's testimony, Blake insisted, because they all concurred that he was unreliable.

"This guy can't even remember when he got married five years ago." Blake added that the "not guilty" verdict was anything but an endorsement of Mackay's innocence.

"No," he insisted. "There was no place on the verdict form to place that word [innocent]," Blake said. "His [Mackay's] hands are not totally clean. Whatever it was, we don't believe he said, 'Gilbert, I want that man killed.'"

In the hallway outside the courtroom, Blake turned to co-prosecutor Mike McLaughlin and extended his sympathies. "You did the best you could with what you had," Blake offered. Then Blake asked McLaughlin if Pauole would lose his sentence deal with the state and get 99 years. "We felt like he had breached it quite a bit," Blake volunteered.

McLaughlin countered that it was unlikely.

Within days, Neil Mackay would head back to Hawaii, a free man. His attorney had even convinced the State of Alaska to pay for his ticket. There was, however, one person who missed the celebration. Absent from the courtroom that Sunday was Marianne Pfeil. She'd left Fairbanks on Thursday when the case went to the jury. Before she left, Pfeil told reporters she had emotionally prepared herself for a not guilty verdict.

"Maybe it's God's will," she said, "to save Scotty's mind, so he can believe his father didn't kill his mother." Two days later, Marianne Pfeil withdrew the wrongful death lawsuit she'd filed against Neil Mackay. She said that she ordered the suit withdrawn because she wanted no further contact with Mackay or his representatives.

Filed in U.S. District Court in Anchorage on Oct. 5, 1987, after Mackay's first trial in the case ended in a mistrial, the action alleged that Robert Pfeil was "shot by agents employed and instigated" by Mackay. The lawsuit asked for $5 million in punitive damages plus $1 million in other damages and medical expenses. Marianne Pfeil said that the suit was filed on the advice of lawyers to preserve the family's legal rights within the two-year statute of limitations in damage cases.

In terminating the civil suit, Marianne said she disagreed with the jury's findings. Told that civil cases require less proof of guilt than criminal cases, she nevertheless said, "It's time to put all that behind me and get on with my life."

What about Gilbert Kapualoha Pauole, Jr.?

With the trial over and done, Junior was finally on the verge of a much-delayed sentencing. Except there was a twist. With Junior Pauole there was always a twist. His attorney Richard Kibby, now Anchorage municipal attorney, let it be known that the sentence Junior would eventually receive did not necessarily have to match his original agreement.

"There was an innuendo," Kibby claimed, "that even though there was a stipulated agreement of 20 years, there would at some point possibly be consideration of a lesser sentence."

Kibby even quoted special prosecutor Timothy Petumenos as saying, "I'm not making any promises."

Quick denials resounded through Judge Greene's courtroom. Petumenos "flatly denied" making any secret deal with Kibby or Pauole. Mike McLaughlin, the assistant district attorney now handling that case for the state, told Greene that he was surprised the issue had been raised and was concerned that the suggestion of secret deals, which were not communicated to the various defendants, might jeopardize the three convictions already returned in the case.

It would also "suggest that the state committed a fraud on the court," McLaughlin said. On June 29, 1988, Pauole's new attorney asked that he be sentenced to ten years, because he was a very cooperative witness for the state. McLaughlin praised Pauole's cooperation but added that the Pfeil murder "represents the worst type of killing. The contract killing of an innocent victim."

"I'm very sorry for what I've done," Pauole told Greene when it came his turn to address the court. "Everything I have said about Mr. Mackay is the truth."

Judge Greene deducted two years from Junior's sentence. Not because of his cooperation in the Neil Mackay case. The state had already given him a "tremendous deal," the judge noted, especially given that the charges started as attempted murder and then ended up as murder in the first-degree. Greene deducted two years because he was also cooperating with federal authorities investigating his former organized crime cronies in Seattle and Arizona.

"Mr. Pauole is the person who set the price on the life of Robert Pfeil," Greene said in pronouncing his sentence. "Mr. Pauole's involvement in this offense is major . . . If it hadn't been for Mr. Pauole, it's pretty doubtful that Mr. Pfeil would have died." Greene further noted that Junior Pauole had been a professional criminal all his life.

She sentenced him to 20 years with two years suspended and five years' probation upon his release from prison. The *Anchorage Daily News* headline read, "Judge trims state witness' sentence to 18 years." The file on the Robert Pfeil killing was now closed.

Marianne Pfeil got the last word. Asked about Pauole's sentence after the hearing, she said it seemed reasonable.

"But nothing was solved," she added. "Nothing was solved."

AFTERWORD

NEIL MACKAY'S BODY WAS FOUND IN his Waikiki condo on September 22, 1994. In poor health, the coroner ruled he died of natural causes. He had been dead for several days before he was found. He had, in other words, died alone. He was 71.

Scotty Mackay was nowhere near when his father died. After his father's acquittal, he left Hawaii for Anchorage, at the invitation of Wayne Anthony Ross. The voluble attorney told reporters he offered the young man "a safe haven after his father was acquitted so he could finish high school." Now calling himself Scott—and sometimes N. Scott Mackay—he graduated from Robert Service high school in 1991, then started college and took a job at the National Bank of Alaska. He eventually jumped to the U.S. Army, arriving at Fort Knox, Ky. in 1998 to complete basic combat training. His last known residence was Marietta, Georgia, north of Atlanta, where he worked as a Physician Assistant.

Marianne Pfeil remarried in August of 1994. Her new husband was Herbert C. Lang. A 1951 graduate of the University of Alaska, Fairbanks, Lang was president of Anchorage Sand and Gravel Co. and former President of the University of Alaska, Anchorage, Board of Regents. Both were widowers, Lang having lost his wife to cancer in 1990.

Carolina Ross Mackay Willis died on April 12, 2012, in Sequim, Washington, at age 86. Her obituary noted that "she held many positions in her lifetime, including work for the Union Pacific Railroad as a yard clerk in Yermo, California." She worked for both the freight and transportation offices of the U.S. Marine Corps, also serving as a school librarian and attendance clerk for the Barstow Unified School District. She retired from the Kenai Chamber of Commerce in Alaska, before moving to the Olympic Peninsula in Washington State.

Her husband Alfred survived her and moved back to Alaska in 2014. Born April 15, 1925, in Barstow, California, he died in Wasilla, Alaska on May 28, 2023, aged 98.

Neil Mackay's lead attorney, James Shallow, died October 29, 2022, at his home in Milwaukee. He was 95. Known for his fierce cross-examination of key witnesses, especially in drug cases, Shellow noted that "the cross-examination must impeach the character of the witness. He must give answers which are implausible or unreasonable. The jury must be encouraged from such responses to find that the witness is biased and untrustworthy and from this infer that his opinions are unreliable."

Blessed with multiple academic achievements – a master's degree in psychology, professional designation as a certified public accountant – his law degree came later in life, at age 35. Criminal defense soon consumed his existence, as well as that of his wife and two daughters. His pro bono work included representation of fair housing and desegregation advocates, as well as Viet Nam war protesters and civil rights activists. He was also a connoisseur of sports cars, owning at various times a Mercedes Benz convertible, a 1966 Ferrari, several Jaguars and a Rolls Royce convertible. He was far from an ascetic.

"My father didn't stop smoking until the day before he died," said daughter Jill in her father's obituary. "He liked very good wine and he drank like a fish. And, frankly, he chased anything in a skirt."

Of Mackay's two attorneys, Jame McComas was the only one to remain in Alaska, moving there after the Mackay case to continue his legal career in Anchorage. Specializing in homicide cases, he defended multiple Alaskans accused of murder, winning many an acquittal. In May 2002, Jim became the first recipient of the annual Jim McComas Alaskan Champion of Liberty Award, created by the Alaska Academy of Trial Lawyers and the Alaska Criminal Defense Bar. McComas and his wife, a speech-language pathologist, retired in 2008 and relocated to the far north of Wisconsin.

Judge Mary Elaine "Meg" Greene died in 2019 at the Fairbanks Pioneer home from Alzheimer's disease. She was 69 years old. By then she had driven all the roads in Alaska in her red Toyota truck and journeyed to Dawson to gamble twice each summer. She was known for taking on complex cases, including the Mental Health Lands Case, whose documents filled an entire room of filing cabinets. After 17 years on the bench, she moved to the University of Alaska legal office. She was instrumental in creating Raven Landing, so that Fairbanks seniors could retire in their home community.

The other judge involved with this case, Judge Kabua Kabua, was charged with manslaughter in October 1975, before the Scotty Mackay affair. The charge arose out a presumed assault of his wife. Kabua was acquitted by Trust Territory Associate Justice Arvin H. Brown after a weeklong trial.

Rodger and Marie Cotting, charged with contempt in the wake of the Scotty Mackay case, also faced a high visibility trial. The Cotting's soon had a high-priced attorney, Russell Walker, paid by Neil Mackay. Walker managed to disqualify the judge, quash the search warrant, and suppress the evidence recovered during that search. The charges were ultimately dropped. The Cottings eventually left Majuro for Washington, D.C., where Rodger took a job with the Office of Surface Mining, Reclamation, and Enforcement.

By the end of 1987, meanwhile, the APD Homicide Response Team had found their rhythm. In 47 homicide investigations conducted from mid-1985 through that year, only ten remained unsolved. Of the remaining 37, all but one was charged and convicted. The sole outlier was Neil Sutherland Mackay. "He was tried in the court of public opinion, and he was tried in a court of law," said Assistant District Attorney Steve Branchflower of Mackay's death. "Now he's going to answer to a higher authority. I'd love to hear that verdict."

The abiding contrasts, however, belong to the co-conspirators.

After Neil Mackay's acquittal, Gilbert Kapualoha Pauole, Jr., declared he was ready to testify all over again. In a July 1988 telephone interview with journalist Sheila Toomey, Pauole also said he understood why a Fairbanks jury didn't believe him. "There was too many other things talked about instead of what ought to be talked about," he declared. Even with that, he wanted one more chance to convince a jury he was telling the truth—should Marianne Pfeil choose to do so.

"If she goes to federal court and does something, I'll do it all over—for her, for me, for whatever reasons," he said. "For her not to give up. I'm not going to give up . . . My motive is to clear my conscience maybe, but I just don't feel comfortable about the whole thing."

"Let's do it again," he added, "but now let's stick to the issues. Let's not talk about Frank Colacurcio and Junior. Let's talk about Neil Mackay and Junior."

His hopes were doomed even as he pronounced them. Marianne Pfeil had long since withdrawn her federal suit against Neil Mackay.

Tyoga Closson, on the other hand, disappeared off the radar. Disappeared, that is, until September 1993. He was found in a *Spokane Spokesman-Review* piece about criminal sentencings for Kootenai County, Idaho. Closson, 26, then living in Pend Oreille, was sentenced to 60 days in jail, 45 days suspended, for possession of a controlled substance and petty theft. He also faced one year on probation.

In July of 1990, meanwhile, Robert Betts once more managed to find himself in trouble. Held at a "special handling" unit at the Spring Creek maximum security prison in Seward, Alaska, Betts refused to return to his cell for the routine 1:30 a.m. bedtime lockdown. Instead, Betts and a second prisoner went on a glass-smashing, fire-setting rampage. Betts brandished a sharpened broom handle while he started his fire. It took two "take down" teams more than an hour to get the two under control.

Two months later, a state appellate court upheld Robert Betts' 50-year sentence.

If there was one candidate with a decent chance at rehabilitation, it was Larry Gentry. He was the one co-conspirator with the full support of his family throughout his trial. Even Judge Greene noticed. Housed at the Mountain Creek medium-security prison in Eagle River, just north of Anchorage, Gentry had eased into a supervisory role for inmates taking care of Iditarod sled dogs dropped off for post-race care. "It's a pleasure to take care of these dogs," Gentry told an *Anchorage Daily News* reporter in March 1996. "It's very therapeutic, a stress reliever. It makes you feel a bit more human."

Gentry was released from prison in 2002. His only court appearance in the years since was a speeding violation in Seward. It cost him $144.00.

John Ian Arthur Bright, not too surprisingly, stayed true to Judge Greene's dire assessment. Greene, in acknowledging John Bright's difficult past, had predicted his arc at sentencing. Calling him "the unfortunate product of a very bad system," she noted that "he is seemingly satisfied with his life of violence." Added that he "does not have the human feelings which he now professes." Concluded that, "I seriously doubt there is anything I could do today that would deter Mr. Bright from the criminal life."

Sentenced to 99 years in jail, his parole eligibility restricted for 40 years, Bright was destined to be in his 60s before he was eligible for release. Like Robert Betts, Bright was jailed at the Spring Creek maximum security prison. In 1991, just four years after his arrival, Bright assaulted another inmate. It was brutal.

According to court records, "The victim of Bright's assault testified at grand jury that Bright threw a caustic liquid into his eyes, then hit him on the side of his head with a heavy object, shattering his skull. As the victim tried to escape from the room, Bright caught him and choked him until he lost consciousness. As a consequence of this attack, the victim suffered long-term damage to his eyes and severe facial injuries (fractures of the jaw and the orbit of the eye)."

Bright's first trial on the charge resulted in a hung jury. He wasn't so lucky the second time around. Found guilty of felony assault, he faced an additional 10-year sentence. Except that . . . a judge ruled he was entitled to a third trial, due to the potential prejudice of holding his first two trials inside the prison. He ended up with time added to his sentence. Originally eligible for parole in 2027, he is currently scheduled for release in 2052.

Little has changed about the man. In 2007, he bragged about his jailhouse assault on national television. In his latest iteration of the event, he claimed to have bitten off a third of his victim's index finger.

"I spit his finger on the floor," Bright declared. He smiled broadly at the memory.

Photo Credit: Lorraine A. Miller

LELAND E. HALE "BACKED INTO" THE true crime genre when he joined Maj. Walter Gilmour to write Butcher, Baker, a bestselling true crime work about Alaska serial killer Robert C. Hansen.

Always the "writer guy," Hale did his first poetry reading at age eleven; he placed third in a regional poetry contest at the tender age of eighteen. After securing his undergraduate degree, he became a ghostwriter—which he now characterizes as his "devil's apprenticeship." Soon thereafter, he took a job at a Washington State agency that once employed serial killer Ted Bundy. It was just a coincidence.

Taking his next job at a trade association, he was called upon to testify before a U.S. Congressional committee chaired by the legendary Rep. John Dingell (MI). Later, Mr. Hale edited a U.S. Atomic Energy Agency volume on the nonproliferation of nuclear weapons. Upon earning a master's degree at the University of Washington School of Engineering, he took a job at The Boeing Company, followed by a decade at Microsoft.

That said, true crime is his true passion. He is presently in his happiest place.

www.ingramcontent.com/pod-product-compliance
Lightning Source LLC
Chambersburg PA
CBHW011724020426
42333CB00024B/2724

* 9 7 8 1 6 8 4 9 2 2 3 8 3 *